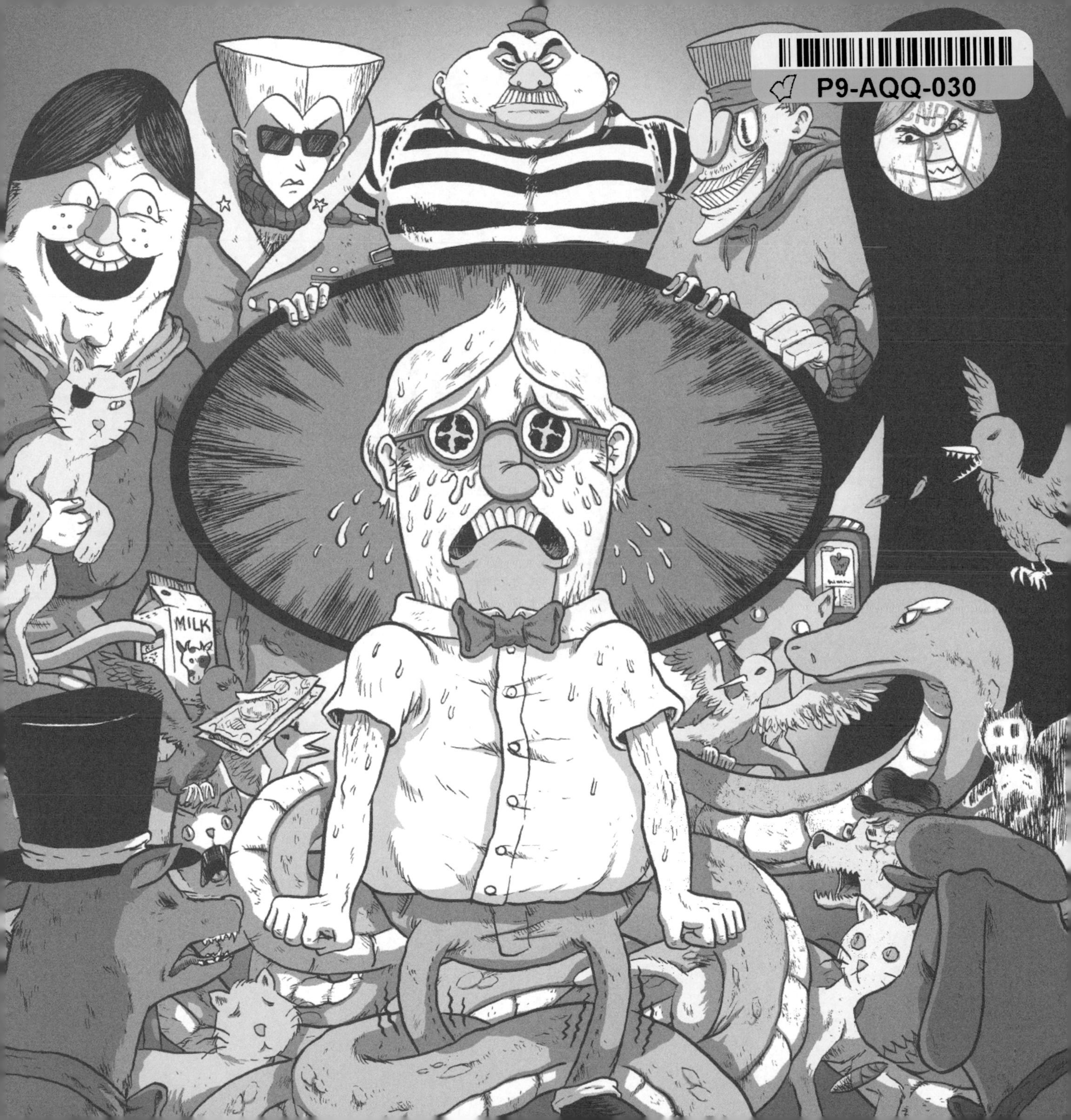
MILK

The Bad-ventures of Bobo Backslack
by Jon Chadurjian

Published by AdHouse Books

ISBN 1-935233-28-9
ISBN 978-1-935233-28-2
10 9 8 7 6 5 4 3 2 1

Design: Pitzer + Chadurjian

AdHouse Books LLC
3905 Brook Road
Richmond, VA 23227 USA
www.adhousebooks.com

First Printing, May 2014

Printed in Malaysia

THE BAD-VENTURES of

Bobo Backslack

A *WRETCHED* TALE PENNED BY
JON CHADURJIAN

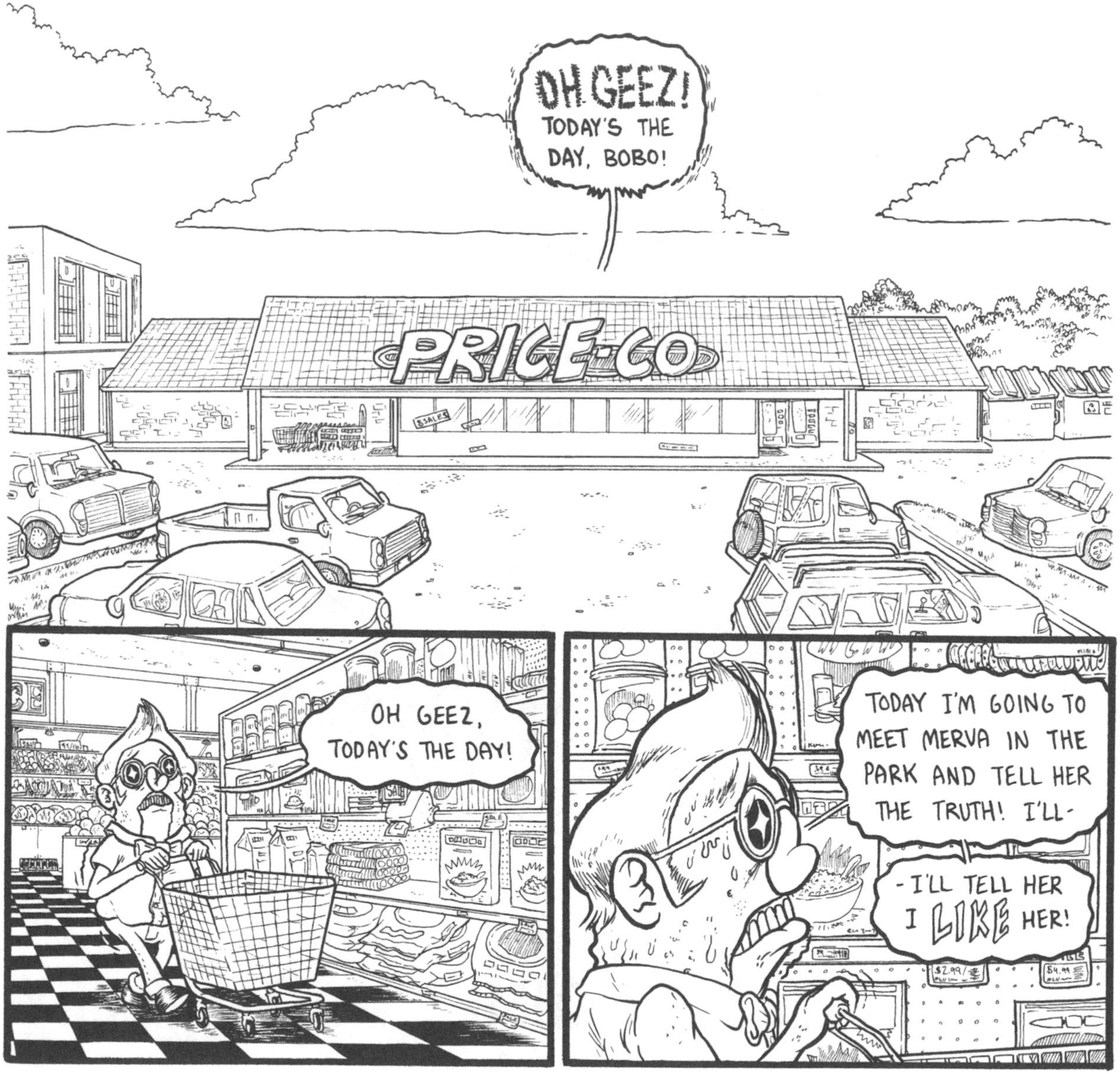
OH GEEZ! TODAY'S THE DAY, BOBO!
PRICE-CO
OH GEEZ, TODAY'S THE DAY!
TODAY I'M GOING TO MEET MERVA IN THE PARK AND TELL HER THE TRUTH! I'LL-
-I'LL TELL HER I LIKE HER!

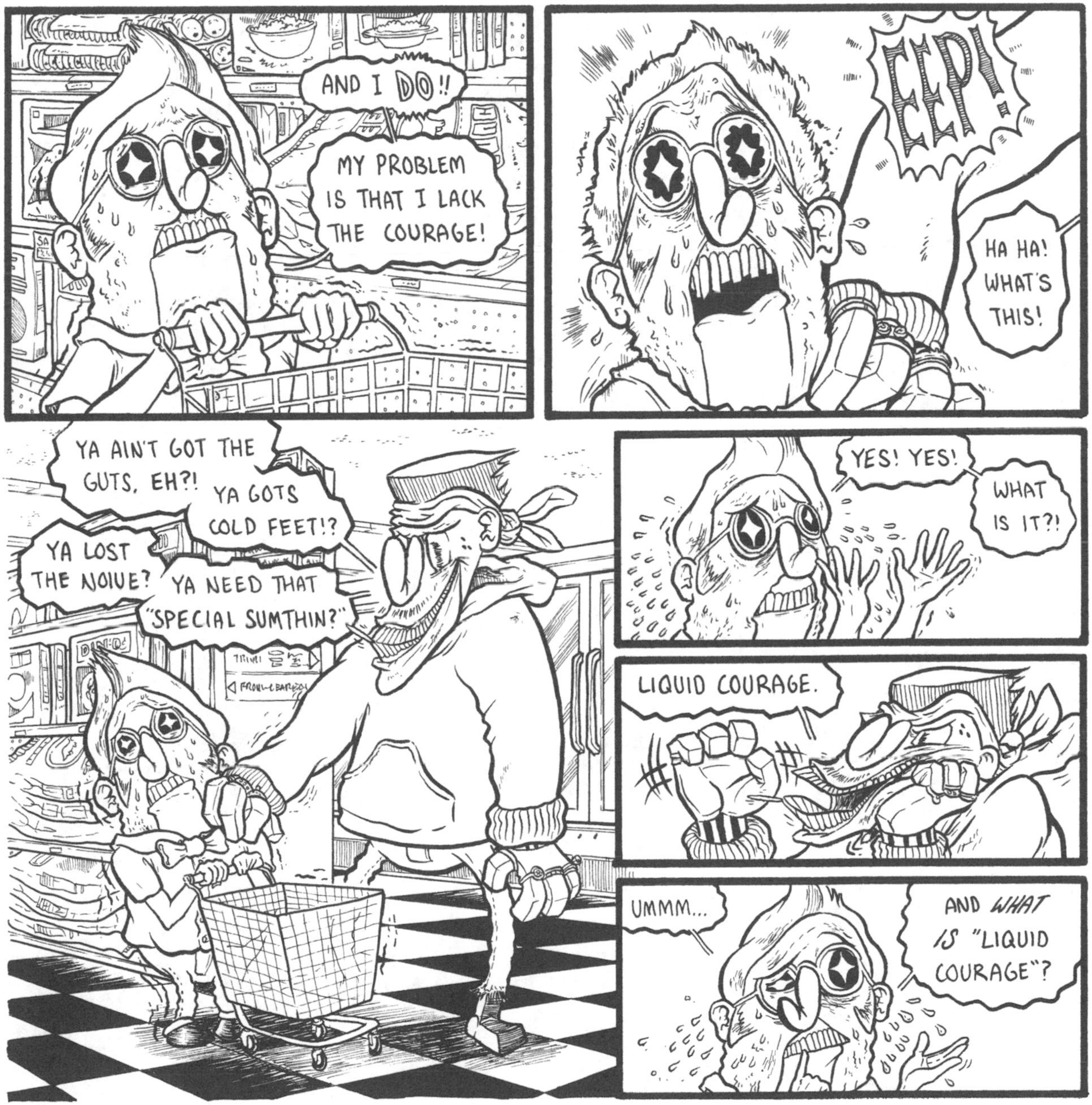
AND I DO!!
MY PROBLEM IS THAT I LACK THE COURAGE!
EEP!
HA HA! WHAT'S THIS!
YA AIN'T GOT THE GUTS, EH?!
YA GOTS COLD FEET!?
YA LOST THE NOIVE?
YA NEED THAT "SPECIAL SUMTHIN?"
YES! YES!
WHAT IS IT?!
LIQUID COURAGE.
UMMM...
AND WHAT IS "LIQUID COURAGE"?

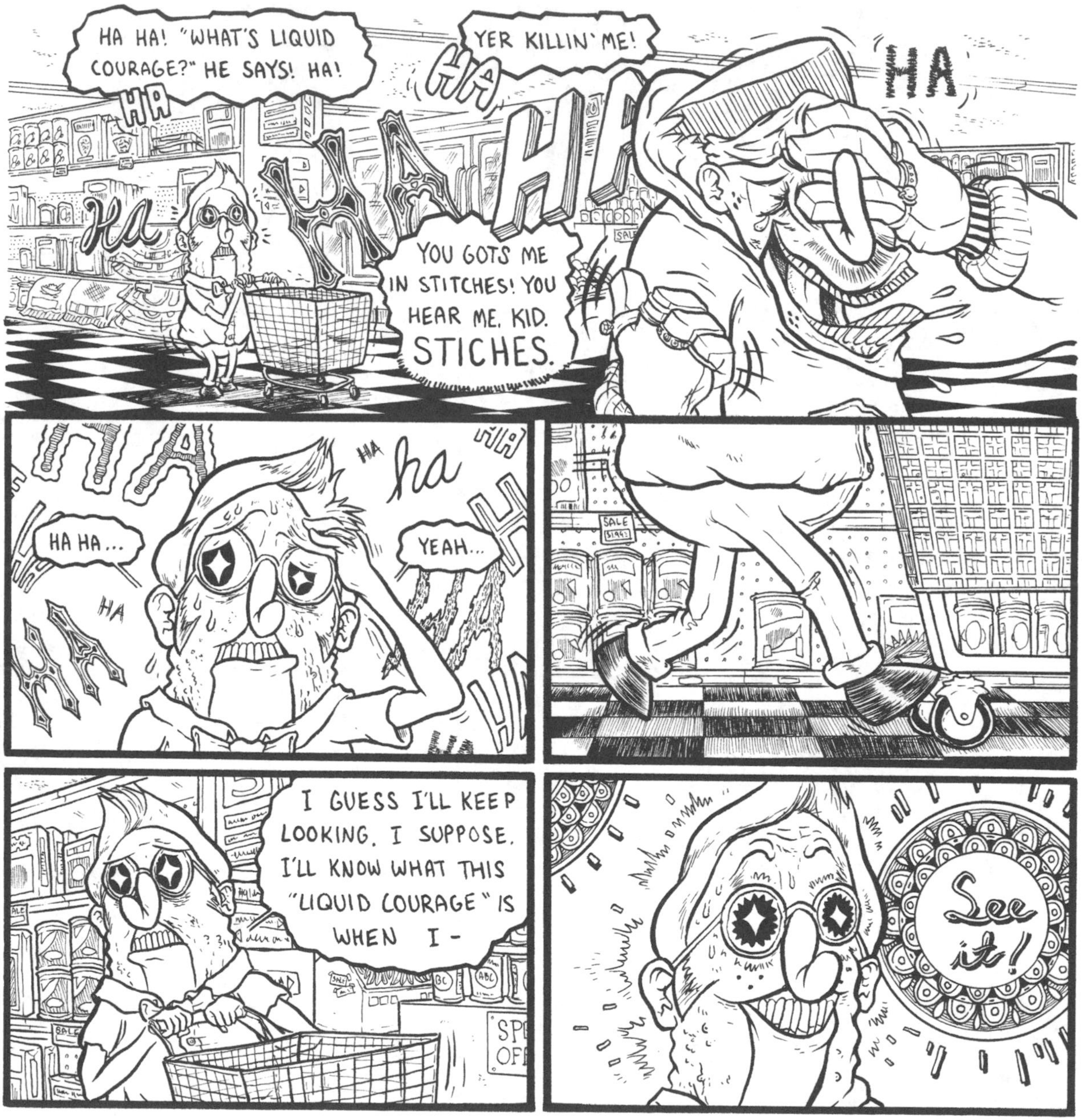
HA HA! "WHAT'S LIQUID COURAGE?" HE SAYS! HA!
YER KILLIN' ME!
HA
HA
HA
HA
HA
HA
HA
YOU GOTS ME IN STITCHES! YOU HEAR ME, KID. STICHES.
HA HA...
YEAH...
HA
ha
HA
I GUESS I'LL KEEP LOOKING. I SUPPOSE. I'LL KNOW WHAT THIS "LIQUID COURAGE" IS WHEN I -
See it!

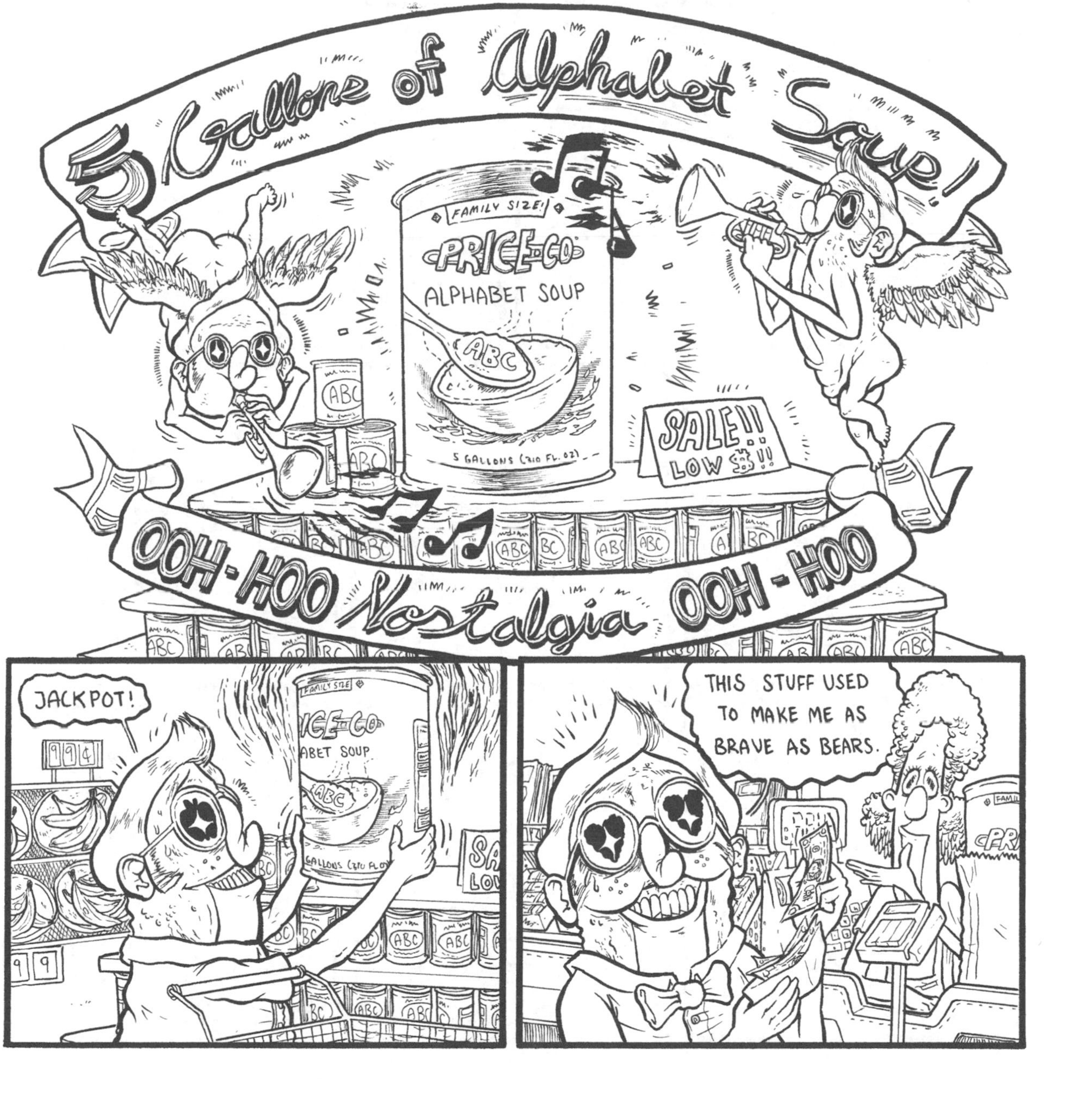
5 Gallons of Alphabet Soup!
FAMILY SIZE!
PRICE-CO
ALPHABET SOUP
ABC
5 GALLONS (310 FL. OZ)
SALE!! LOW $!!
OOH-HOO Nostalgia OOH-HOO
JACKPOT!
99¢
THIS STUFF USED TO MAKE ME AS BRAVE AS BEARS.

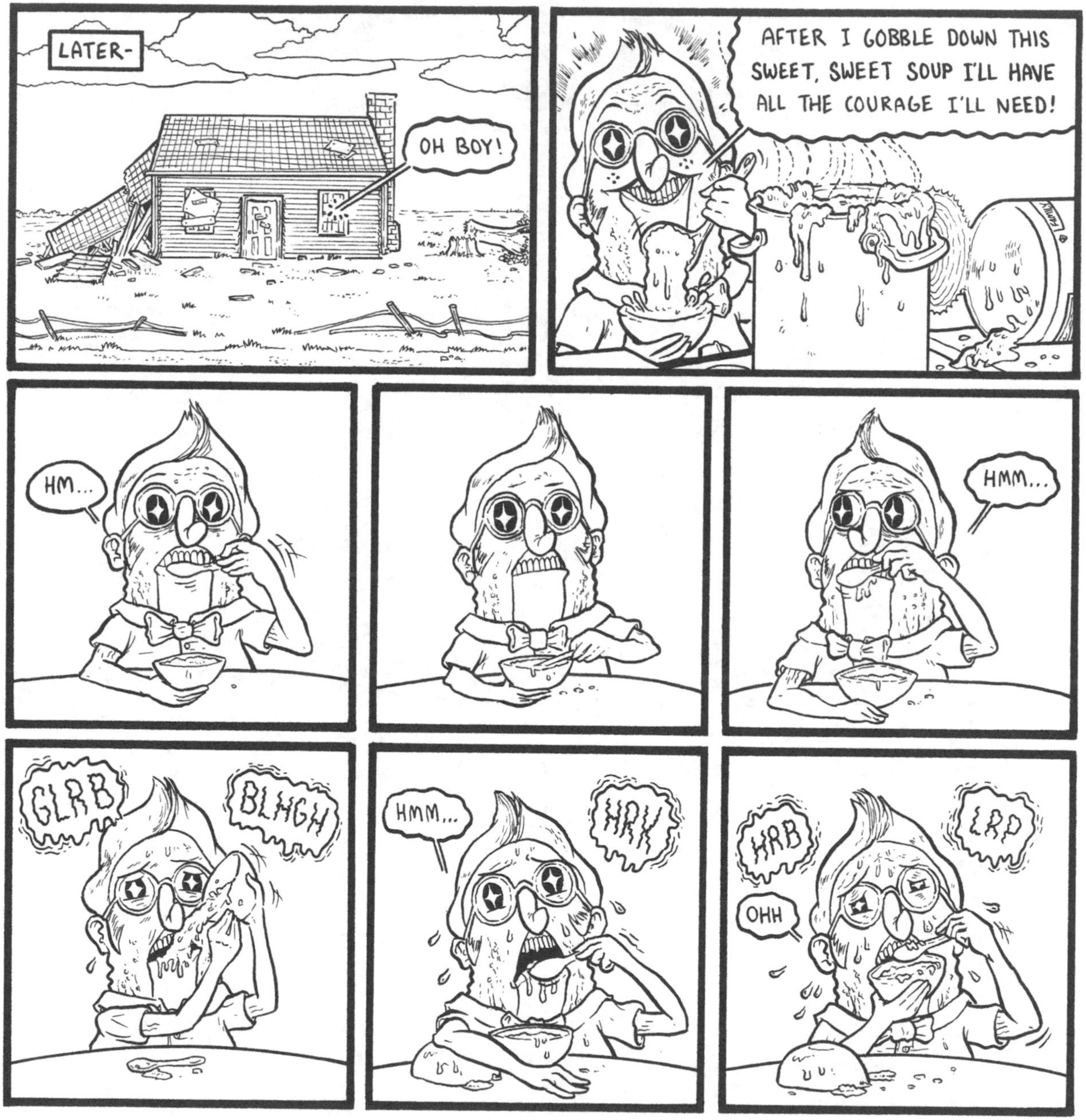
LATER-
OH BOY!
AFTER I GOBBLE DOWN THIS SWEET, SWEET SOUP I'LL HAVE ALL THE COURAGE I'LL NEED!
HM...
HMM...
GLRB
BLHGH
HMM...
HRK
HRB
OHH
LRP

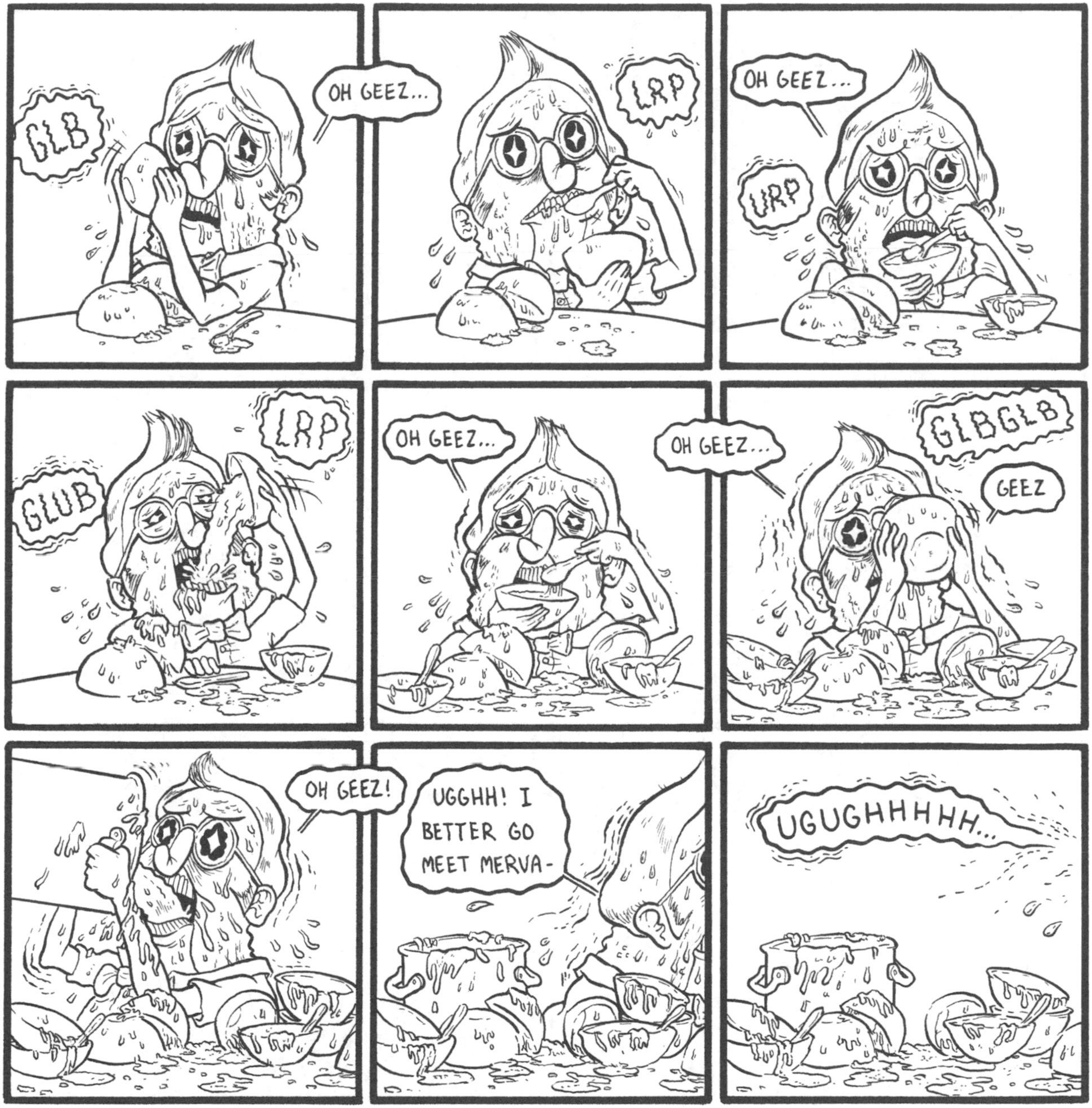
GLB
OH GEEZ...
LRP
OH GEEZ...
URP
GLUB
LRP
OH GEEZ...
OH GEEZ...
GLBGLB
GEEZ
OH GEEZ!
UGGHH! I BETTER GO MEET MERVA-
UGUGHHHHH...

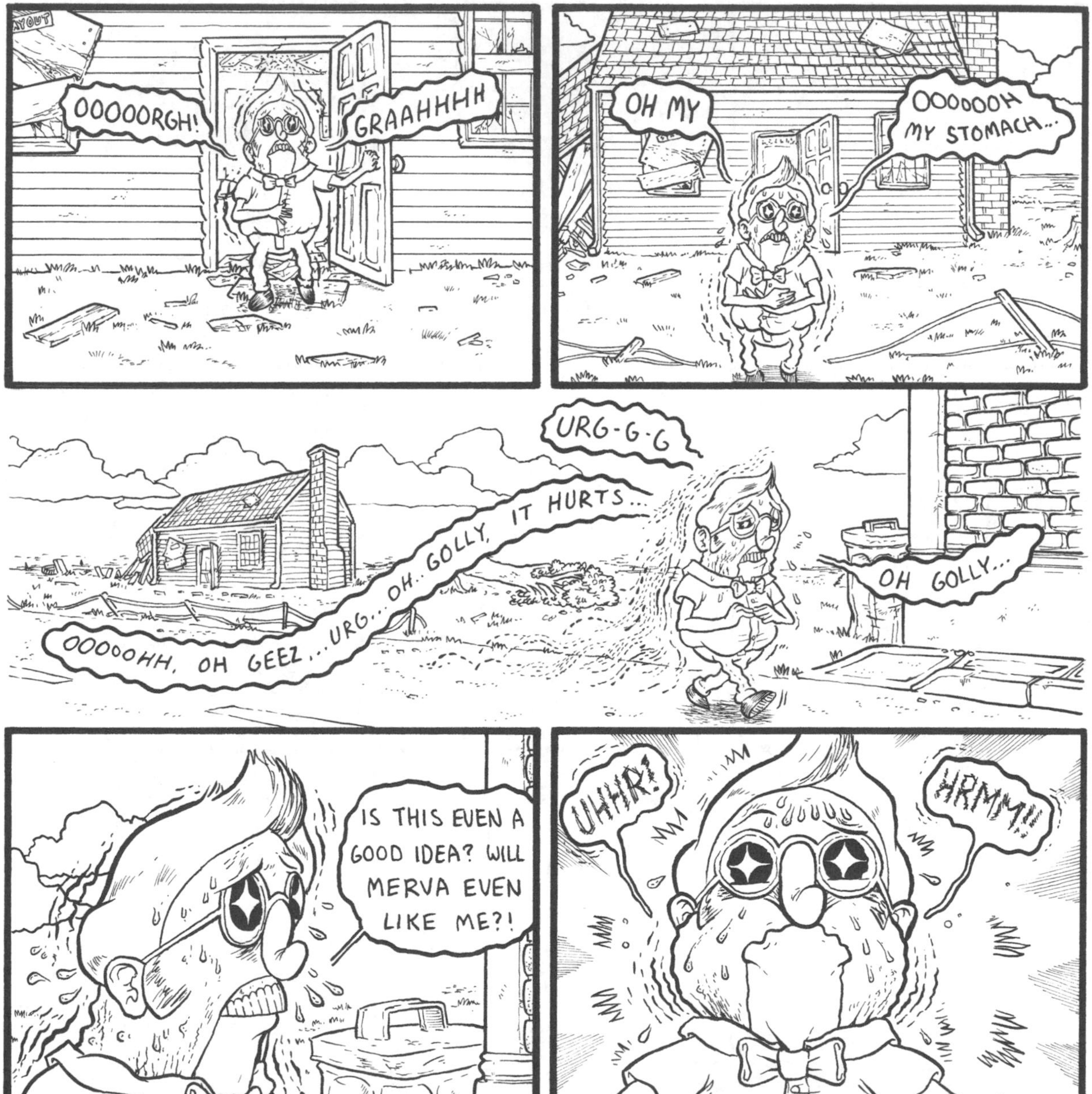
OOOOORGH!
GRAAHHHH
OH MY
OOOOOOH MY STOMACH...
URG-G-G
OOOOOHH, OH GEEZ... URG... OH.. GOLLY, IT HURTS...
OH GOLLY...
IS THIS EVEN A GOOD IDEA? WILL MERVA EVEN LIKE ME?!
UHHR!
HRMM!

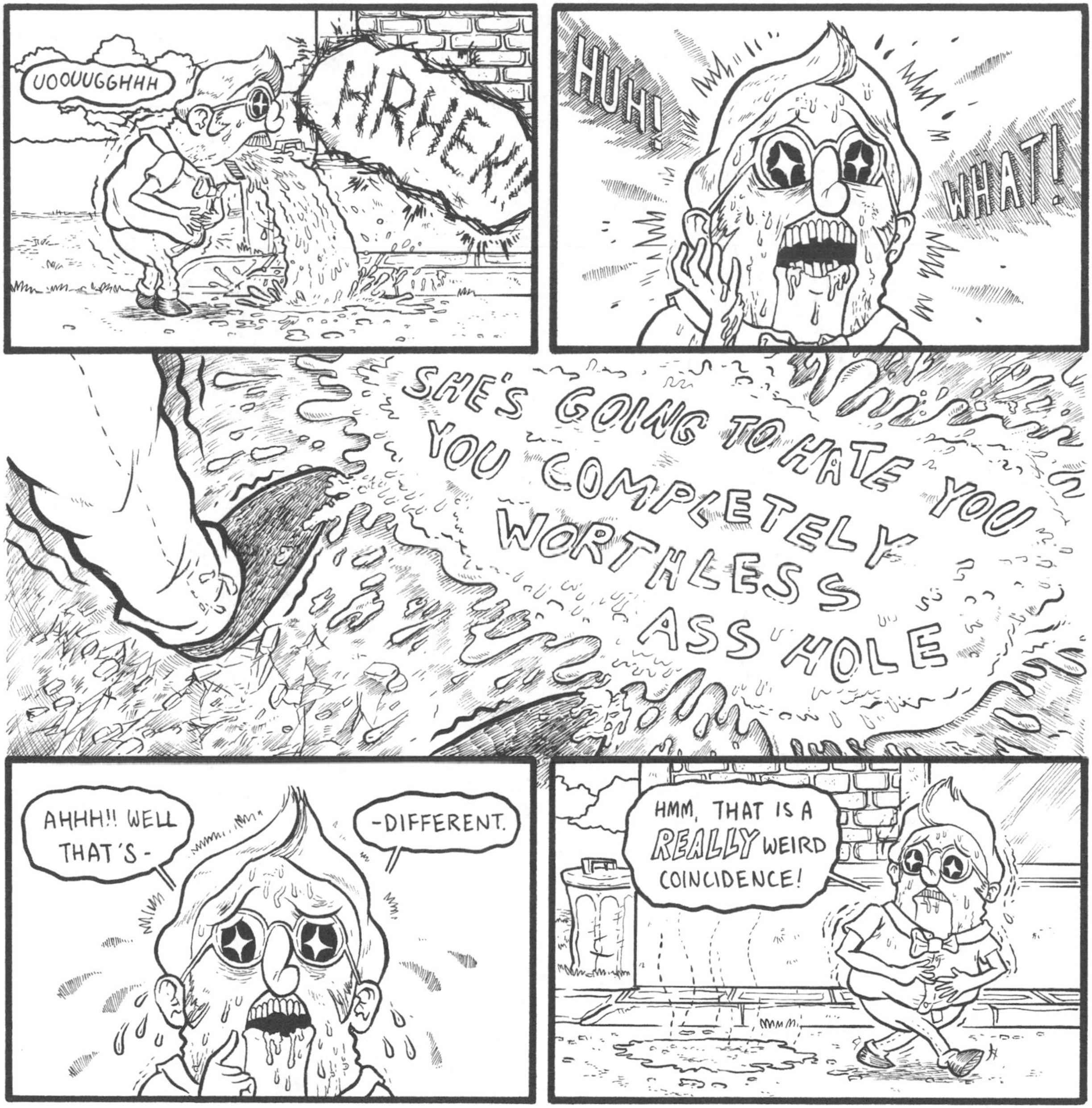
UOOUUGGHHH
HRHEK!
HUH!
WHAT!
SHE'S GOING TO HATE YOU
YOU COMPLETELY
WORTHLESS
ASS HOLE
AHHH!! WELL THAT'S -
-DIFFERENT.
HMM, THAT IS A REALLY WEIRD COINCIDENCE!

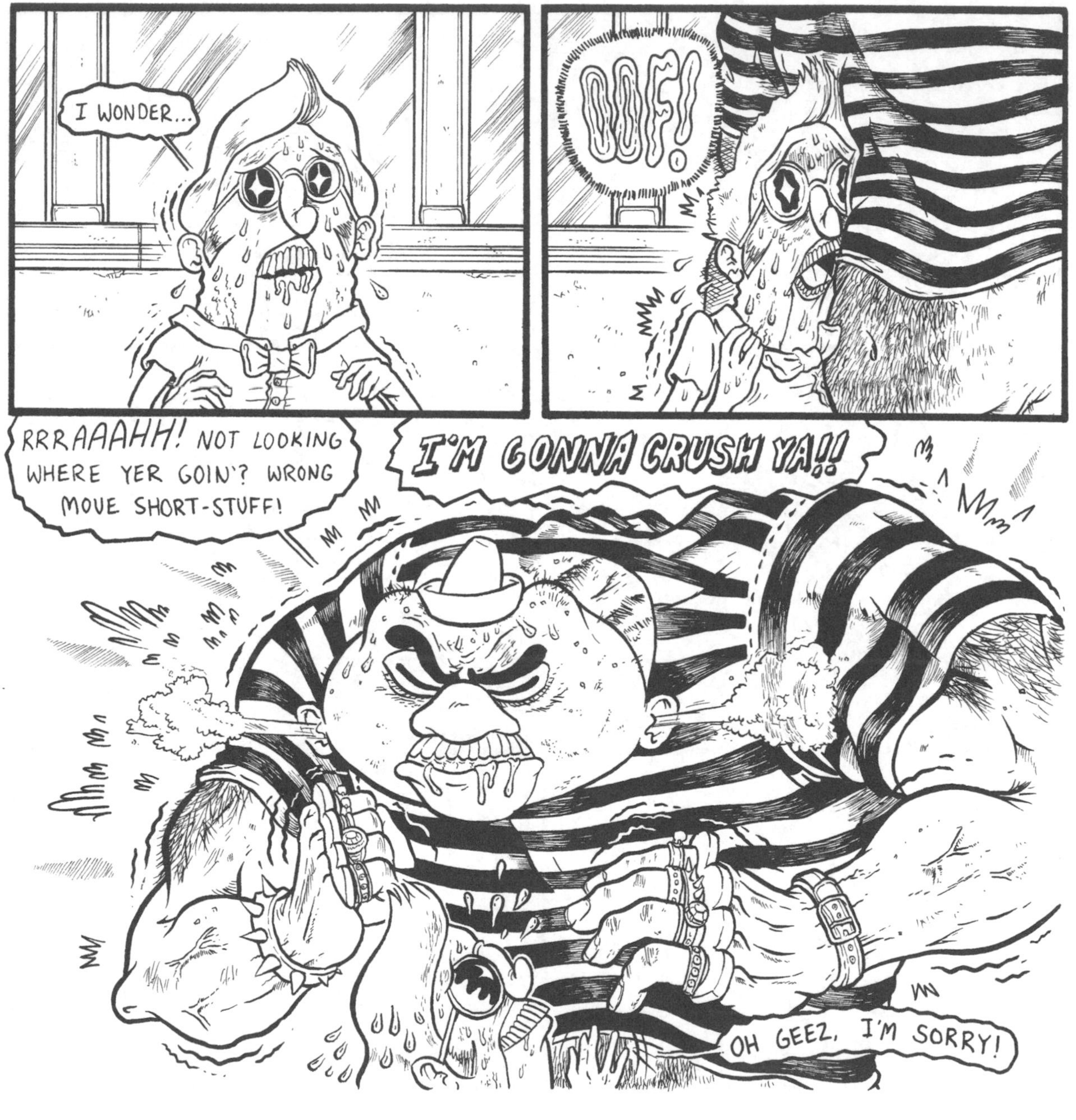
I WONDER...
OOF!
RRRAAAHH! NOT LOOKING WHERE YER GOIN'? WRONG MOVE SHORT-STUFF!
I'M GONNA CRUSH YA!!
OH GEEZ, I'M SORRY!

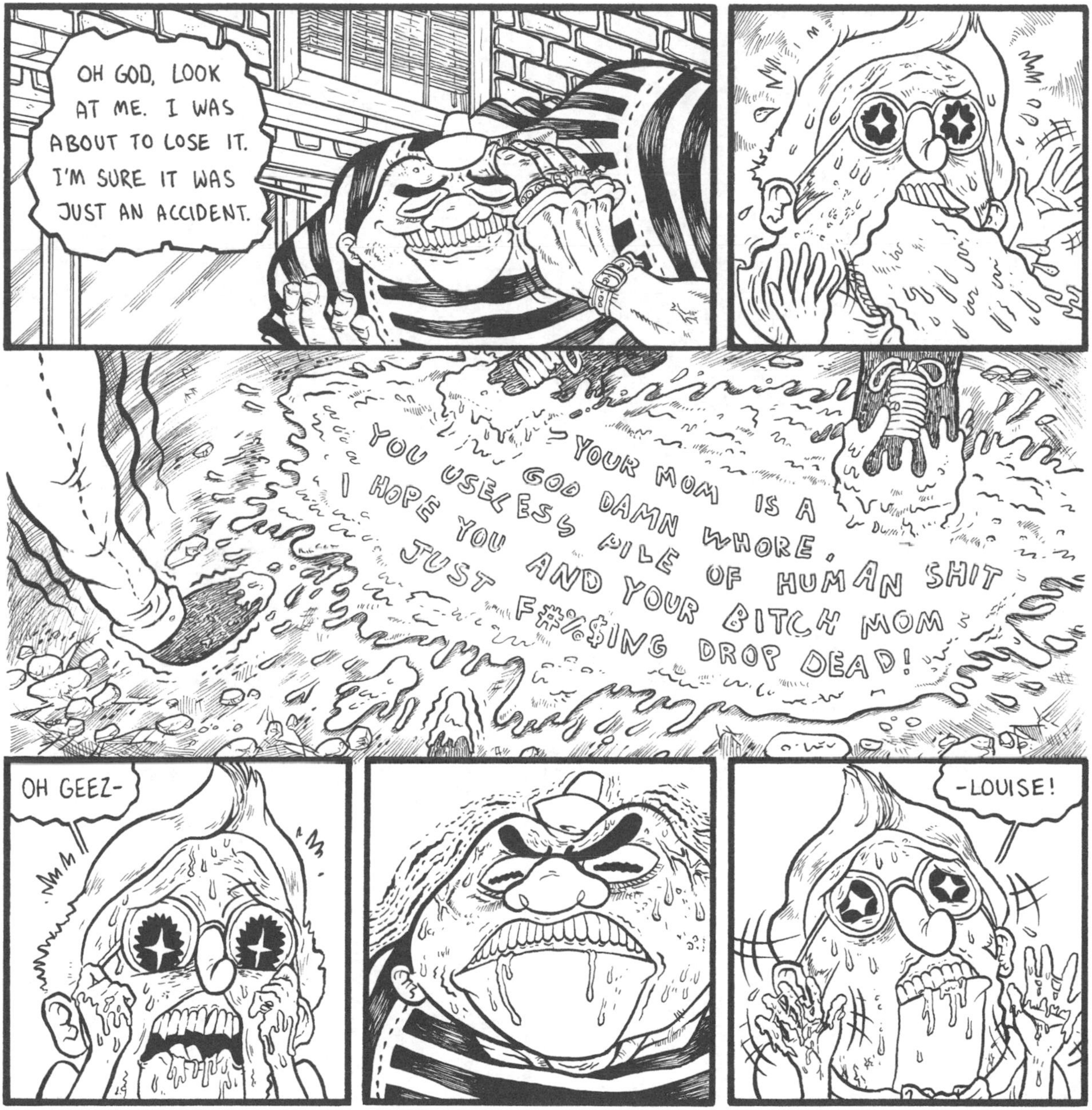
OH GOD, LOOK AT ME. I WAS ABOUT TO LOSE IT. I'M SURE IT WAS JUST AN ACCIDENT.
YOUR MOM IS A GOD DAMN WHORE, YOU USELESS PILE OF HUMAN SHIT I HOPE YOU AND YOUR BITCH MOM JUST F#%$ING DROP DEAD!
OH GEEZ-
-LOUISE!

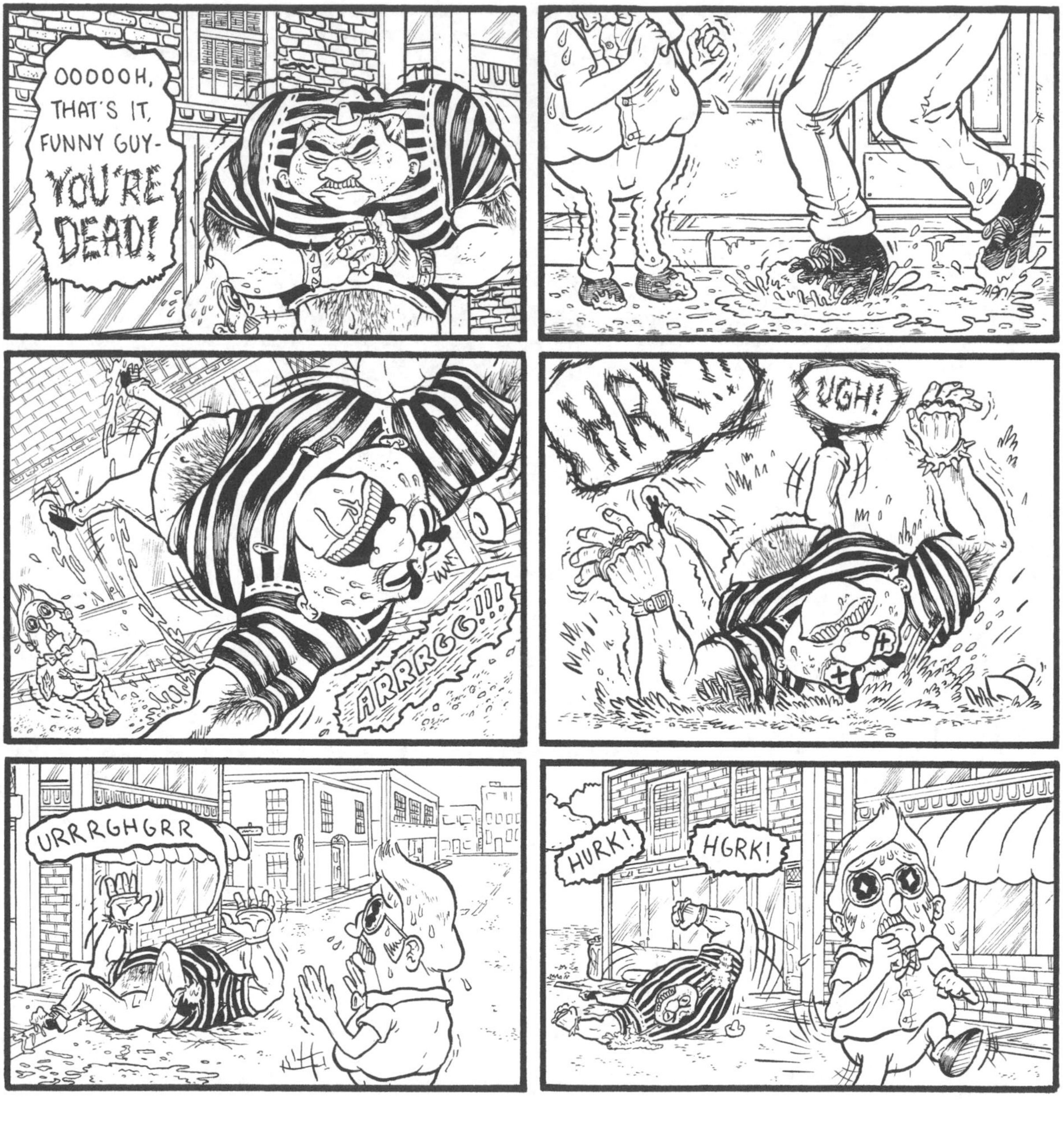
OOOOOH, THAT'S IT, FUNNY GUY- YOU'RE DEAD!
ARRRGG!!!
HRK!
UGH!
URRRGHGRR
HURK!
HGRK!

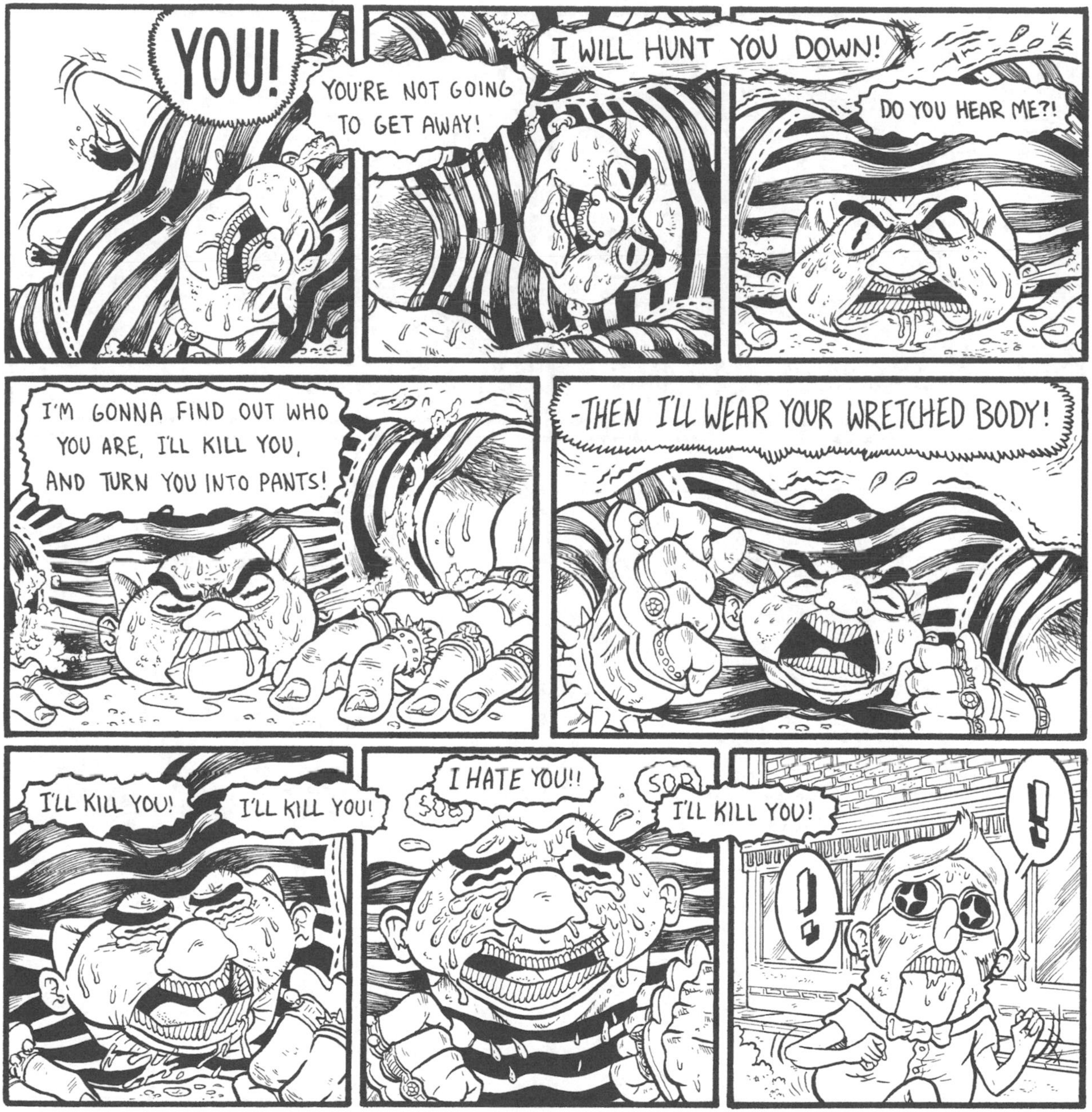
YOU!
YOU'RE NOT GOING TO GET AWAY!
I WILL HUNT YOU DOWN!
DO YOU HEAR ME?!
I'M GONNA FIND OUT WHO YOU ARE, I'LL KILL YOU, AND TURN YOU INTO PANTS!
-THEN I'LL WEAR YOUR WRETCHED BODY!
I'LL KILL YOU!
I'LL KILL YOU!
I HATE YOU!!
SOB
SOB
I'LL KILL YOU!
!
!

DO YOU HEAR ME!?
GOTTA-
-HURRY-
-CAN'T-
I'M GONNA WEAR YOU!!
-BE LATE-
-FOR MERVA!
RAY'S
PARK
Huff
Huff
Huff
Huff
Huff
Huff
Huff
PARK

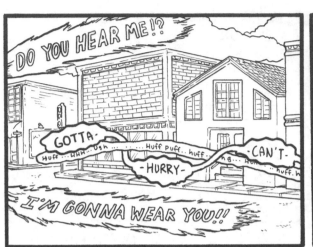

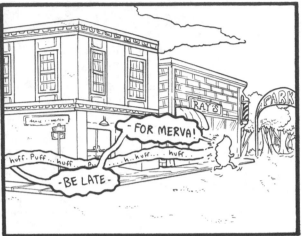

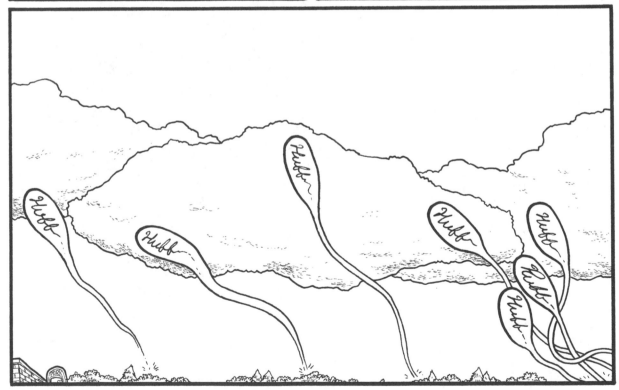

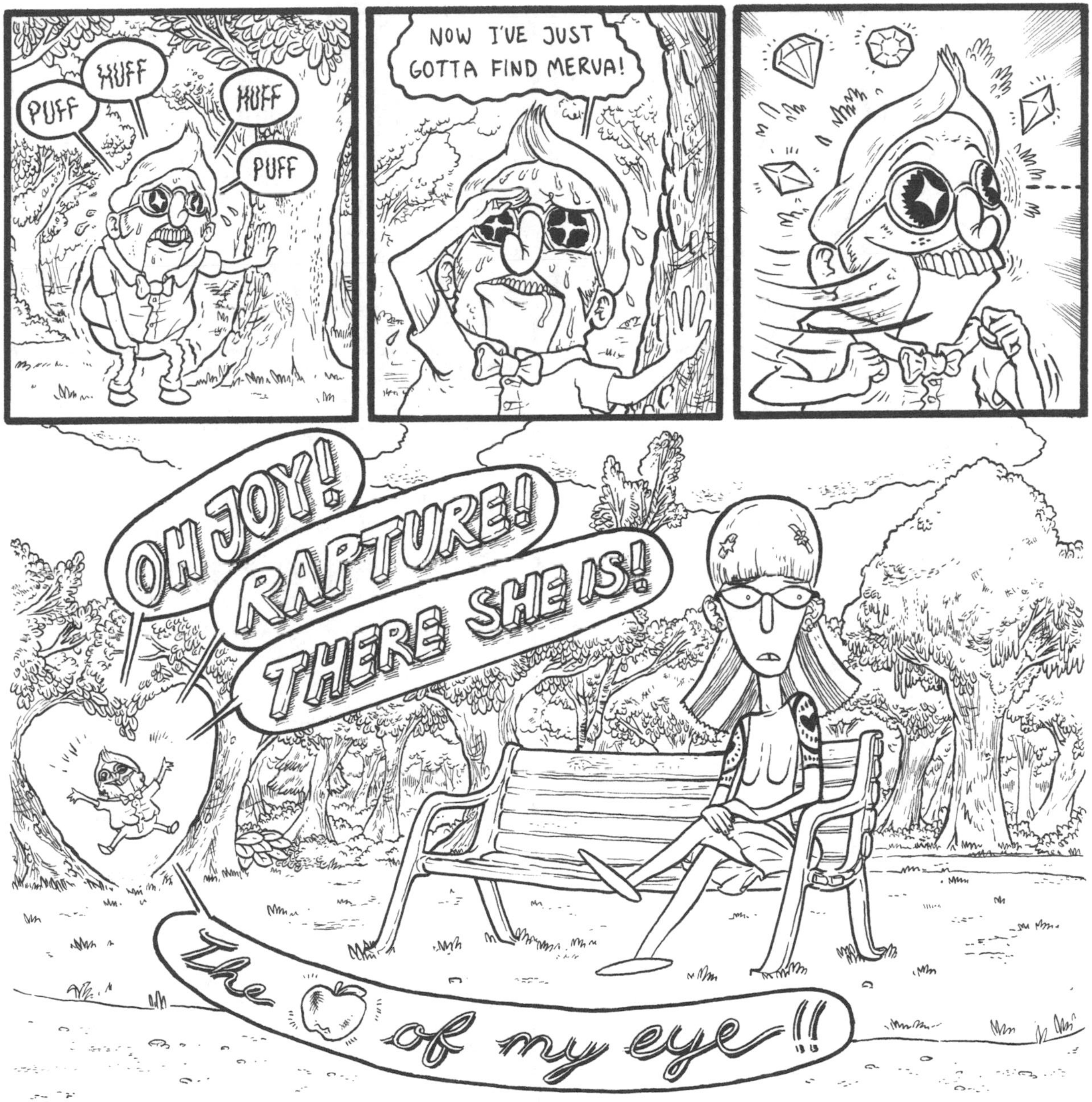
PUFF
HUFF
HUFF
PUFF
NOW I'VE JUST GOTTA FIND MERVA!
OH JOY!
RAPTURE!
THERE SHE IS!
The [apple] of my eye!!

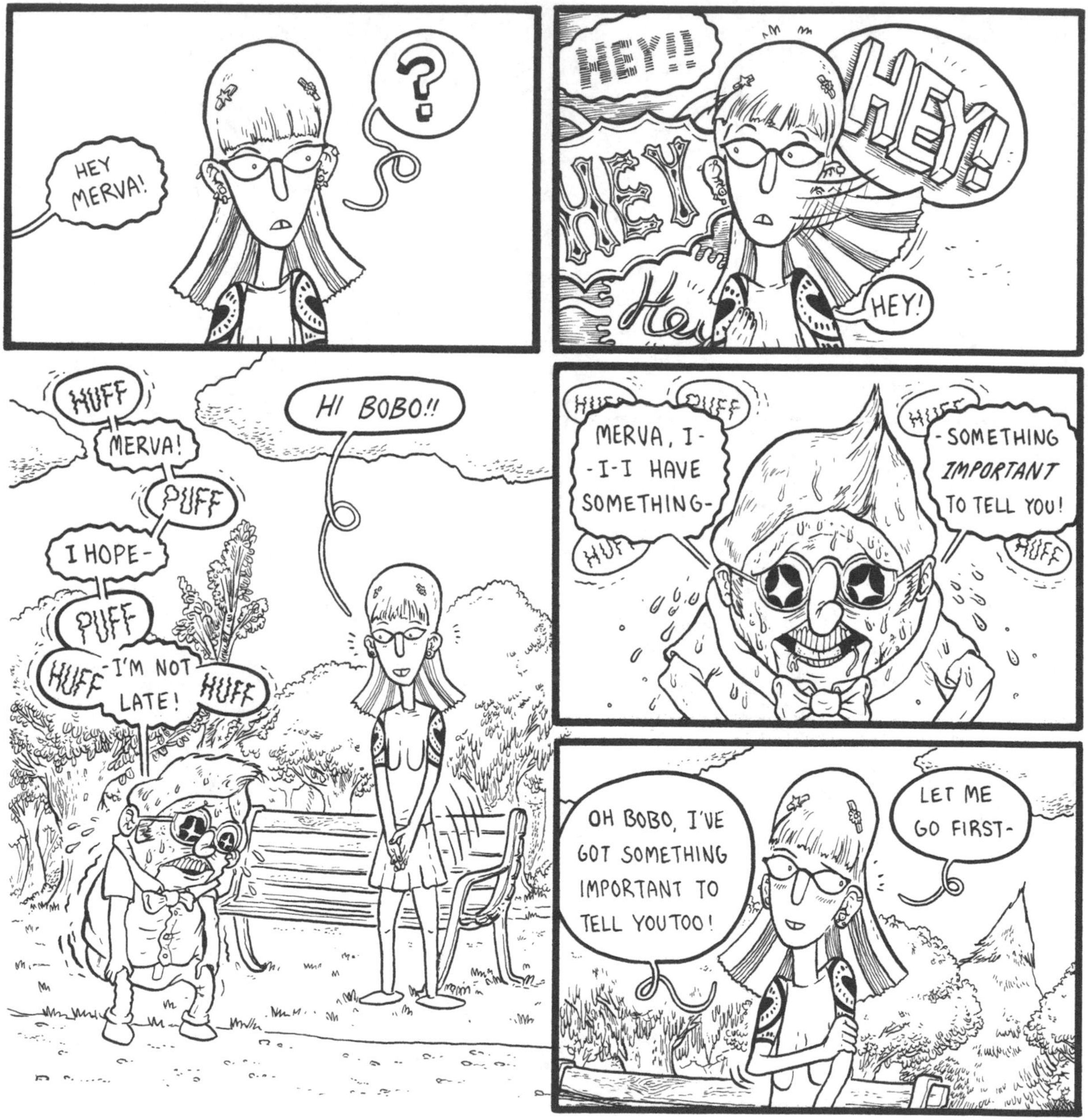
HEY MERVA!
?
HEY!!
HEY
Hey
HEY!
HEY!
HUFF
MERVA!
PUFF
I HOPE-
PUFF
HUFF
-I'M NOT LATE!
HUFF
HI BOBO!!
MERVA, I- -I-I HAVE SOMETHING-
-SOMETHING IMPORTANT TO TELL YOU!
HUFF
OH BOBO, I'VE GOT SOMETHING IMPORTANT TO TELL YOU TOO!
LET ME GO FIRST-

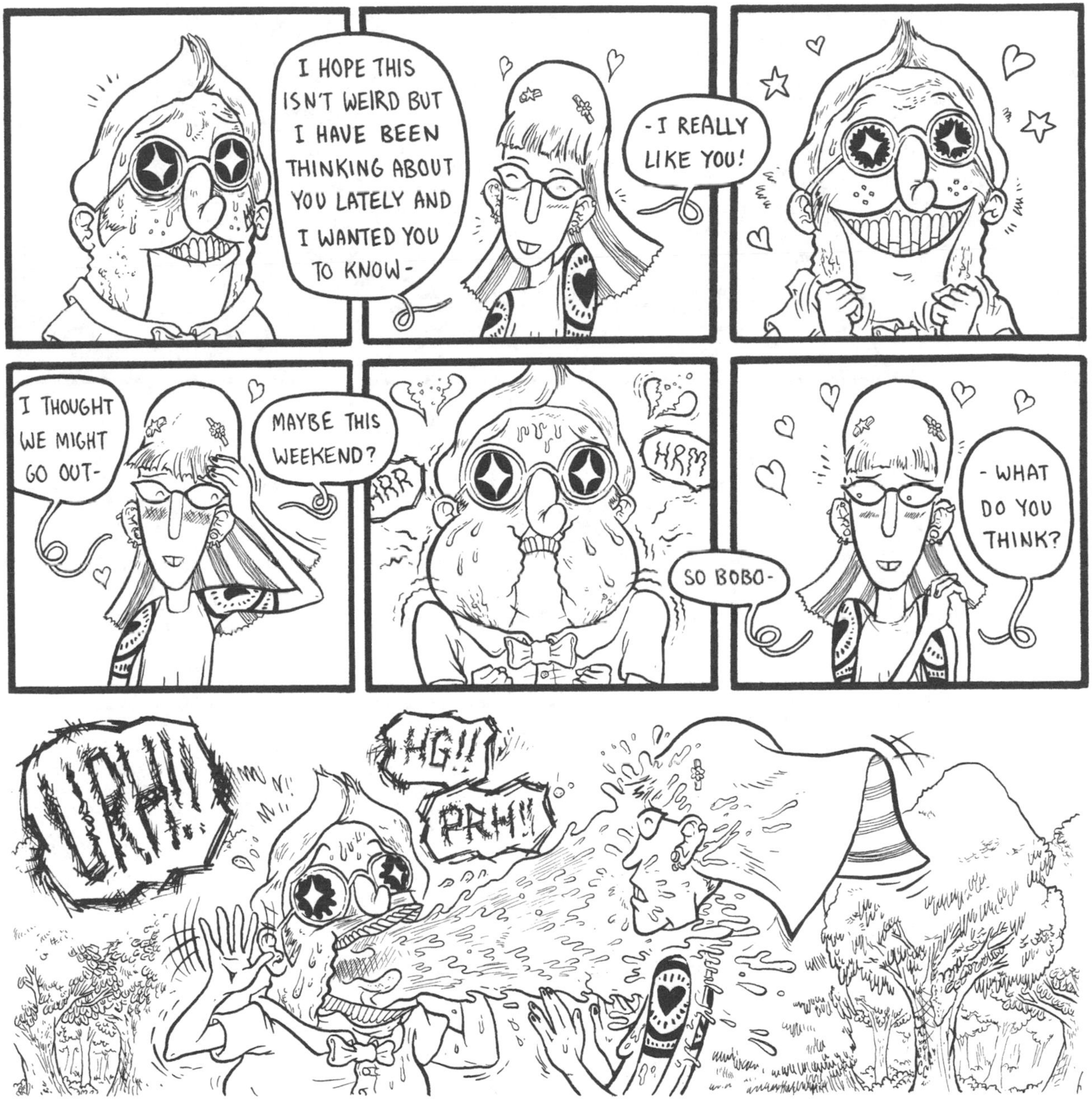
I HOPE THIS ISN'T WEIRD BUT I HAVE BEEN THINKING ABOUT YOU LATELY AND I WANTED YOU TO KNOW-
-I REALLY LIKE YOU!
I THOUGHT WE MIGHT GO OUT-
MAYBE THIS WEEKEND?
HRR
HRM
SO BOBO-
-WHAT DO YOU THINK?
URH!!
HG!!
PRH!!

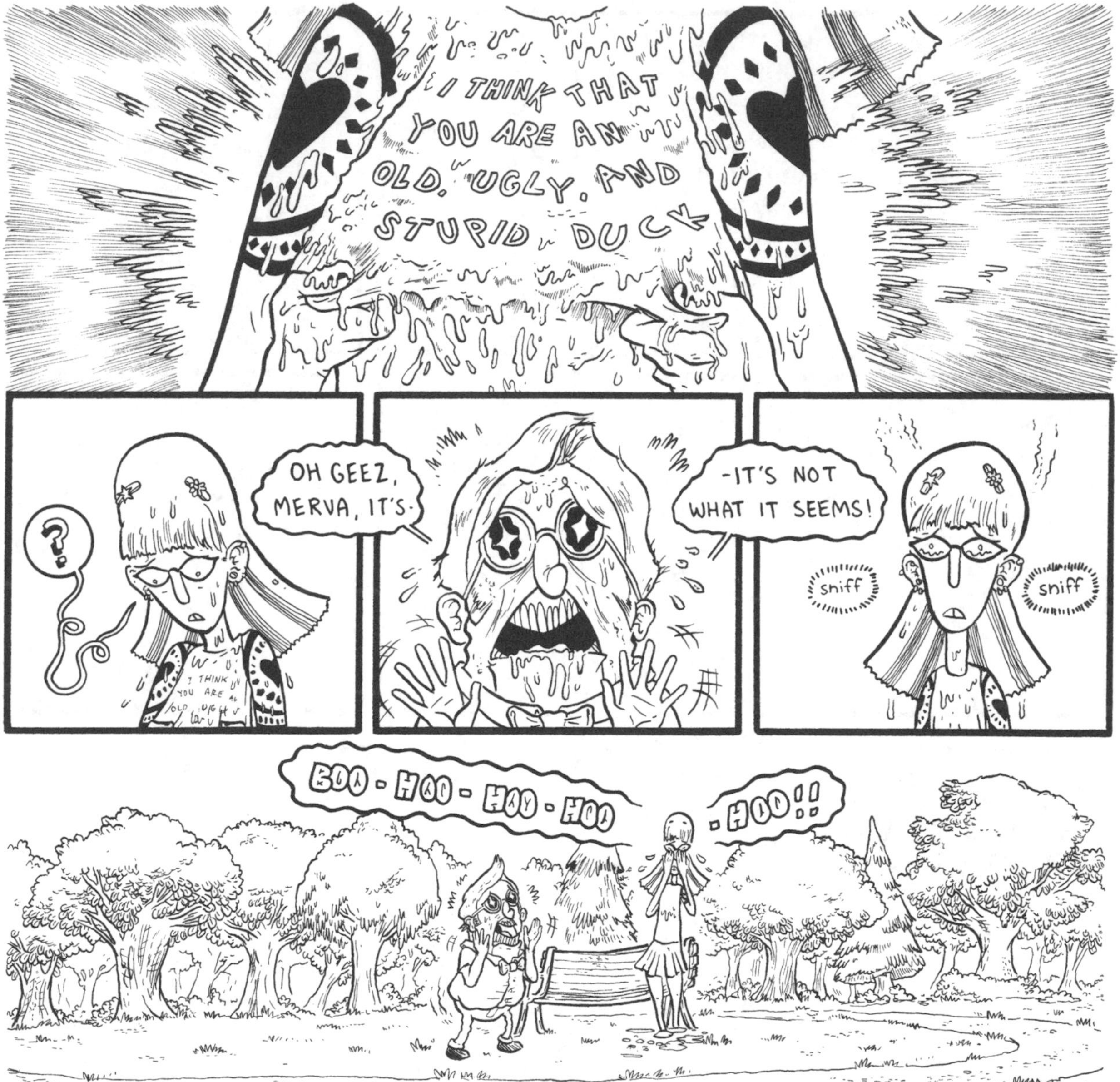
I THINK THAT YOU ARE AN OLD, UGLY, AND STUPID DUCK
?
OH GEEZ, MERVA, IT'S-
-IT'S NOT WHAT IT SEEMS!
sniff
sniff
BOO-HOO-HOO-HOO-HOO-HOO!!

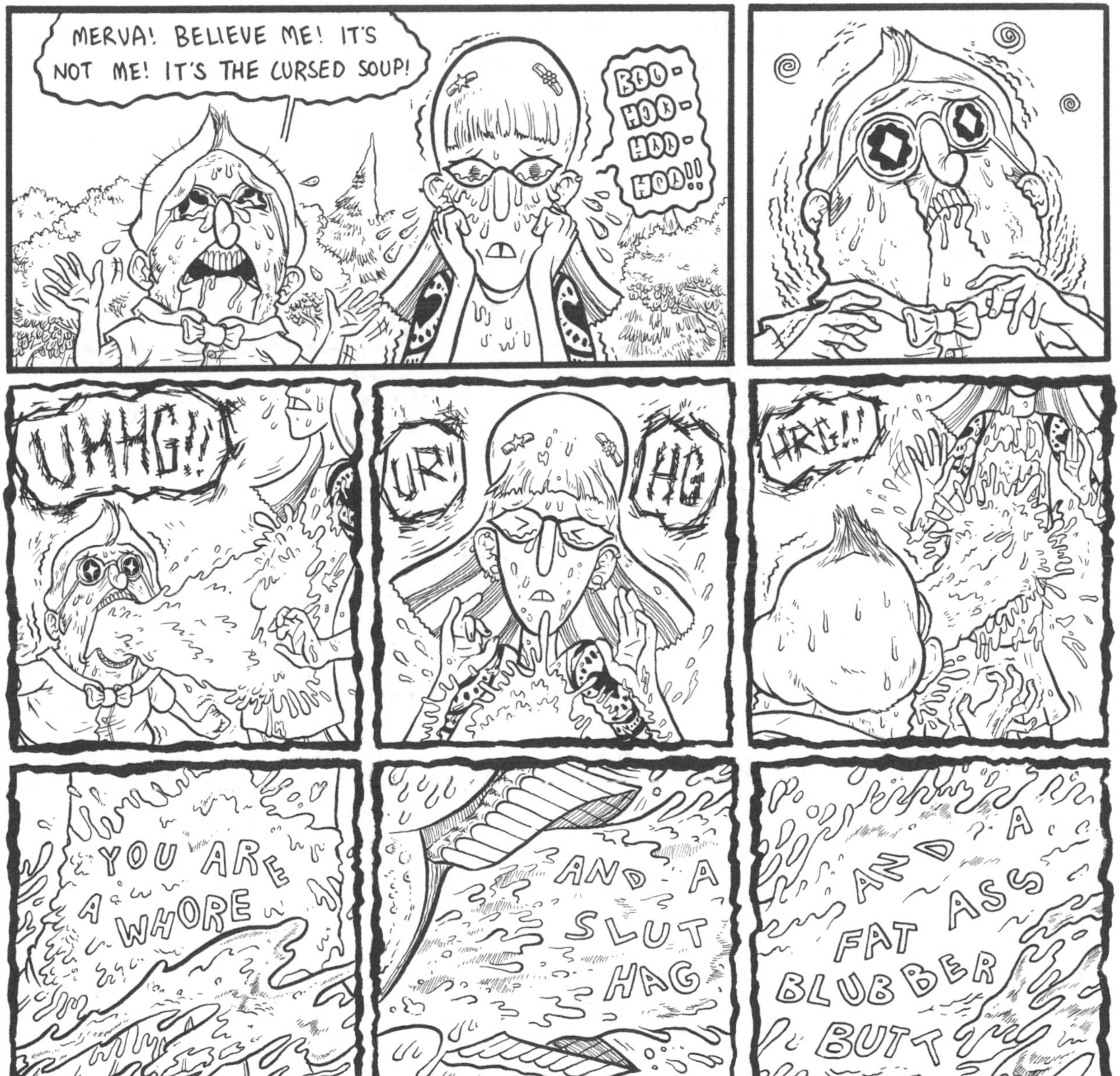
MERVA! BELIEVE ME! IT'S NOT ME! IT'S THE CURSED SOUP!
BOO-HOO-HOO-HOO!!
UHHG!!
UR!
HG
HRG!!
YOU ARE A WHORE
AND A SLUT HAG
AND A FAT ASS BLUBBER BUTT

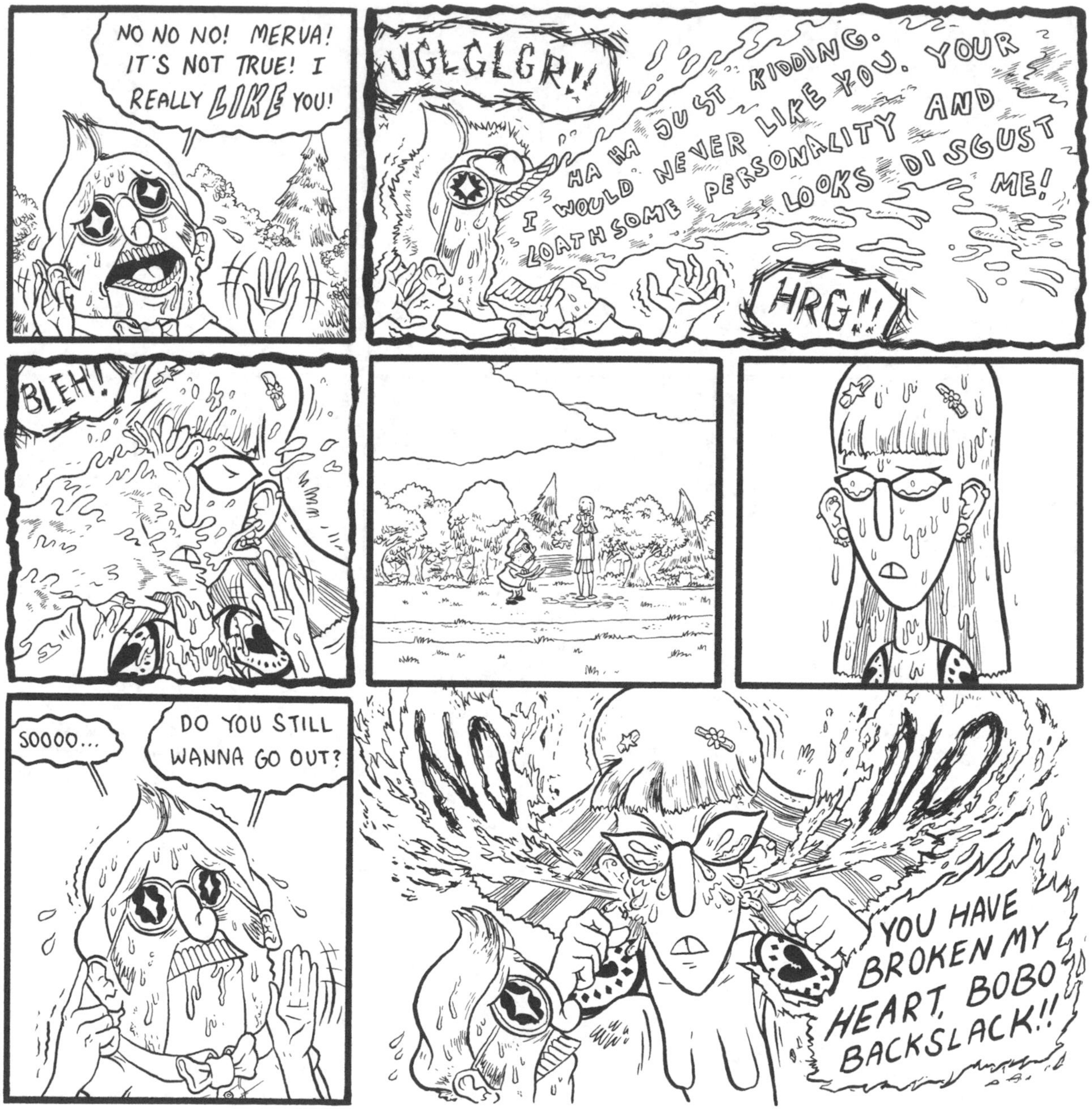
NO NO NO! MERVA! IT'S NOT TRUE! I REALLY LIKE YOU!
UGLGLGR!!
HA HA JUST KIDDING. I WOULD NEVER LIKE YOU. YOUR LOATHSOME PERSONALITY AND LOOKS DISGUST ME!
HRG!!
BLEH!
SOOOO...
DO YOU STILL WANNA GO OUT?
NO NO
YOU HAVE BROKEN MY HEART, BOBO BACKSLACK!!

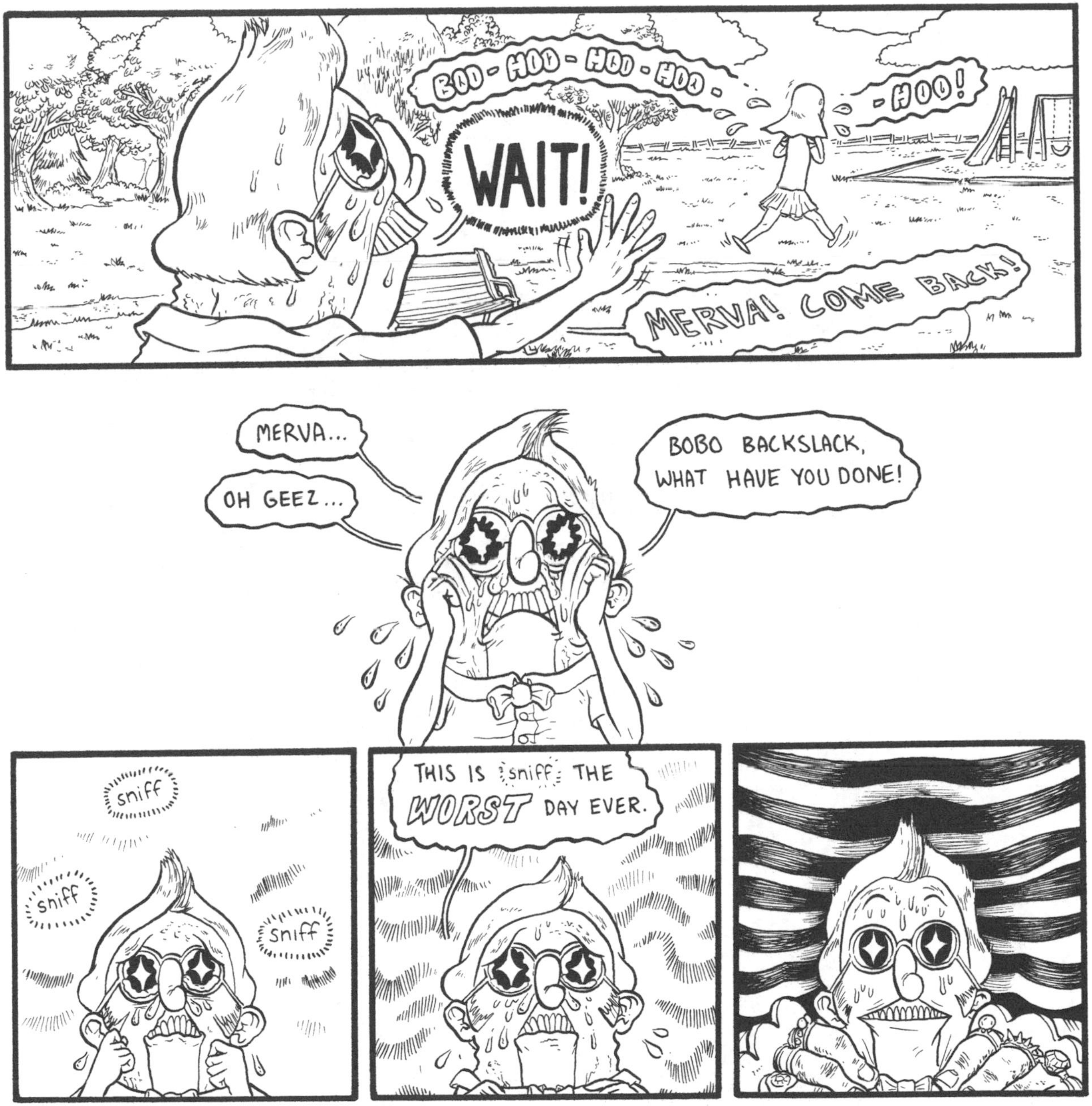
BOO-HOO-HOO-HOO-
-HOO!
WAIT!
MERVA! COME BACK!
MERVA...
OH GEEZ...
BOBO BACKSLACK, WHAT HAVE YOU DONE!
sniff
sniff
sniff
THIS IS sniff THE WORST DAY EVER.

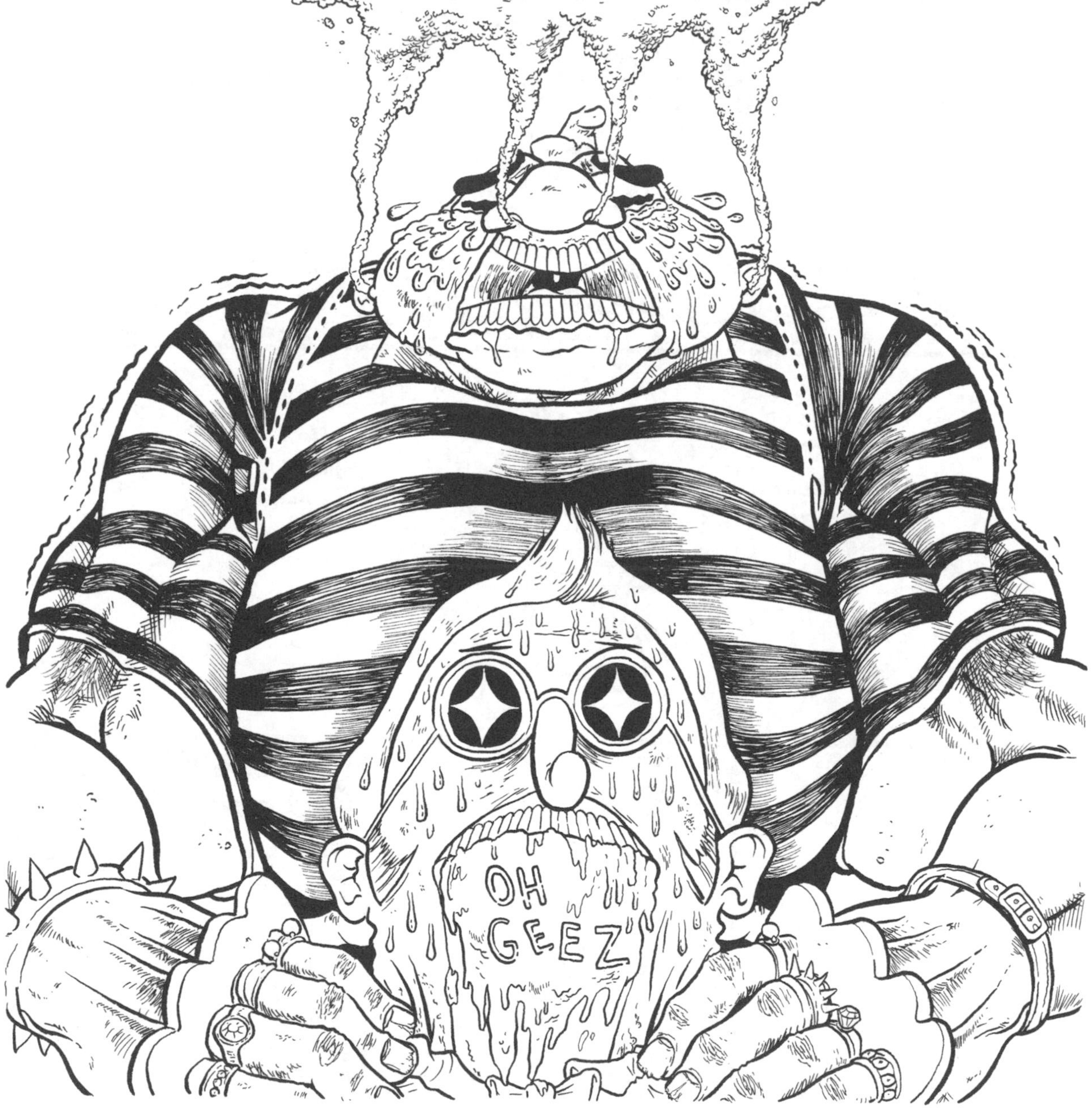
OH
GEEZ

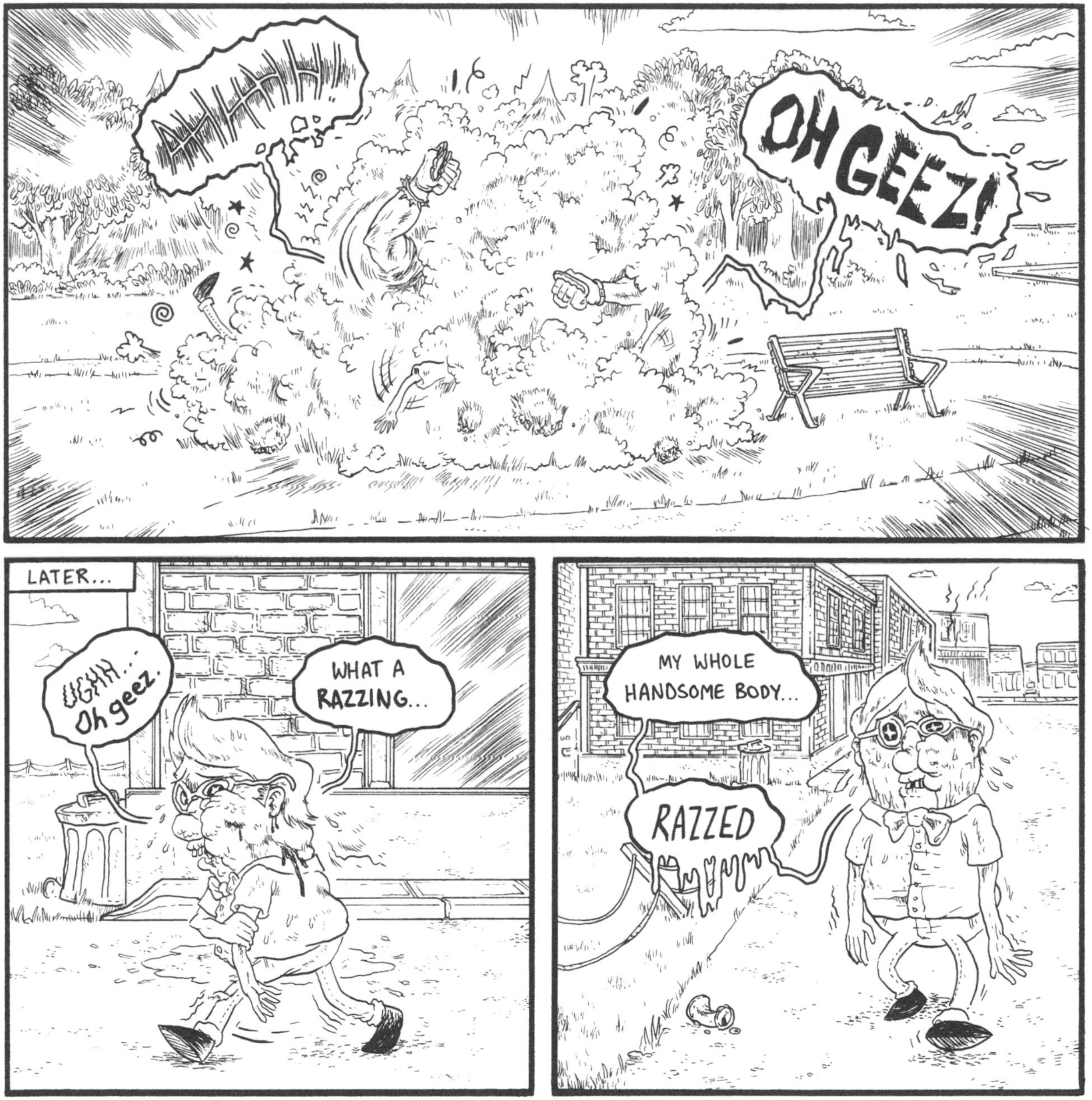
AHHHH!!
OH GEEZ!
LATER...
UGHH... Oh geez.
WHAT A RAZZING...
MY WHOLE HANDSOME BODY...
RAZZED

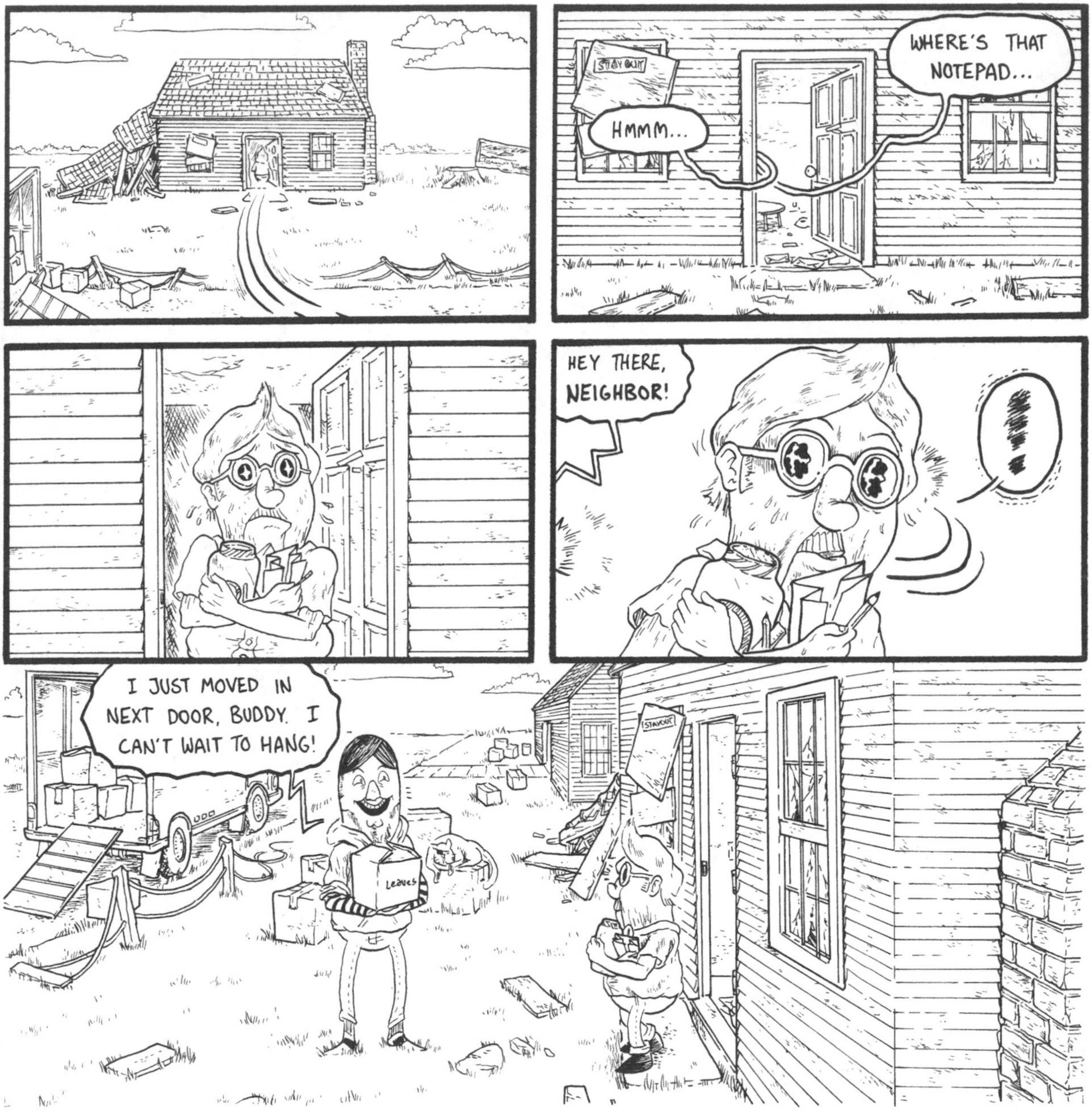
STAY OUT
HMMM...
WHERE'S THAT NOTEPAD...
HEY THERE, NEIGHBOR!
!
I JUST MOVED IN NEXT DOOR, BUDDY. I CAN'T WAIT TO HANG!
STAY OUT
Leaves

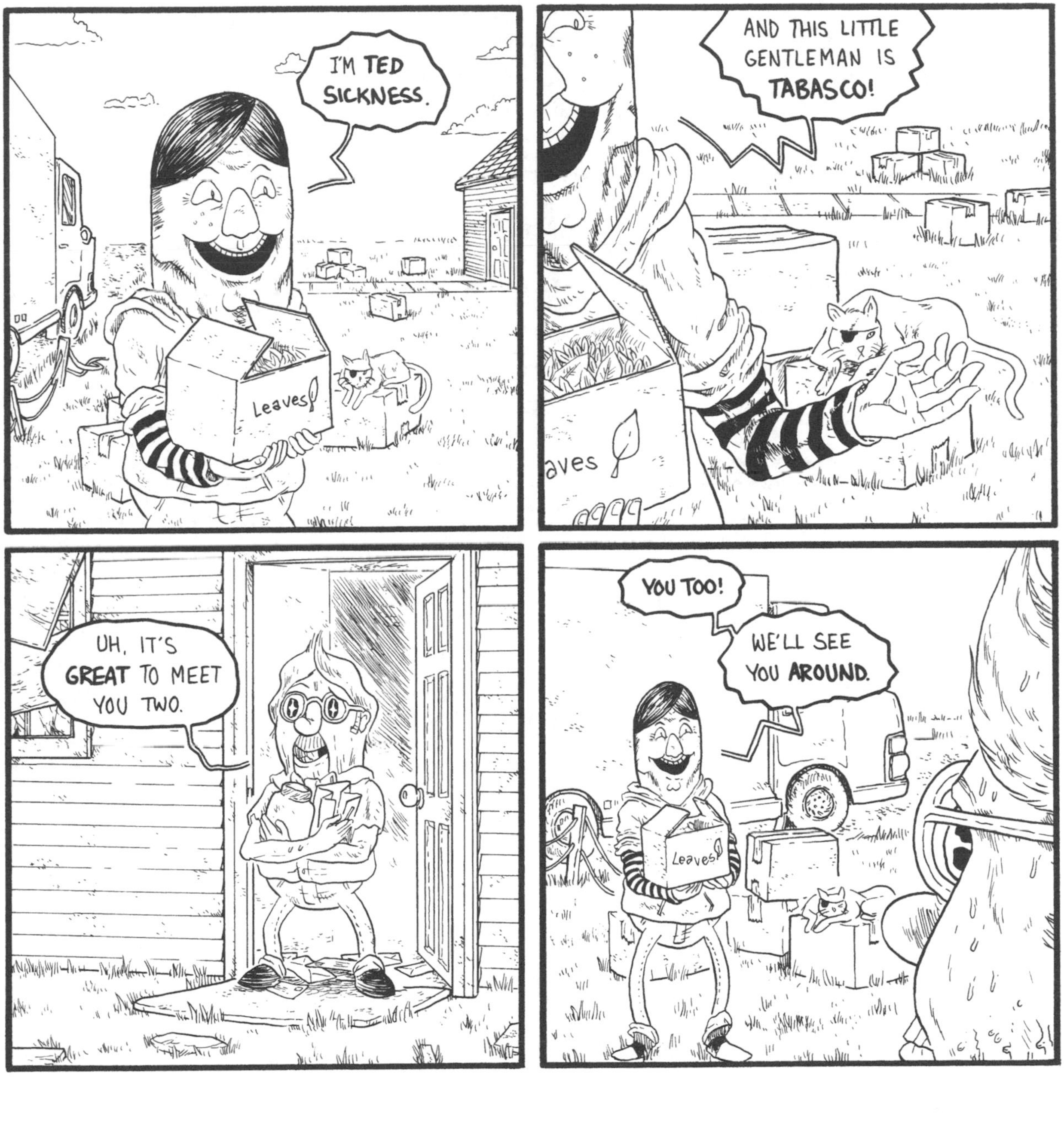
I'M TED SICKNESS.
Leaves
AND THIS LITTLE GENTLEMAN IS TABASCO!
aves
UH, IT'S GREAT TO MEET YOU TWO.
YOU TOO!
WE'LL SEE YOU AROUND.
Leaves

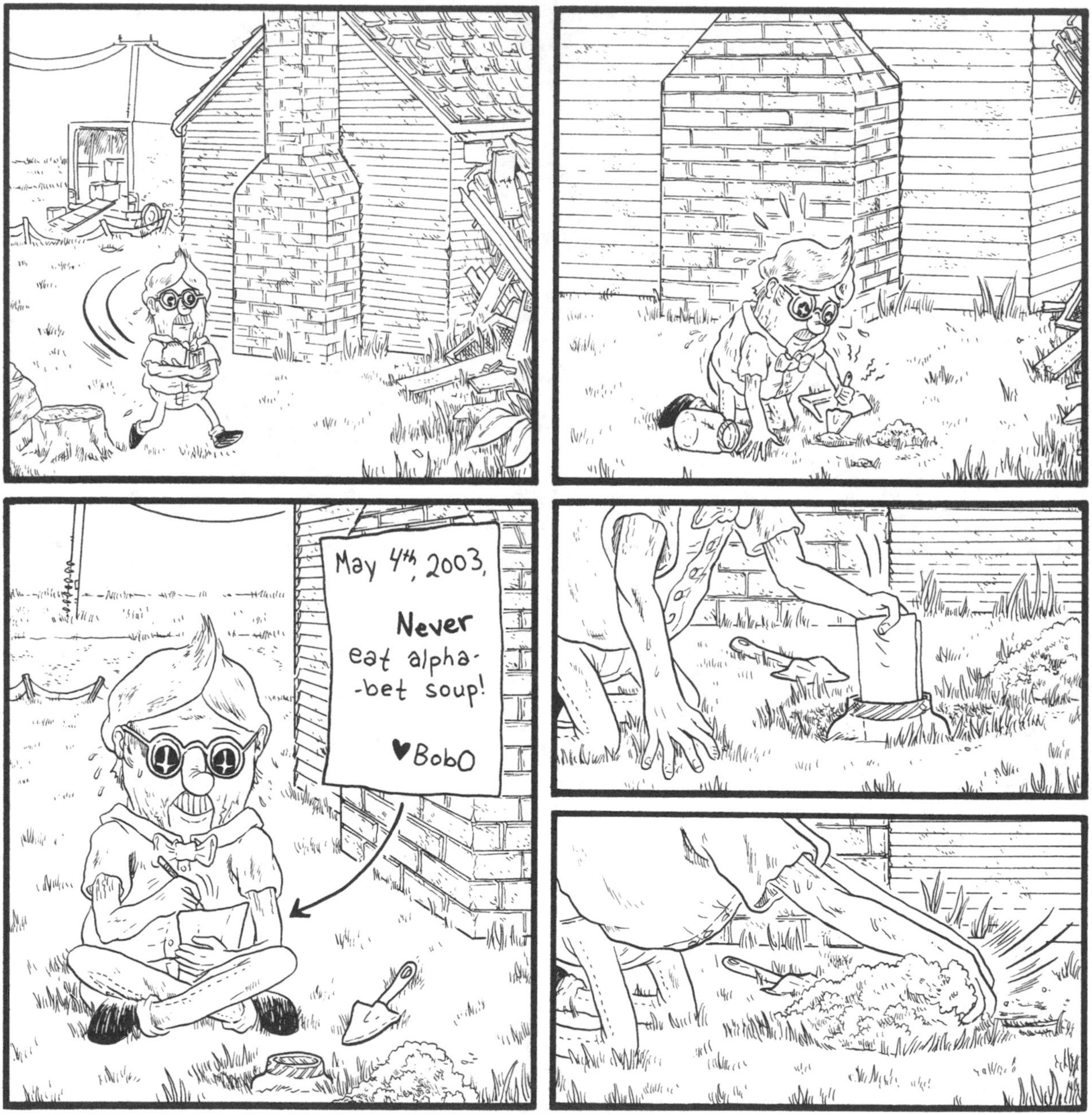
May 4th, 2003,
Never eat alpha-bet soup!
♥BobO

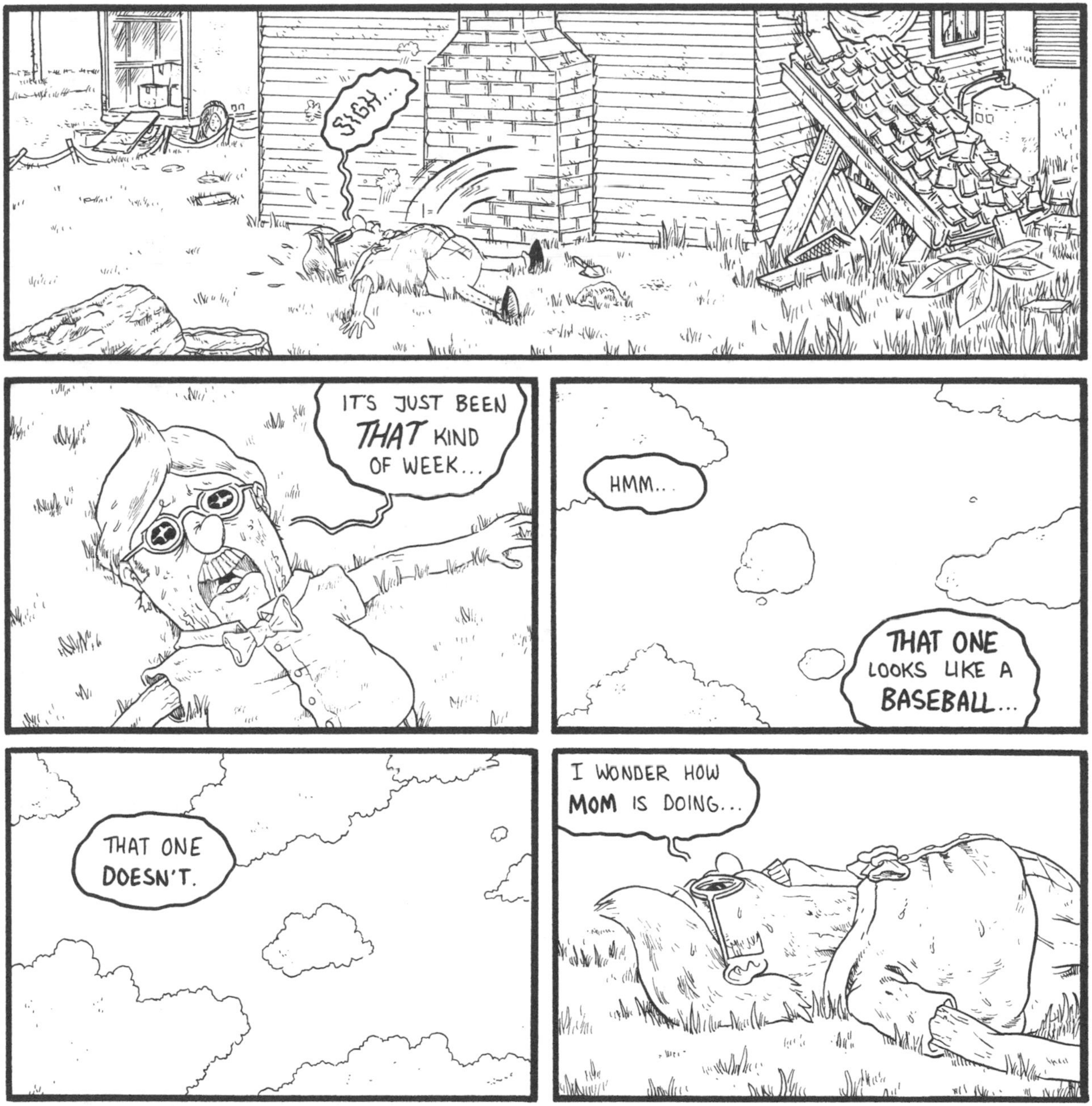
SIGH...
IT'S JUST BEEN THAT KIND OF WEEK...
HMM..
THAT ONE LOOKS LIKE A BASEBALL...
THAT ONE DOESN'T.
I WONDER HOW MOM IS DOING...

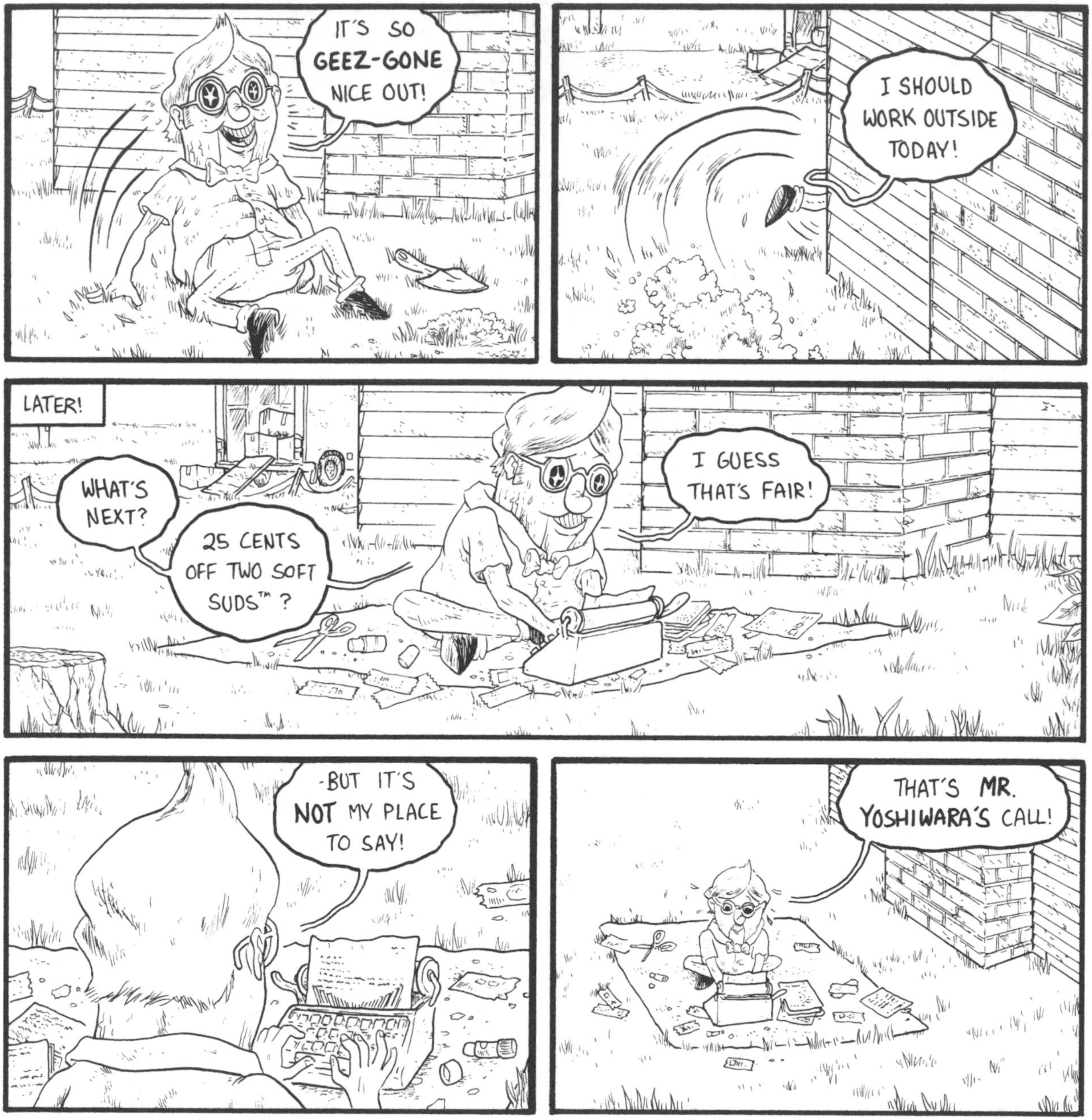
IT'S SO GEEZ-GONE NICE OUT!
I SHOULD WORK OUTSIDE TODAY!
LATER!
WHAT'S NEXT?
25 CENTS OFF TWO SOFT SUDS™ ?
I GUESS THAT'S FAIR!
-BUT IT'S NOT MY PLACE TO SAY!
THAT'S MR. YOSHIWARA'S CALL!

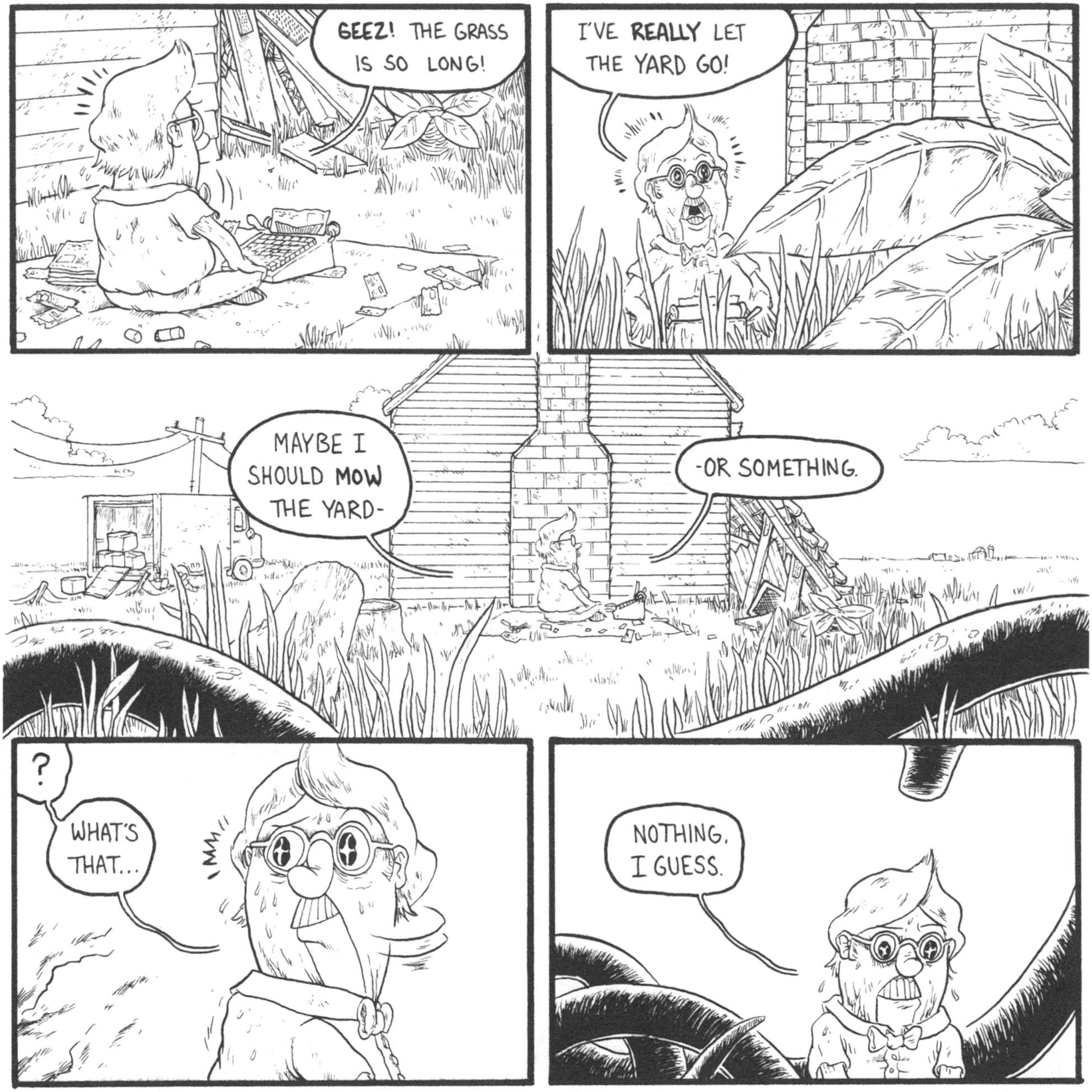
GEEZ! THE GRASS IS SO LONG!
I'VE REALLY LET THE YARD GO!
MAYBE I SHOULD MOW THE YARD-
-OR SOMETHING.
?
WHAT'S THAT...
MM
NOTHING, I GUESS.

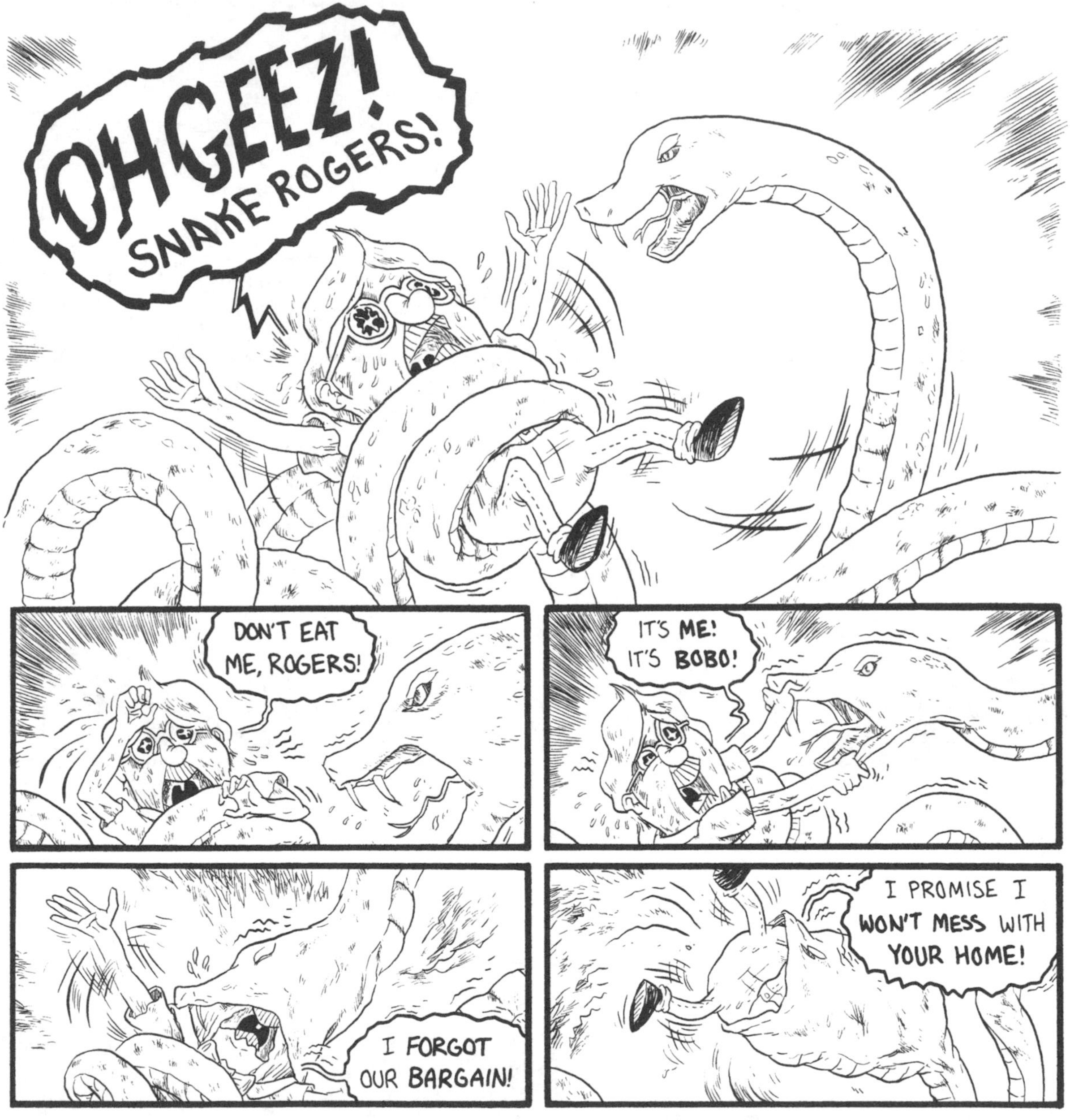
OH GEEZ! SNAKE ROGERS!
DON'T EAT ME, ROGERS!
IT'S ME! IT'S BOBO!
I FORGOT OUR BARGAIN!
I PROMISE I WON'T MESS WITH YOUR HOME!

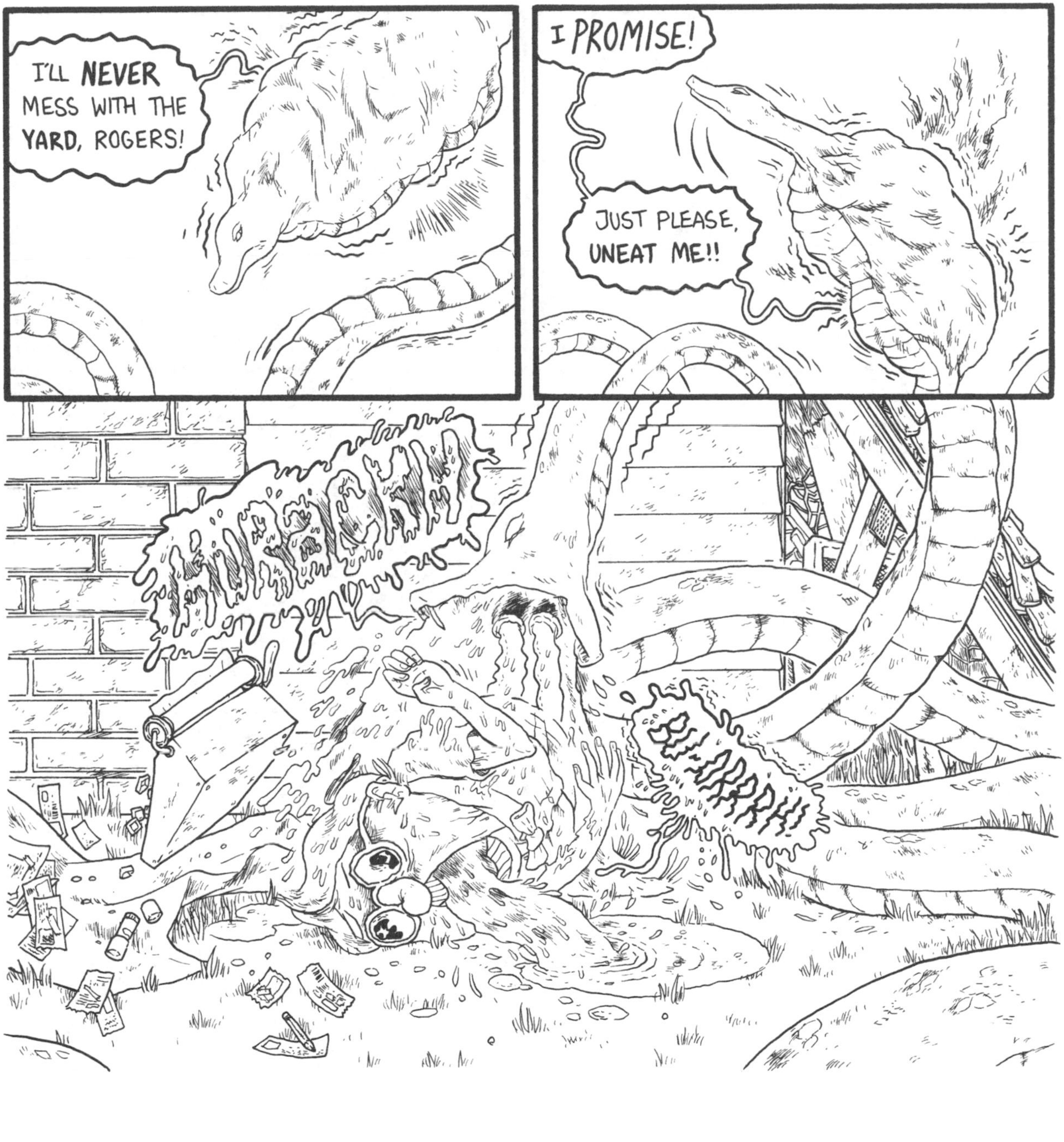
I'LL NEVER MESS WITH THE YARD, ROGERS!
I PROMISE!
JUST PLEASE, UNEAT ME!!

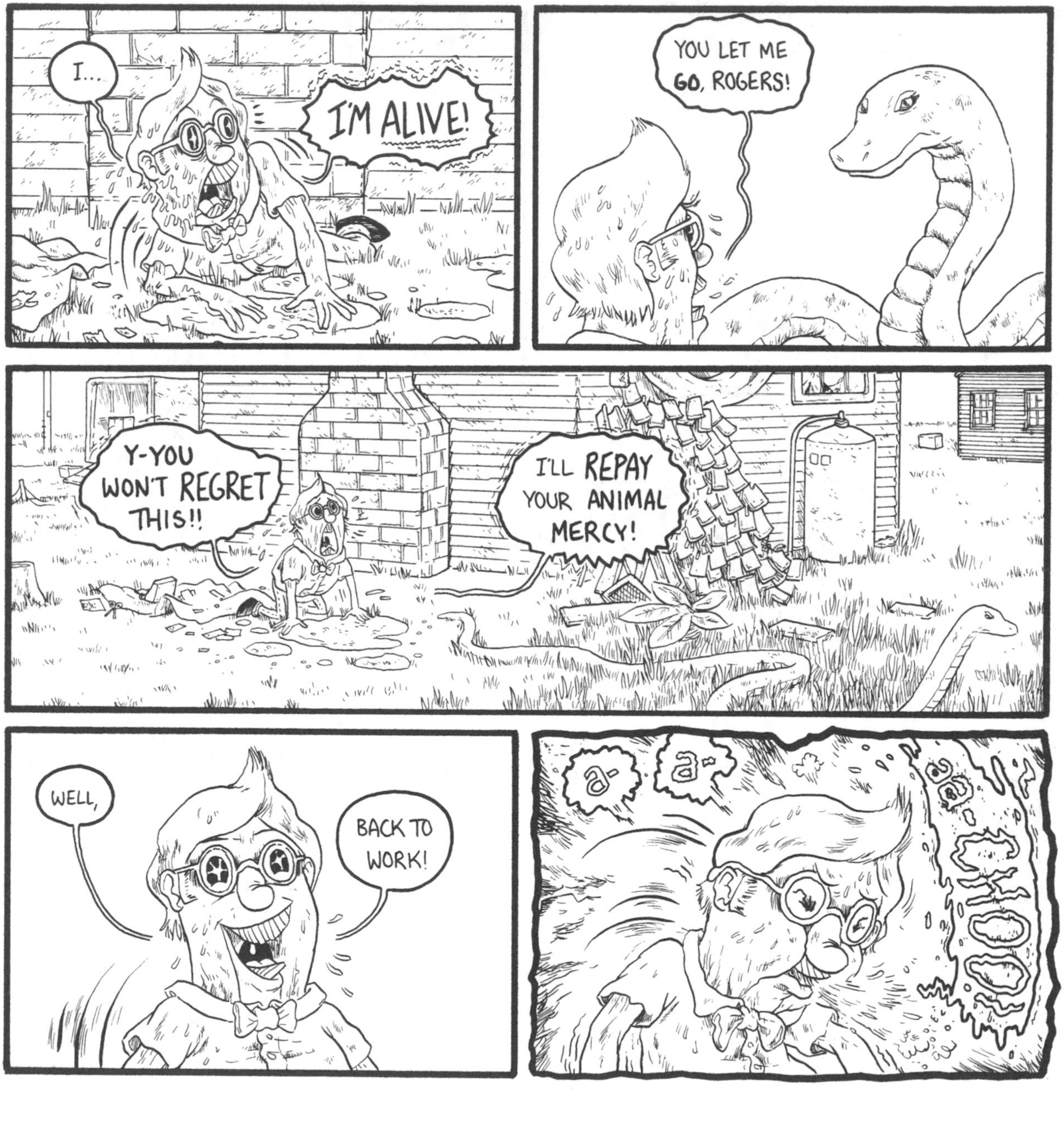
I...
I'M ALIVE!
YOU LET ME GO, ROGERS!
Y-YOU WON'T REGRET THIS!!
I'LL REPAY YOUR ANIMAL MERCY!
WELL,
BACK TO WORK!
a-
a-
aaCHOO

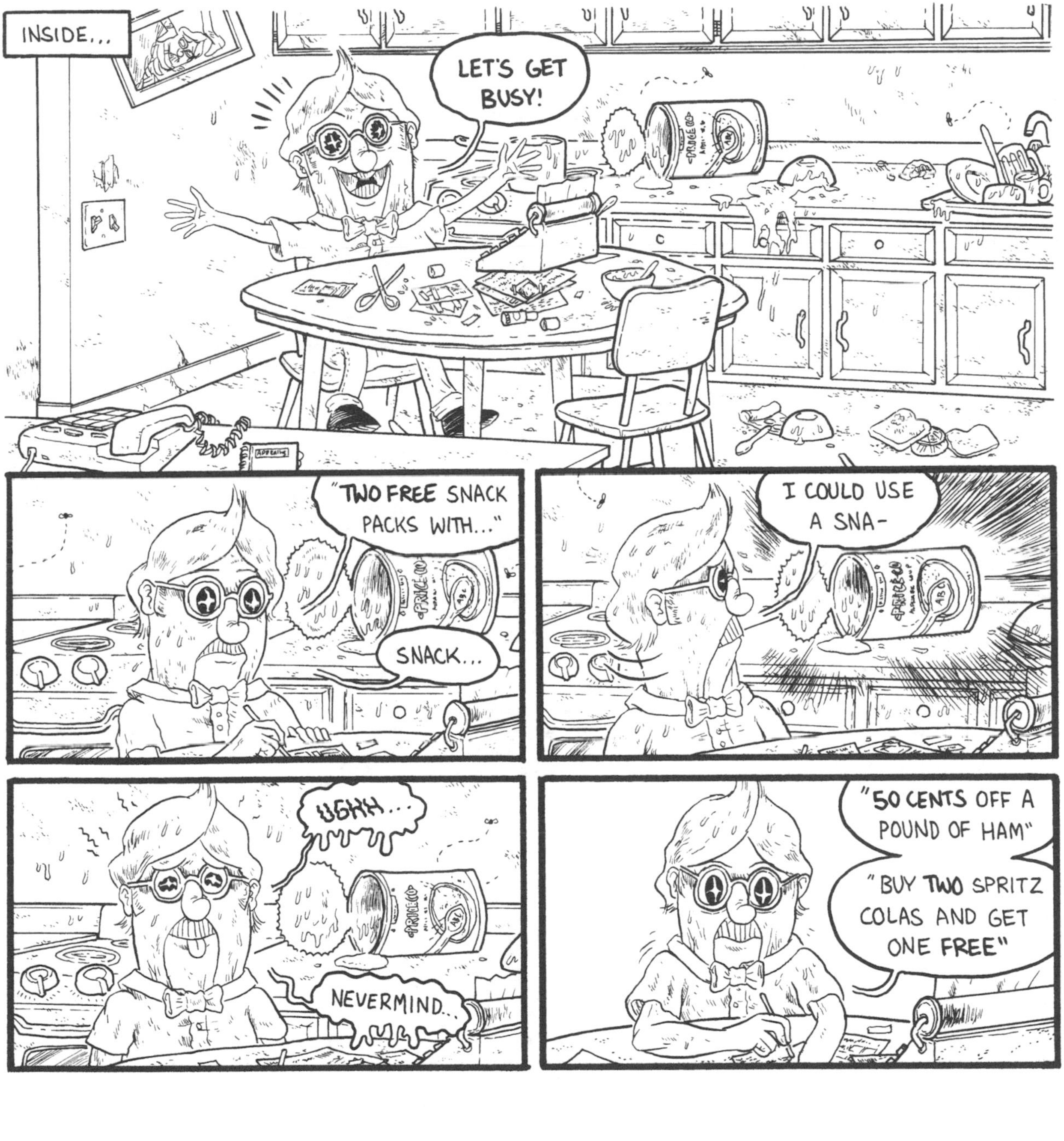
INSIDE...
LET'S GET BUSY!
"TWO FREE SNACK PACKS WITH..."
SNACK...
I COULD USE A SNA-
UGHH...
NEVERMIND...
"50 CENTS OFF A POUND OF HAM"
"BUY TWO SPRITZ COLAS AND GET ONE FREE"

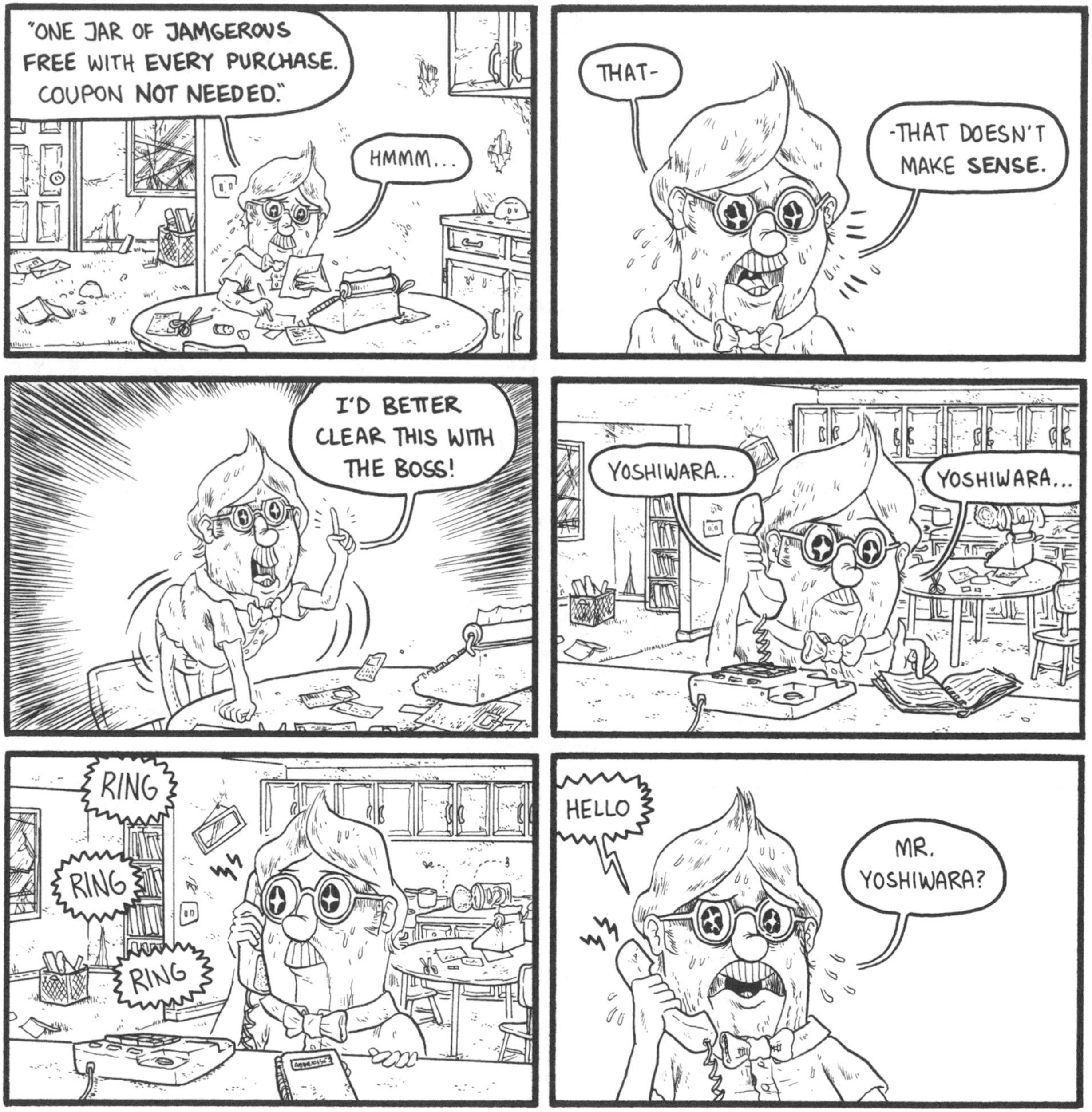
"ONE JAR OF JAMGEROUS FREE WITH EVERY PURCHASE. COUPON NOT NEEDED."
HMMM...
THAT-
-THAT DOESN'T MAKE SENSE.
I'D BETTER CLEAR THIS WITH THE BOSS!
YOSHIWARA...
YOSHIWARA...
RING
RING
RING
HELLO
MR. YOSHIWARA?

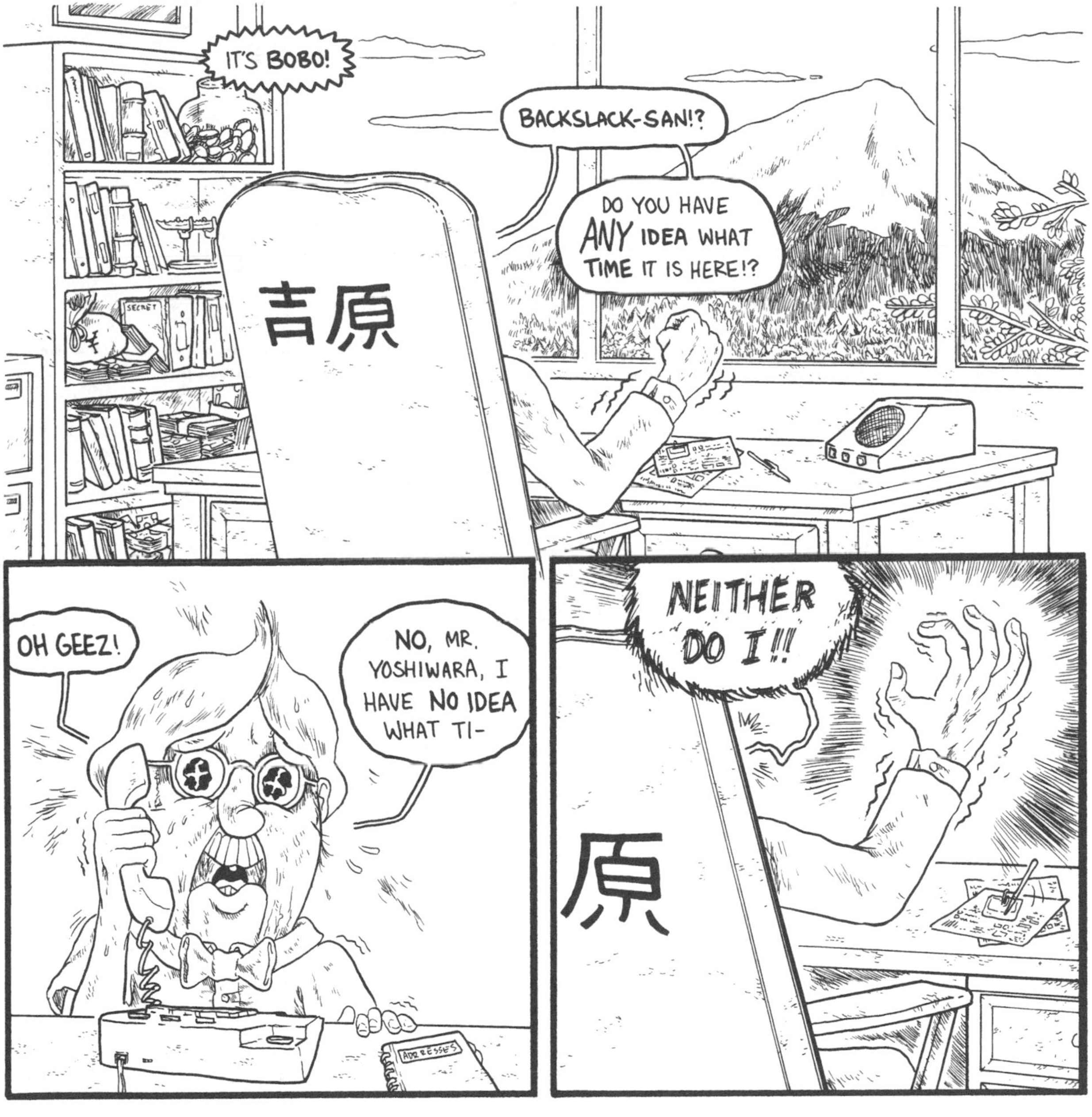
IT'S BOBO!
BACKSLACK-SAN!?
DO YOU HAVE ANY IDEA WHAT TIME IT IS HERE!?
吉原
OH GEEZ!
NO, MR. YOSHIWARA, I HAVE NO IDEA WHAT TI-
NEITHER DO I!!
原
SECRET
ADDRESSES

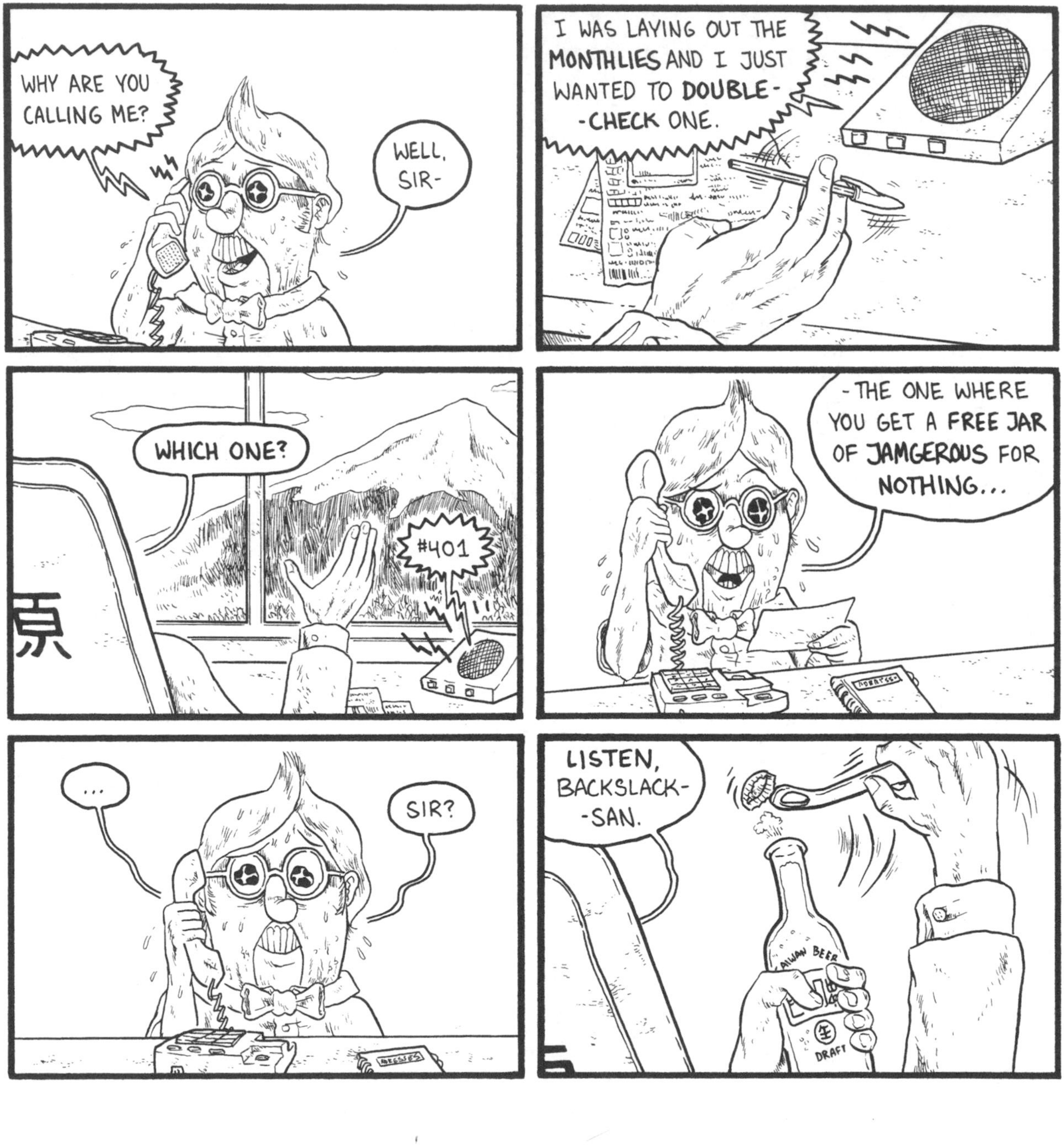
WHY ARE YOU CALLING ME?
WELL, SIR-
I WAS LAYING OUT THE MONTHLIES AND I JUST WANTED TO DOUBLE- -CHECK ONE.
WHICH ONE?
#401
- THE ONE WHERE YOU GET A FREE JAR OF JAMGEROUS FOR NOTHING...
...
SIR?
LISTEN, BACKSLACK- -SAN.
TAIWAN BEER
DRAFT

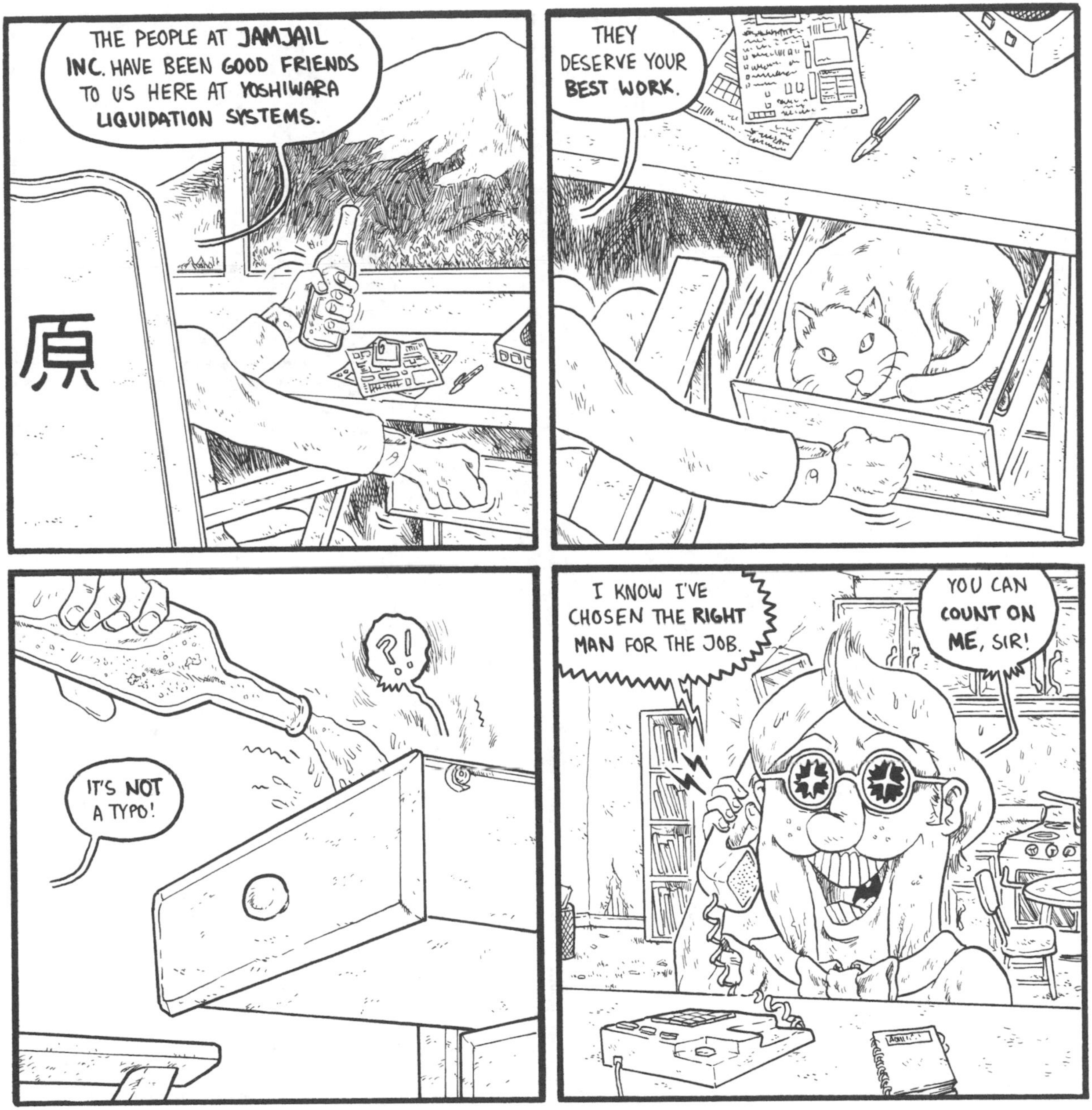
THE PEOPLE AT JAMJAIL INC. HAVE BEEN GOOD FRIENDS TO US HERE AT YOSHIWARA LIQUIDATION SYSTEMS.
原
THEY DESERVE YOUR BEST WORK.
?!
IT'S NOT A TYPO!
I KNOW I'VE CHOSEN THE RIGHT MAN FOR THE JOB.
YOU CAN COUNT ON ME, SIR!

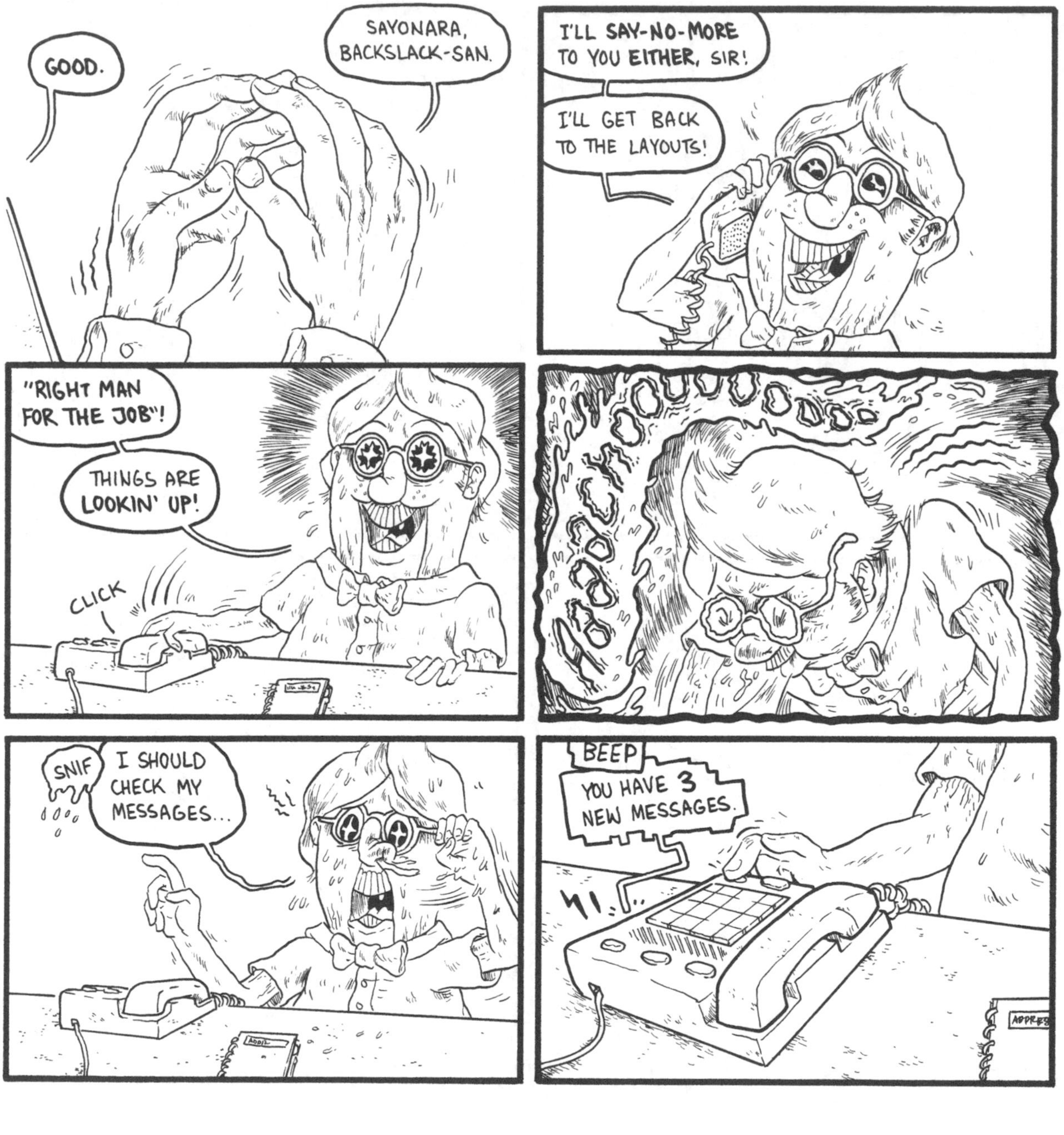
GOOD.
SAYONARA, BACKSLACK-SAN.
I'LL SAY-NO-MORE TO YOU EITHER, SIR!
I'LL GET BACK TO THE LAYOUTS!
"RIGHT MAN FOR THE JOB"!
THINGS ARE LOOKIN' UP!
CLICK
SNIF
I SHOULD CHECK MY MESSAGES...
BEEP
YOU HAVE 3 NEW MESSAGES.

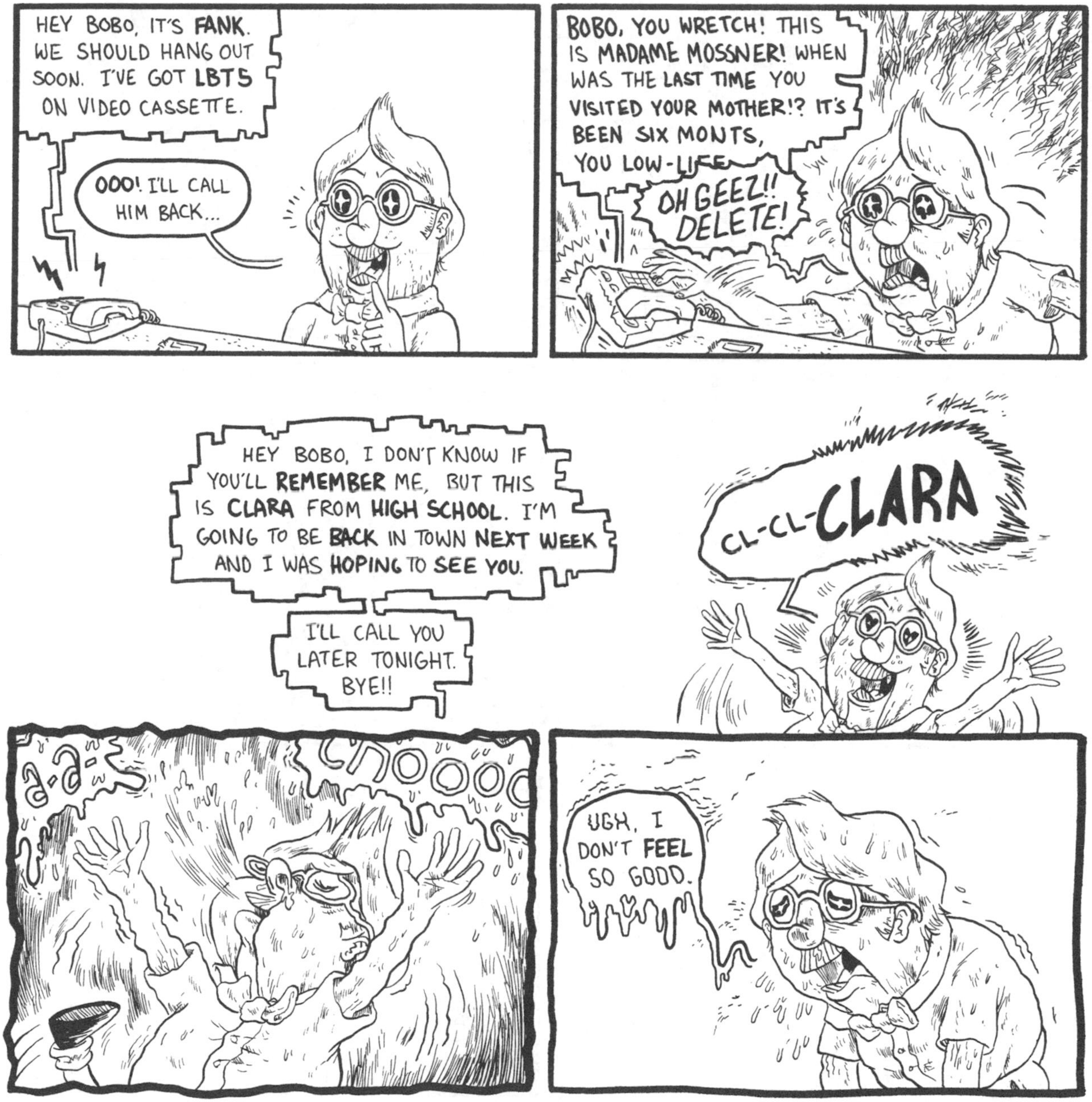
HEY BOBO, IT'S FANK. WE SHOULD HANG OUT SOON. I'VE GOT LBT5 ON VIDEO CASSETTE.
OOO! I'LL CALL HIM BACK...
BOBO, YOU WRETCH! THIS IS MADAME MOSSNER! WHEN WAS THE LAST TIME YOU VISITED YOUR MOTHER!? IT'S BEEN SIX MONTS, YOU LOW-LIFE
OH GEEZ!! DELETE!
HEY BOBO, I DON'T KNOW IF YOU'LL REMEMBER ME, BUT THIS IS CLARA FROM HIGH SCHOOL. I'M GOING TO BE BACK IN TOWN NEXT WEEK AND I WAS HOPING TO SEE YOU.
I'LL CALL YOU LATER TONIGHT. BYE!!
CL-CL-CLARA
A-A-
CHOOOO
UGH, I DON'T FEEL SO GOOD.

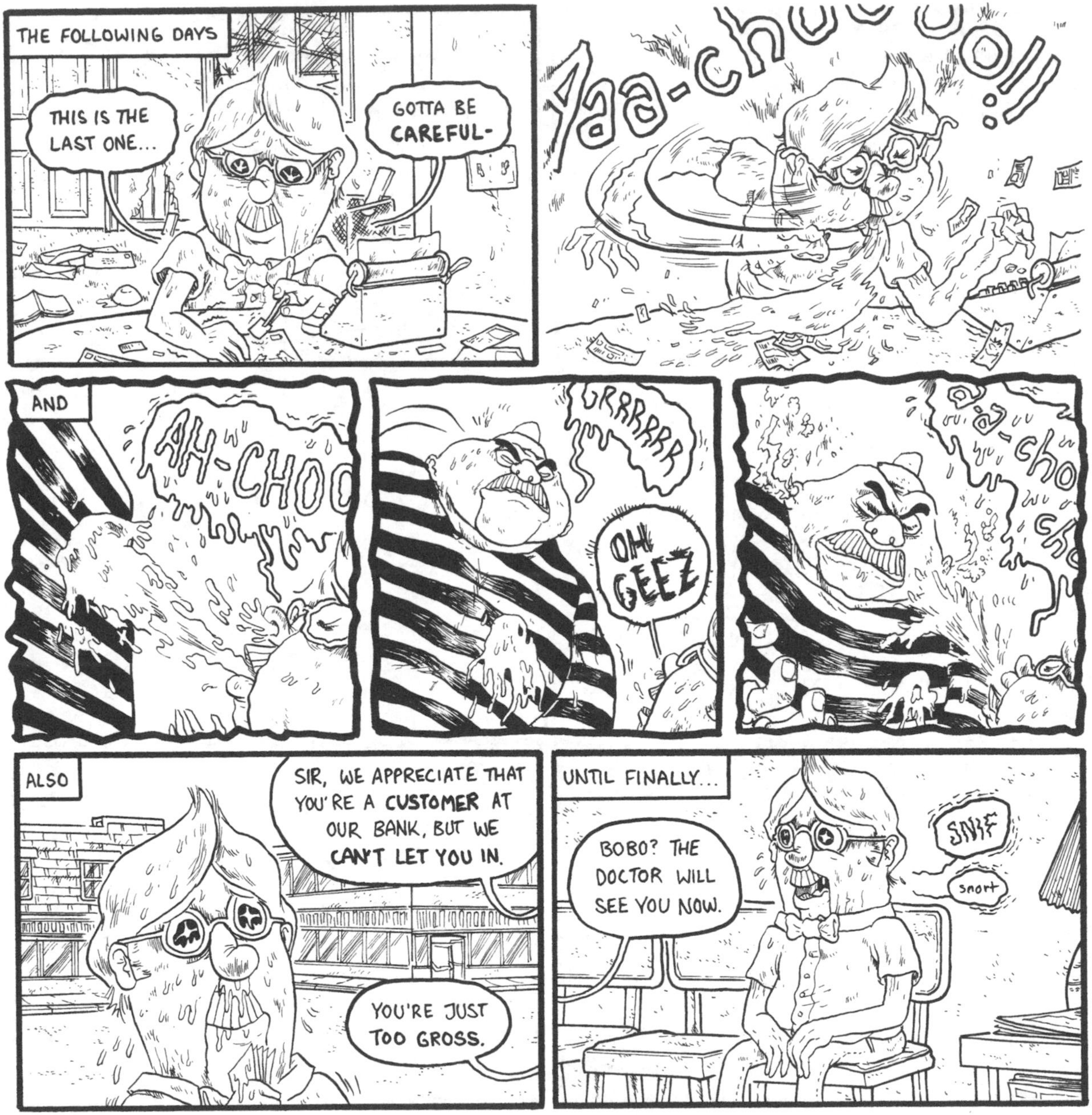
THE FOLLOWING DAYS
THIS IS THE LAST ONE...
GOTTA BE CAREFUL-
Yaa-choo!!
AND
AH-CHOO
GRRRRRR
OH GEEZ
a-a-choo
ALSO
SIR, WE APPRECIATE THAT YOU'RE A CUSTOMER AT OUR BANK, BUT WE CAN'T LET YOU IN.
YOU'RE JUST TOO GROSS.
UNTIL FINALLY...
BOBO? THE DOCTOR WILL SEE YOU NOW.
SNIF
snort

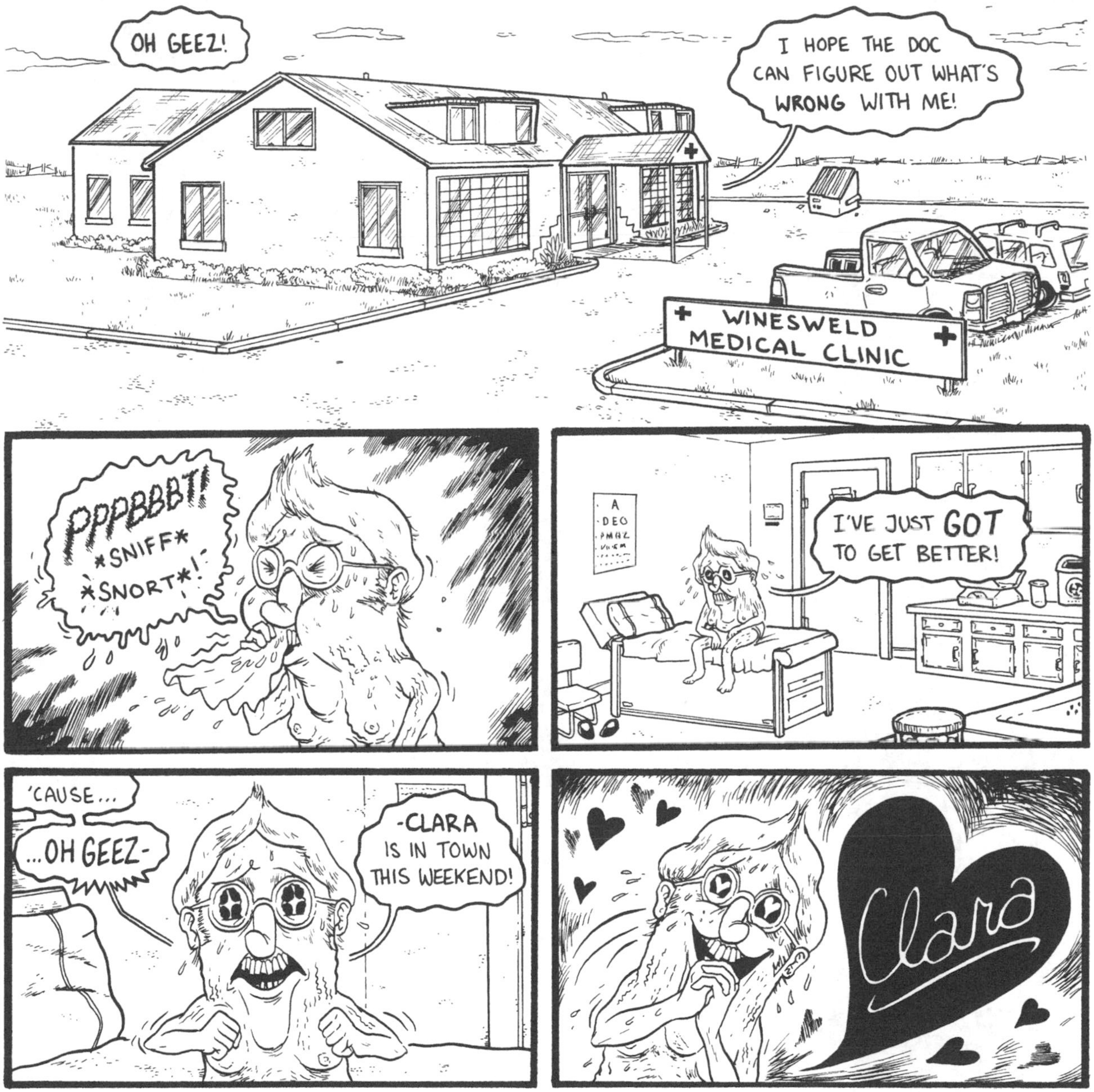
OH GEEZ!
I HOPE THE DOC CAN FIGURE OUT WHAT'S WRONG WITH ME!
WINESWELD MEDICAL CLINIC
PPPBBBT! *SNIFF* *SNORT*!
I'VE JUST GOT TO GET BETTER!
'CAUSE...
...OH GEEZ-
-CLARA IS IN TOWN THIS WEEKEND!
Clara

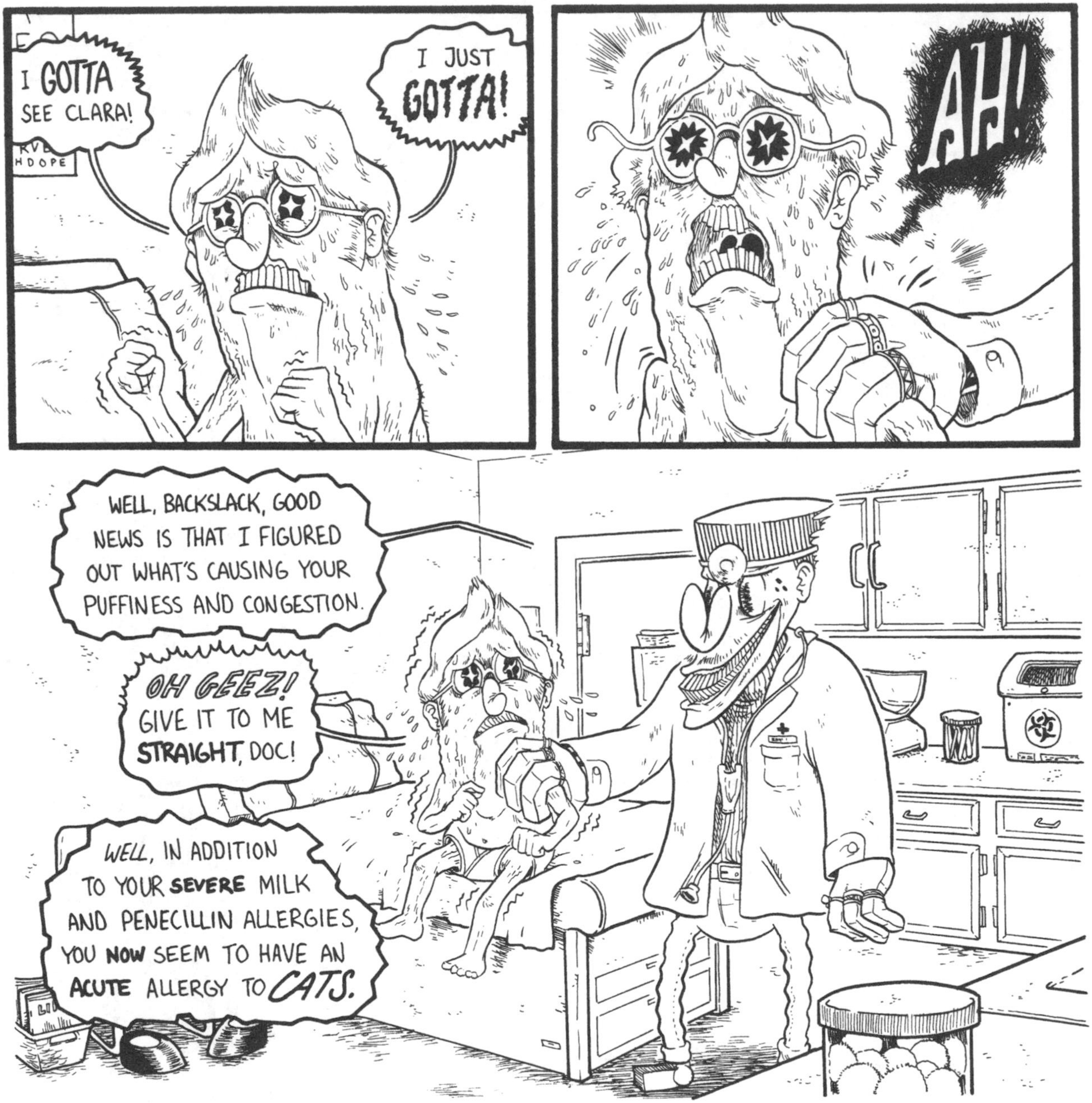

I GOTTA SEE CLARA!
I JUST GOTTA!
AH!
WELL, BACKSLACK, GOOD NEWS IS THAT I FIGURED OUT WHAT'S CAUSING YOUR PUFFINESS AND CONGESTION.
OH GEEZ! GIVE IT TO ME STRAIGHT, DOC!
WELL, IN ADDITION TO YOUR SEVERE MILK AND PENECILLIN ALLERGIES, YOU NOW SEEM TO HAVE AN ACUTE ALLERGY TO CATS.

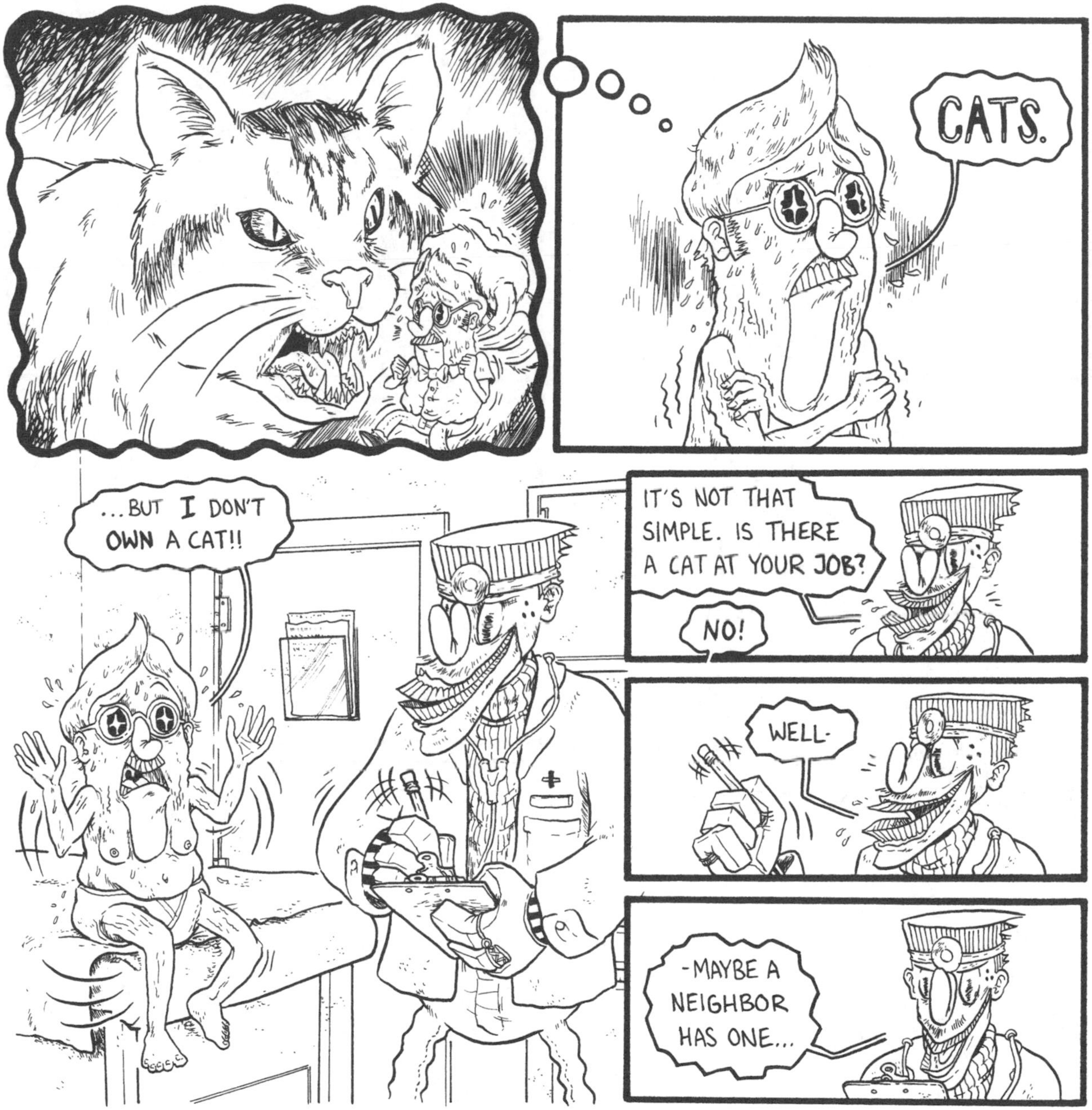
CATS.
...BUT I DON'T OWN A CAT!!
IT'S NOT THAT SIMPLE. IS THERE A CAT AT YOUR JOB?
NO!
WELL-
-MAYBE A NEIGHBOR HAS ONE...

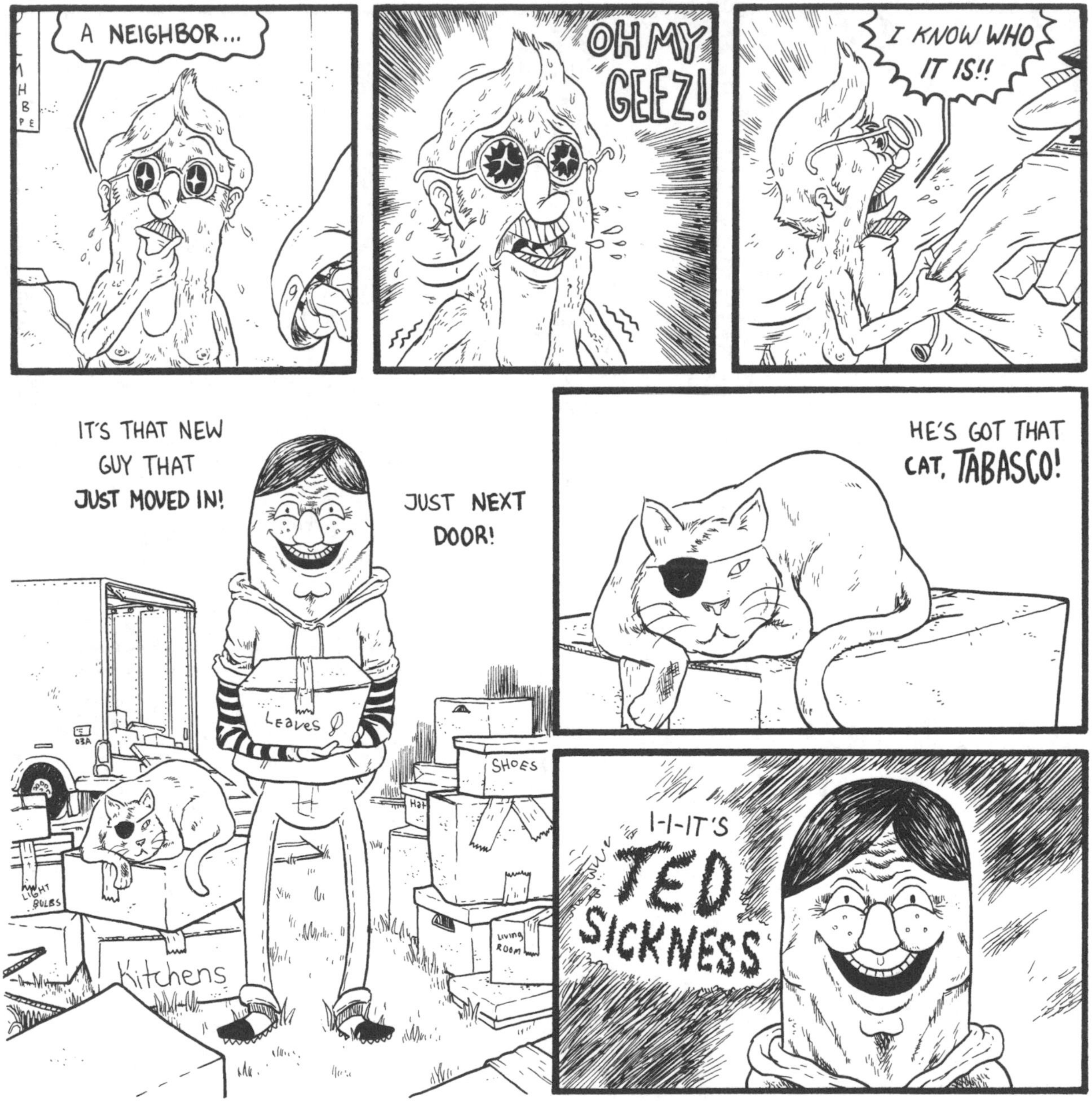

A NEIGHBOR...
OH MY GEEZ!
I KNOW WHO IT IS!!
IT'S THAT NEW GUY THAT JUST MOVED IN!
JUST NEXT DOOR!
Leaves
SHOES
LIGHT BULBS
Kitchens
LIVING ROOM
HE'S GOT THAT CAT, TABASCO!
I-I-IT'S TED SICKNESS

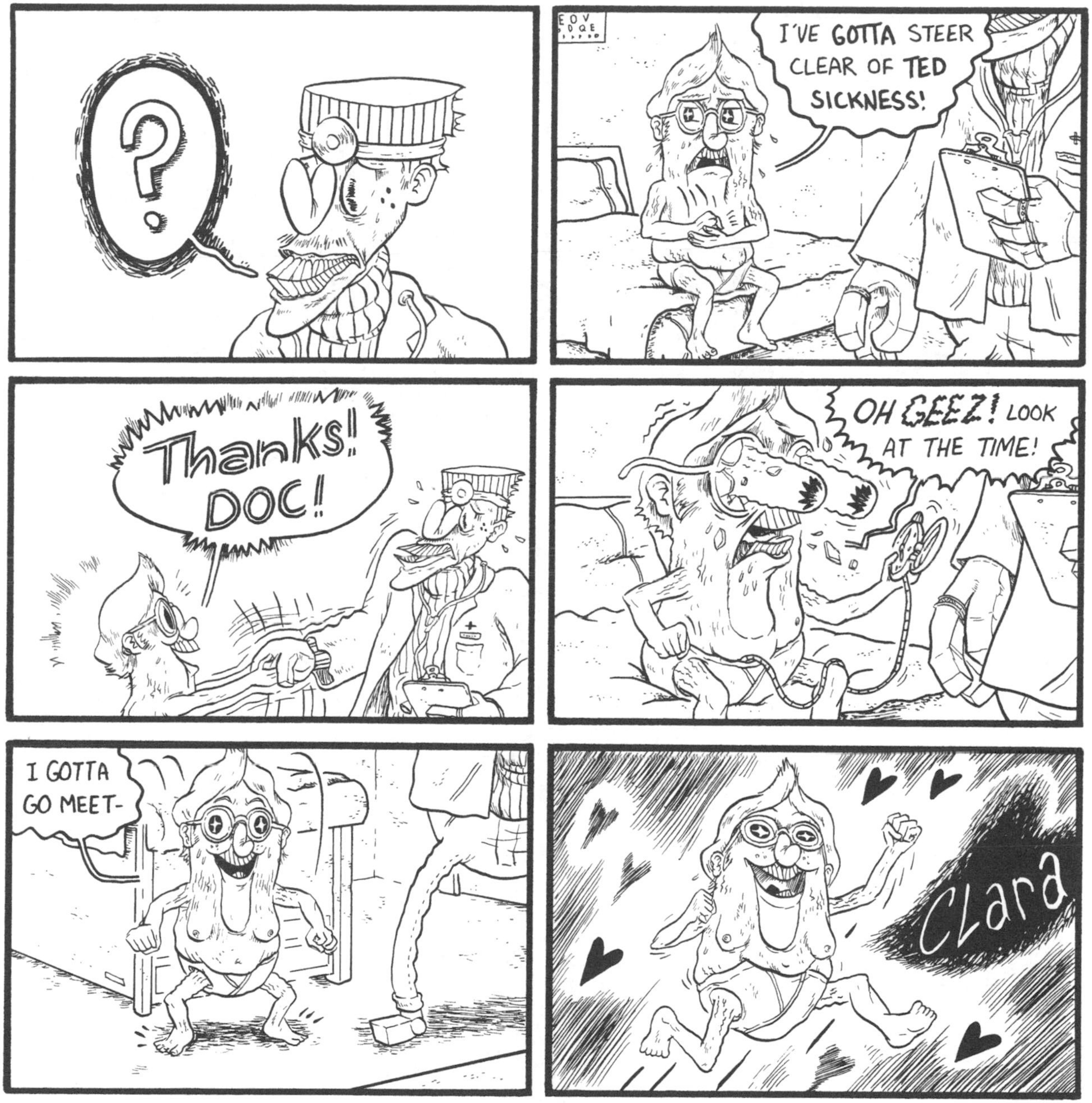
?
I'VE GOTTA STEER CLEAR OF TED SICKNESS!
Thanks! DOC!
OH GEEZ! LOOK AT THE TIME!
I GOTTA GO MEET-
Clara

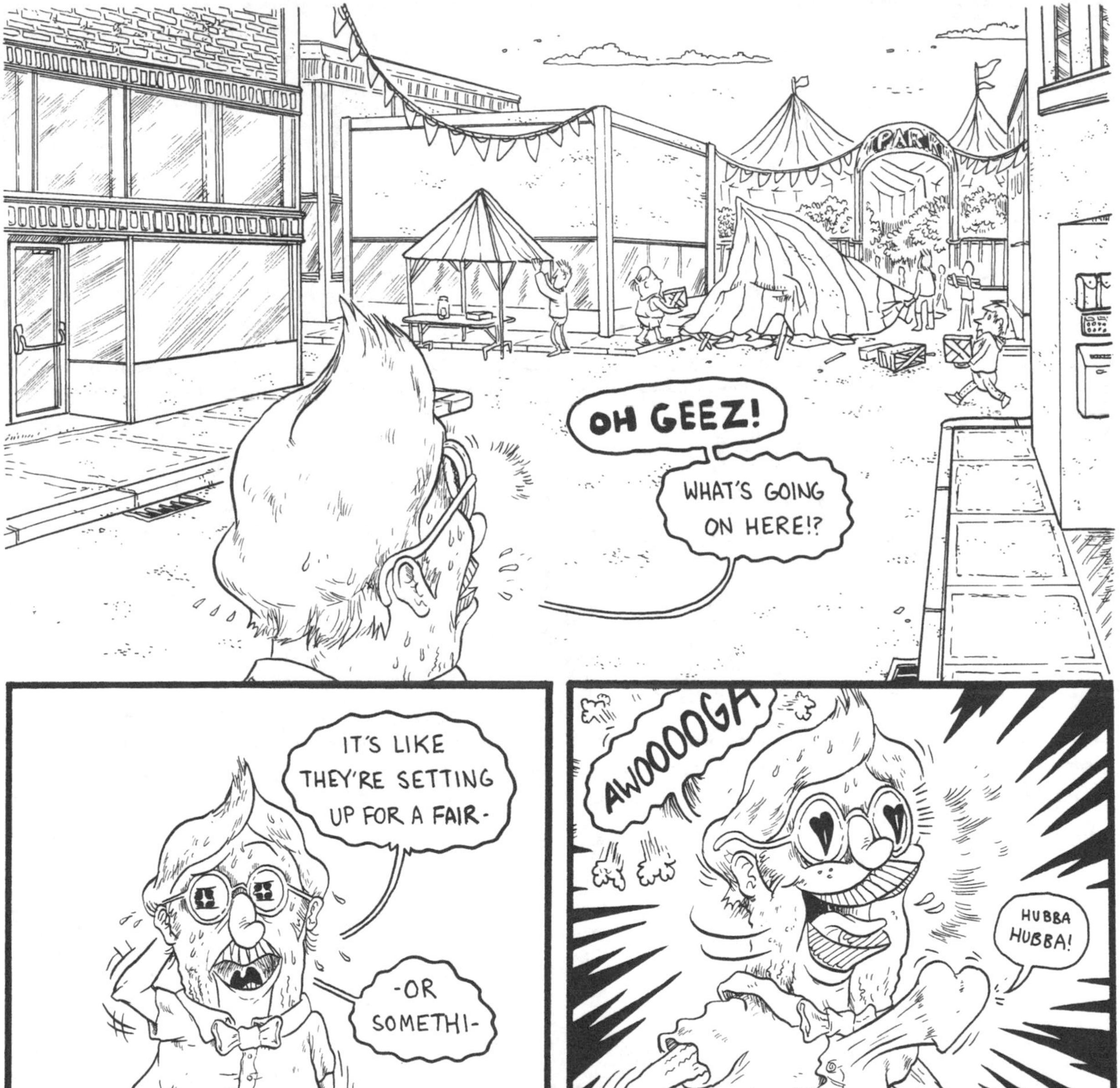
PARK
OH GEEZ!
WHAT'S GOING ON HERE!?
IT'S LIKE THEY'RE SETTING UP FOR A FAIR-
-OR SOMETHI-
AWOOOOGA
HUBBA HUBBA!

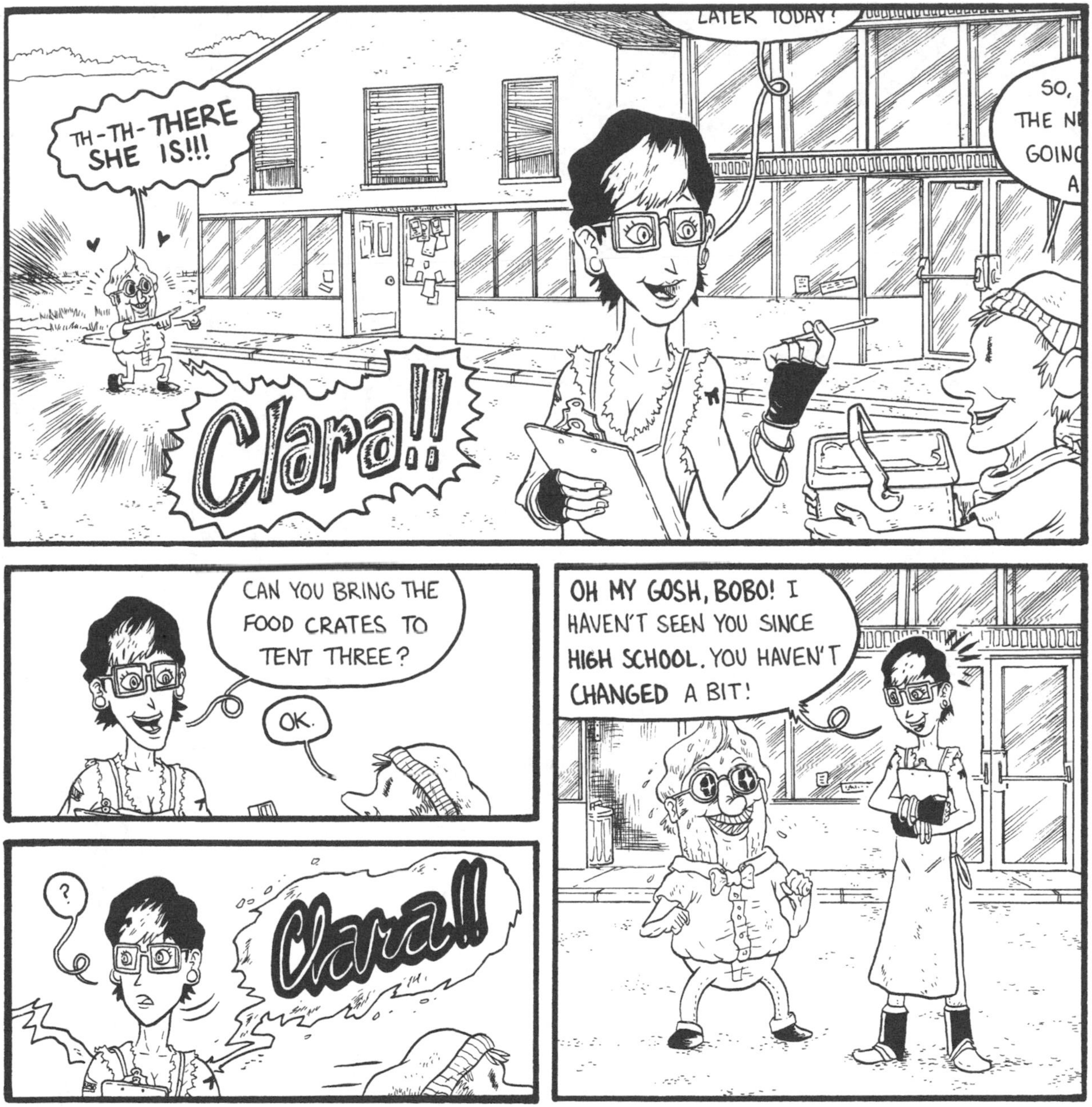
LATER TODAY?
SO,
TH-TH-THERE SHE IS!!!
Clara!!
CAN YOU BRING THE FOOD CRATES TO TENT THREE?
OK.
?
Clara!!
OH MY GOSH, BOBO! I HAVEN'T SEEN YOU SINCE HIGH SCHOOL. YOU HAVEN'T CHANGED A BIT!

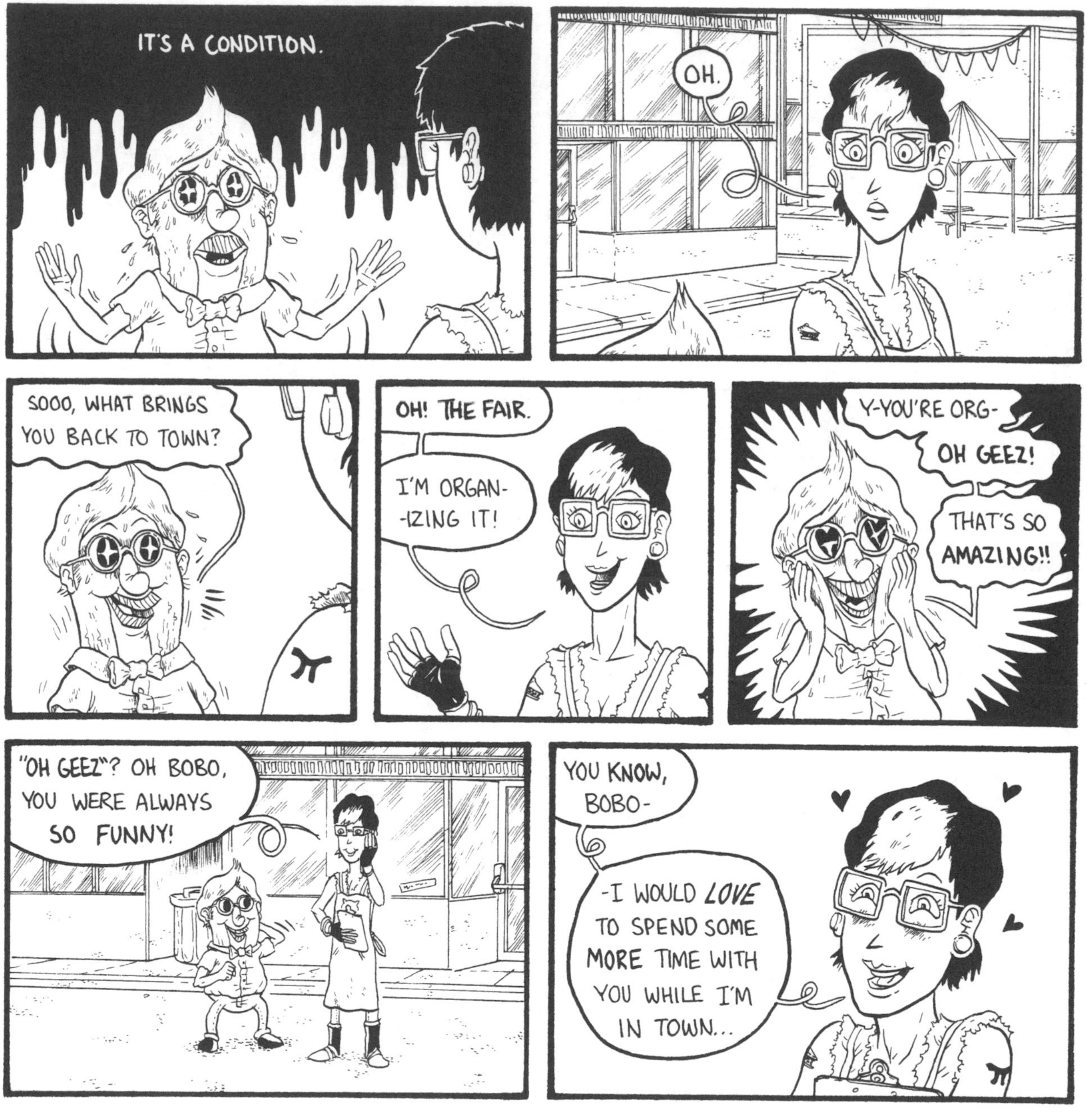
IT'S A CONDITION.
OH.
SOOO, WHAT BRINGS YOU BACK TO TOWN?
OH! THE FAIR.
I'M ORGAN- -IZING IT!
Y-YOU'RE ORG-
OH GEEZ!
THAT'S SO AMAZING!!
"OH GEEZ"? OH BOBO, YOU WERE ALWAYS SO FUNNY!
YOU KNOW, BOBO-
-I WOULD LOVE TO SPEND SOME MORE TIME WITH YOU WHILE I'M IN TOWN...

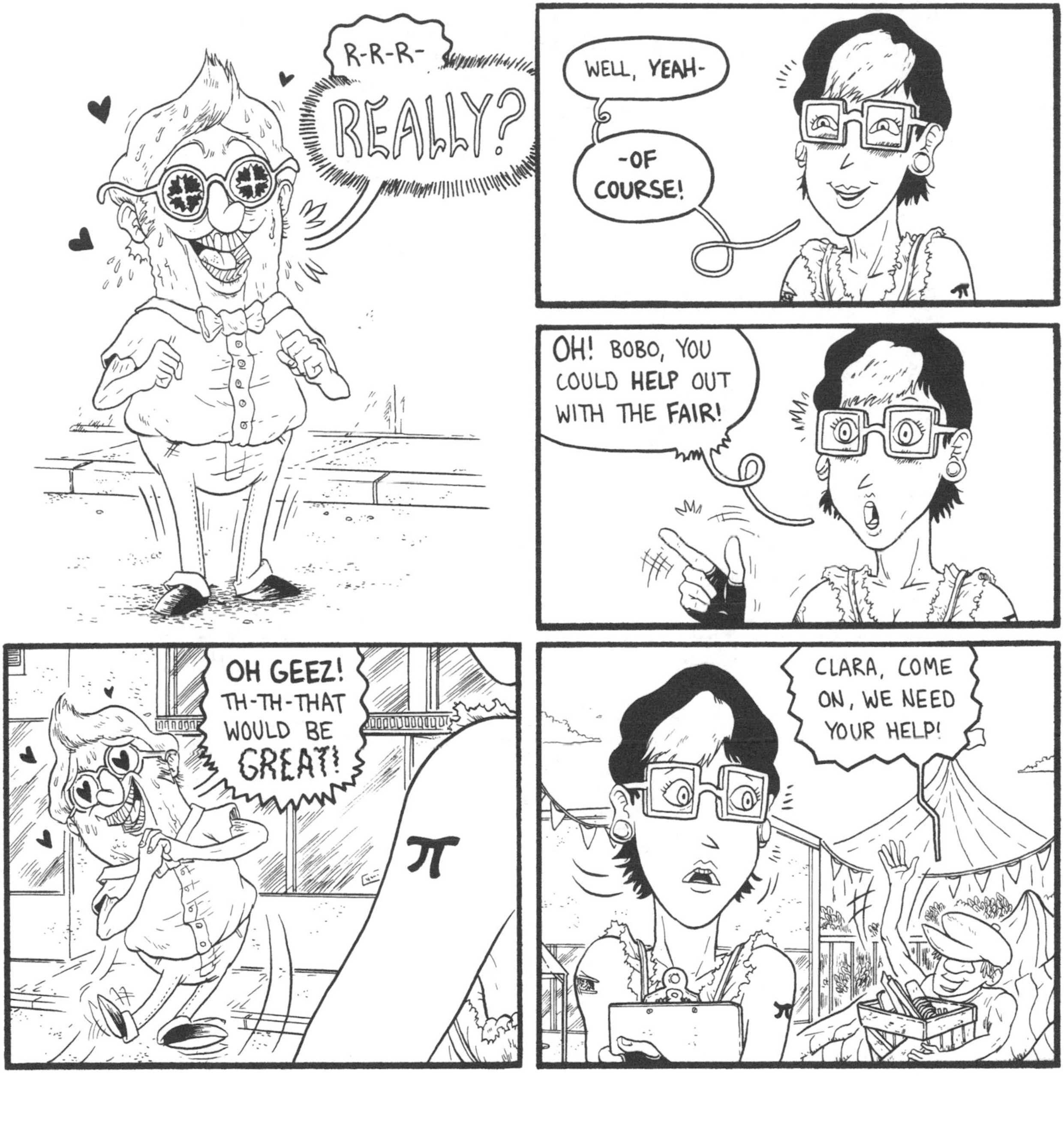
R-R-R-
REALLY?
WELL, YEAH-
-OF COURSE!
OH! BOBO, YOU COULD HELP OUT WITH THE FAIR!
OH GEEZ! TH-TH-THAT WOULD BE GREAT!
CLARA, COME ON, WE NEED YOUR HELP!

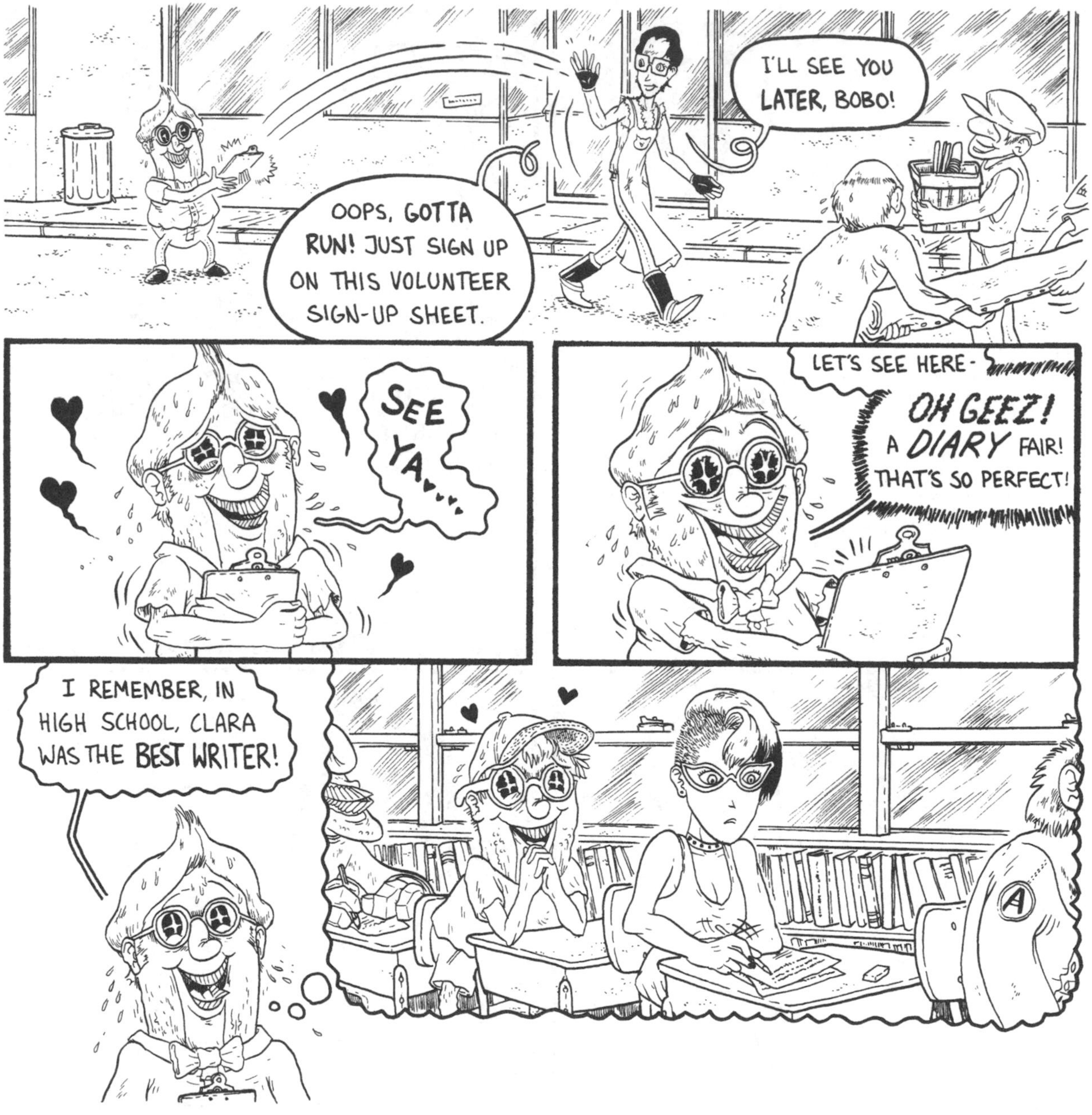
OOPS, GOTTA RUN! JUST SIGN UP ON THIS VOLUNTEER SIGN-UP SHEET.
I'LL SEE YOU LATER, BOBO!
SEE YA...
LET'S SEE HERE-
OH GEEZ! A DIARY FAIR! THAT'S SO PERFECT!
I REMEMBER, IN HIGH SCHOOL, CLARA WAS THE BEST WRITER!

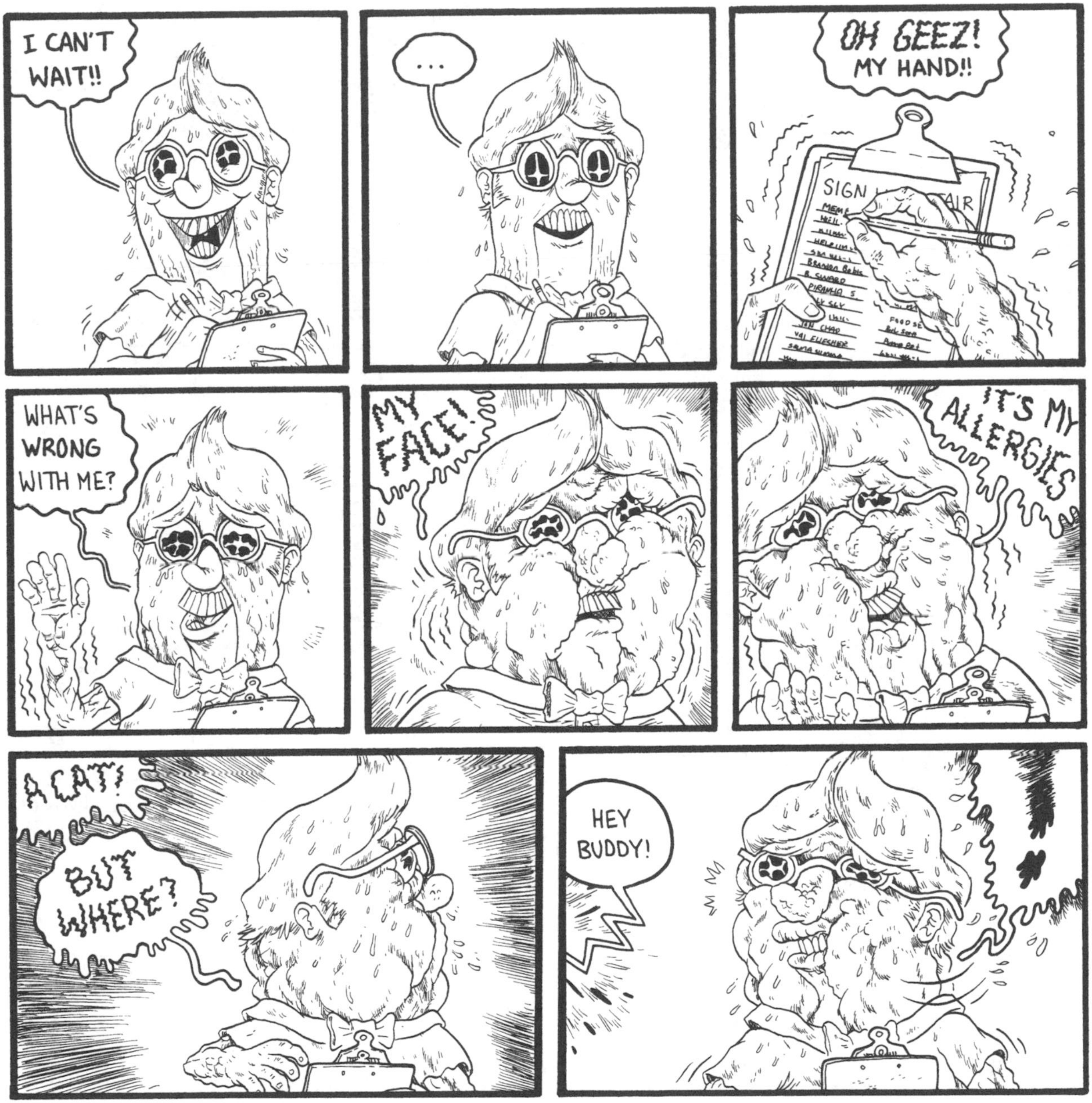
I CAN'T WAIT!!
...
OH GEEZ! MY HAND!!
SIGN
FAIR
WHAT'S WRONG WITH ME?
MY FACE!
IT'S MY ALLERGIES
A CAT!
BUT WHERE?
HEY BUDDY!

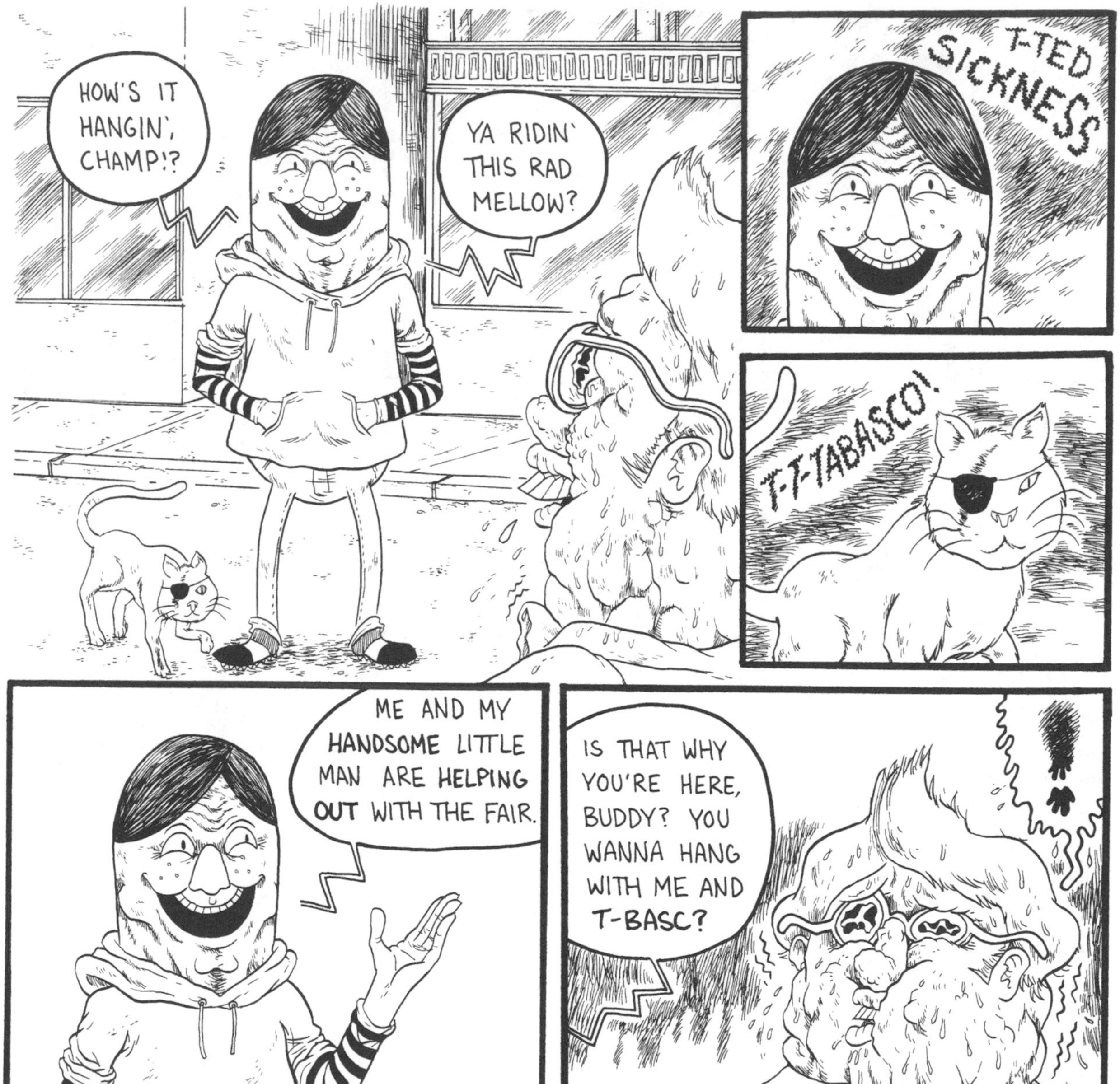
HOW'S IT HANGIN', CHAMP!?
YA RIDIN' THIS RAD MELLOW?
T-TED SICKNESS
T-T-TABASCO!
ME AND MY HANDSOME LITTLE MAN ARE HELPING OUT WITH THE FAIR.
IS THAT WHY YOU'RE HERE, BUDDY? YOU WANNA HANG WITH ME AND T-BASC?
!

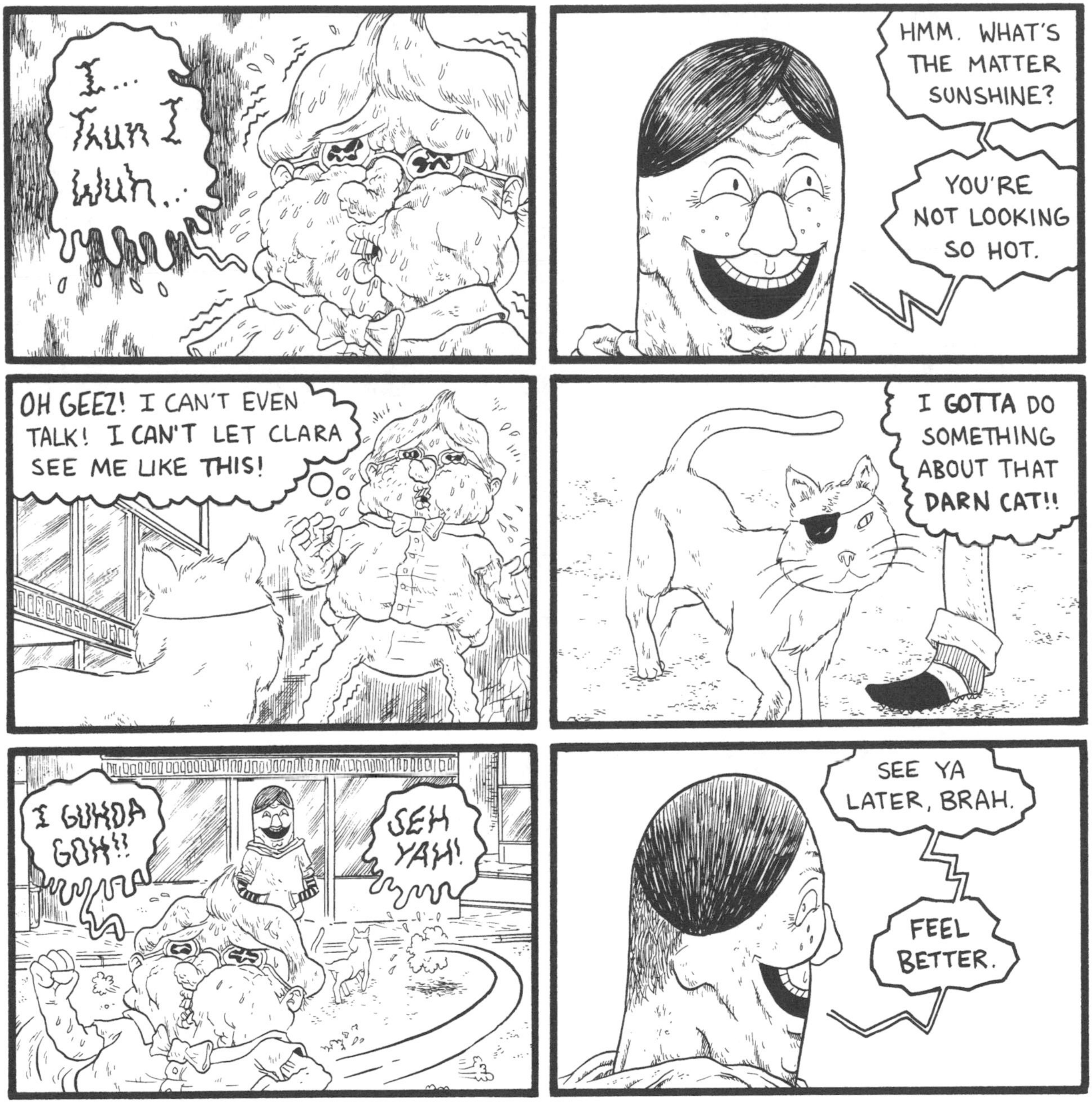
I... Thun I Wuh...
HMM. WHAT'S THE MATTER SUNSHINE?
YOU'RE NOT LOOKING SO HOT.
OH GEEZ! I CAN'T EVEN TALK! I CAN'T LET CLARA SEE ME LIKE THIS!
I GOTTA DO SOMETHING ABOUT THAT DARN CAT!!
I GUHDA GOH!!
SEH YAH!
SEE YA LATER, BRAH.
FEEL BETTER.

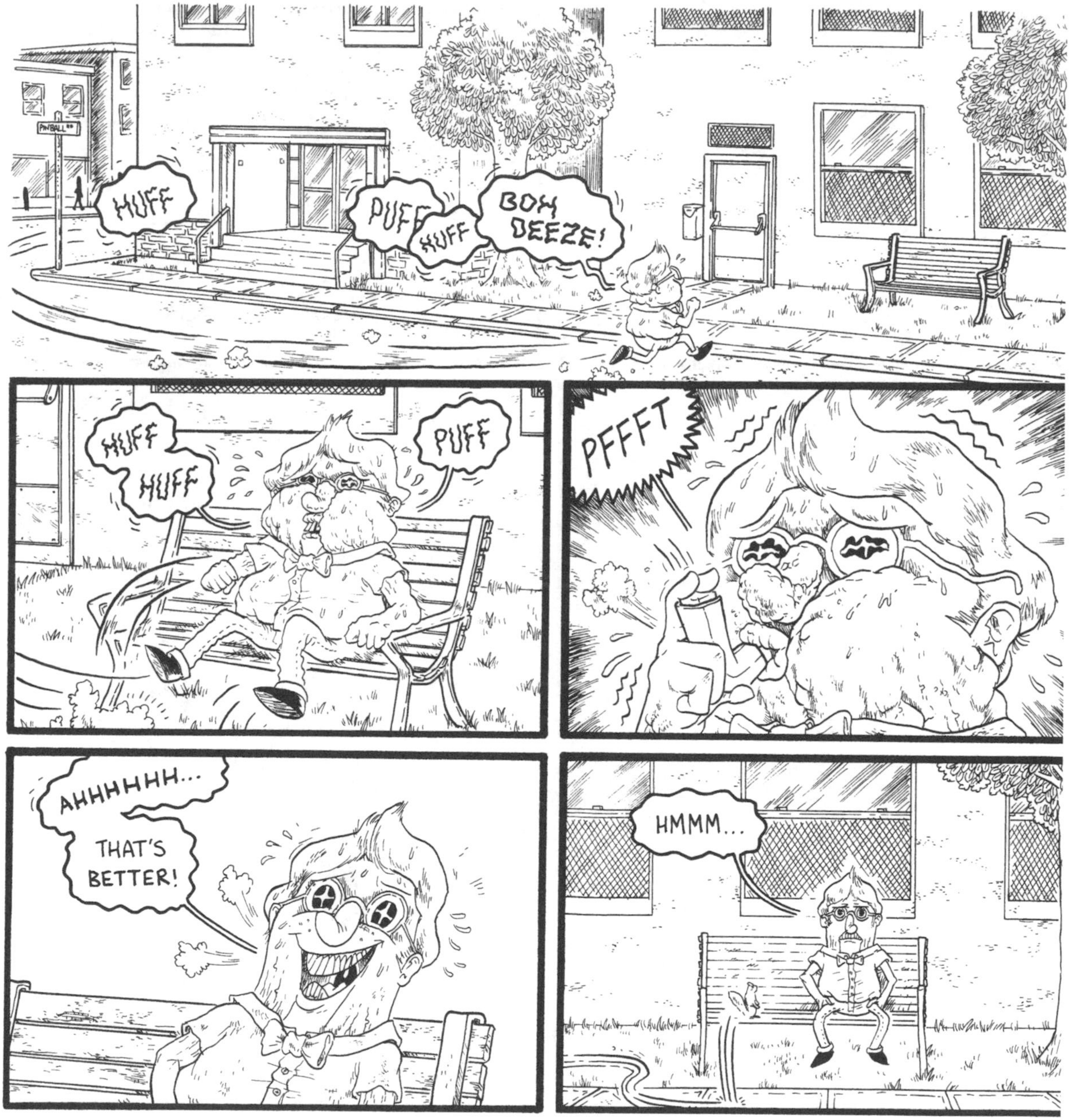
PINBALL
HUFF
PUFF
HUFF
BOH DEEZE!
HUFF
HUFF
PUFF
PFFFT
AHHHHHH...
THAT'S BETTER!
HMMM...

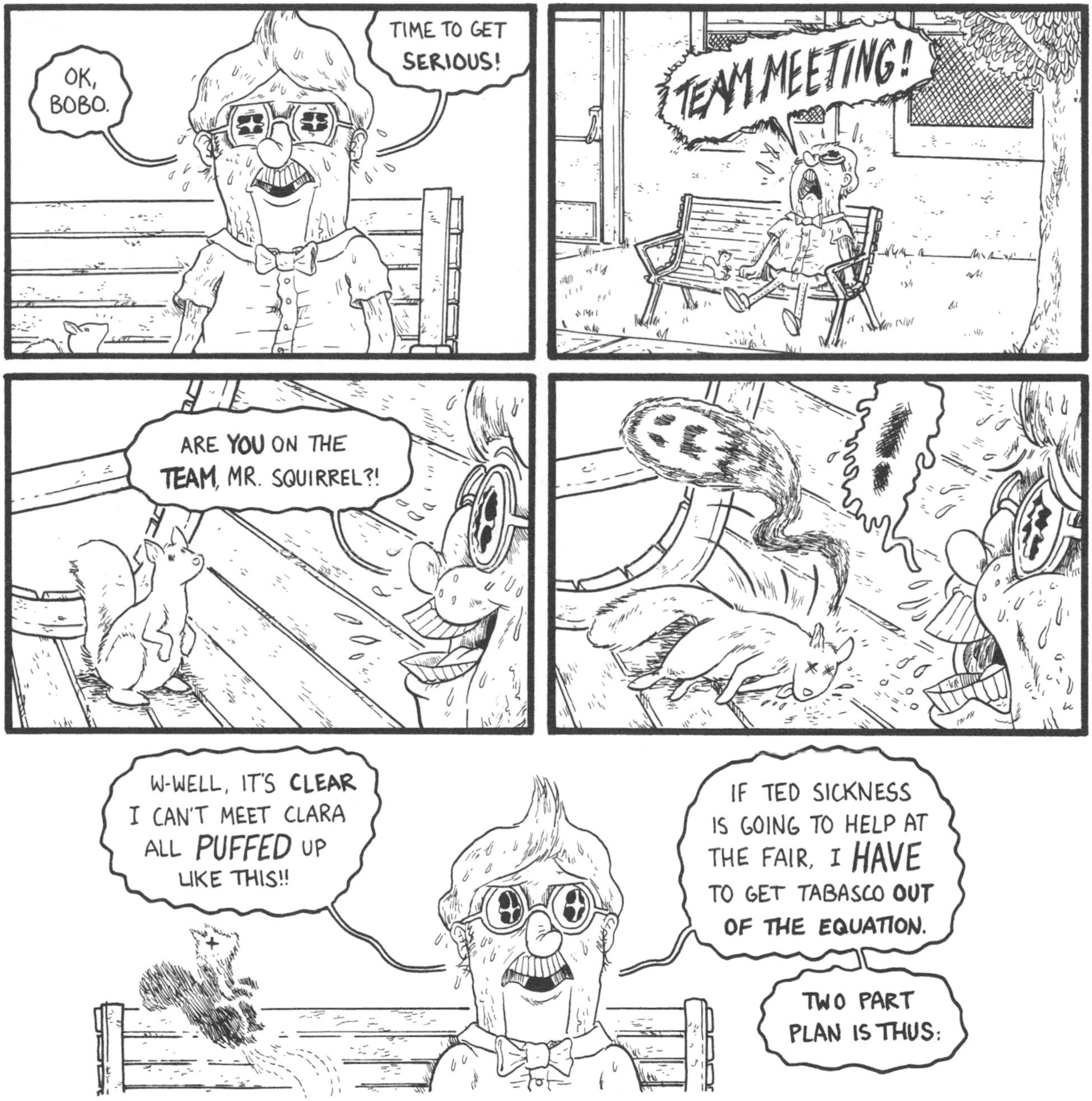
OK, BOBO.
TIME TO GET SERIOUS!
TEAM MEETING!
ARE YOU ON THE TEAM, MR. SQUIRREL?!
!
W-WELL, IT'S CLEAR I CAN'T MEET CLARA ALL PUFFED UP LIKE THIS!!
IF TED SICKNESS IS GOING TO HELP AT THE FAIR, I HAVE TO GET TABASCO OUT OF THE EQUATION.
TWO PART PLAN IS THUS:

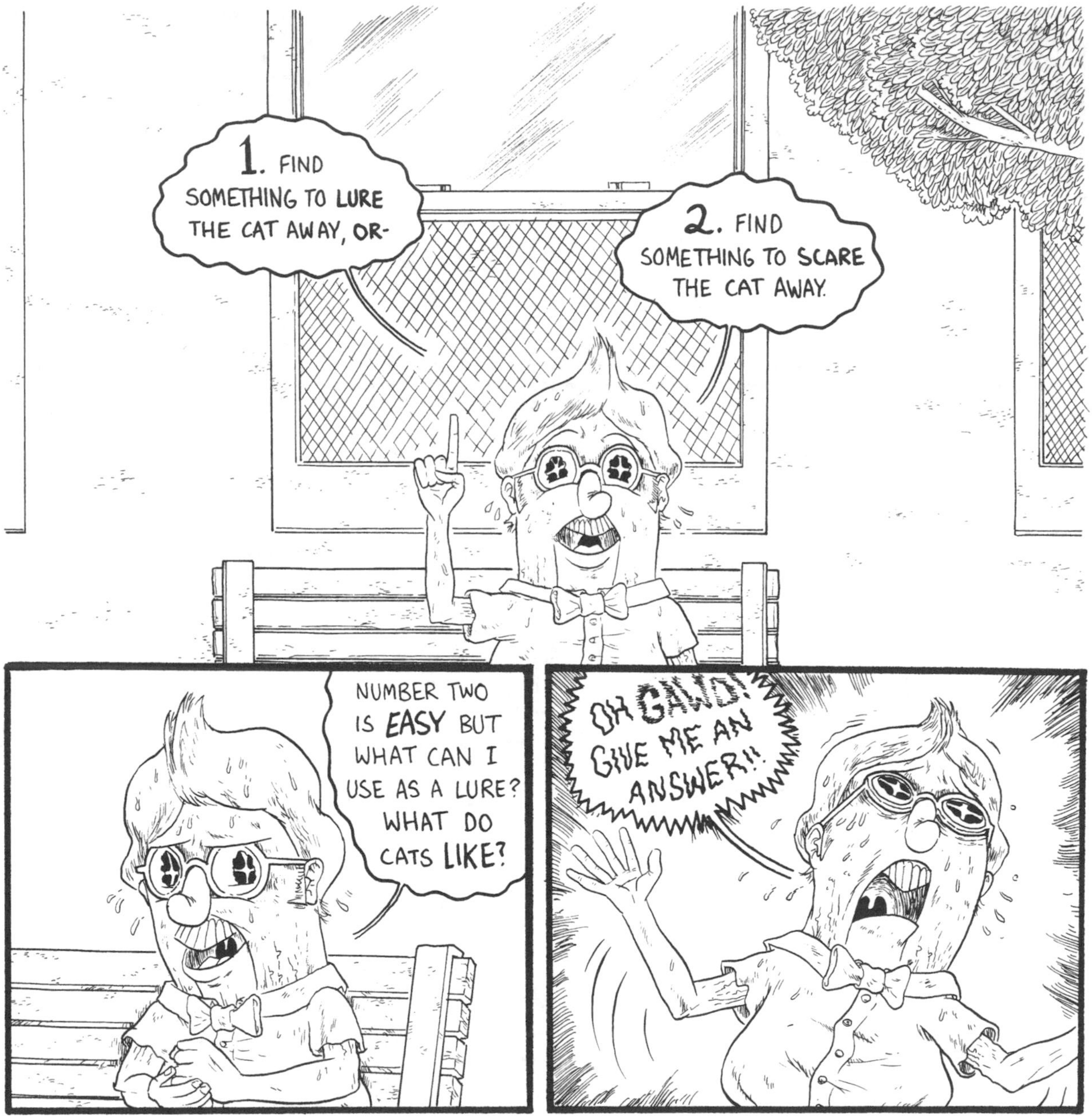
1. FIND SOMETHING TO LURE THE CAT AWAY, OR-
2. FIND SOMETHING TO SCARE THE CAT AWAY.
NUMBER TWO IS EASY BUT WHAT CAN I USE AS A LURE? WHAT DO CATS LIKE?
OH GAWD! GIVE ME AN ANSWER!!

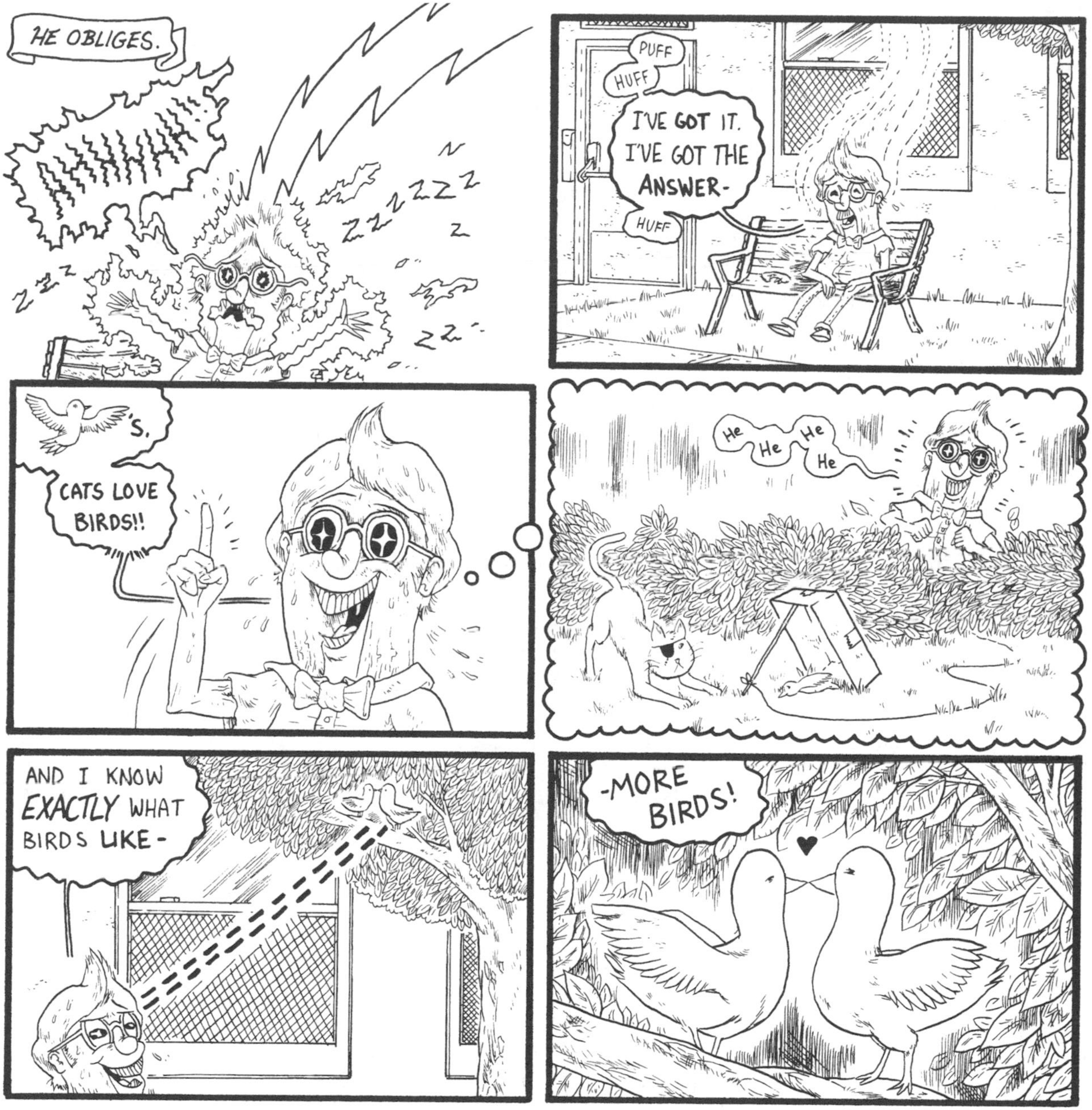
HE OBLIGES.
ARWWHA!!
PUFF
HUFF
I'VE GOT IT. I'VE GOT THE ANSWER-
HUFF
'S.
CATS LOVE BIRDS!!
He He He He
AND I KNOW EXACTLY WHAT BIRDS LIKE-
-MORE BIRDS!

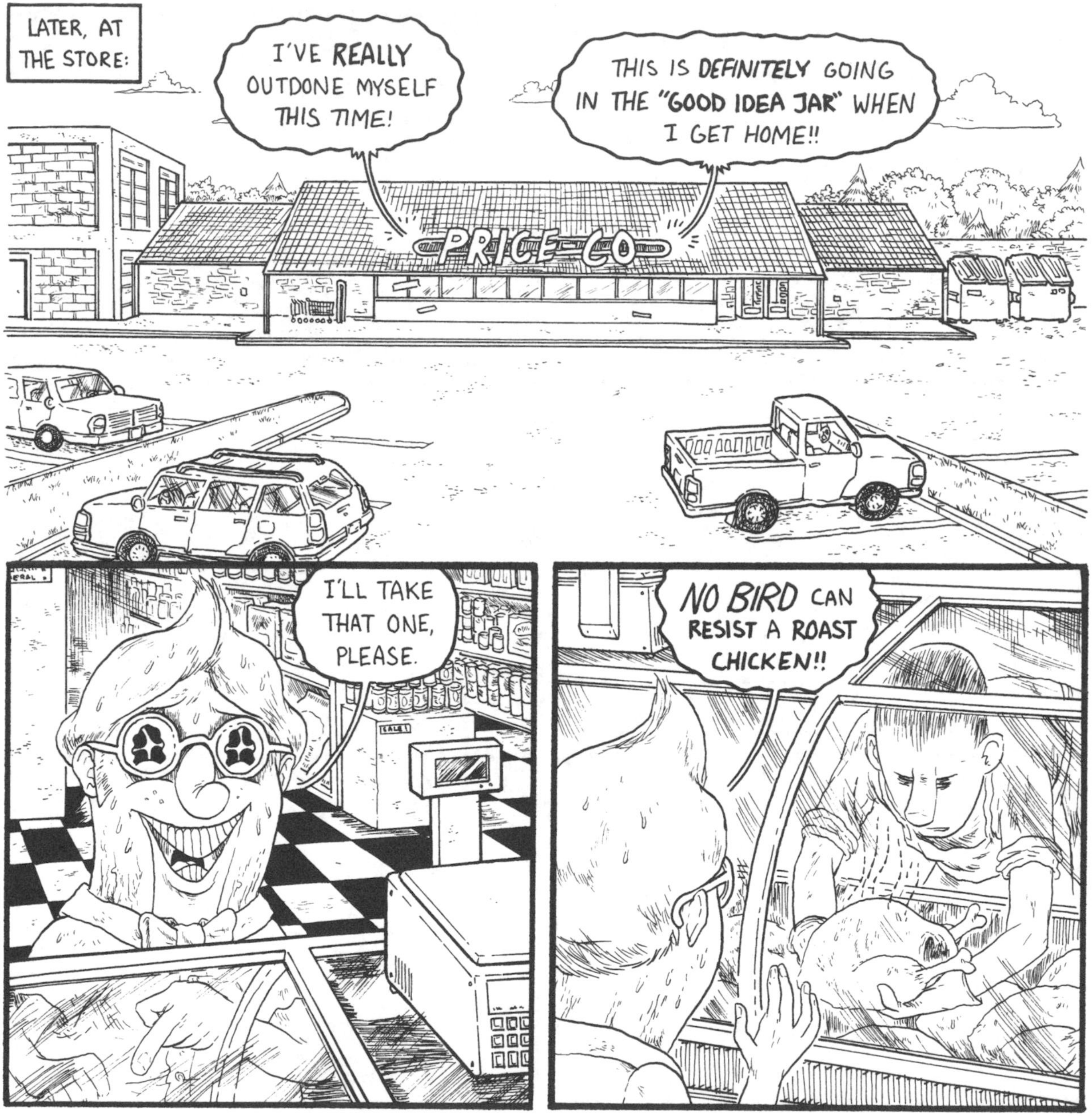
LATER, AT THE STORE:
I'VE REALLY OUTDONE MYSELF THIS TIME!
THIS IS DEFINITELY GOING IN THE "GOOD IDEA JAR" WHEN I GET HOME!!
PRICE-CO
I'LL TAKE THAT ONE, PLEASE.
NO BIRD CAN RESIST A ROAST CHICKEN!!

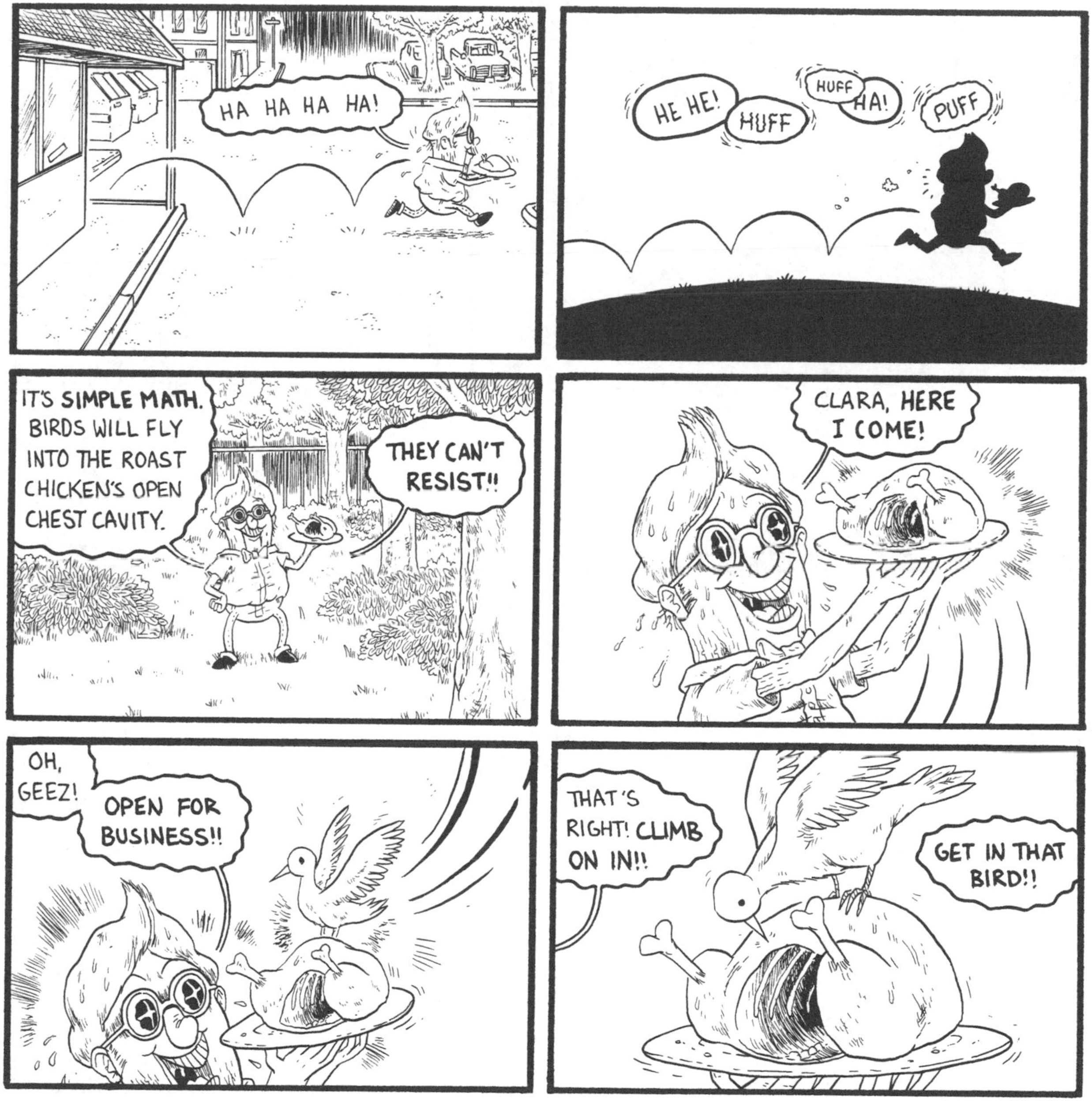
HA HA HA HA!
HE HE!
HUFF
HUFF
HA!
PUFF
IT'S SIMPLE MATH. BIRDS WILL FLY INTO THE ROAST CHICKEN'S OPEN CHEST CAVITY.
THEY CAN'T RESIST!!
CLARA, HERE I COME!
OH, GEEZ!
OPEN FOR BUSINESS!!
THAT'S RIGHT! CLIMB ON IN!!
GET IN THAT BIRD!!

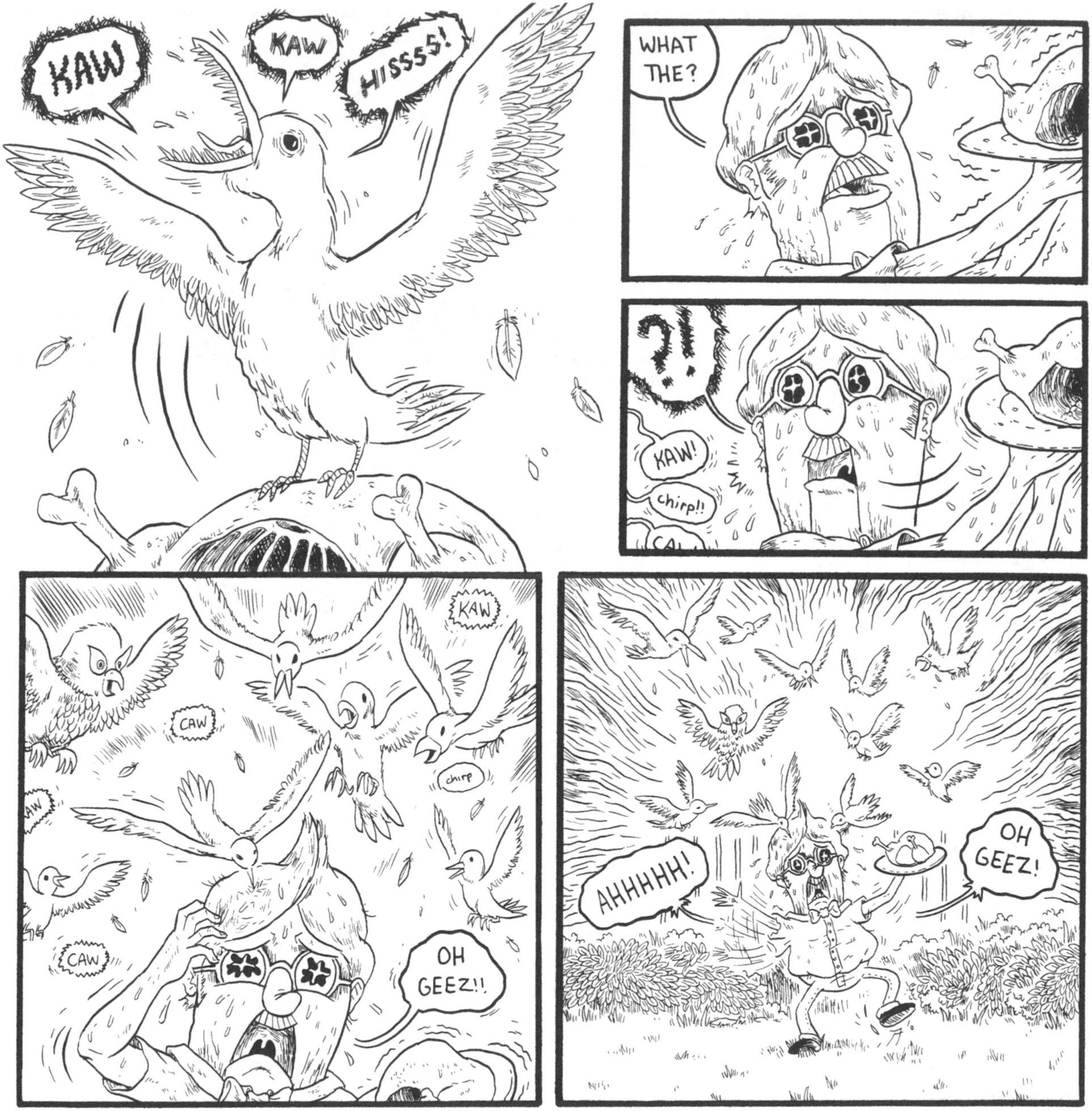
KAW
KAW
HISSSS!
WHAT THE?
?!
KAW!
chirp!!
KAW
CAW
chirp
CAW
OH GEEZ!!
AHHHHH!
OH GEEZ!

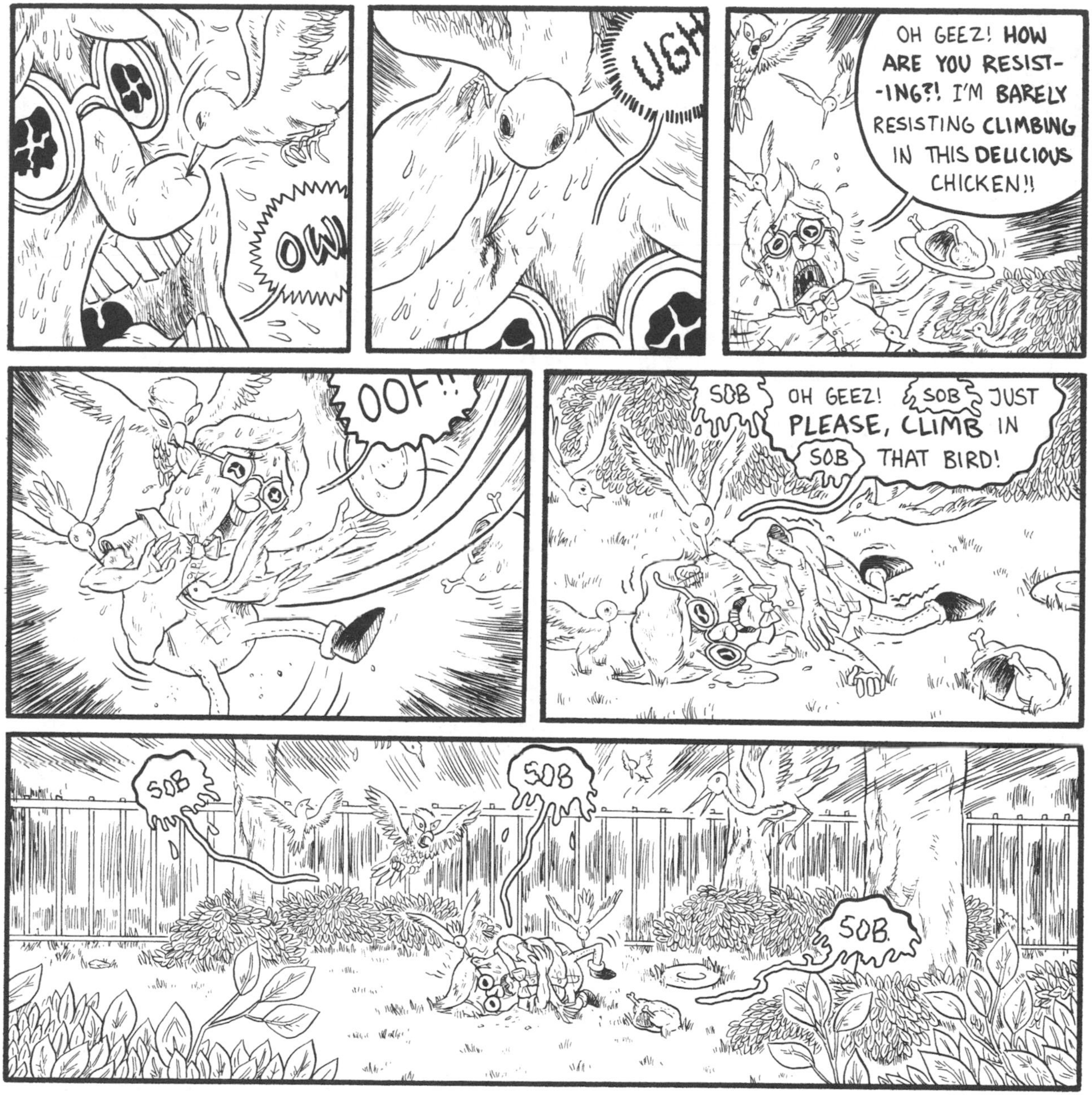
OW
UGH
OH GEEZ! HOW ARE YOU RESIST--ING?! I'M BARELY RESISTING CLIMBING IN THIS DELICIOUS CHICKEN!!
OOF!!
SOB
OH GEEZ! SOB JUST PLEASE, CLIMB IN SOB THAT BIRD!
SOB
SOB
SOB.

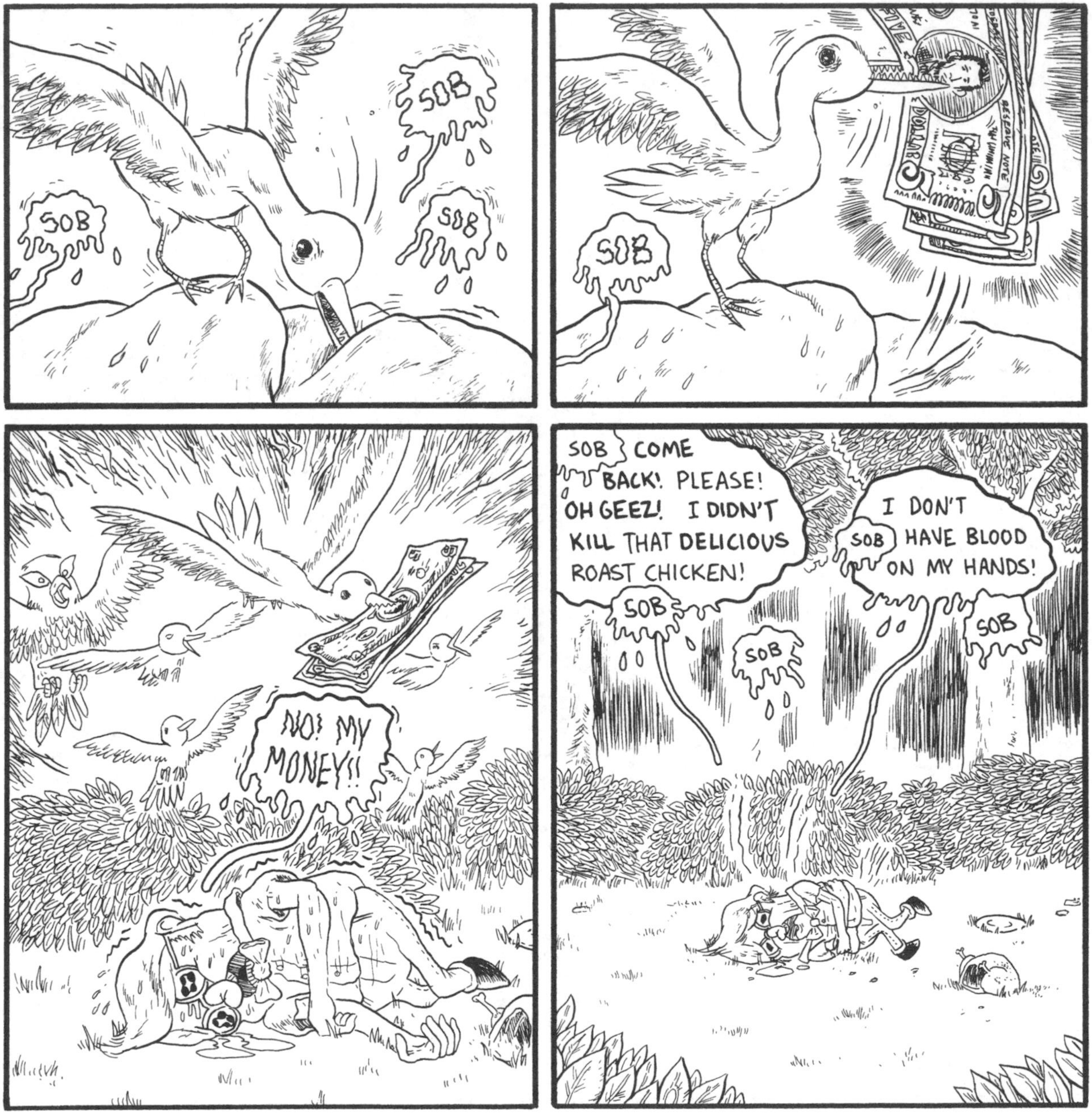
SOB
SOB
SOB
SOB
NO! MY MONEY!!
SOB
COME BACK! PLEASE! OH GEEZ! I DIDN'T KILL THAT DELICIOUS ROAST CHICKEN!
SOB
I DON'T HAVE BLOOD ON MY HANDS!
SOB
SOB
SOB
SOB

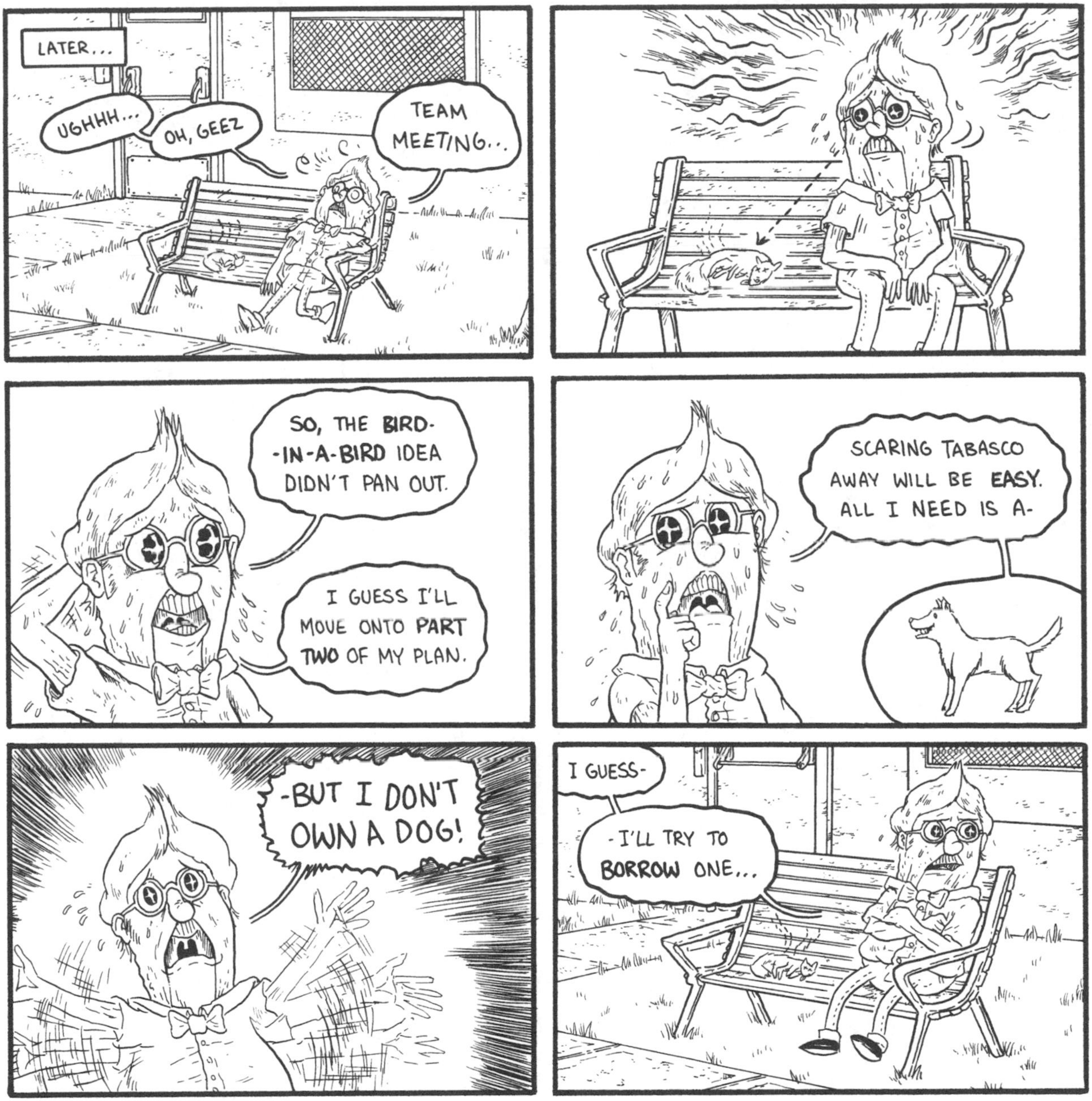
LATER...
UGHHH...
OH, GEEZ
TEAM MEETING...
SO, THE BIRD-
-IN-A-BIRD IDEA DIDN'T PAN OUT.
I GUESS I'LL MOVE ONTO PART TWO OF MY PLAN.
SCARING TABASCO AWAY WILL BE EASY. ALL I NEED IS A-
-BUT I DON'T OWN A DOG!
I GUESS-
-I'LL TRY TO BORROW ONE...

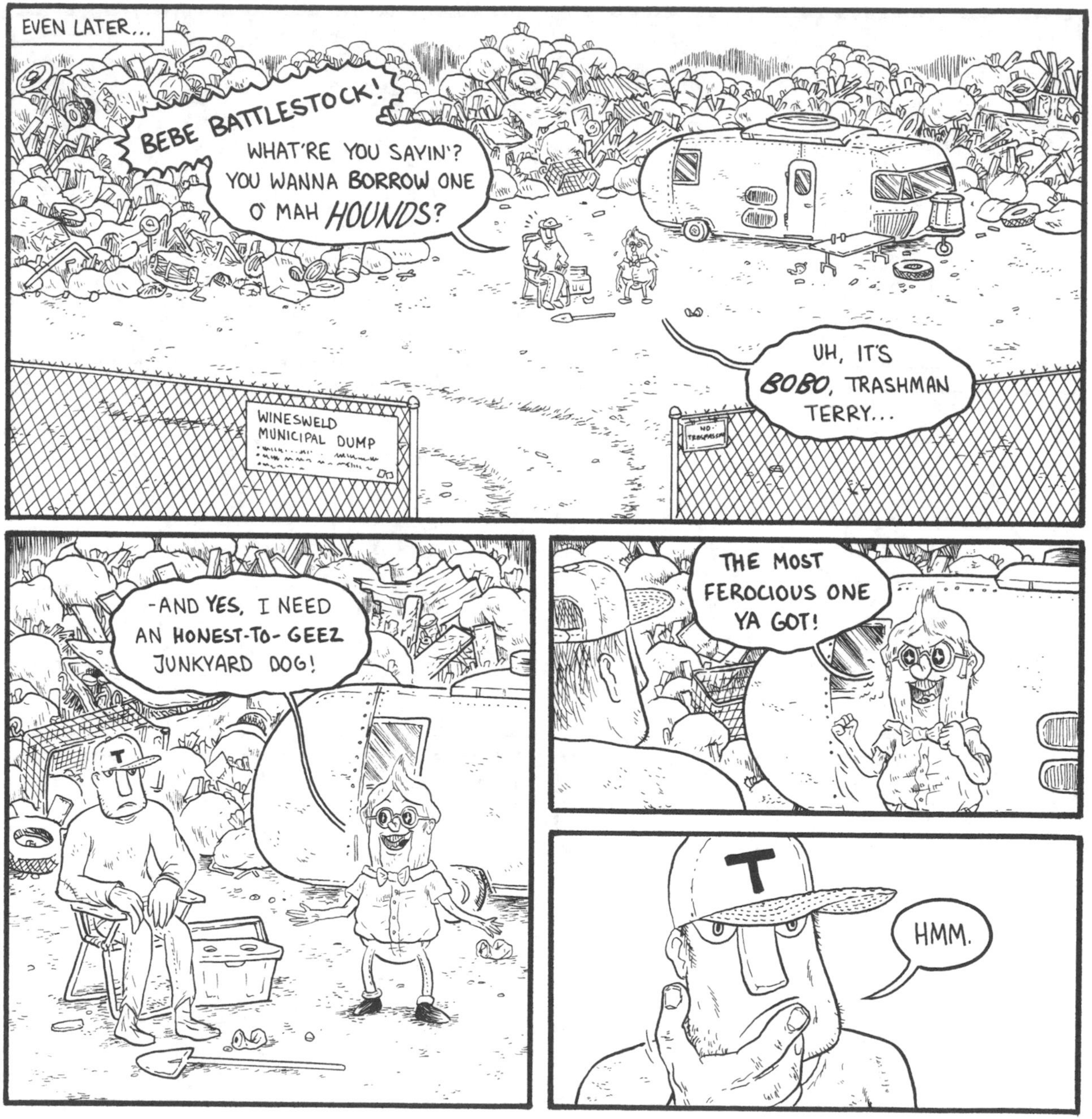
EVEN LATER...
BEBE BATTLESTOCK!
WHAT'RE YOU SAYIN'? YOU WANNA BORROW ONE O' MAH HOUNDS?
WINESWELD MUNICIPAL DUMP
UH, IT'S BOBO, TRASHMAN TERRY...
-AND YES, I NEED AN HONEST-TO-GEEZ JUNKYARD DOG!
THE MOST FEROCIOUS ONE YA GOT!
T
HMM.

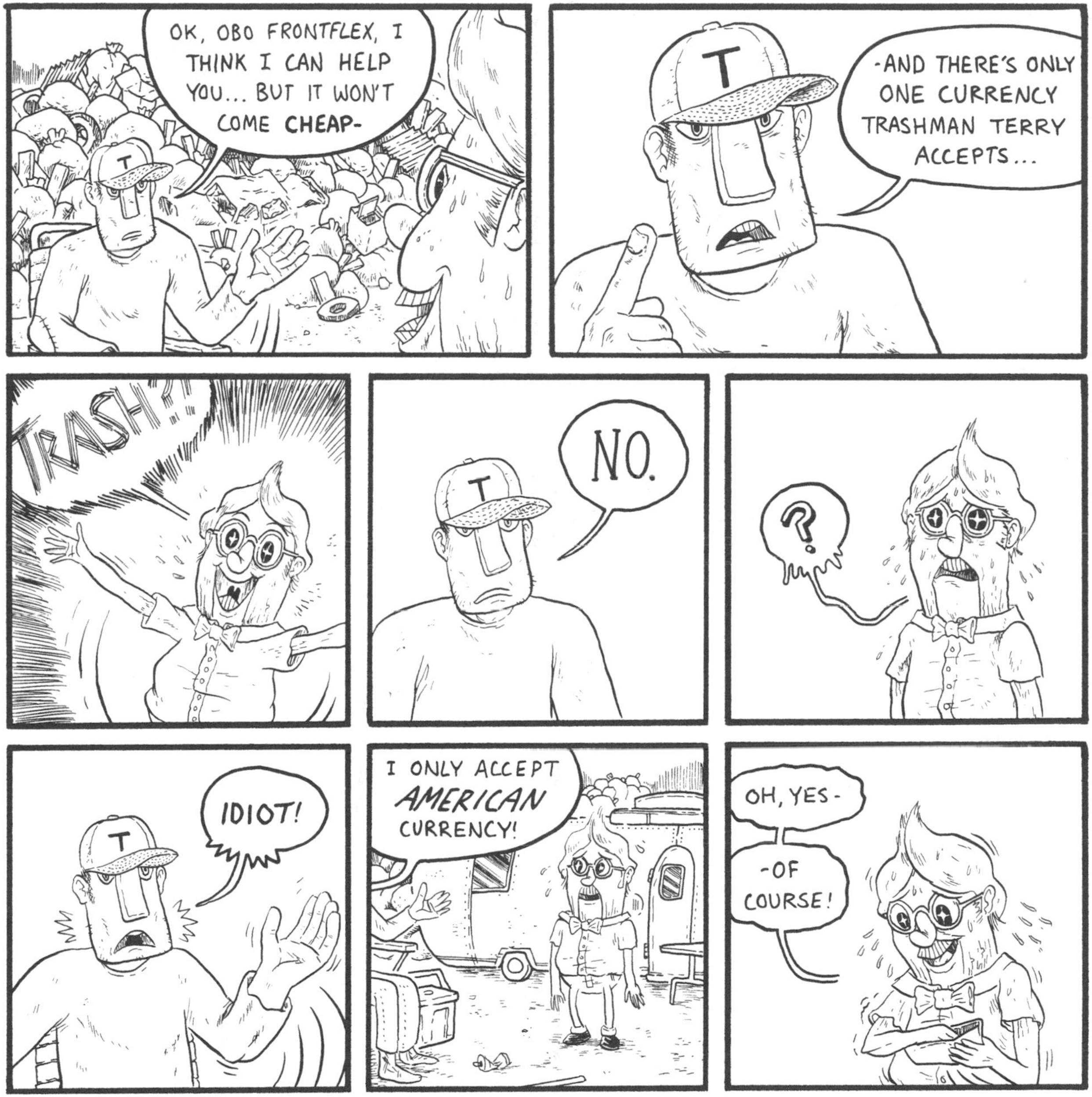
OK, OBO FRONTFLEX, I THINK I CAN HELP YOU... BUT IT WON'T COME CHEAP-
-AND THERE'S ONLY ONE CURRENCY TRASHMAN TERRY ACCEPTS...
TRASH?!
NO.
?
IDIOT!
I ONLY ACCEPT AMERICAN CURRENCY!
OH, YES-
-OF COURSE!

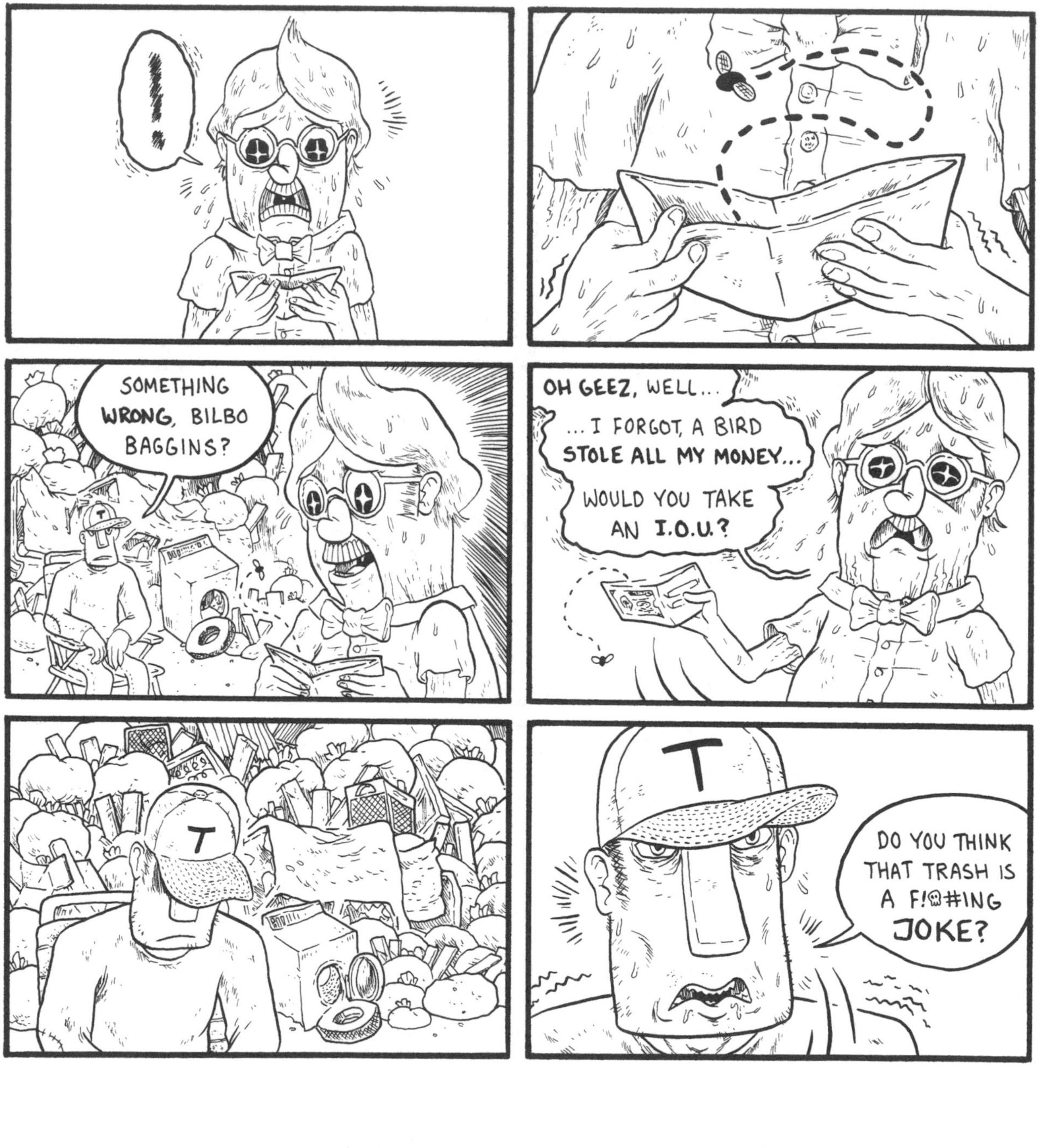
!
SOMETHING WRONG, BILBO BAGGINS?
OH GEEZ, WELL...
...I FORGOT, A BIRD STOLE ALL MY MONEY...
WOULD YOU TAKE AN I.O.U.?
DO YOU THINK THAT TRASH IS A F!☠#ING JOKE?

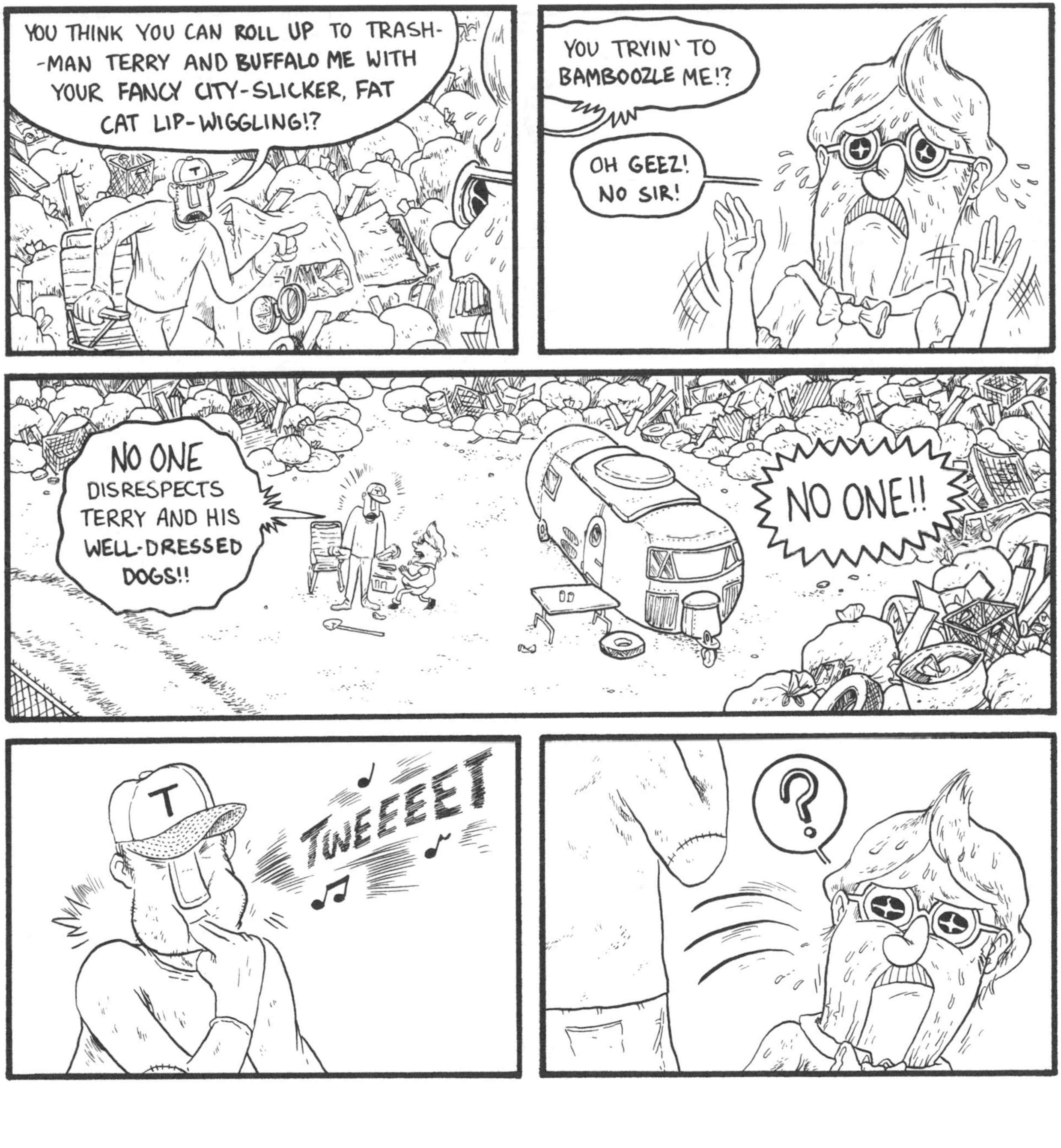

YOU THINK YOU CAN ROLL UP TO TRASH- -MAN TERRY AND BUFFALO ME WITH YOUR FANCY CITY-SLICKER, FAT CAT LIP-WIGGLING!?
YOU TRYIN' TO BAMBOOZLE ME!?
OH GEEZ! NO SIR!
NO ONE DISRESPECTS TERRY AND HIS WELL-DRESSED DOGS!!
NO ONE!!
TWEEEEET
?

WROOF
WROOF
WURF
WROUF
AHHHHHHHH!!
AND DON'T COME BACK!
UFF
WRUF

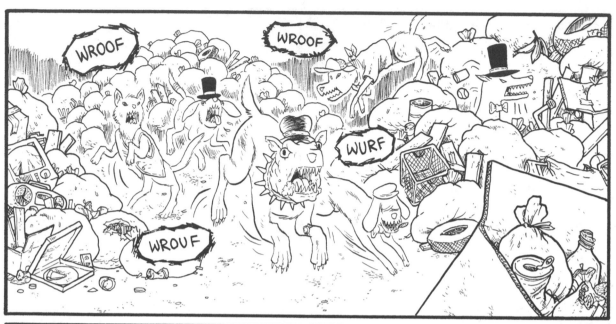

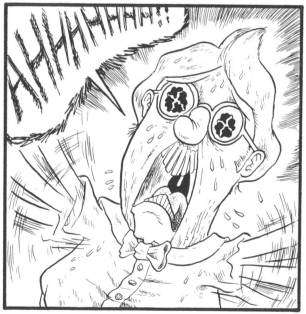

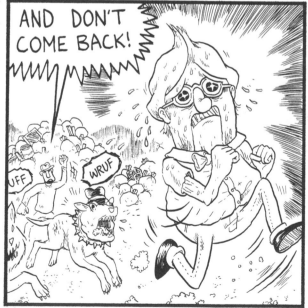

RUFF
AHHHHHHHHHHY
WRUF
ARFF
OH GEEZ!
HUFF
THESE DOGS-
HUFF
WURPH
PUFF
THEY'RE SO FASHIONABLE!
HUFF
PUFF
OH GEEZ!
HUFF
OH GEEZ!
HUFF
OH GEEZ!
WHO LET THE DOGS OUT!?
WUUF
WRAF
WURF

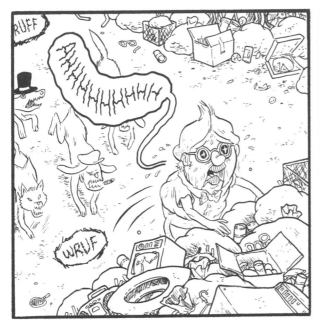

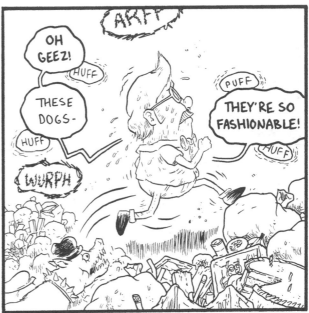

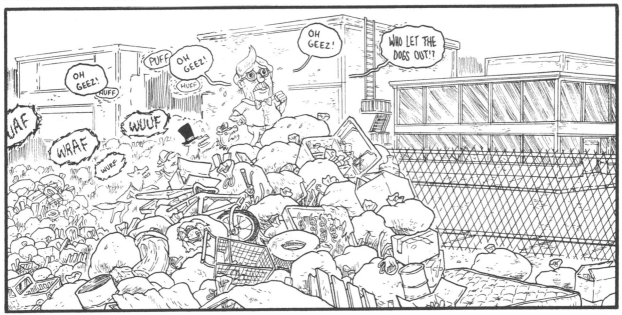

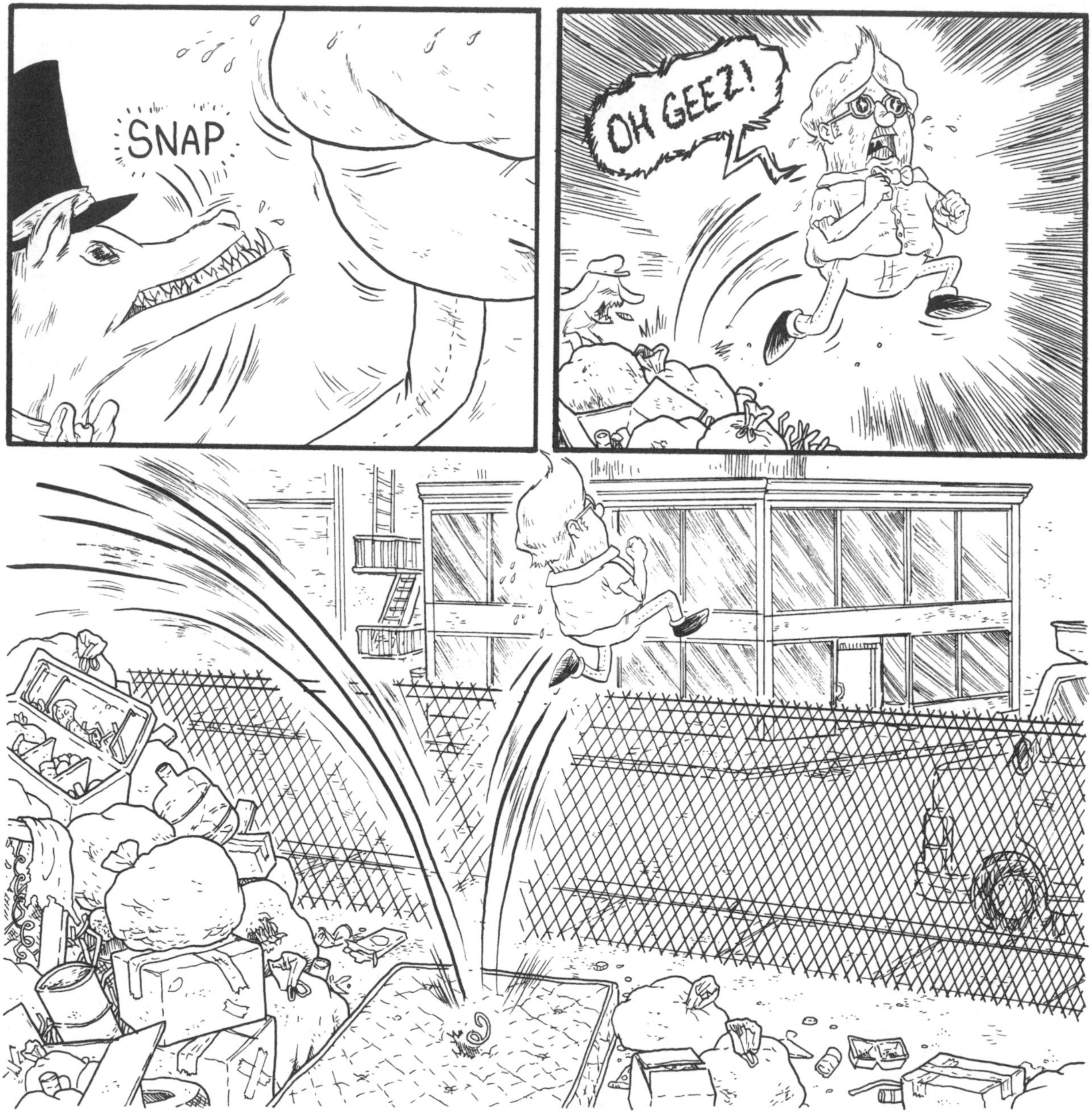
SNAP
OH GEEZ!

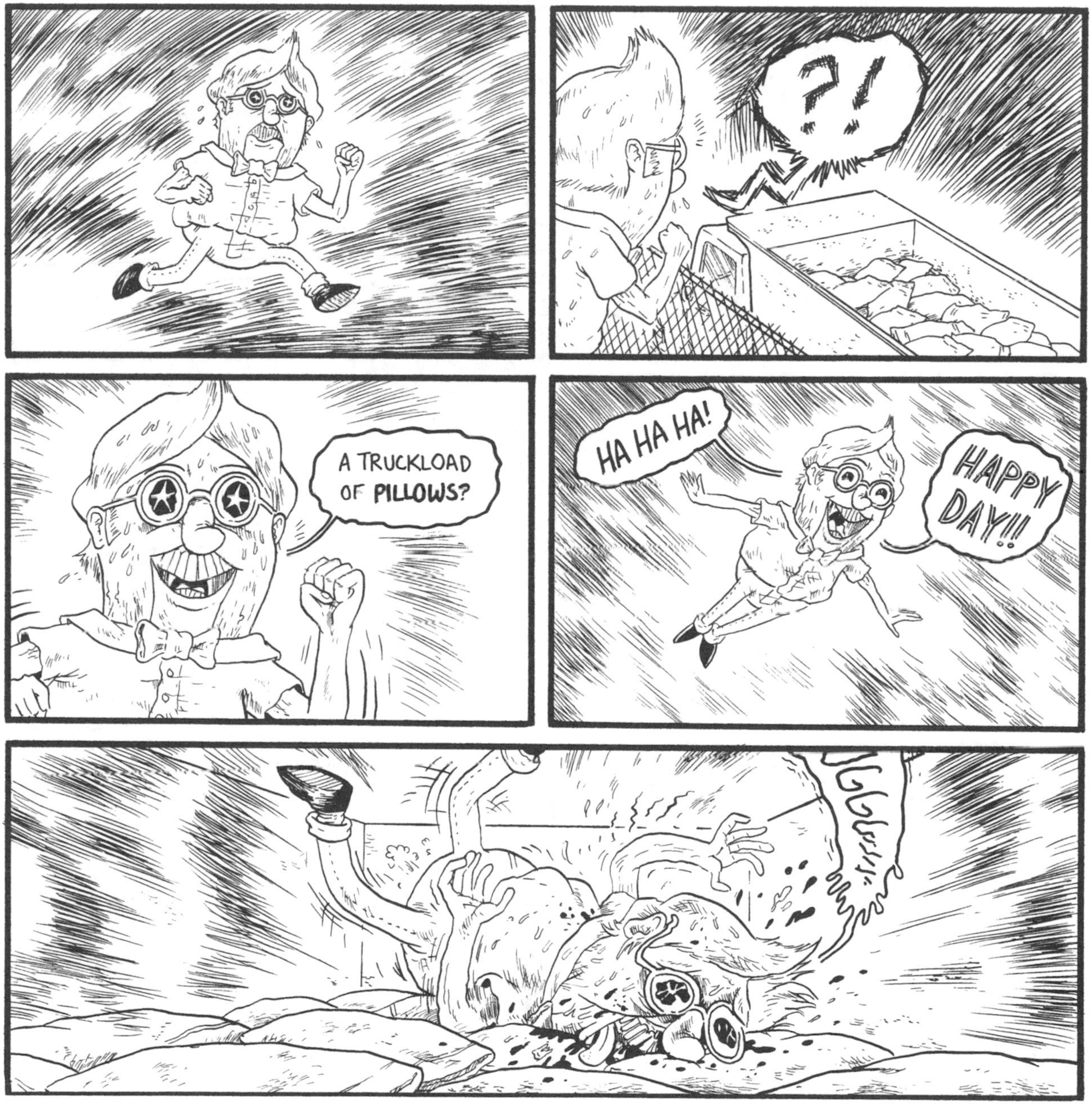
?!
A TRUCKLOAD OF PILLOWS?
HA HA HA!
HAPPY DAY!!

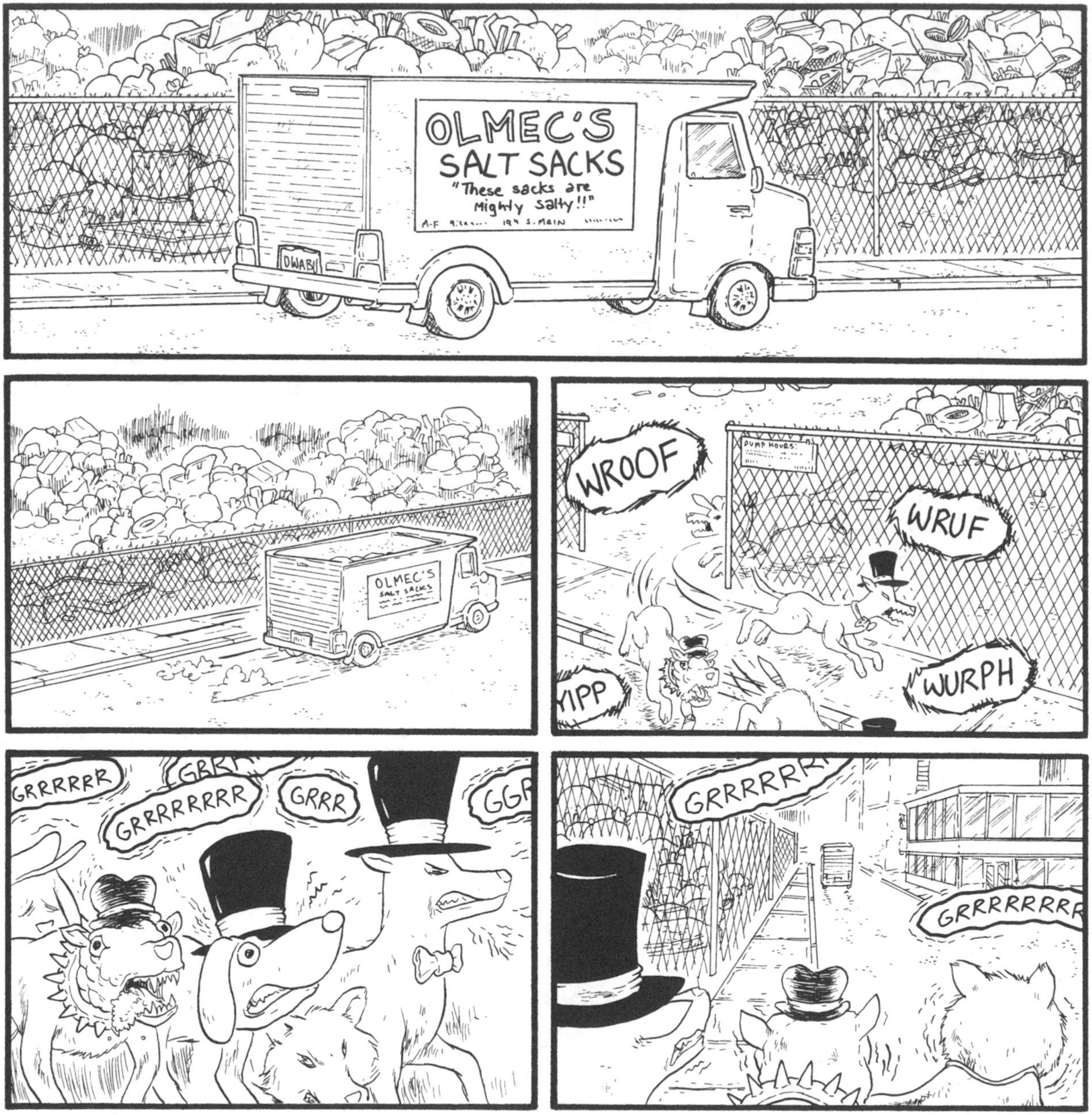
OLMEC'S
SALT SACKS
"These sacks are Mighty salty!!"
OLMEC'S
SALT SACKS
WROOF
DUMP HOURS:
WRUF
YIPP
WURPH
GRRRRRR
GRRRRRRRR
GRRR
GRRRRRR
GRRRRRRRR

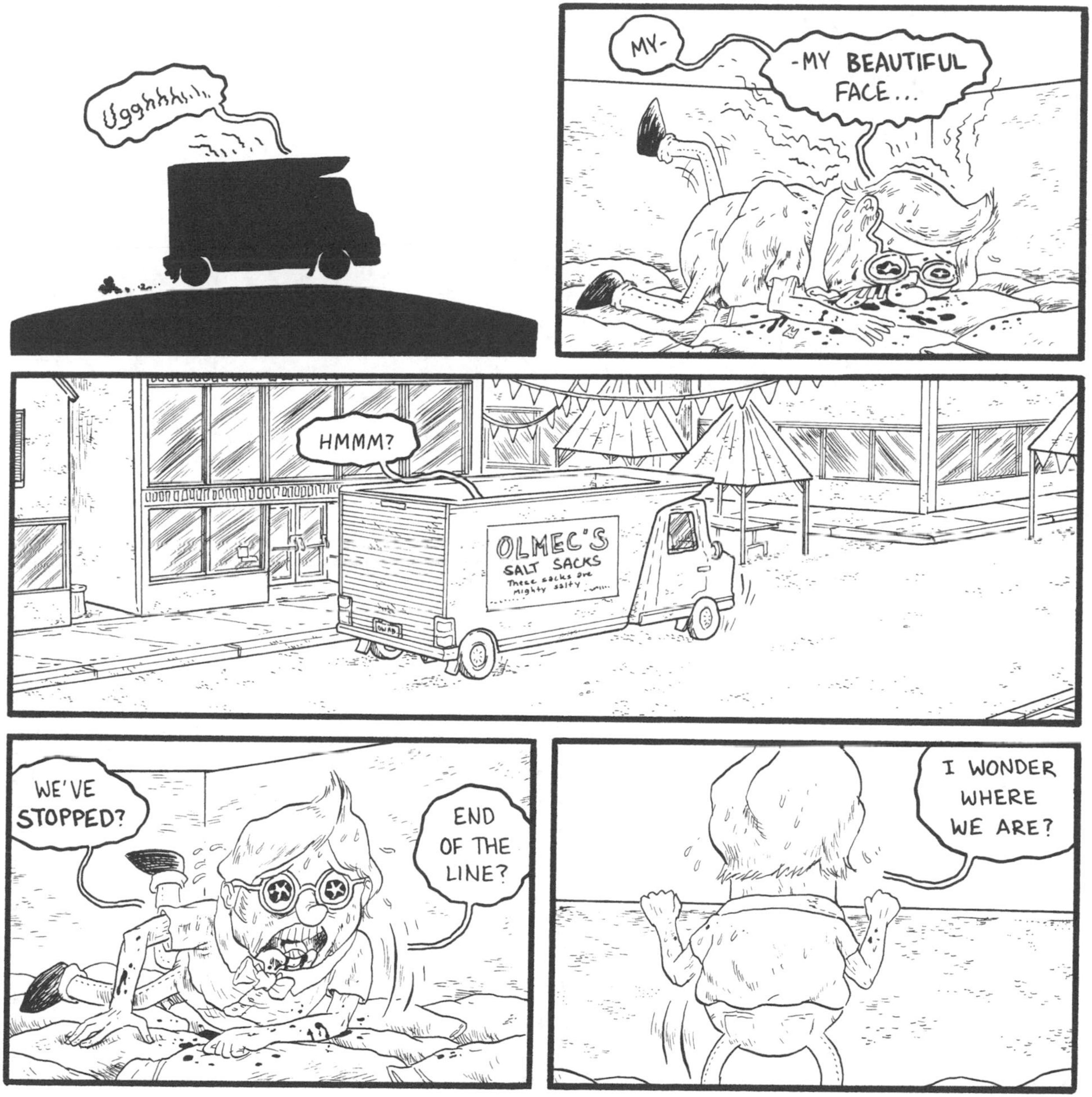
Ugghhh...
MY-
-MY BEAUTIFUL FACE...
HMMM?
OLMEC'S
SALT SACKS
These sacks are mighty salty
WE'VE STOPPED?
END OF THE LINE?
I WONDER WHERE WE ARE?

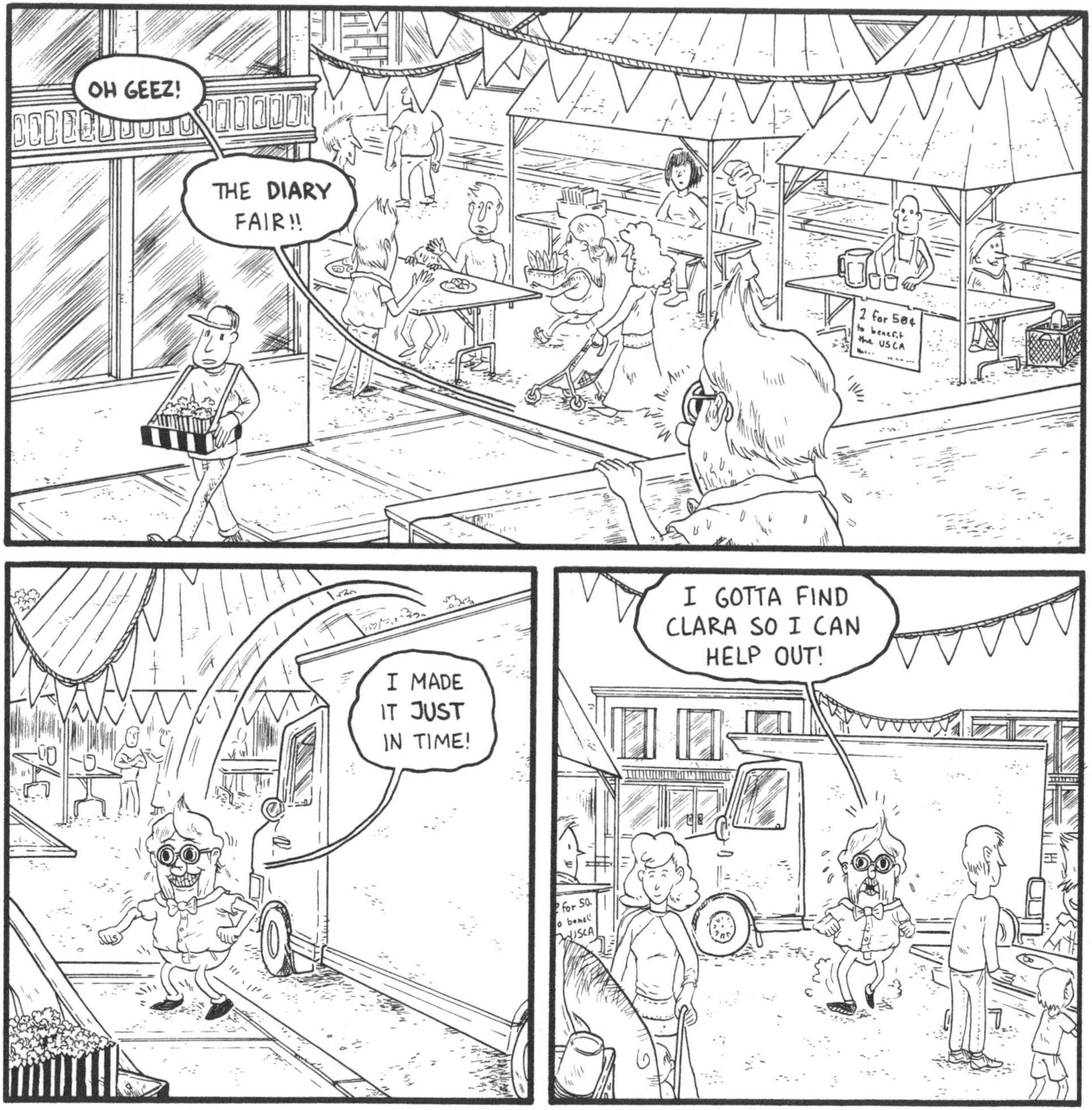
OH GEEZ!
THE DIARY FAIR!!
2 for 50¢ to benefit the USCA
I MADE IT JUST IN TIME!
I GOTTA FIND CLARA SO I CAN HELP OUT!

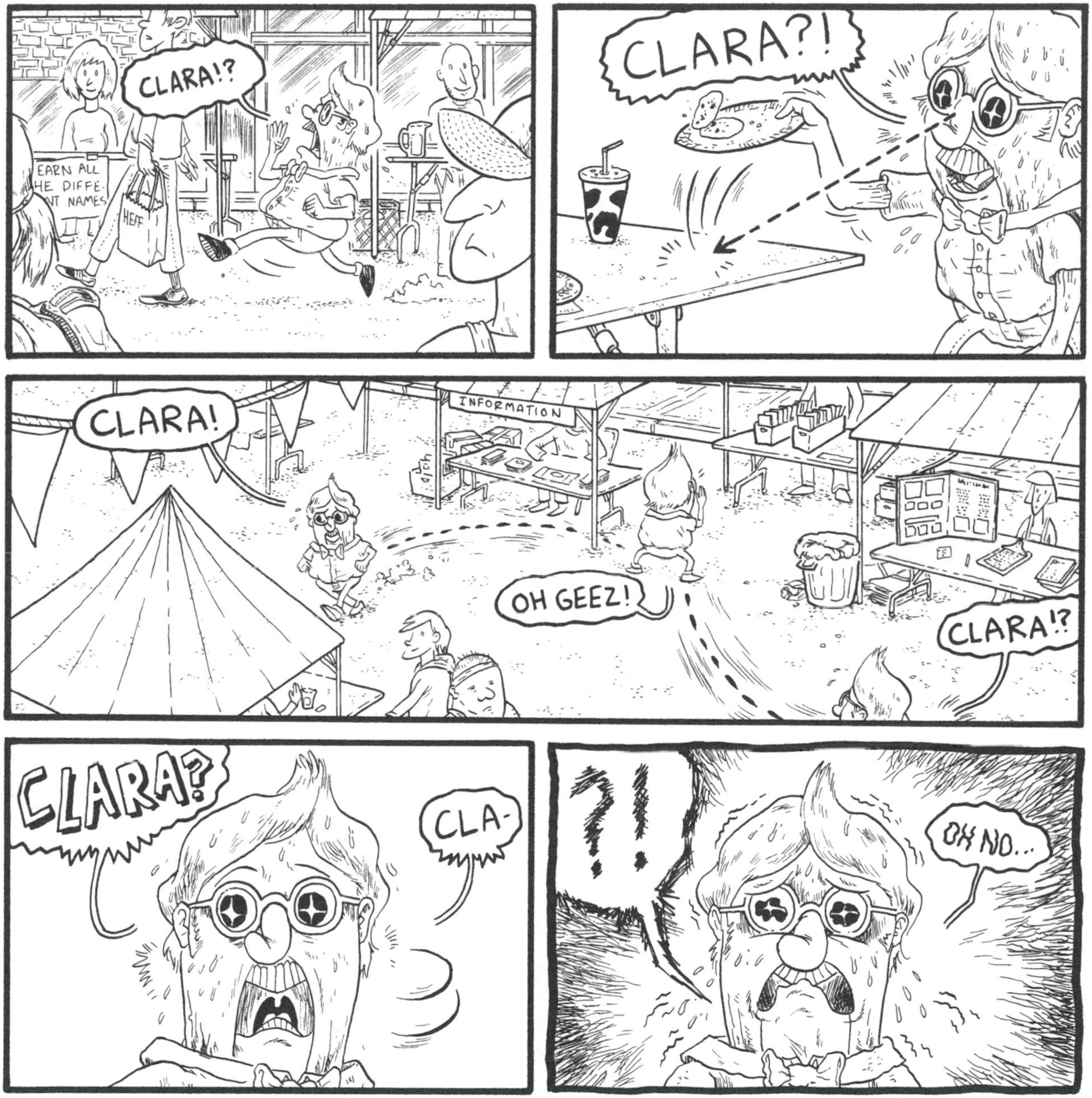
CLARA!?
CLARA?!
CLARA!
INFORMATION
OH GEEZ!
CLARA!?
CLARA?
CLA-
?!
OH NO...

KISSING BOOTH
Kiss a cat? Why not.
$1 For a smooch
RATS AND BATS!!
KISSING BOOTH
IT'S TED AND TABASCO!
Kiss a cat? Why NOT?!
$1 For a smooch!
OH GEEZ!!
I HAVE TO CHEESE IT BEFORE I PUFF UP!

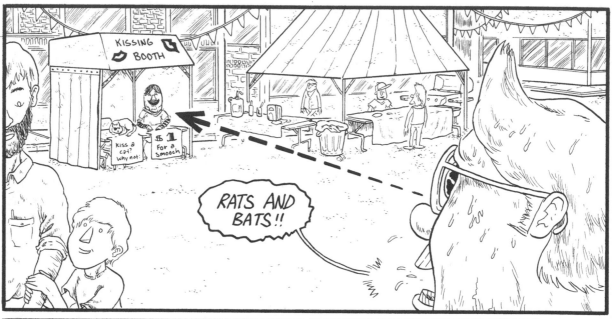

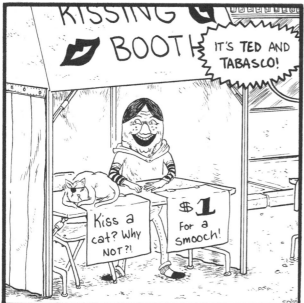

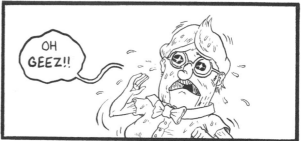

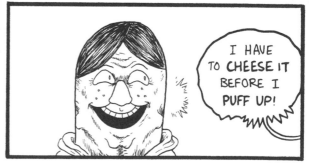

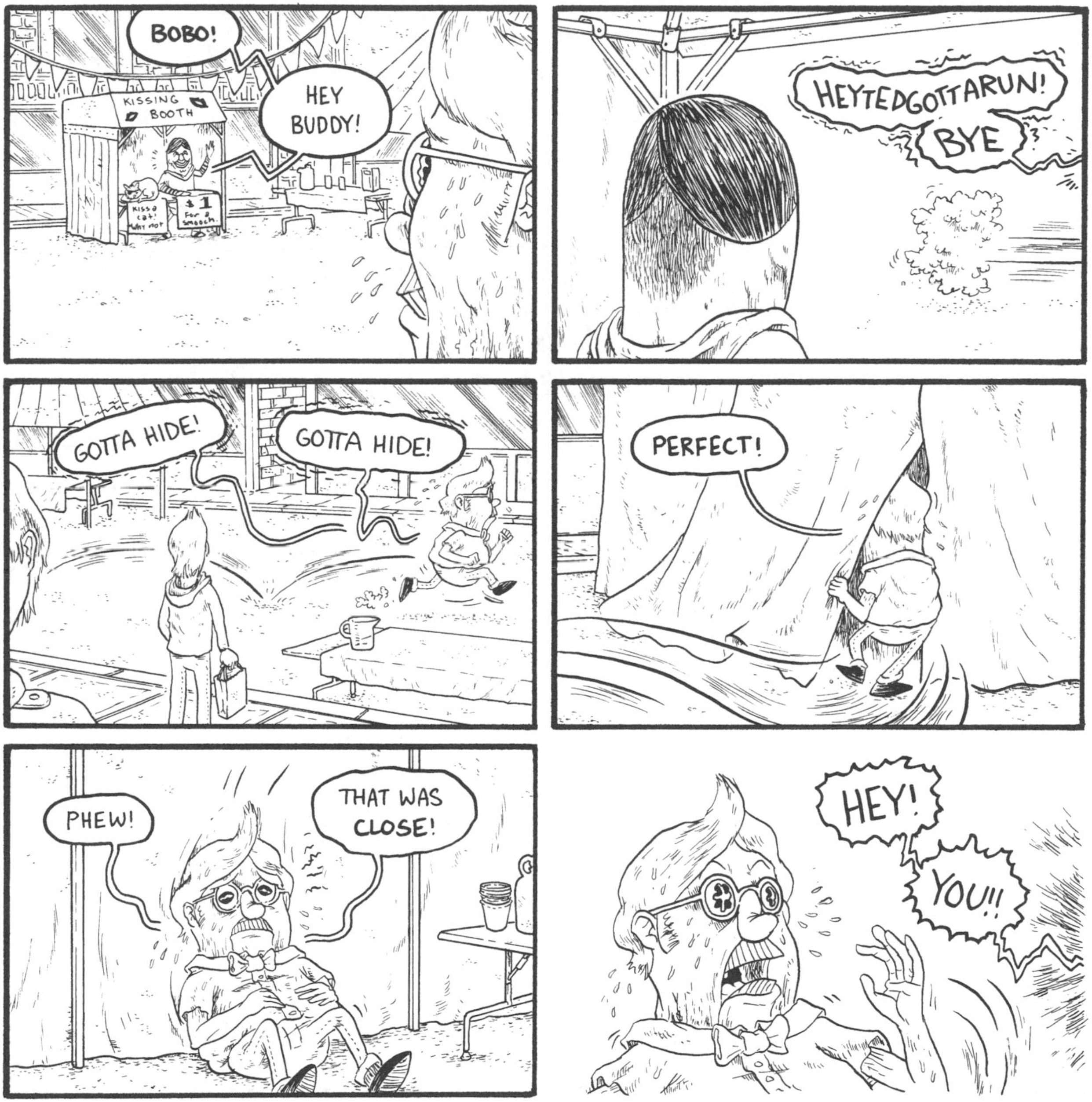
BOBO!
HEY BUDDY!
KISSING BOOTH
Kiss a cat! Why not
$1 For a smooch
HEYTEDGOTTARUN!
BYE
GOTTA HIDE!
GOTTA HIDE!
PERFECT!
PHEW!
THAT WAS CLOSE!
HEY!
YOU!!

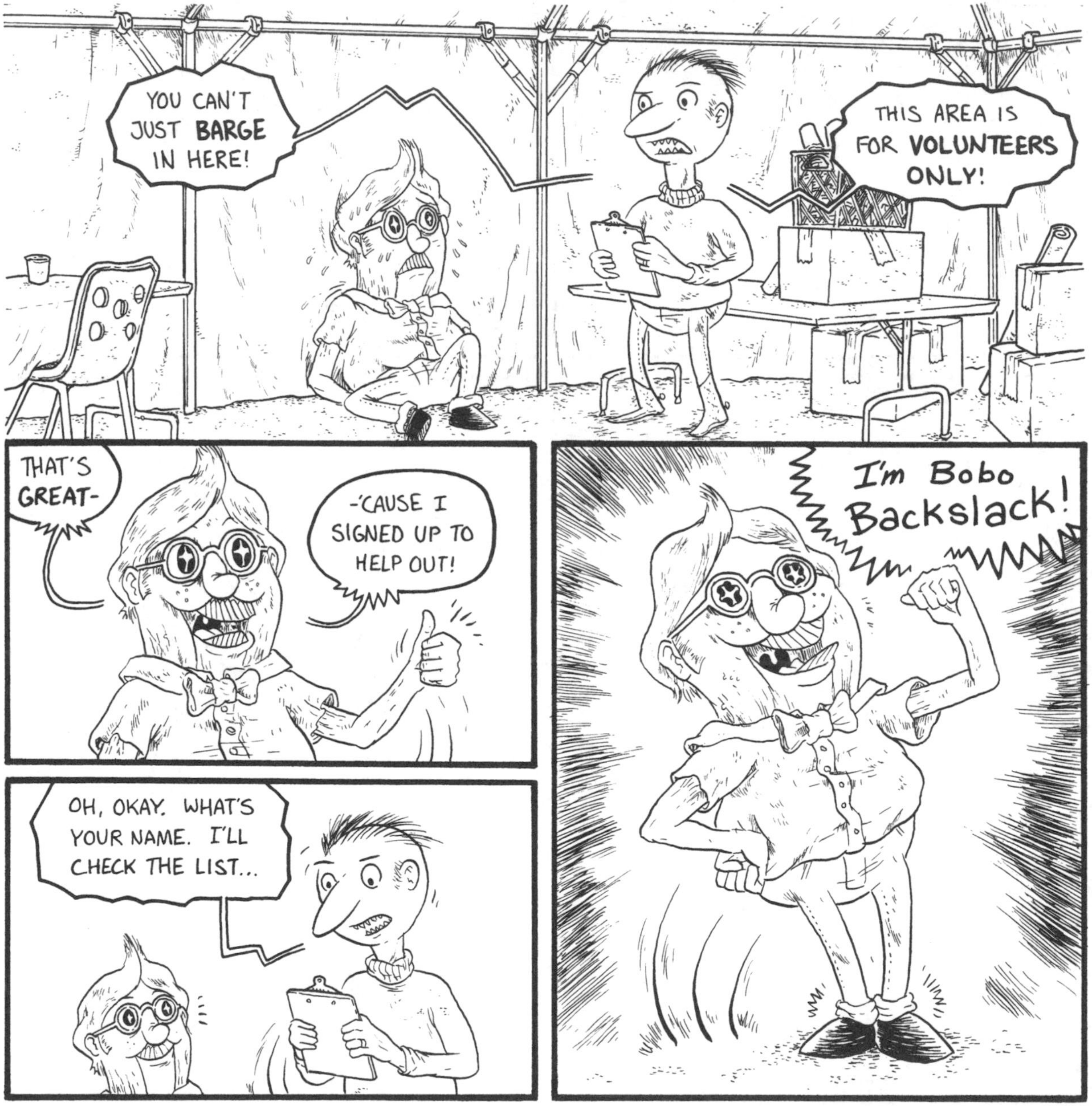
YOU CAN'T JUST BARGE IN HERE!
THIS AREA IS FOR VOLUNTEERS ONLY!
THAT'S GREAT-
-'CAUSE I SIGNED UP TO HELP OUT!
OH, OKAY. WHAT'S YOUR NAME. I'LL CHECK THE LIST...
I'm Bobo Backslack!

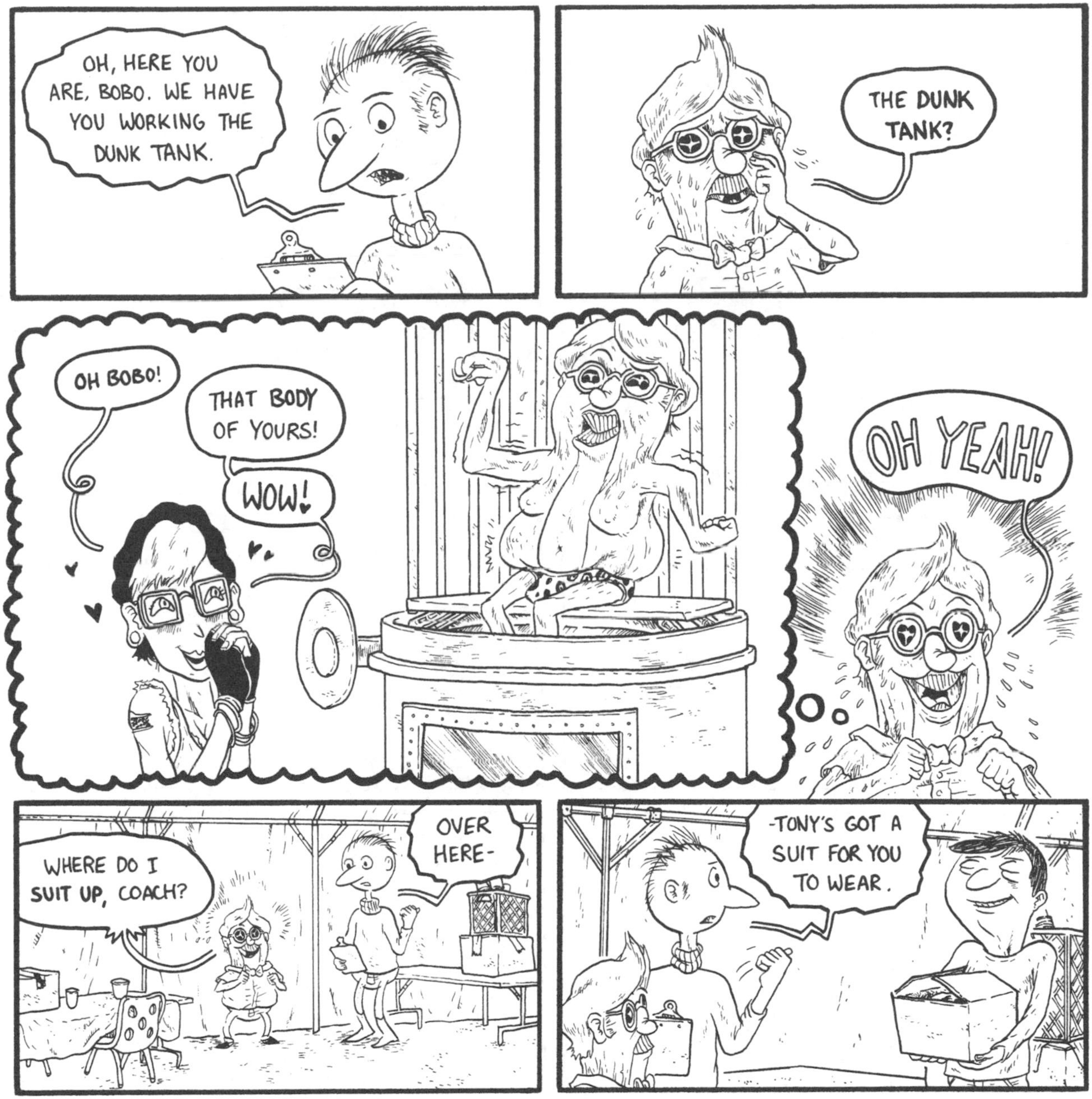
OH, HERE YOU ARE, BOBO. WE HAVE YOU WORKING THE DUNK TANK.
THE DUNK TANK?
OH BOBO!
THAT BODY OF YOURS!
WOW!
OH YEAH!
WHERE DO I SUIT UP, COACH?
OVER HERE-
-TONY'S GOT A SUIT FOR YOU TO WEAR.

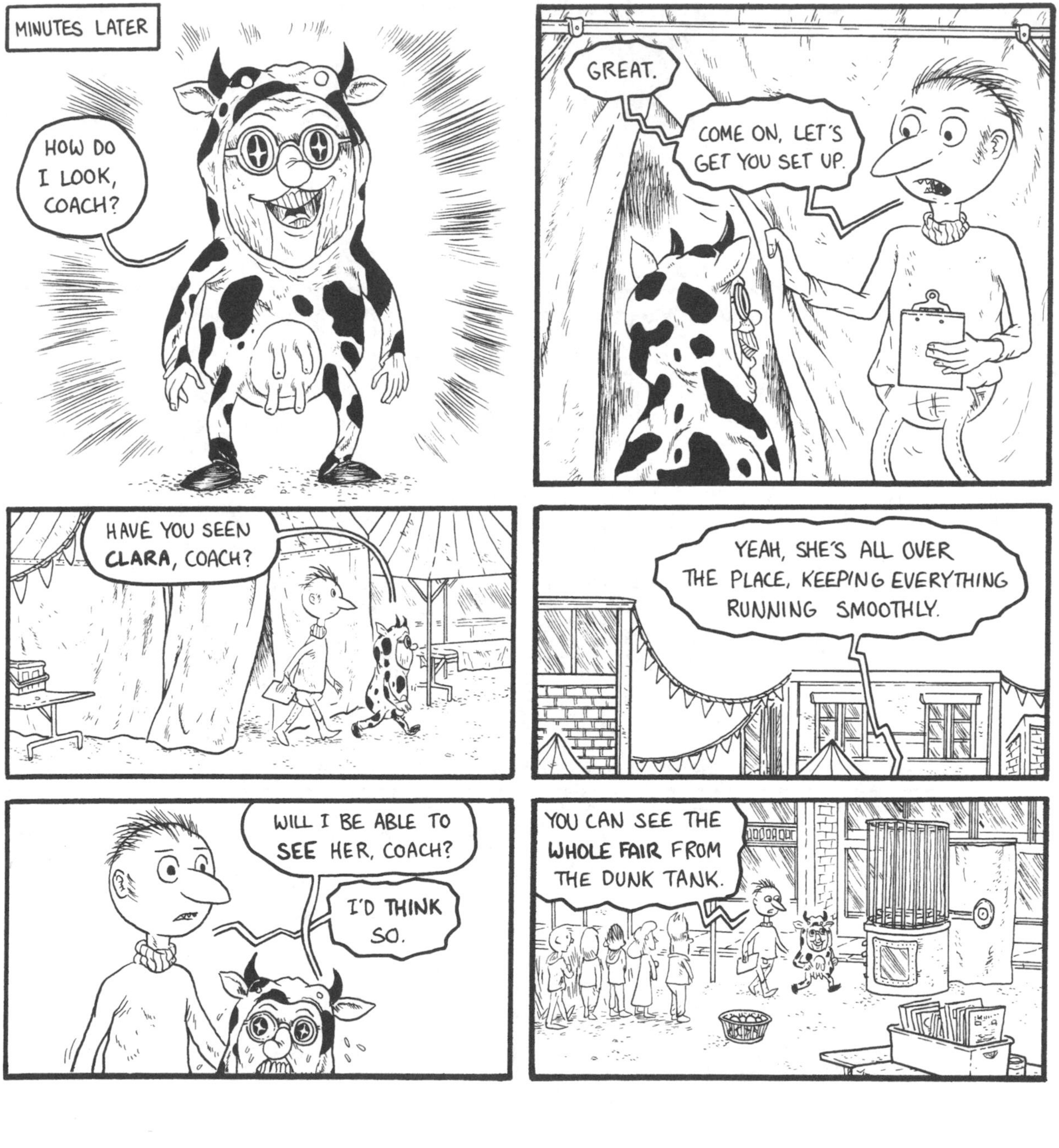
MINUTES LATER
HOW DO I LOOK, COACH?
GREAT.
COME ON, LET'S GET YOU SET UP.
HAVE YOU SEEN **CLARA**, COACH?
YEAH, SHE'S ALL OVER THE PLACE, KEEPING EVERYTHING RUNNING SMOOTHLY.
WILL I BE ABLE TO **SEE** HER, COACH?
I'D **THINK** SO.
YOU CAN SEE THE **WHOLE FAIR** FROM THE DUNK TANK.

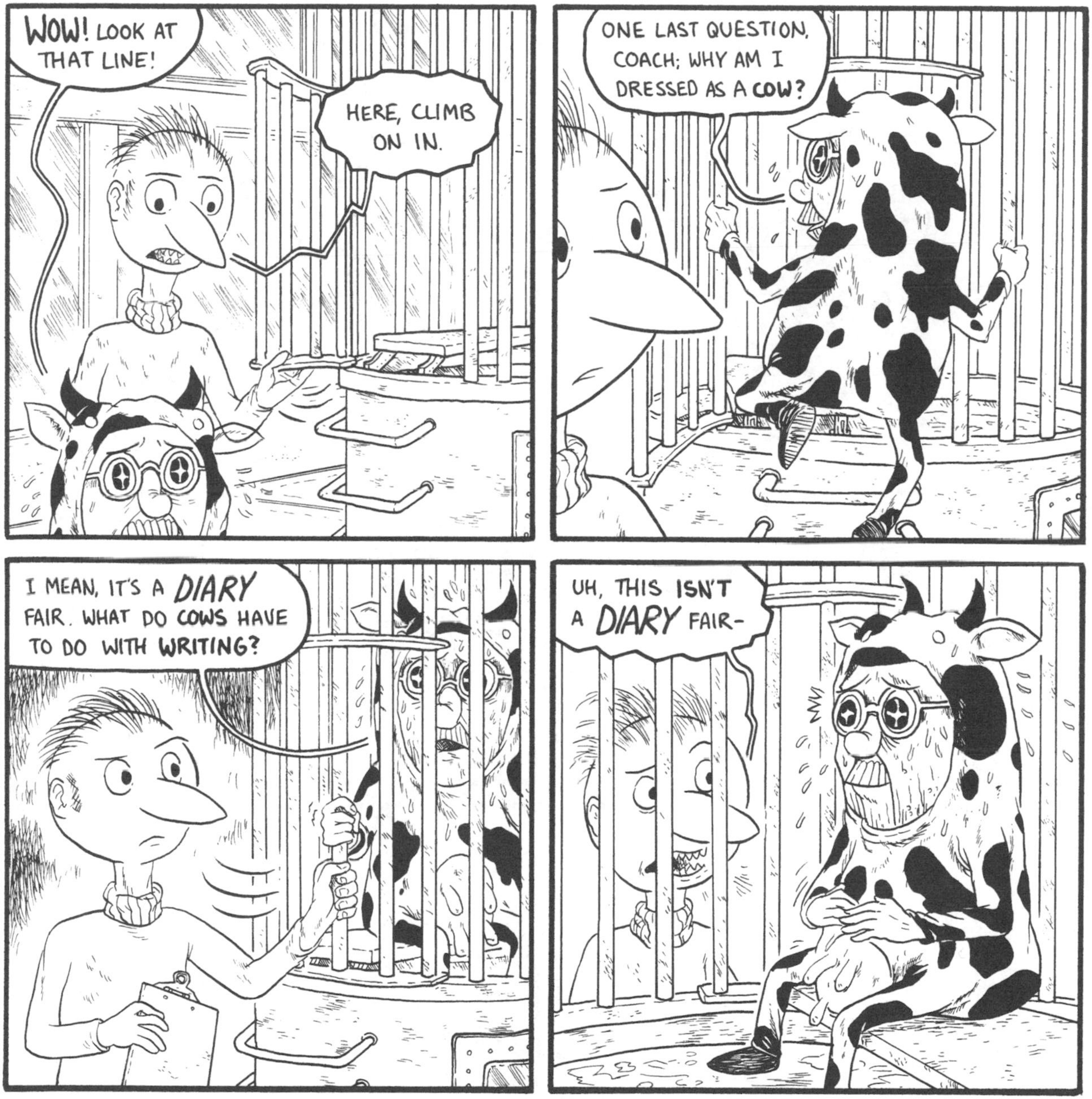
WOW! LOOK AT THAT LINE!
HERE, CLIMB ON IN.
ONE LAST QUESTION, COACH; WHY AM I DRESSED AS A COW?
I MEAN, IT'S A DIARY FAIR. WHAT DO COWS HAVE TO DO WITH WRITING?
UH, THIS ISN'T A DIARY FAIR-

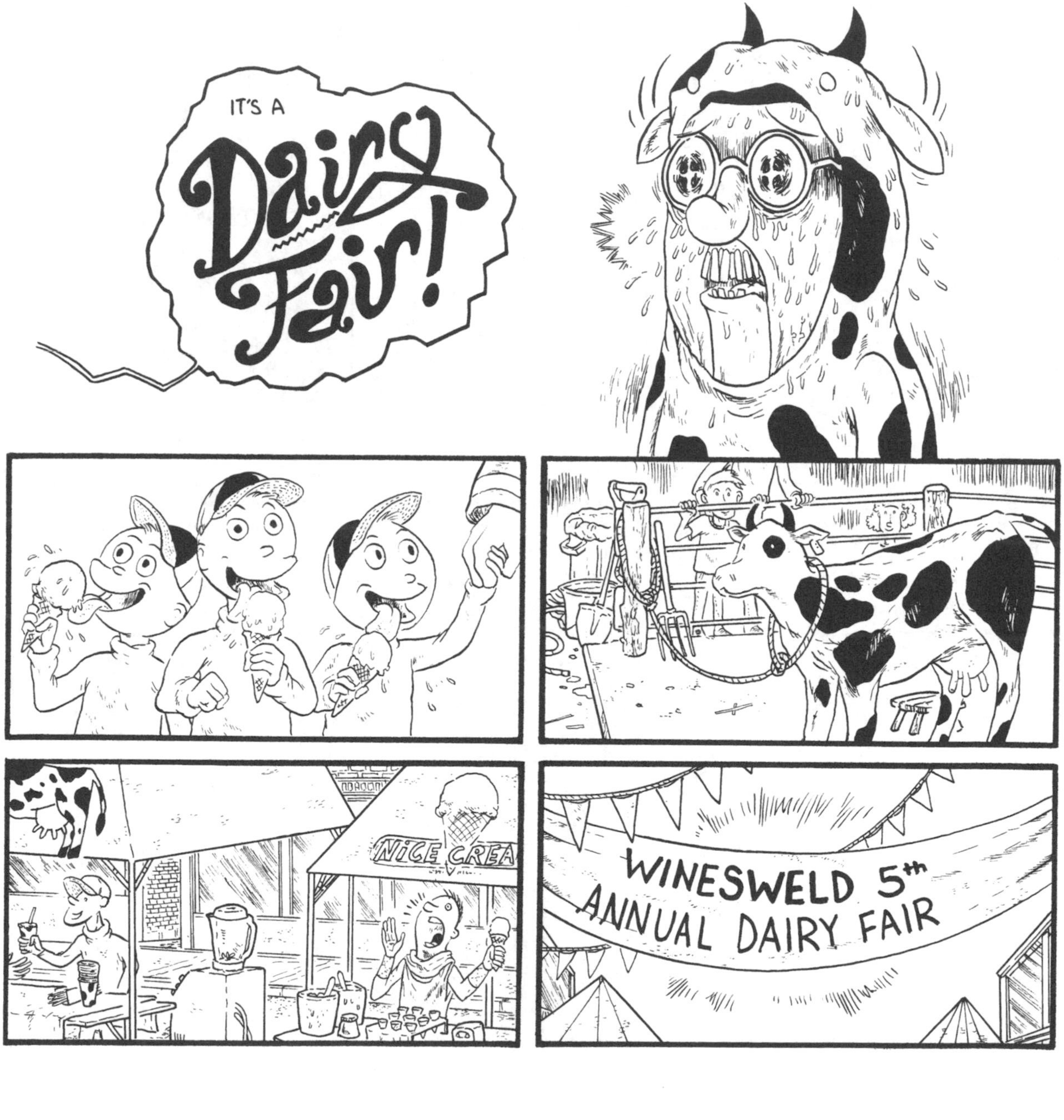
IT'S A
Dairy Fair!
NICE CREA
WINESWELD 5th ANNUAL DAIRY FAIR

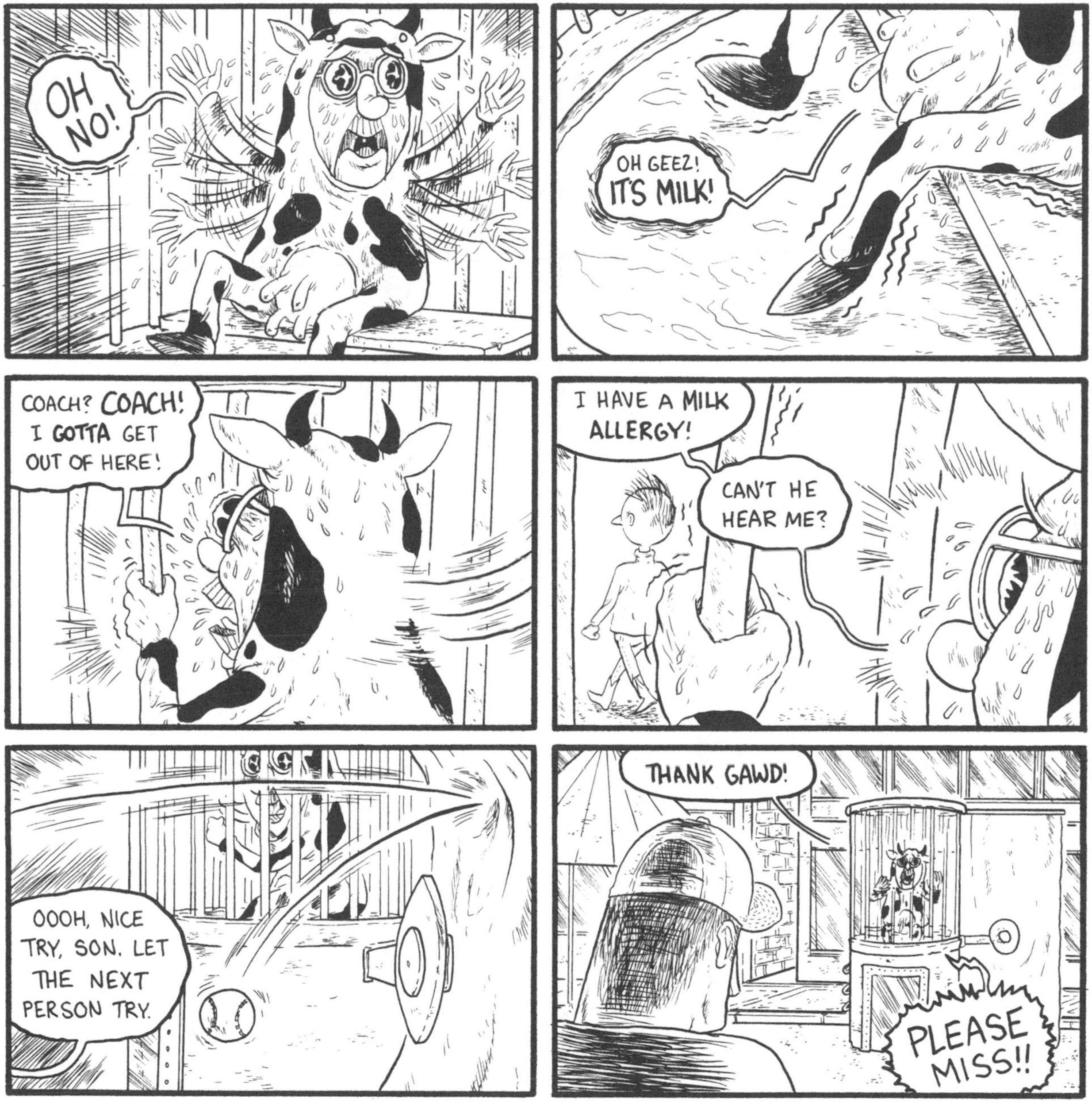
OH NO!
OH GEEZ! IT'S MILK!
COACH? COACH! I GOTTA GET OUT OF HERE!
I HAVE A MILK ALLERGY!
CAN'T HE HEAR ME?
OOOH, NICE TRY, SON. LET THE NEXT PERSON TRY.
THANK GAWD!
PLEASE MISS!!

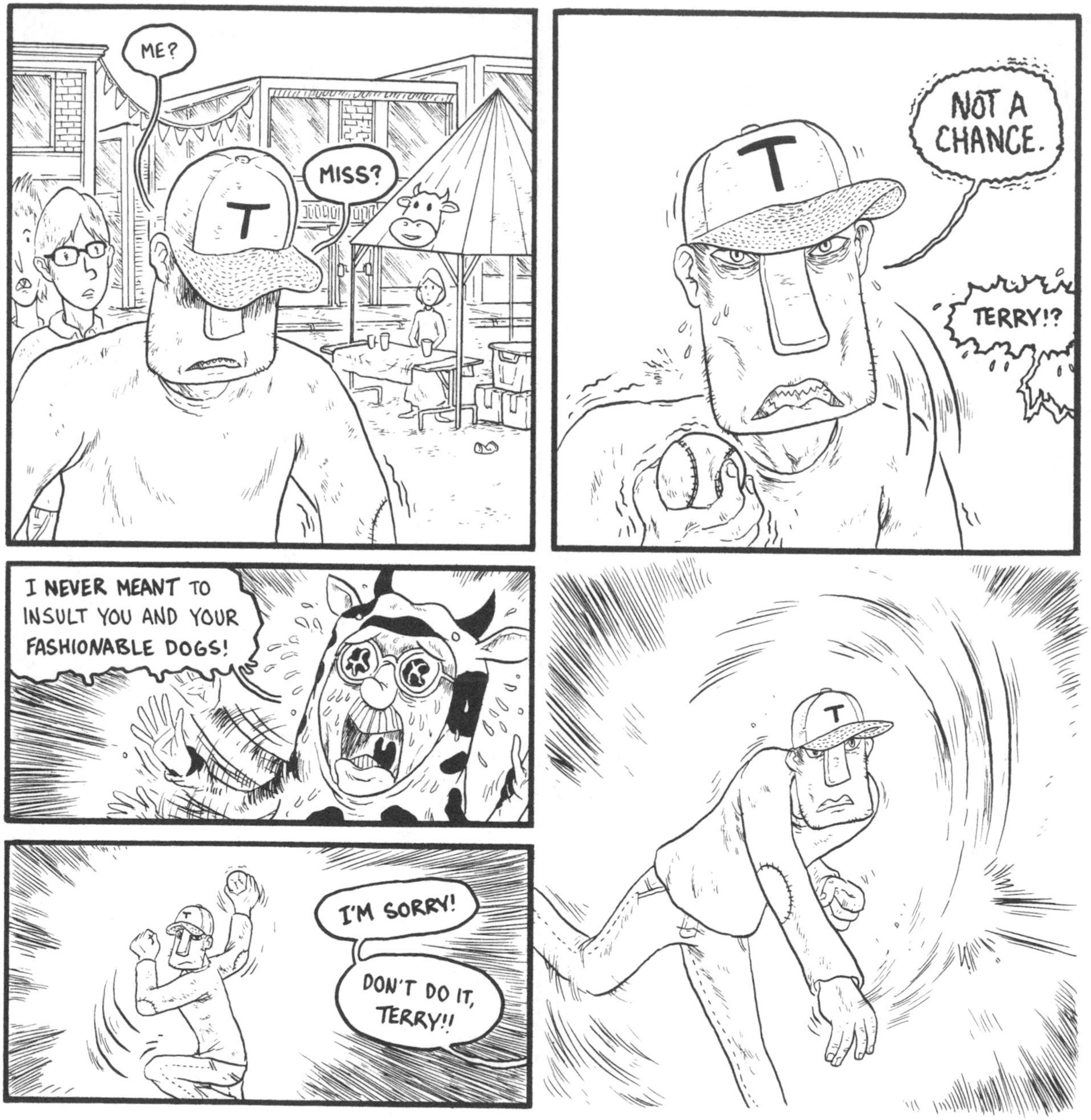
ME?
MISS?
NOT A CHANCE.
TERRY!?
I NEVER MEANT TO INSULT YOU AND YOUR FASHIONABLE DOGS!
I'M SORRY!
DON'T DO IT, TERRY!!

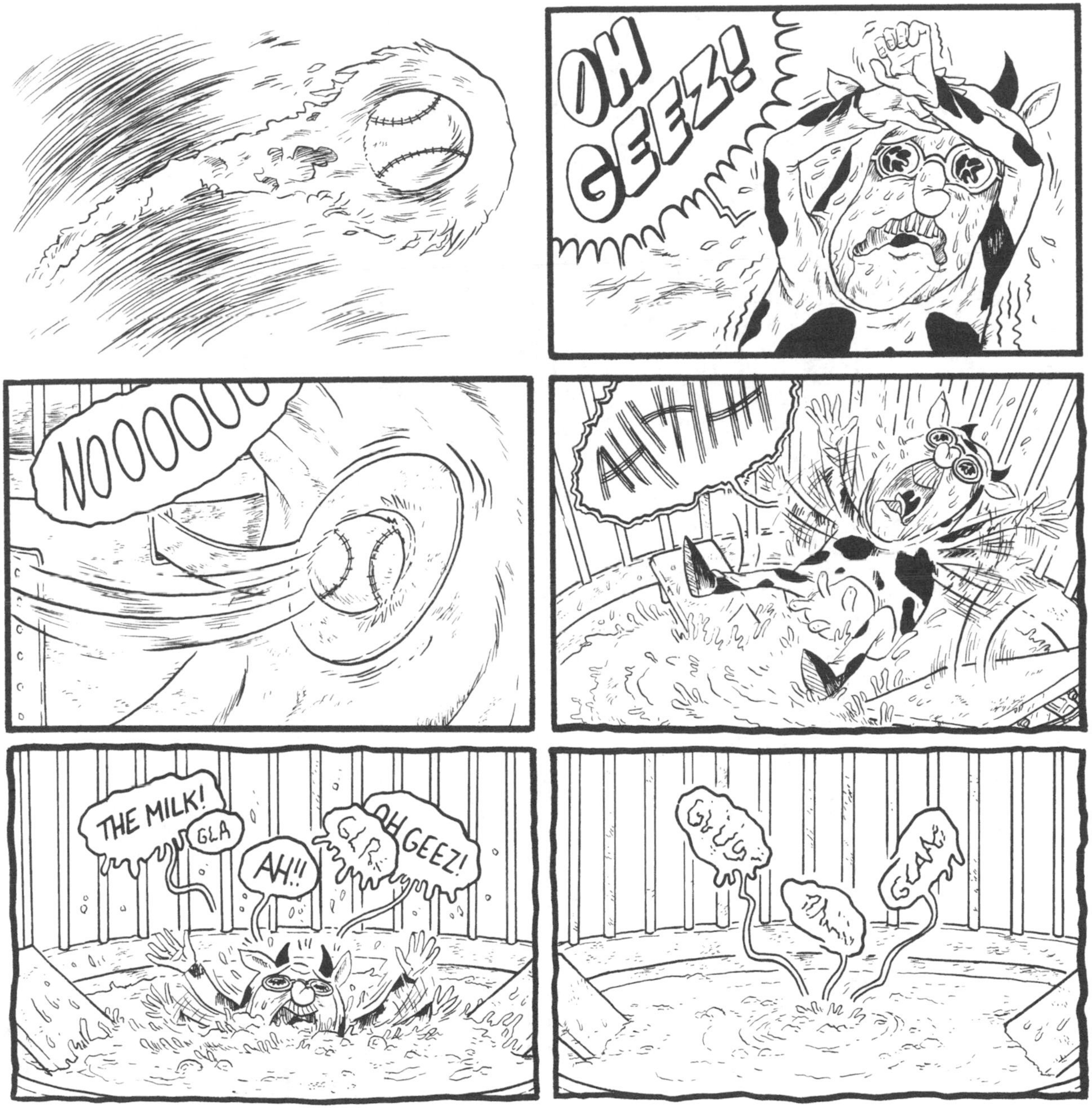
OH GEEZ!
NOOOOO
AHHHH
THE MILK!
GLA
AH!!
GLR
OH GEEZ!
GLUG

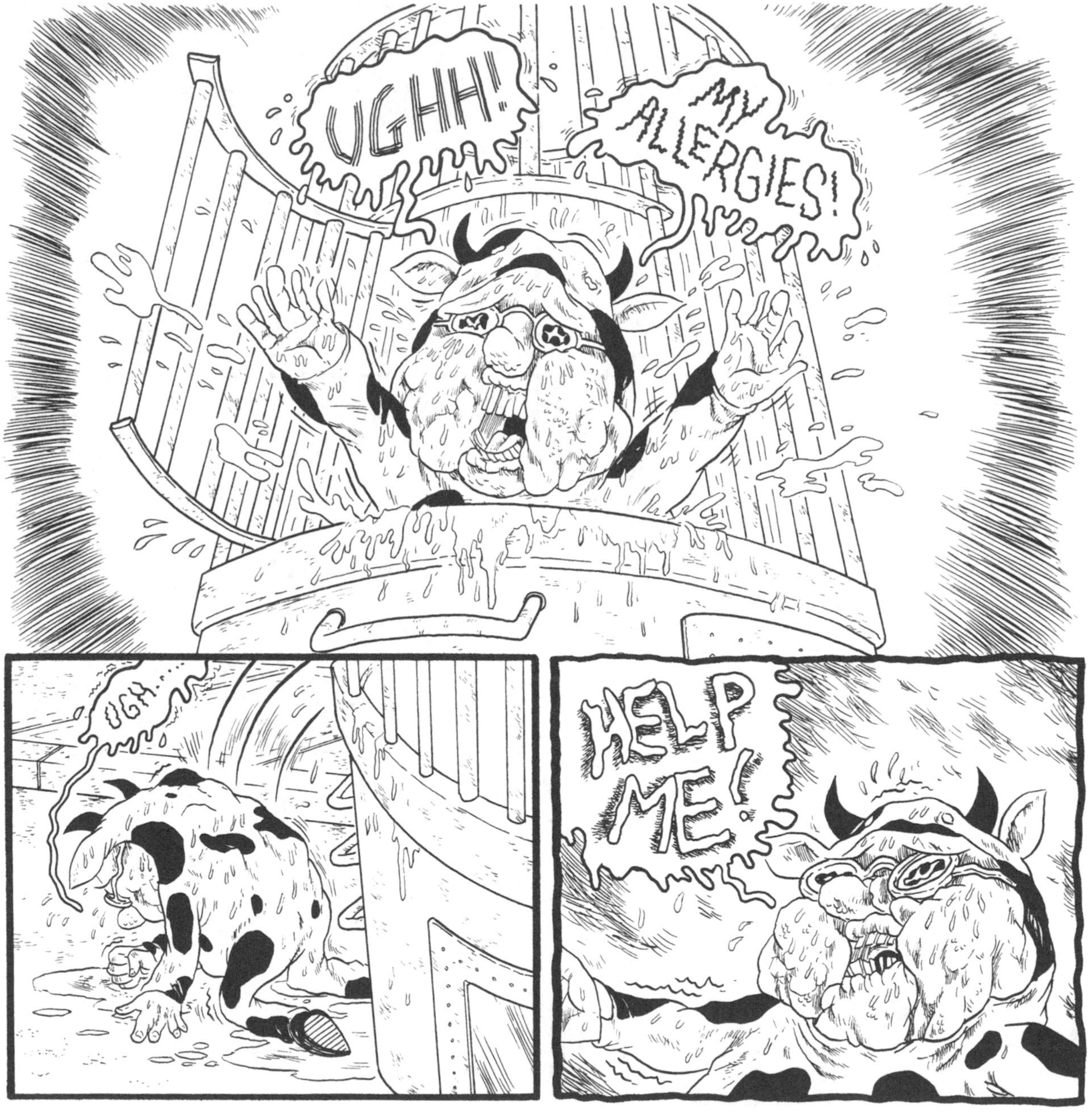
UGHH!
MY ALLERGIES!
UGH...
HELP ME!

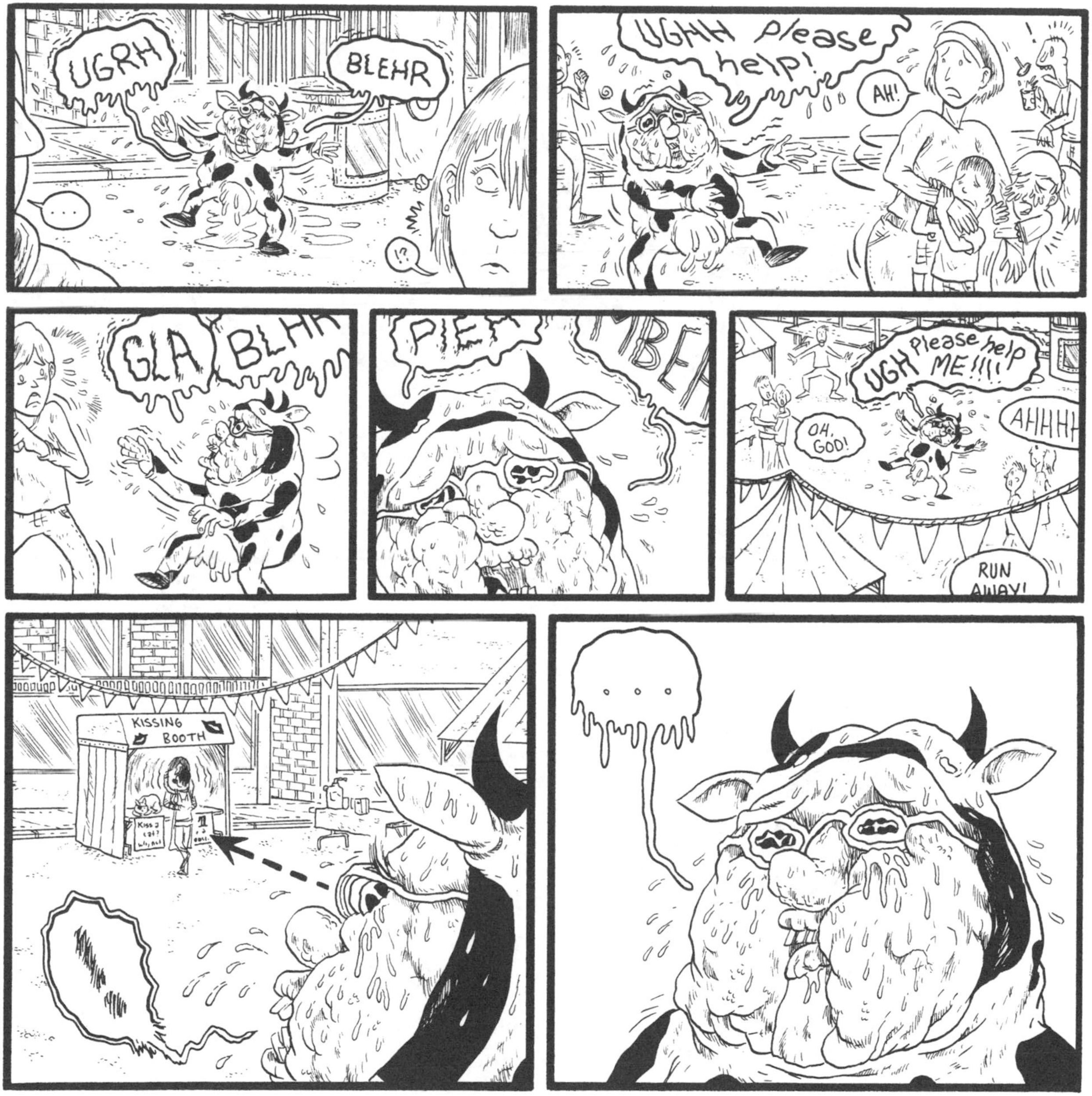

UGRH
BLEHR
...
!?
UGHH please help!
AH!
GLA
BLHR
PIER
MBER
UGH Please help ME!!!!
OH, GOD!
AHHHH
RUN AWAY!
KISSING BOOTH
...

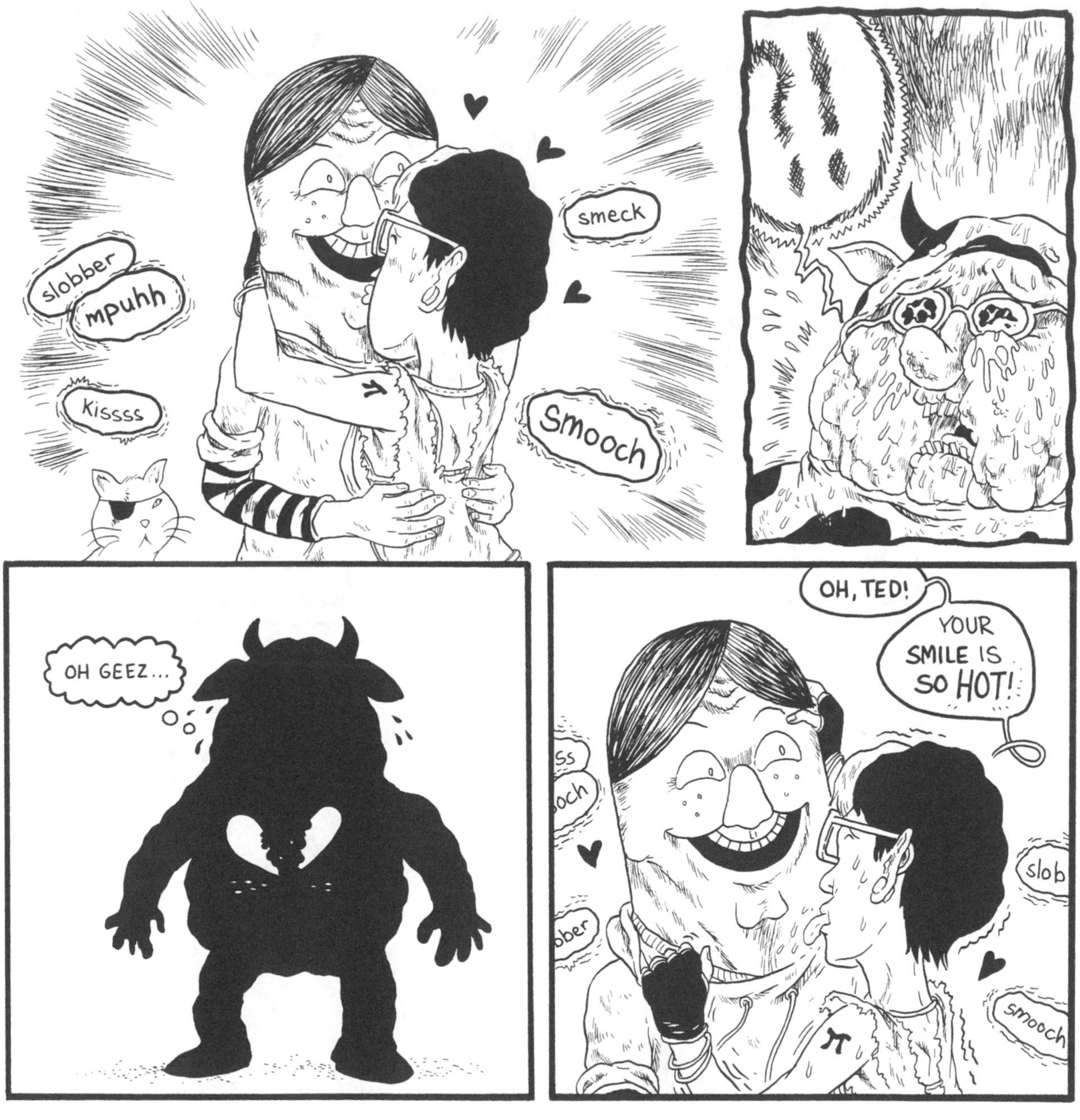
slobber
mpuhh
kissss
smeck
Smooch
OH GEEZ...
OH, TED!
YOUR SMILE IS SO HOT!
slob
smooch

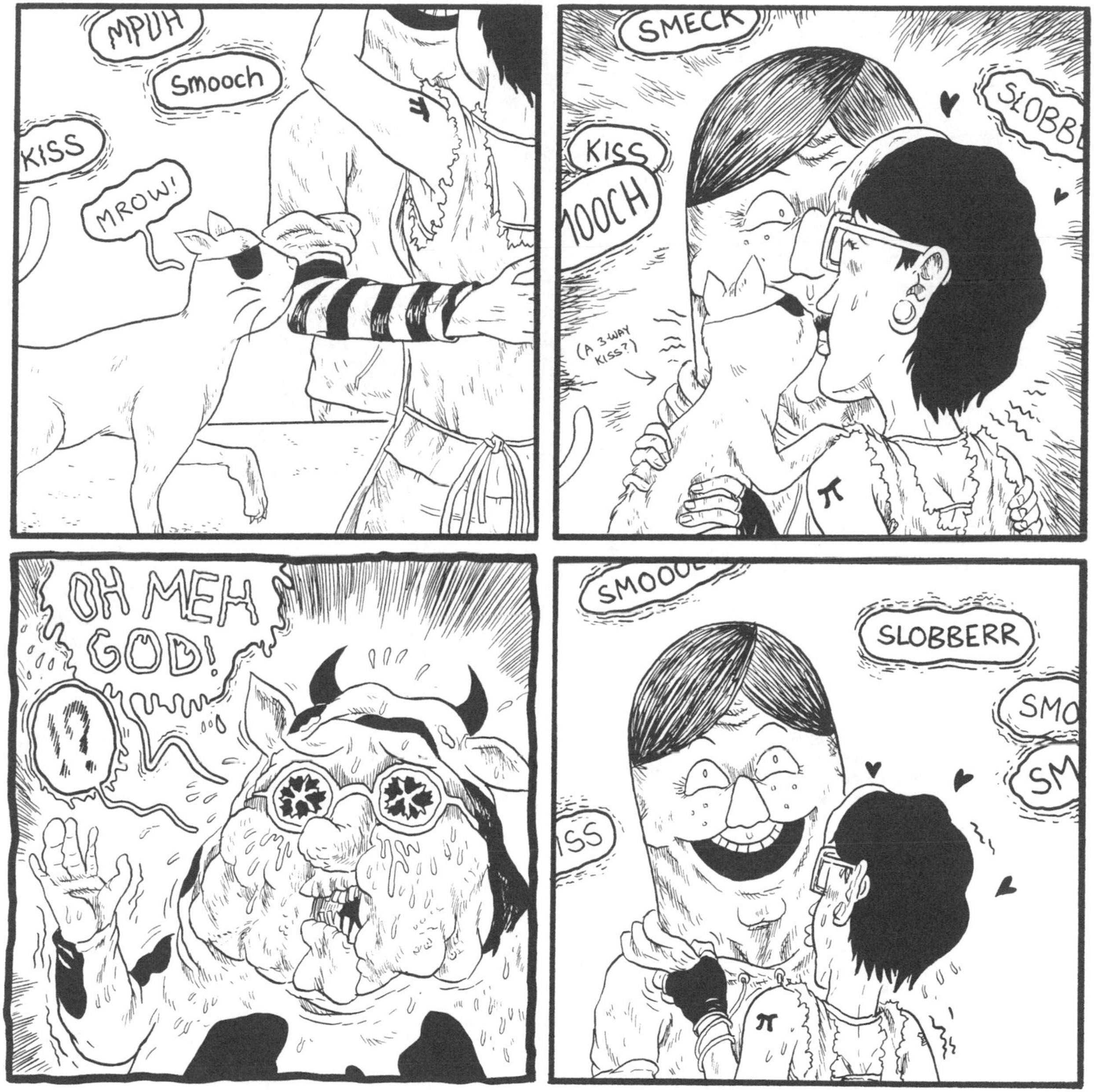
MPUH
Smooch
KISS
MROW!
SMECK
SLOBB
KISS
MOOCH
(A 3-WAY KISS?)
OH MEH GOD!
!?
SMOOO
SLOBBERR
SMO
SM
ISS

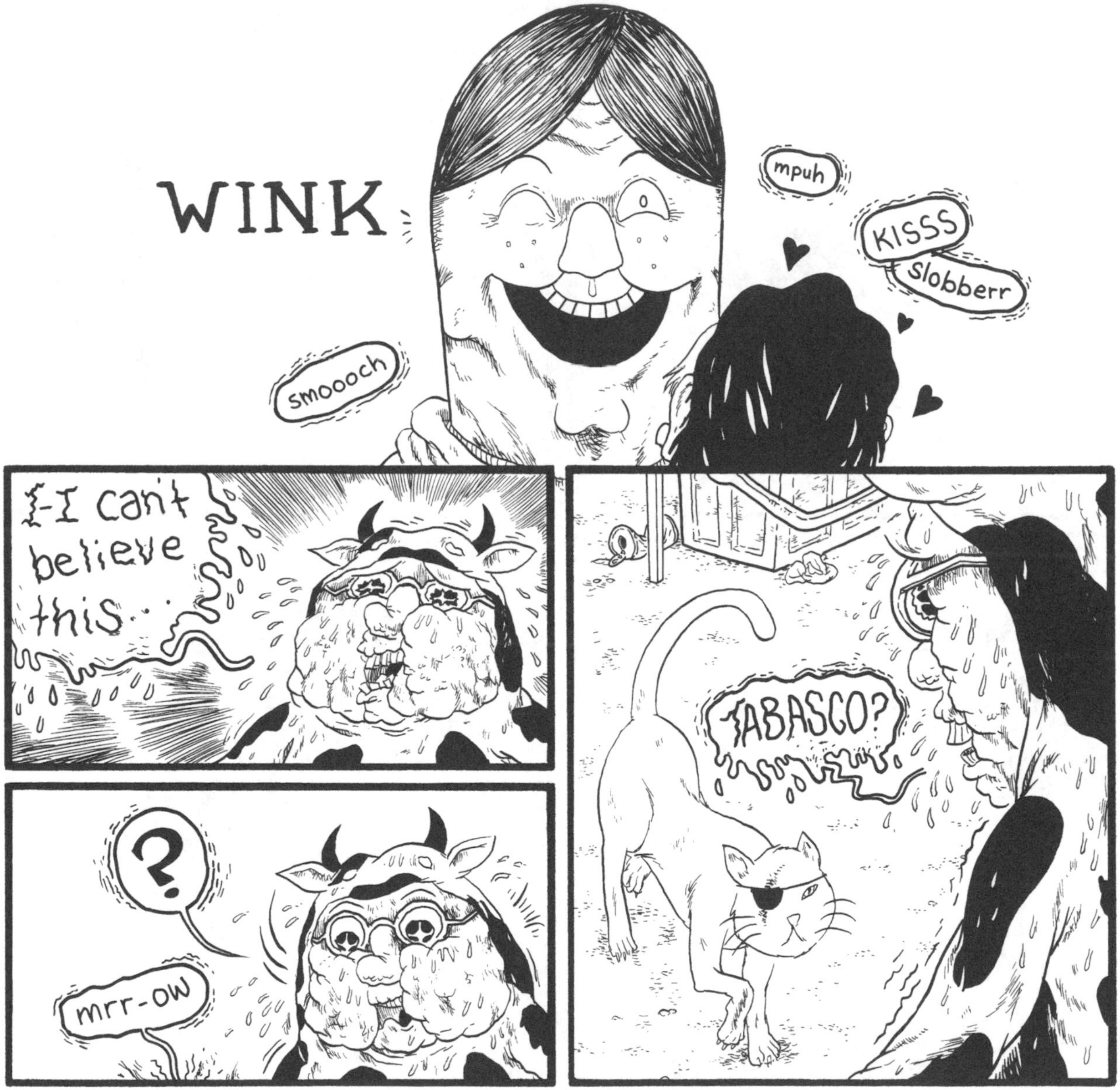
WINK
mpuh
KISSS
slobberr
smoooch
I-I can't believe this...
?
mrr-ow
TABASCO?

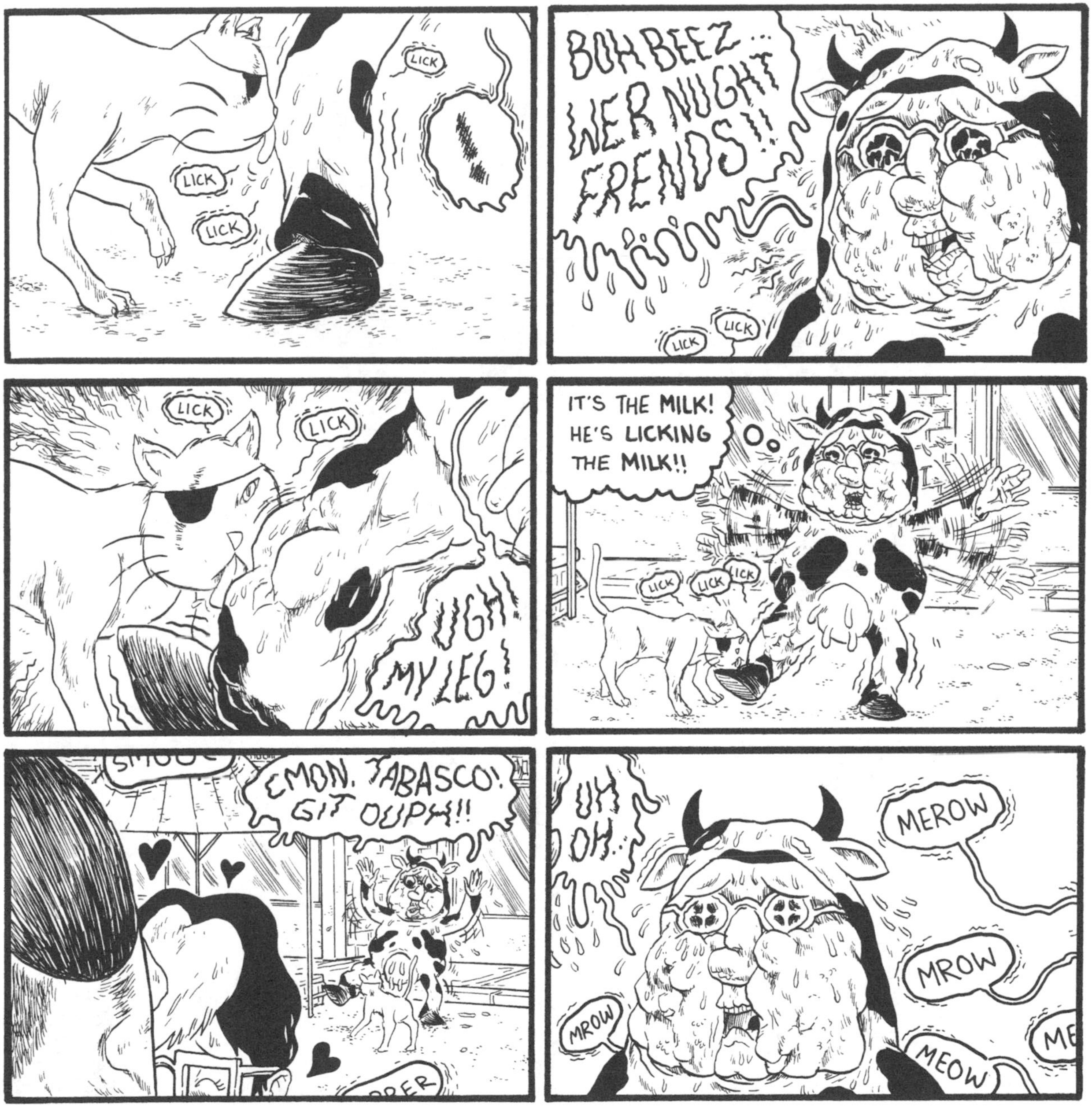
LICK
LICK
LICK
BOH BEEZ... WER NUGHT FRENDS!!
LICK
LICK
LICK
LICK
UGH! MY LEG!
IT'S THE MILK! HE'S LICKING THE MILK!!
LICK
LICK
LICK
CMON. TABASCO! GIT OUPH!!
UH OH...
MEROW
MROW
MROW
MEOW

AHHH!!
MROW
MROW
LICK
TU MENY CATS!!
LICK
MROW
LICK
LICK
MEOW
UGHHHH
LICK LICK
LICK
LICK
LICK
THIS CAN'T GET *ANY* WORSE!!
LICK
LICK LICK

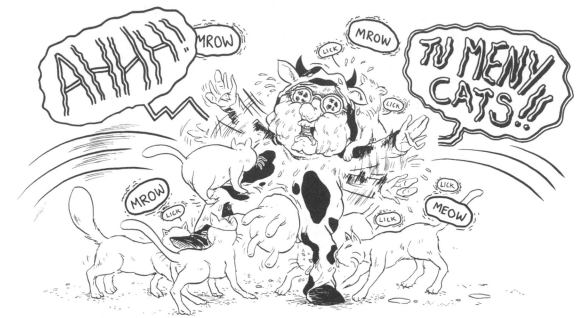

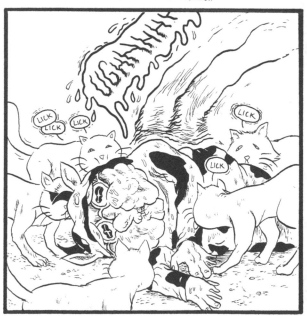

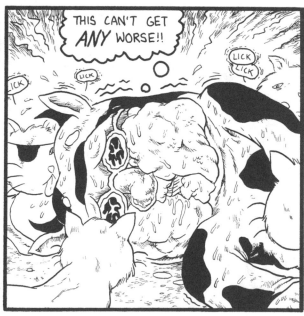

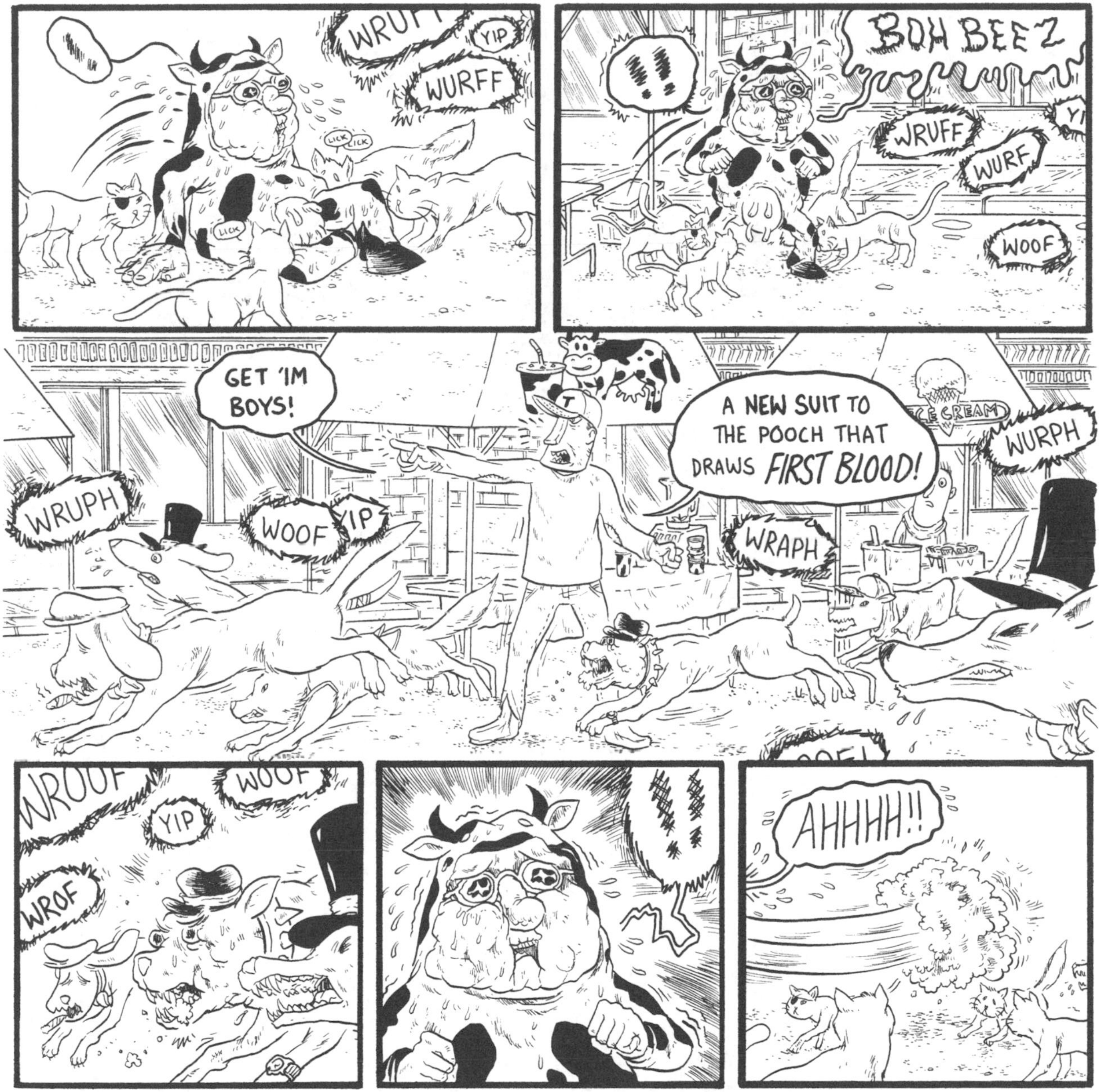

WRUFF
YIP
WURFF
LICK
LICK
LICK
BOH BEEZ
!!
WRUFF
WURF
WOOF
GET 'IM BOYS!
A NEW SUIT TO THE POOCH THAT DRAWS FIRST BLOOD!
ICE CREAM
WURPH
WRUPH
WOOF
YIP
WRAPH
WROOF
WOOF
YIP
WROF
AHHHH!!

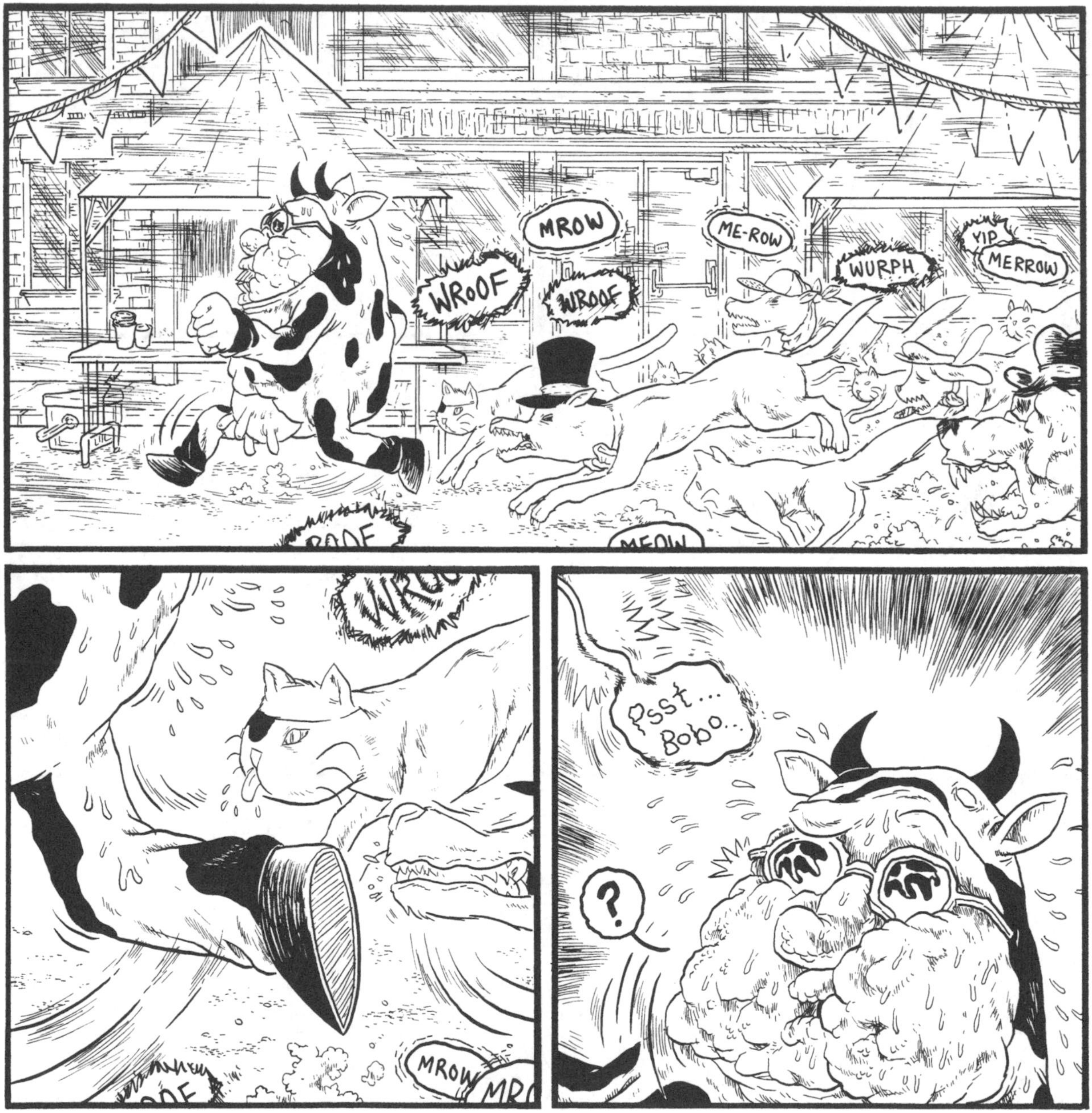
WROOF
MROW
WROOF
ME-ROW
WURPH
YIP
MERROW
MROW
Psst... Bobo...
?

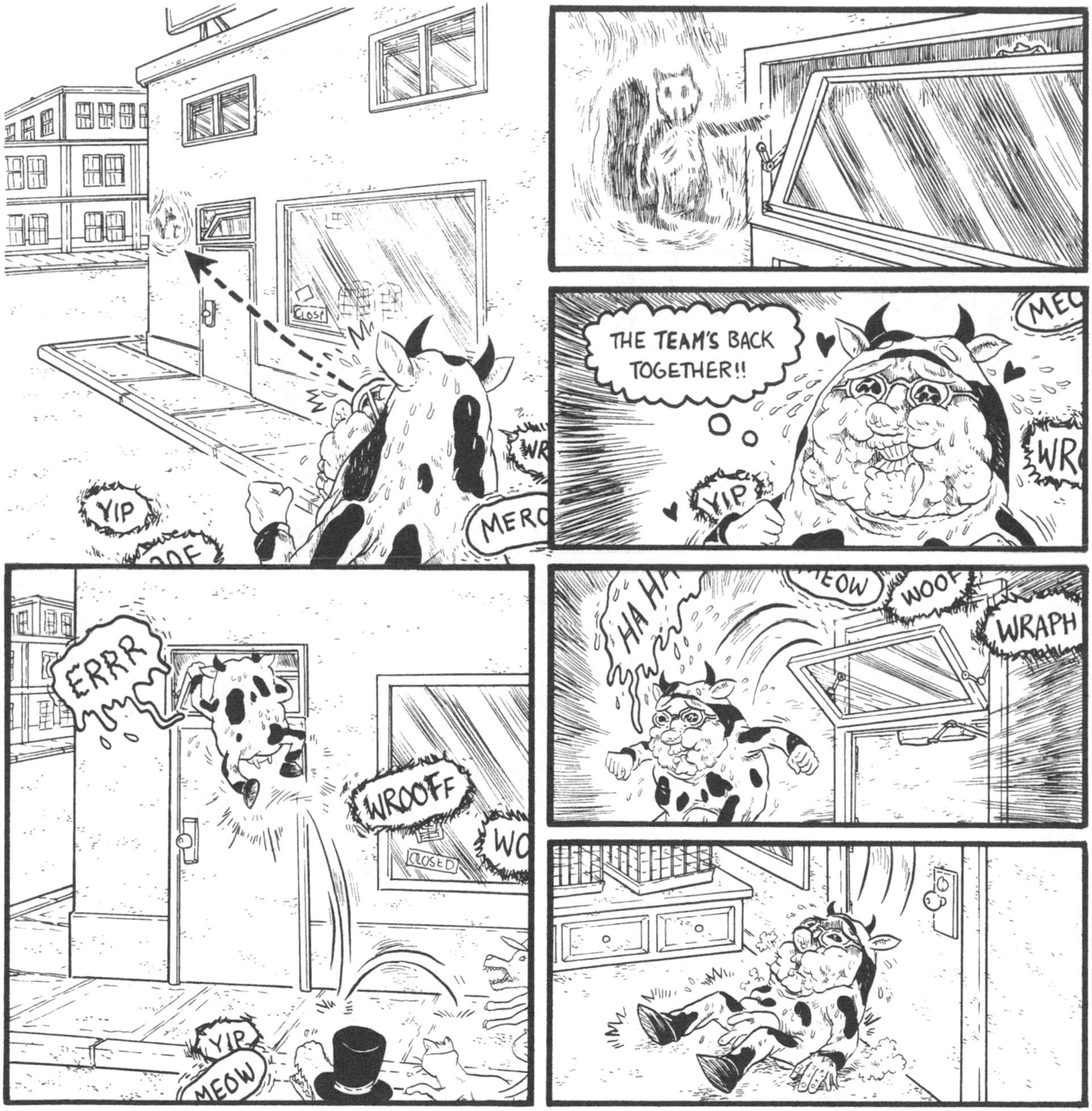
YIP
THE TEAM'S BACK TOGETHER!!
YIP
ERRR
WROOFF
YIP
MEOW
HA HA
WOOF
WRAPH

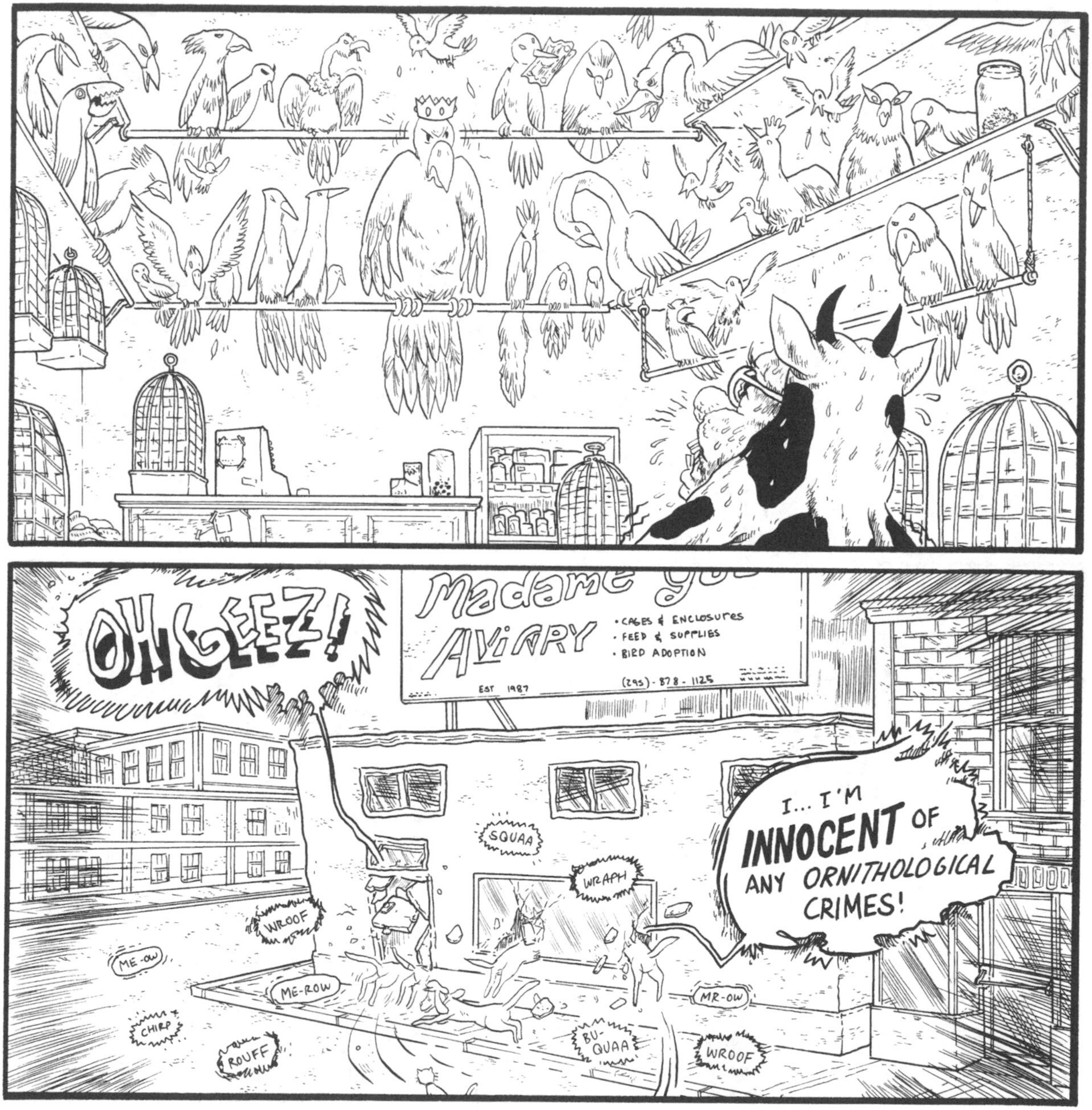
OH GEEZ!
Madame
AVIARY
• CAGES & ENCLOSURES
• FEED & SUPPLIES
• BIRD ADOPTION
EST 1987
(295)-878-1125
I... I'M INNOCENT OF ANY ORNITHOLOGICAL CRIMES!
SQUAA
WRAPH
WROOF
ME-OW
ME-ROW
MR-OW
CHIRP
ROUFF
BU-QUAA
WROOF

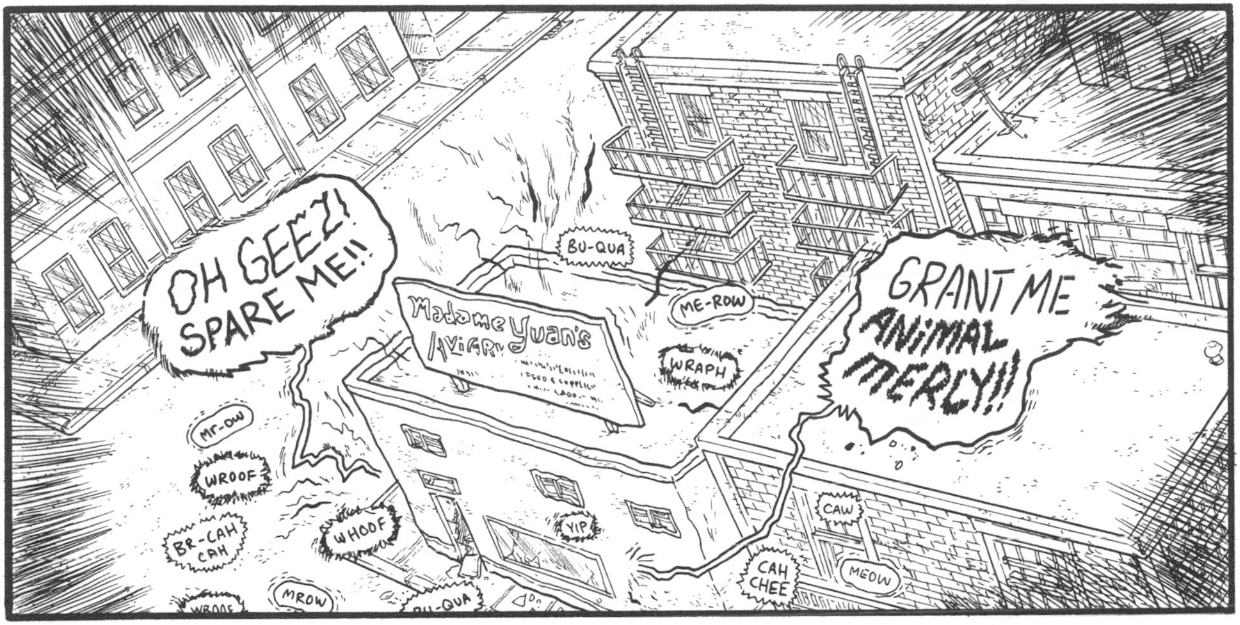
OH GEEZ! SPARE ME!!
BU-QUA
Madame Yuan's Aviary
ME-ROW
WRAPH
GRANT ME ANIMAL MERCY!!
Mr-OW
WROOF
BR-CAH CAH
WHOOF
YIP
CAW
CAH CHEE
MEOW
MROW
BU-QUA

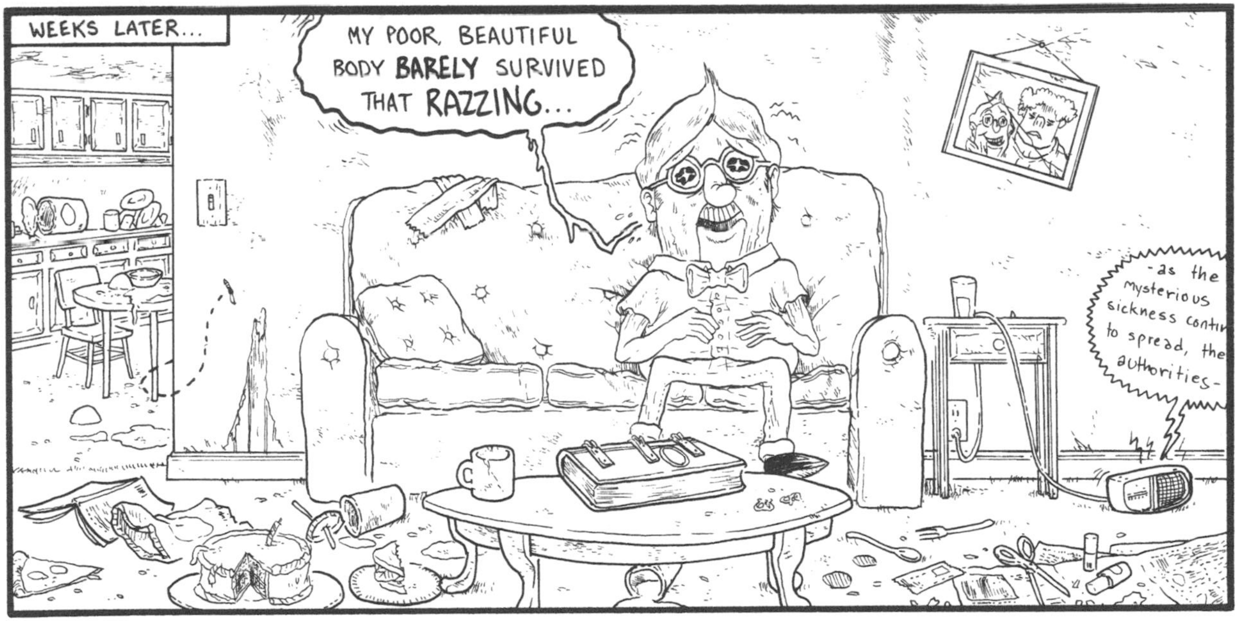
WEEKS LATER...
MY POOR, BEAUTIFUL BODY BARELY SURVIVED THAT RAZZING...
-as the mysterious sickness conti to spread, the authorities-

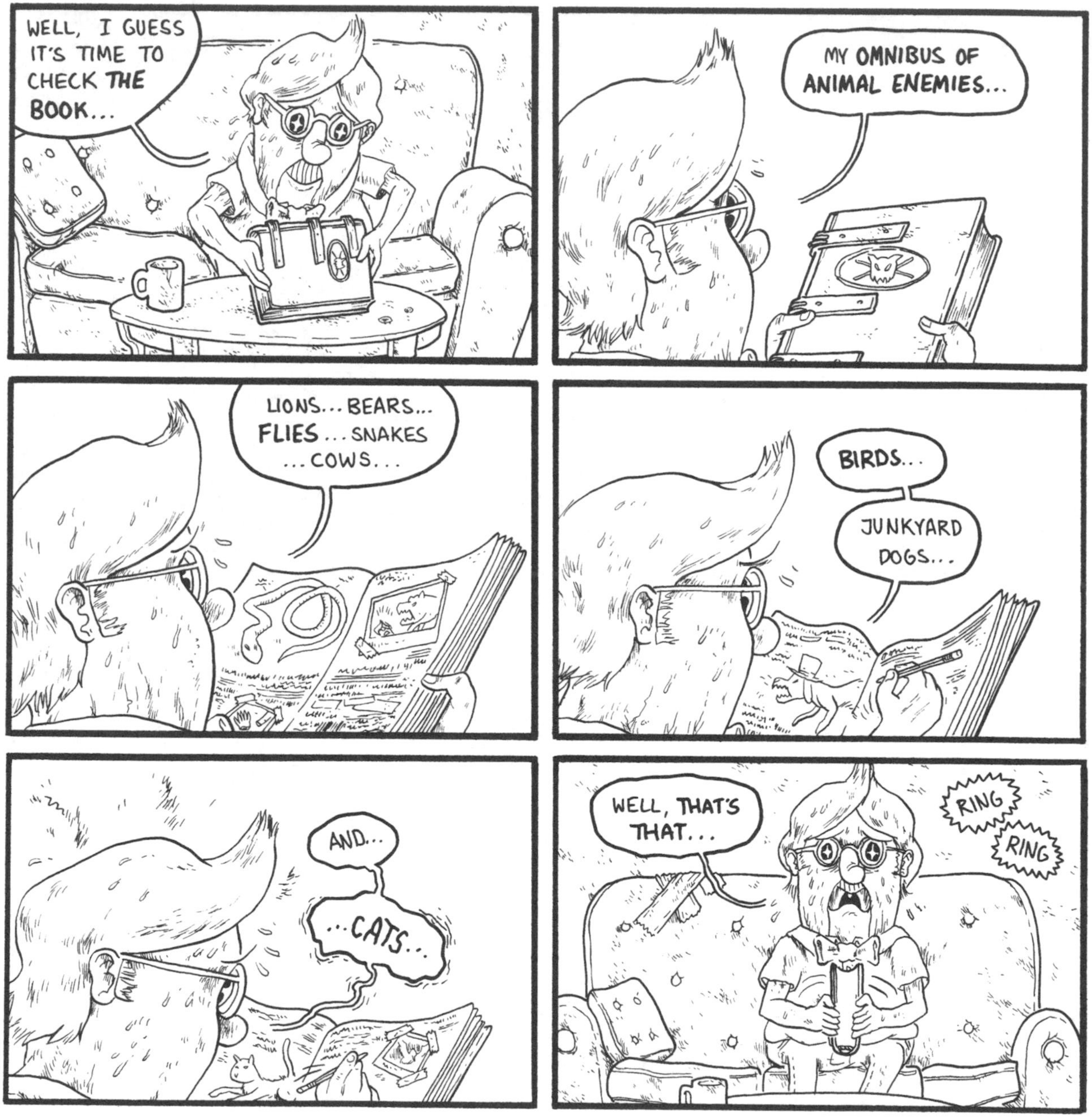
WELL, I GUESS IT'S TIME TO CHECK THE BOOK...
MY OMNIBUS OF ANIMAL ENEMIES...
LIONS... BEARS... FLIES... SNAKES ... COWS...
BIRDS...
JUNKYARD DOGS...
AND...
...CATS...
WELL, THAT'S THAT...
RING
RING

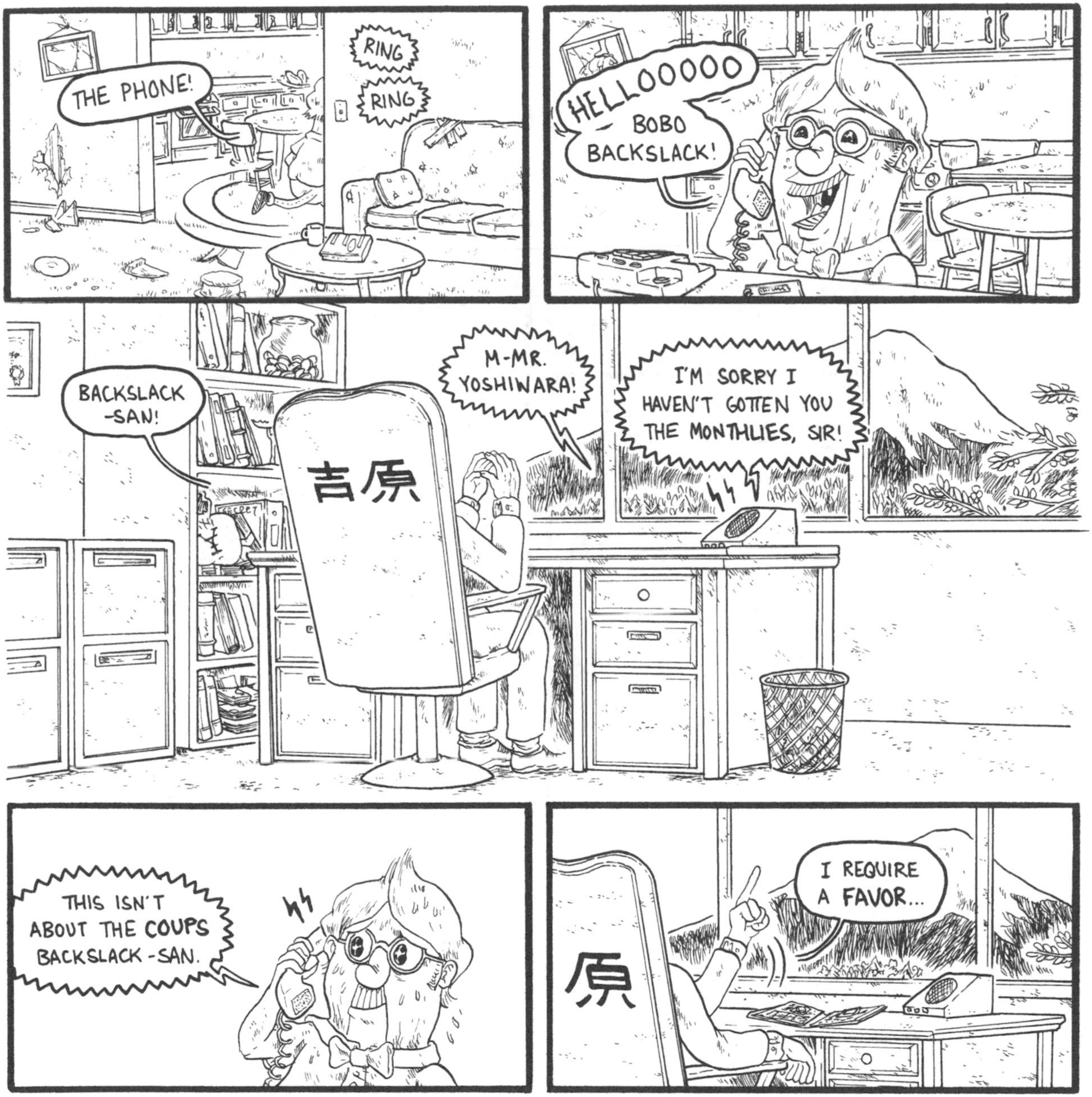
THE PHONE!
RING
RING
HELLOOOOO BOBO BACKSLACK!
BACKSLACK -SAN!
M-MR. YOSHIWARA!
I'M SORRY I HAVEN'T GOTTEN YOU THE MONTHLIES, SIR!
吉原
THIS ISN'T ABOUT THE COUPS BACKSLACK-SAN.
原
I REQUIRE A FAVOR...

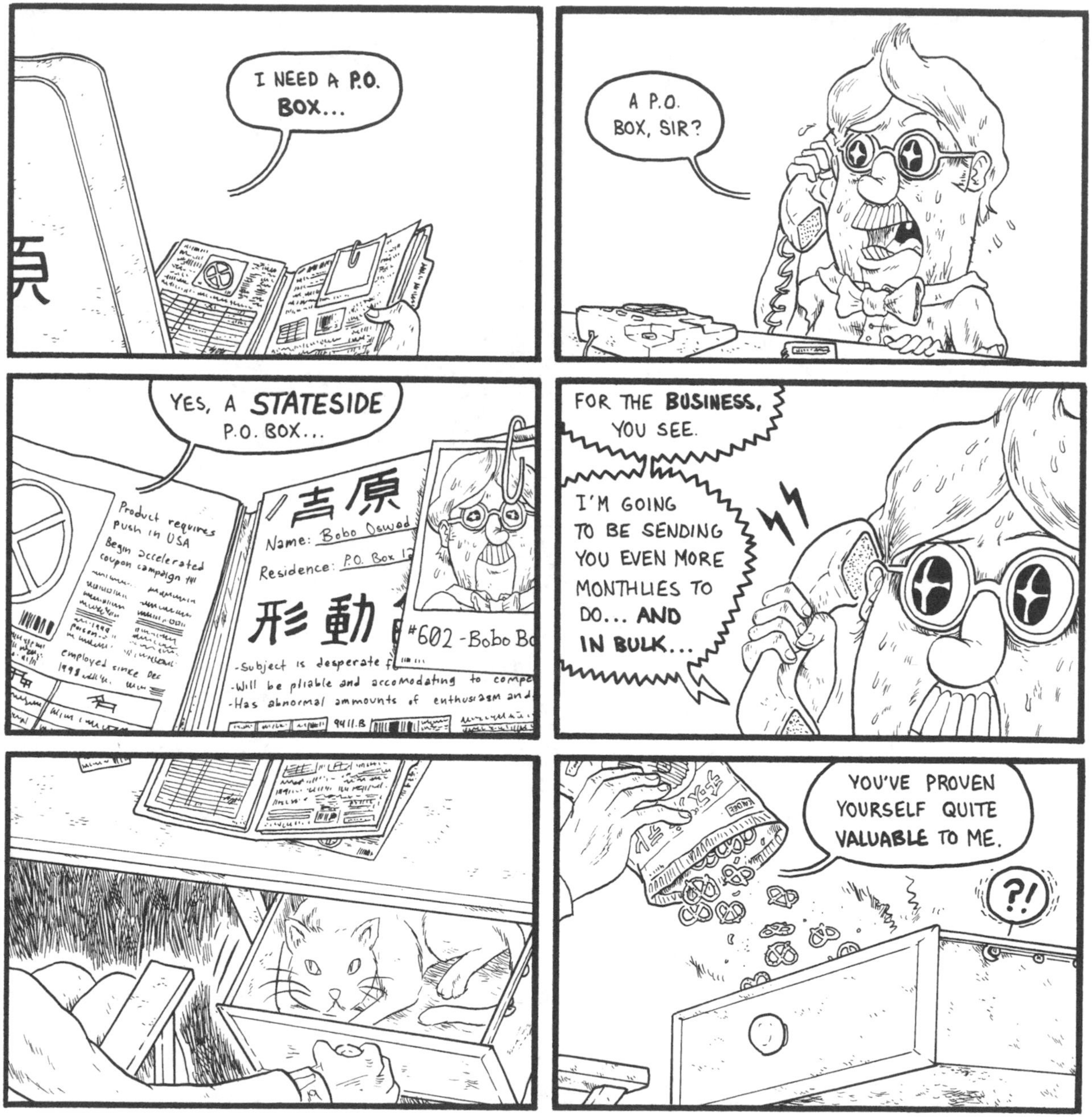

I NEED A P.O. BOX...
A P.O. BOX, SIR?
YES, A STATESIDE P.O. BOX...
FOR THE BUSINESS, YOU SEE.
I'M GOING TO BE SENDING YOU EVEN MORE MONTHLIES TO DO... AND IN BULK...
YOU'VE PROVEN YOURSELF QUITE VALUABLE TO ME.
?!

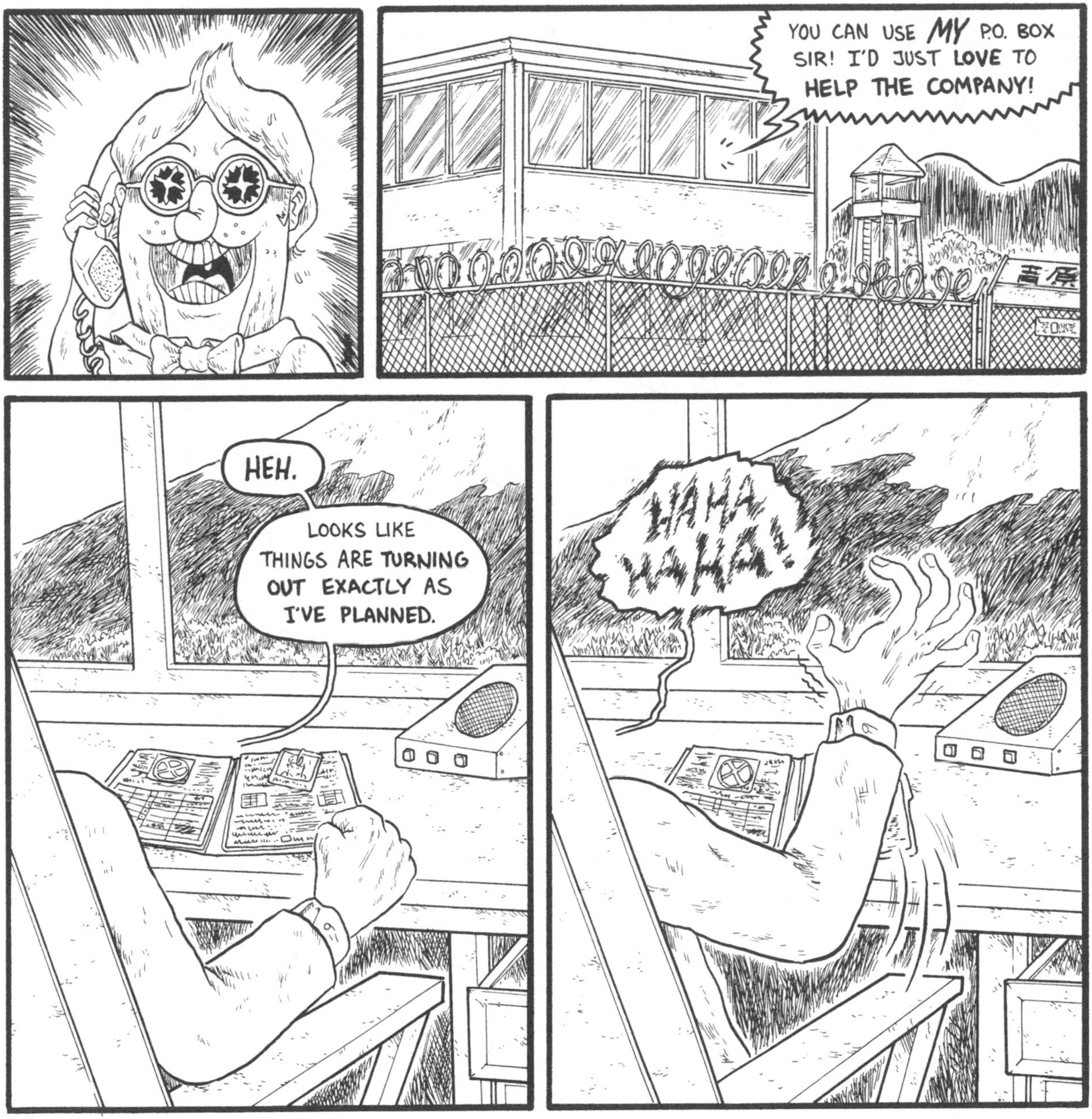
YOU CAN USE MY P.O. BOX SIR! I'D JUST LOVE TO HELP THE COMPANY!
HEH.
LOOKS LIKE THINGS ARE TURNING OUT EXACTLY AS I'VE PLANNED.
HAHA HAHA!

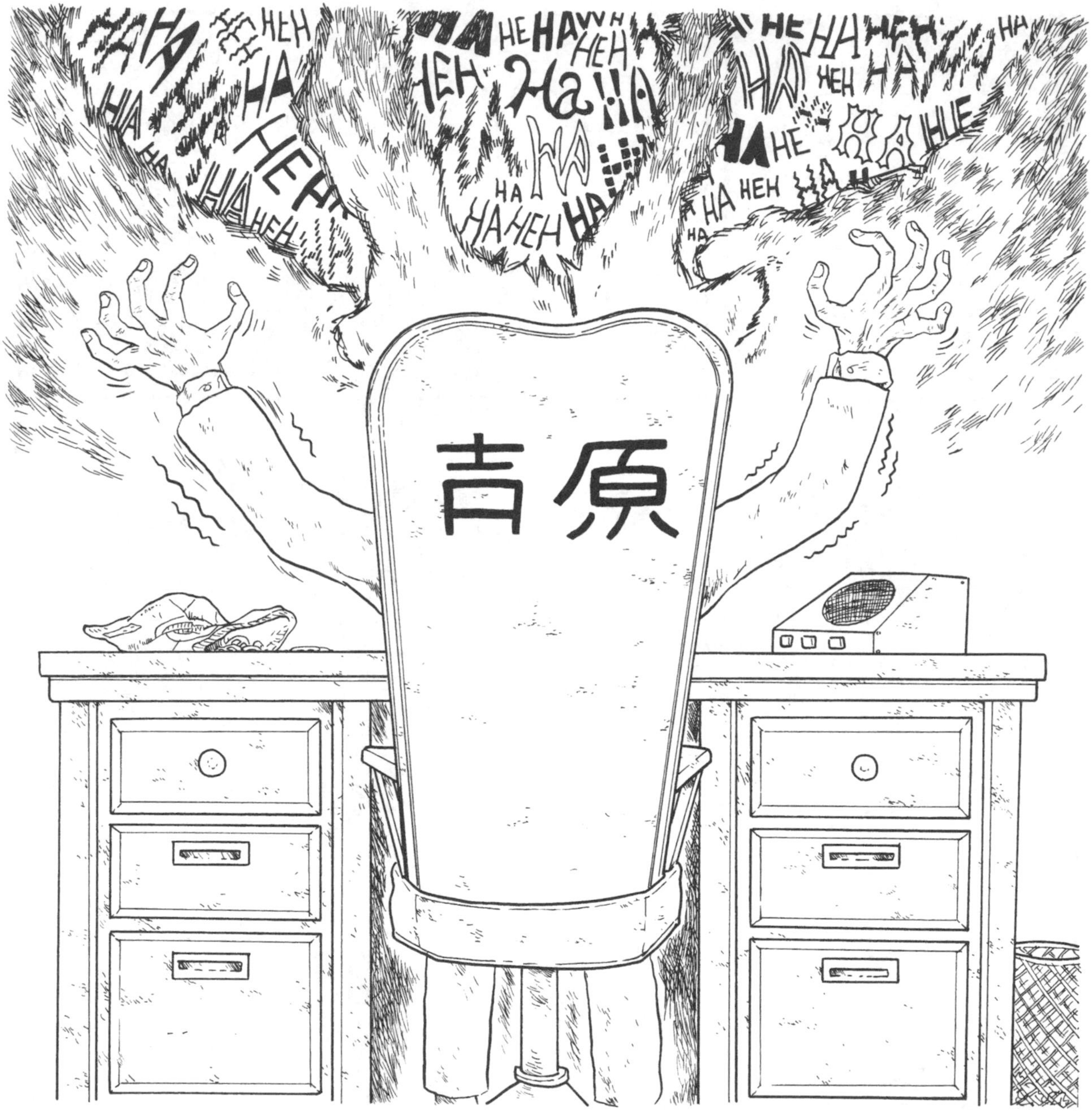
HA HEH
HE HA HEH
HA HEH
HA HE
HA HEH
吉原

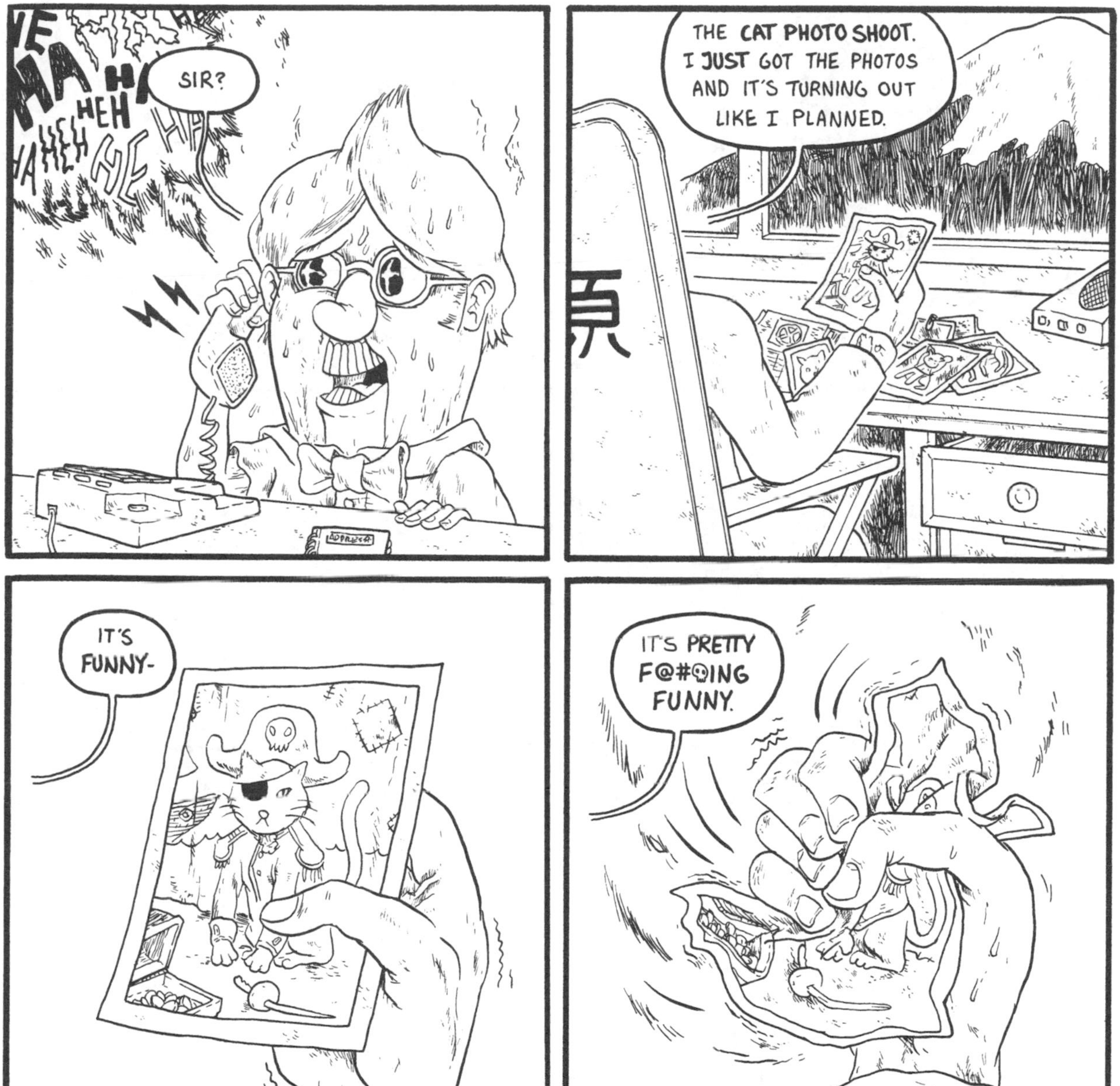
HA HA HEH HEH HE HA
SIR?
THE CAT PHOTO SHOOT. I JUST GOT THE PHOTOS AND IT'S TURNING OUT LIKE I PLANNED.
IT'S FUNNY-
IT'S PRETTY F@#☠ING FUNNY.

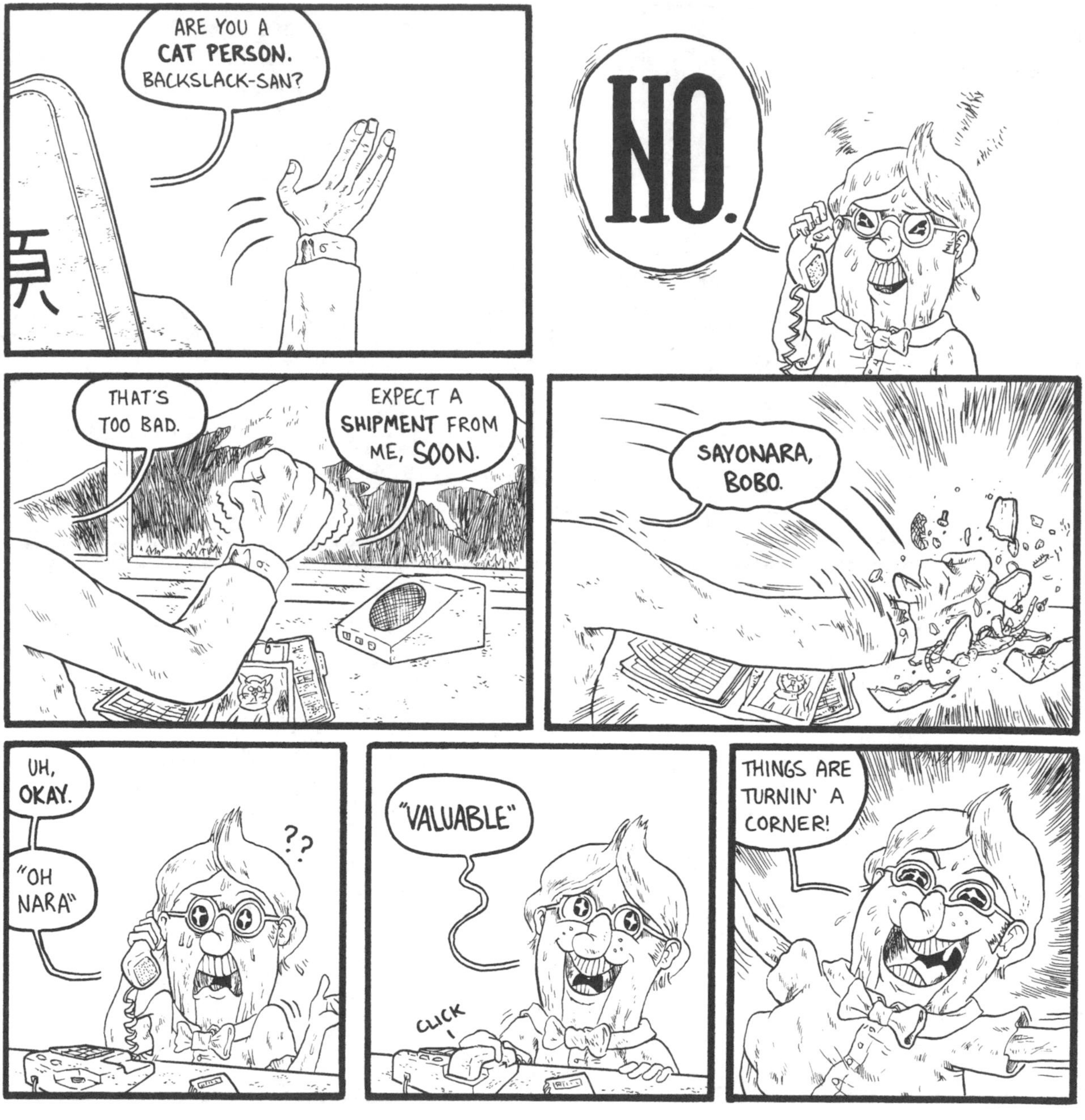
ARE YOU A CAT PERSON. BACKSLACK-SAN?
NO.
THAT'S TOO BAD.
EXPECT A SHIPMENT FROM ME, SOON.
SAYONARA, BOBO.
UH, OKAY.
"OH NARA"
??
"VALUABLE"
CLICK
THINGS ARE TURNIN' A CORNER!

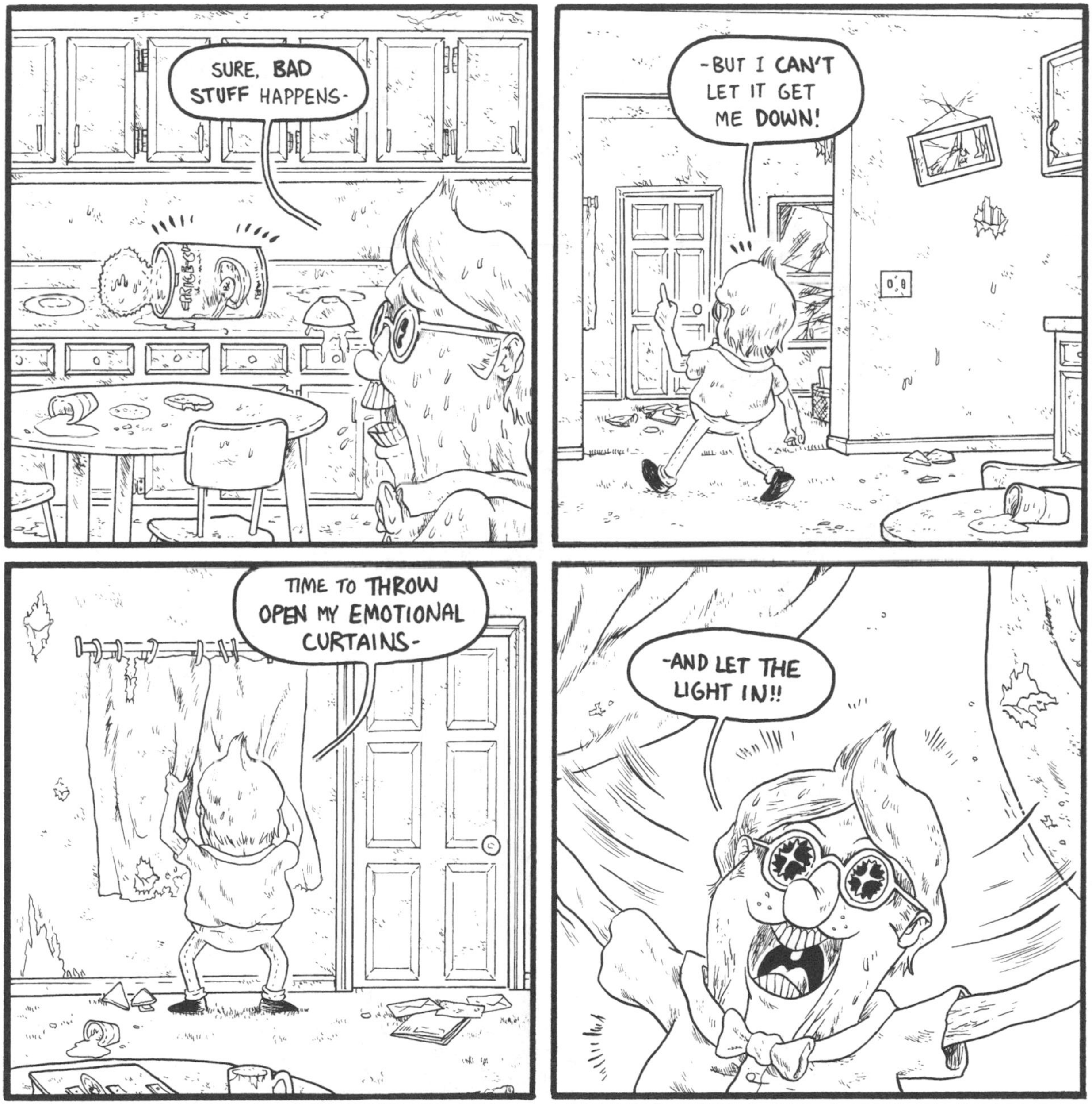
SURE, BAD STUFF HAPPENS-
-BUT I CAN'T LET IT GET ME DOWN!
TIME TO THROW OPEN MY EMOTIONAL CURTAINS-
-AND LET THE LIGHT IN!!

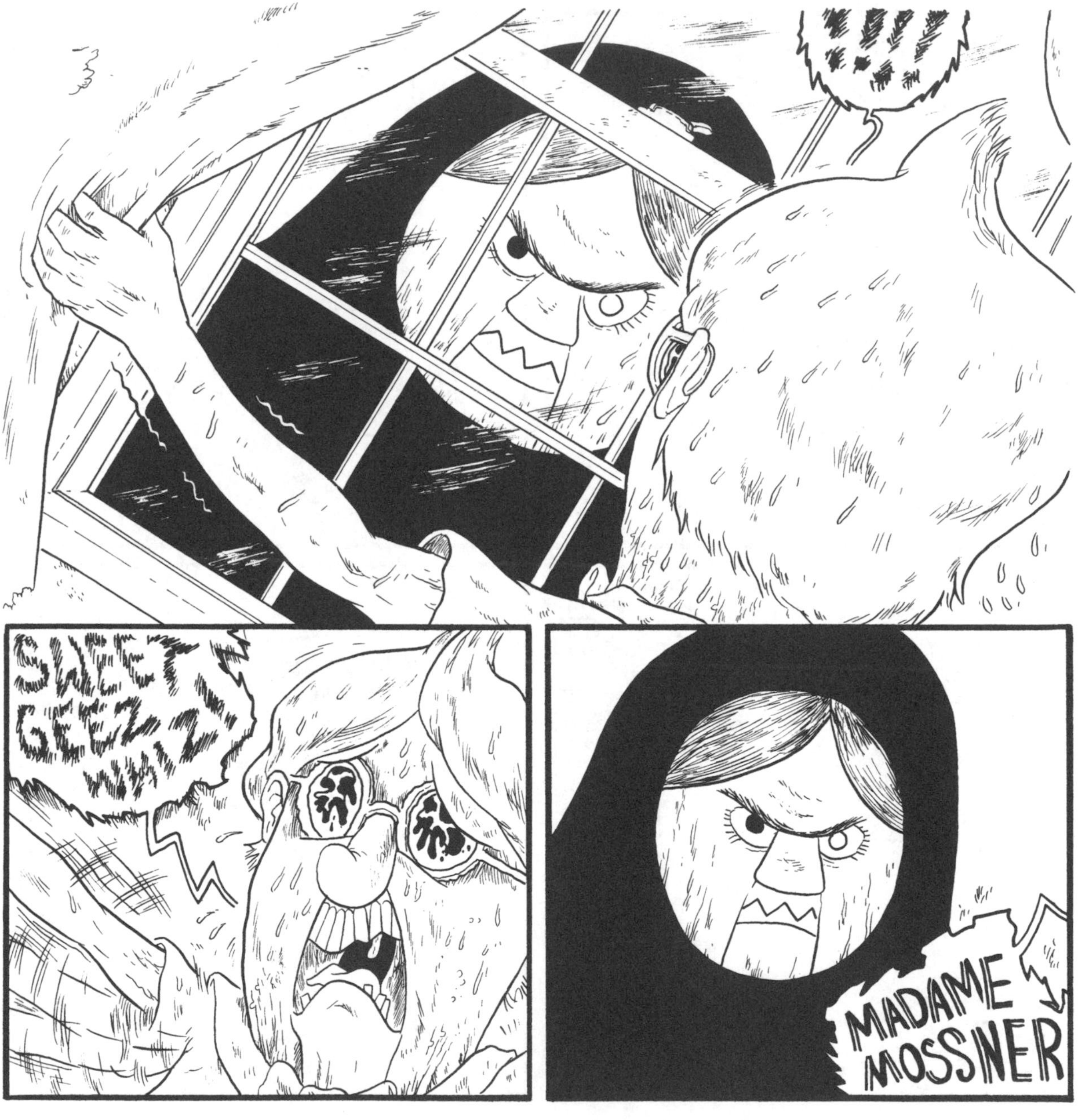
SWEET GEEZ WHIZ!
MADAME MOSSNER

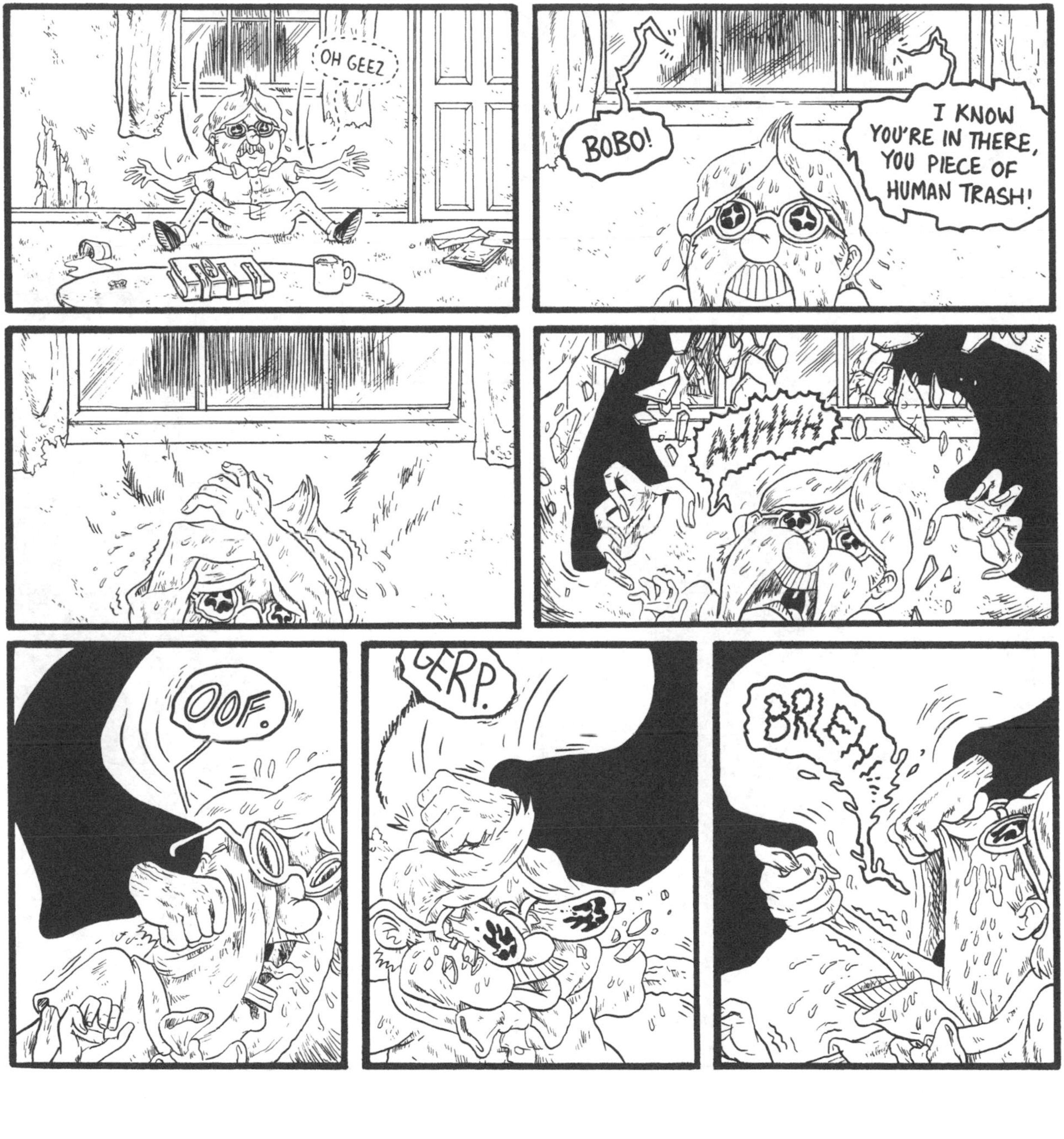
OH GEEZ
BOBO!
I KNOW YOU'RE IN THERE, YOU PIECE OF HUMAN TRASH!
AHHHH
OOF.
GERP.
BRLEH!

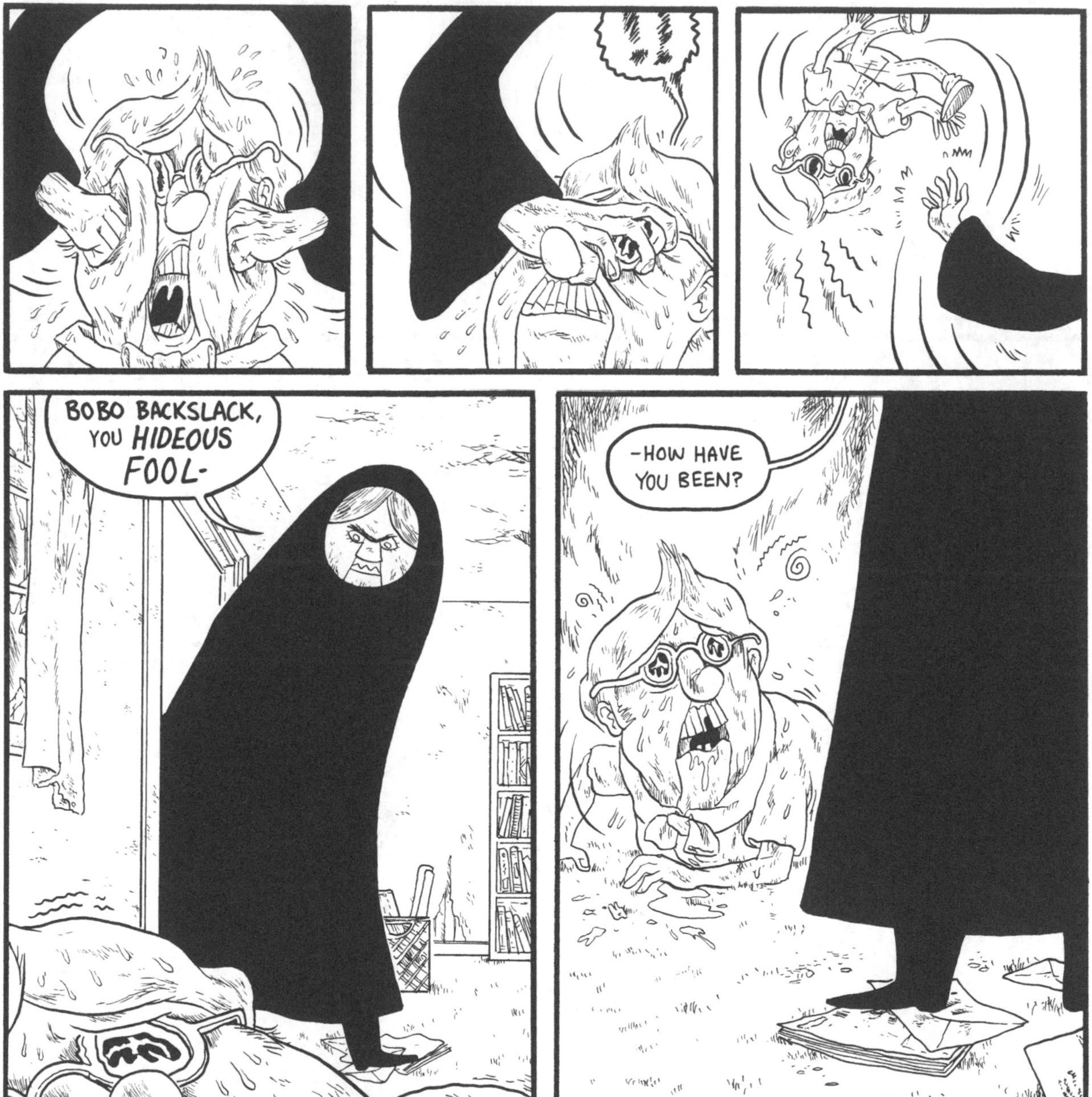
BOBO BACKSLACK, YOU HIDEOUS FOOL-
-HOW HAVE YOU BEEN?

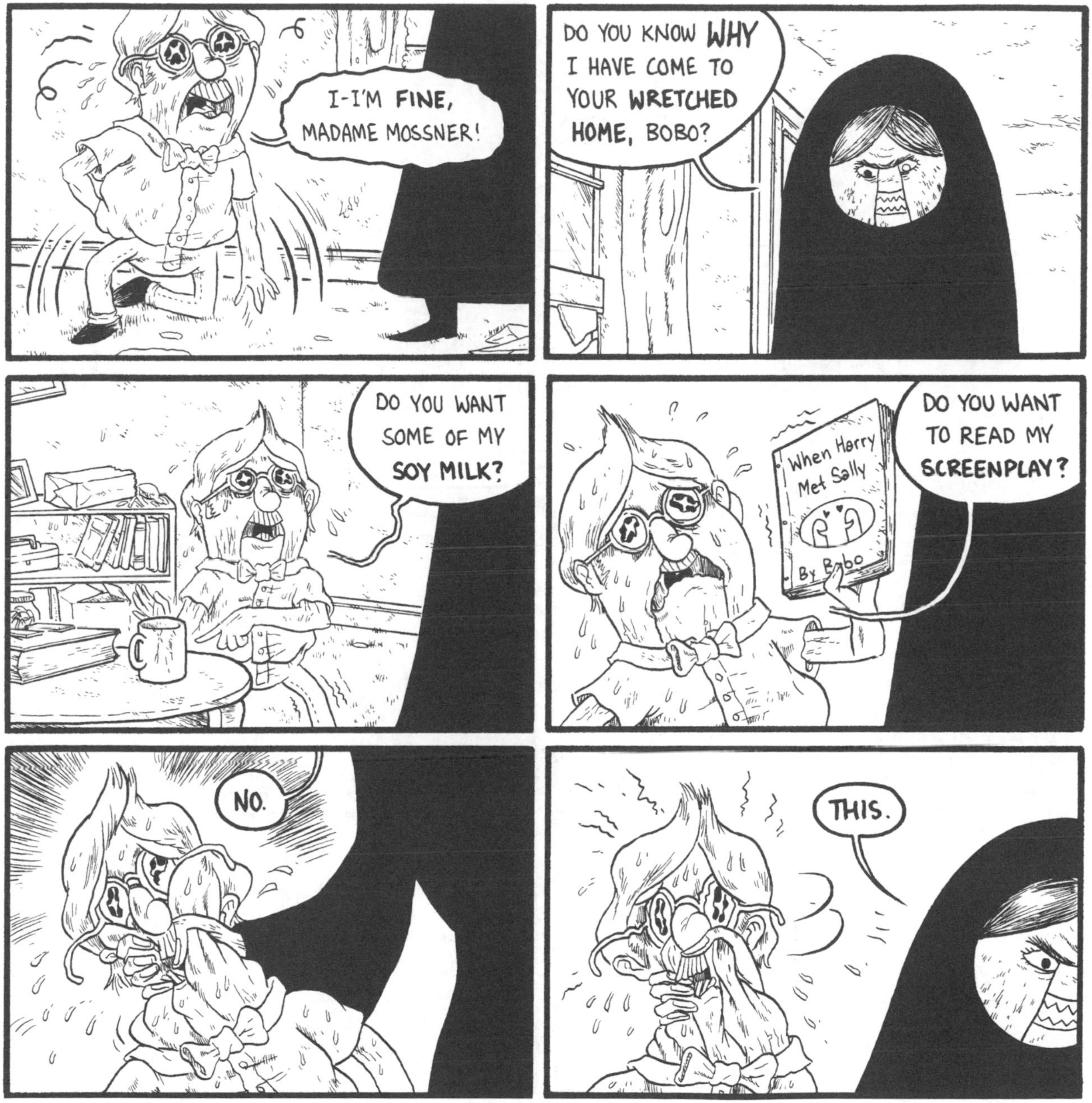
I-I'M FINE, MADAME MOSSNER!
DO YOU KNOW WHY I HAVE COME TO YOUR WRETCHED HOME, BOBO?
DO YOU WANT SOME OF MY SOY MILK?
When Harry Met Sally
By Bobo
DO YOU WANT TO READ MY SCREENPLAY?
NO.
THIS.

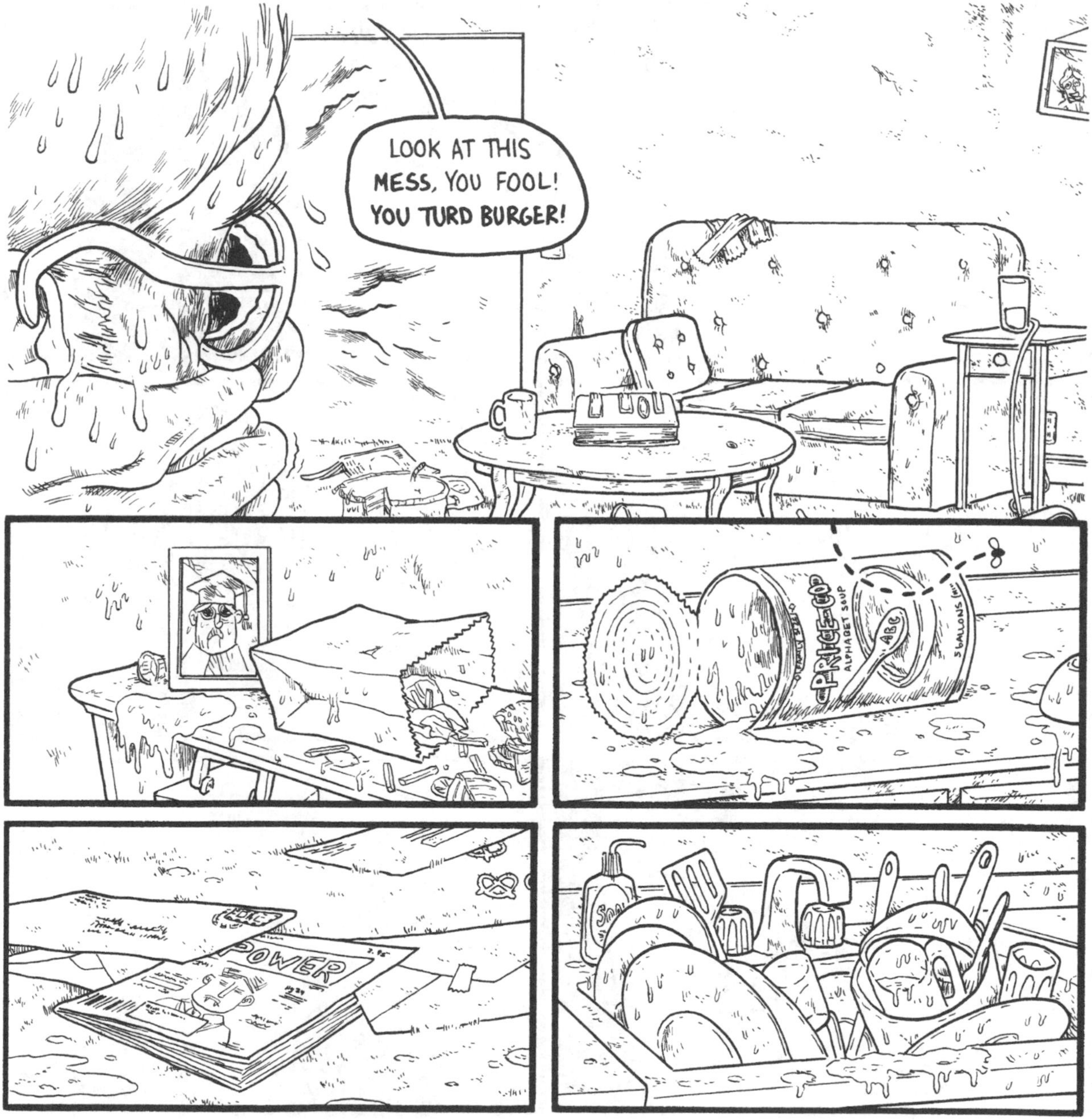
LOOK AT THIS MESS, YOU FOOL! YOU TURD BURGER!
ALPHABET SOUP
POWER

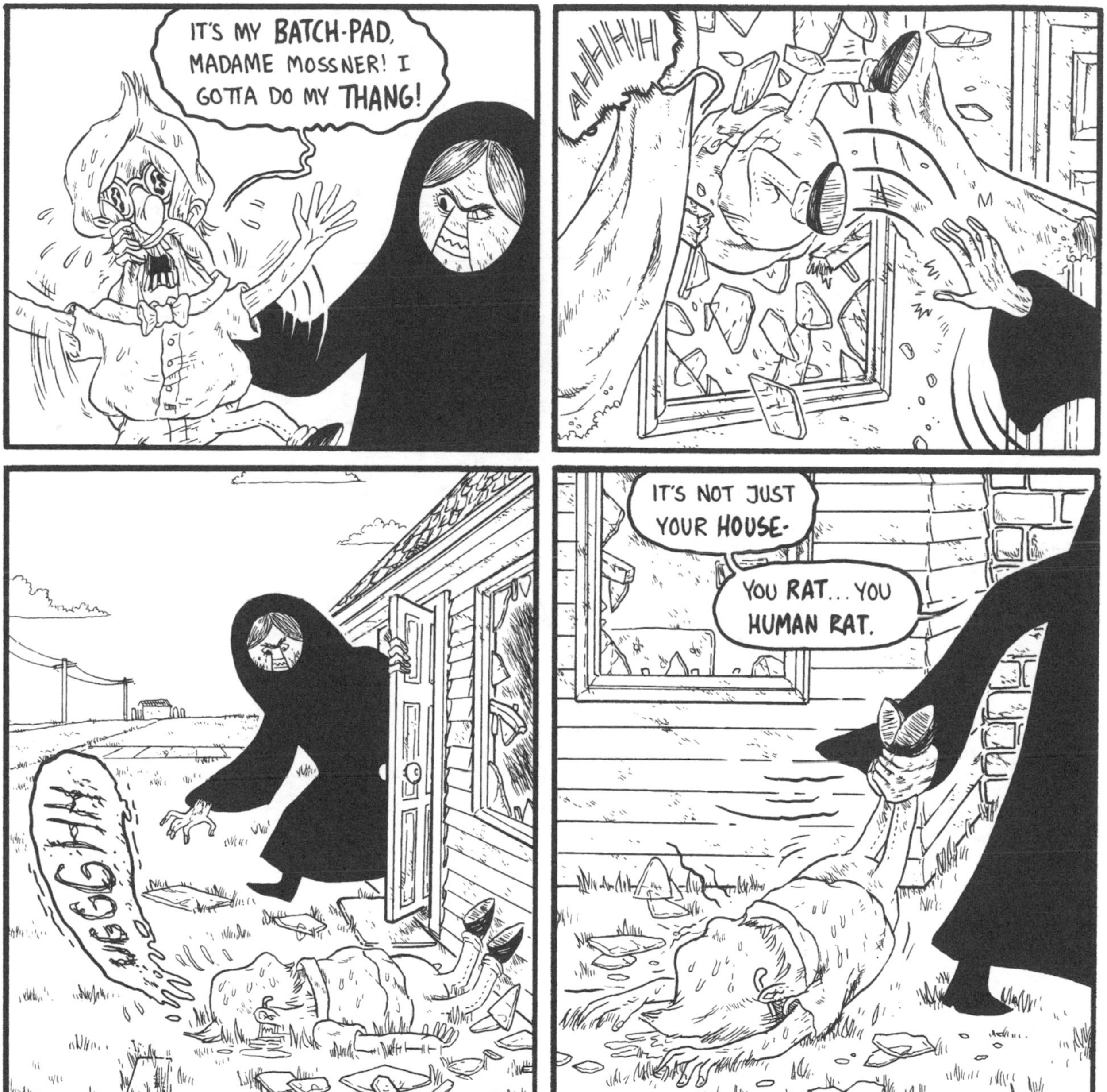
IT'S MY BATCH-PAD, MADAME MOSSNER! I GOTTA DO MY THANG!
AHHHHH
UGGGHHH
IT'S NOT JUST YOUR HOUSE-
YOU RAT... YOU HUMAN RAT.

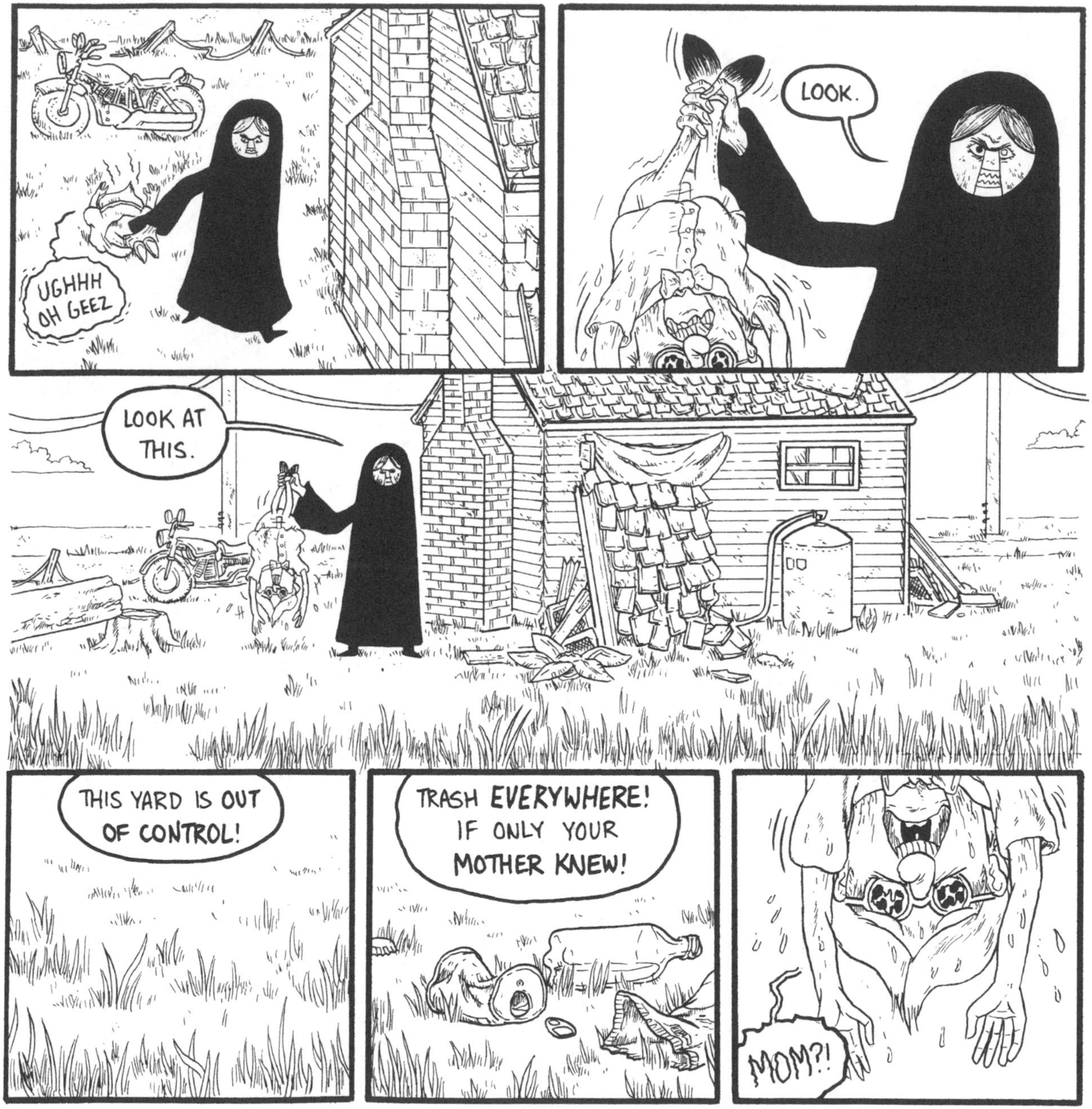
UGHHH OH GEEZ
LOOK.
LOOK AT THIS.
THIS YARD IS OUT OF CONTROL!
TRASH EVERYWHERE! IF ONLY YOUR MOTHER KNEW!
MOM?!

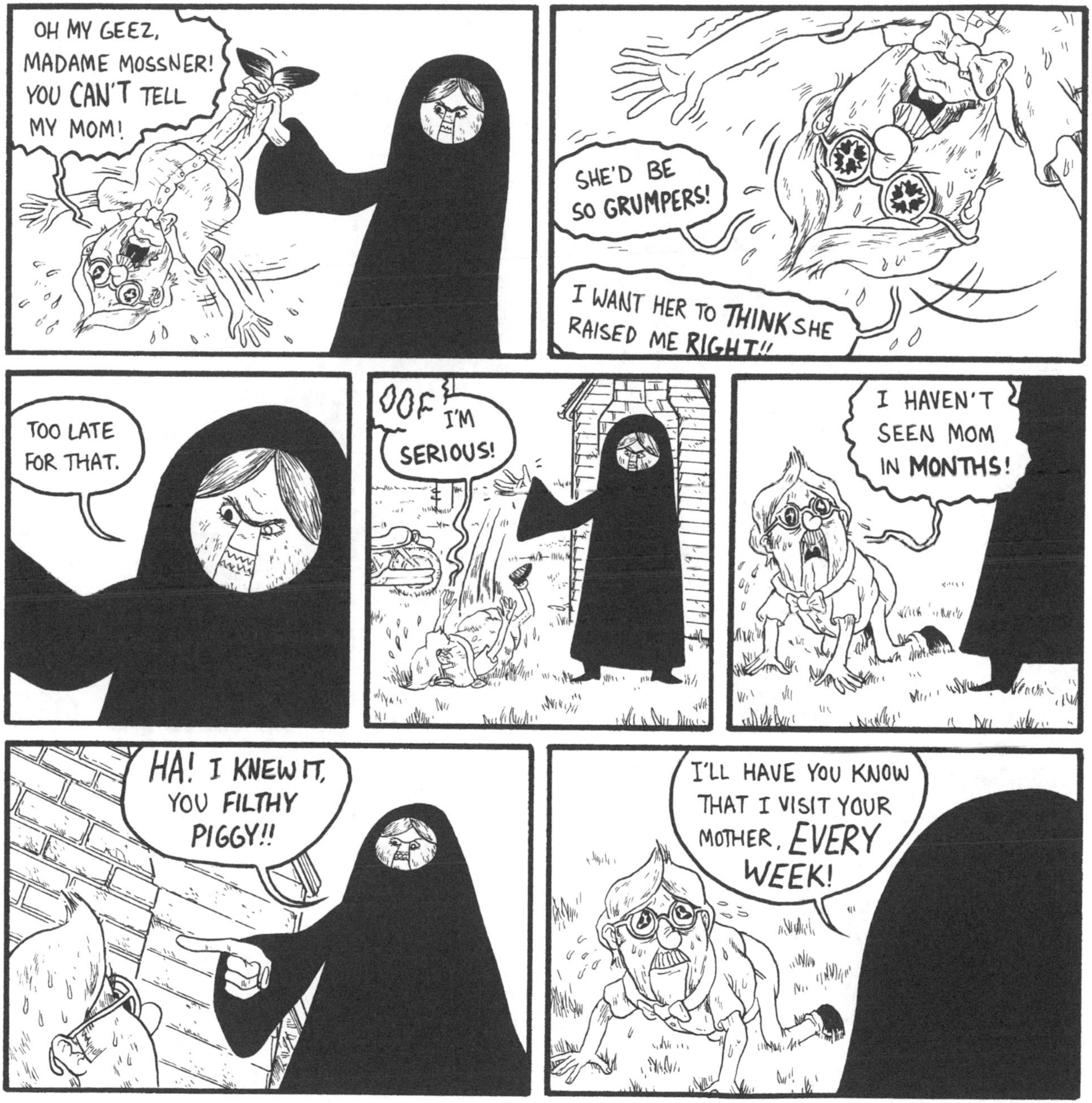
OH MY GEEZ, MADAME MOSSNER! YOU CAN'T TELL MY MOM!
SHE'D BE SO GRUMPERS!
I WANT HER TO THINK SHE RAISED ME RIGHT!!
TOO LATE FOR THAT.
OOF
I'M SERIOUS!
I HAVEN'T SEEN MOM IN MONTHS!
HA! I KNEW IT, YOU FILTHY PIGGY!!
I'LL HAVE YOU KNOW THAT I VISIT YOUR MOTHER, EVERY WEEK!

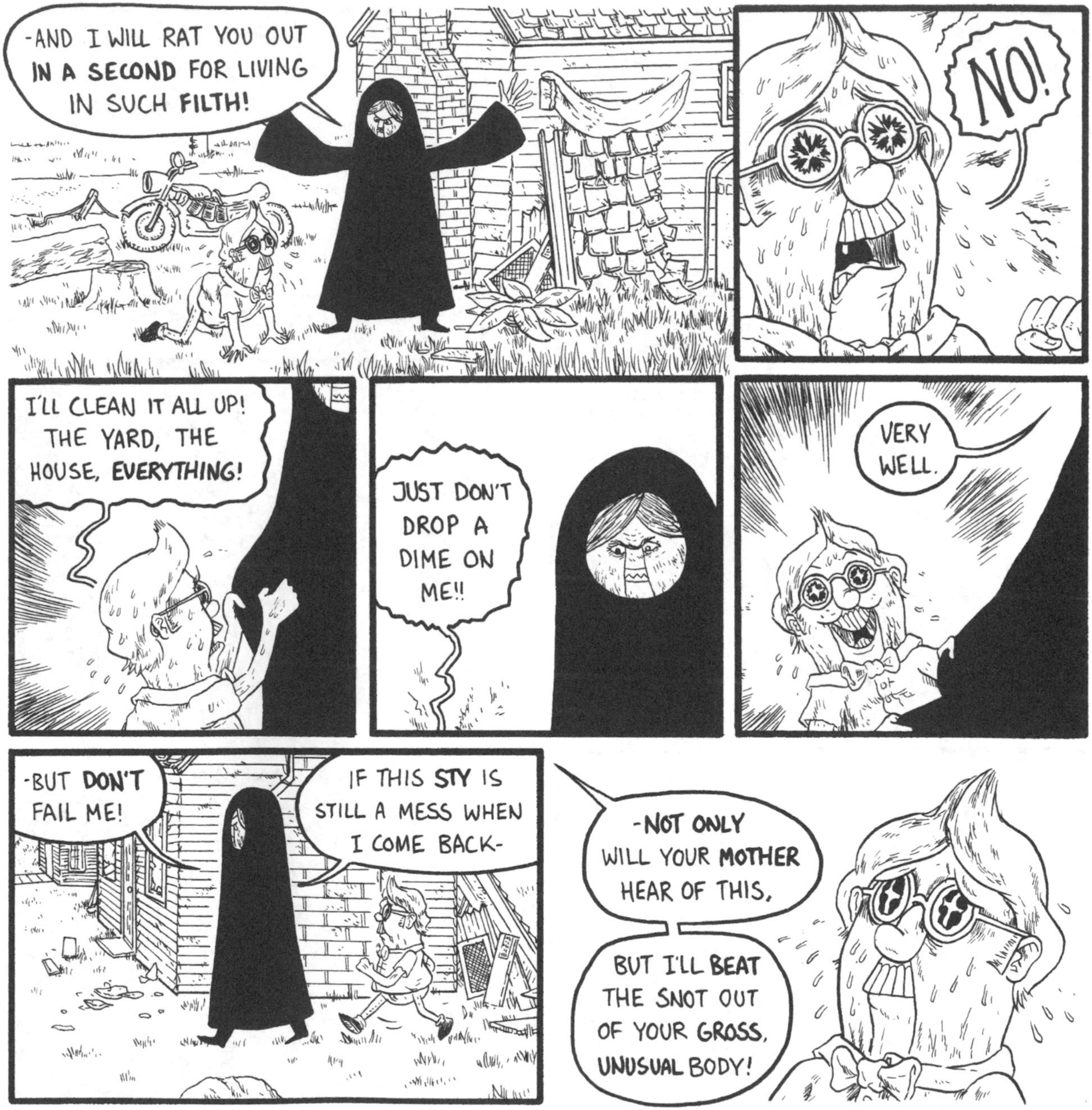
-AND I WILL RAT YOU OUT IN A SECOND FOR LIVING IN SUCH FILTH!
NO!
I'LL CLEAN IT ALL UP! THE YARD, THE HOUSE, EVERYTHING!
JUST DON'T DROP A DIME ON ME!!
VERY WELL.
-BUT DON'T FAIL ME!
IF THIS STY IS STILL A MESS WHEN I COME BACK-
-NOT ONLY WILL YOUR MOTHER HEAR OF THIS,
BUT I'LL BEAT THE SNOT OUT OF YOUR GROSS, UNUSUAL BODY!

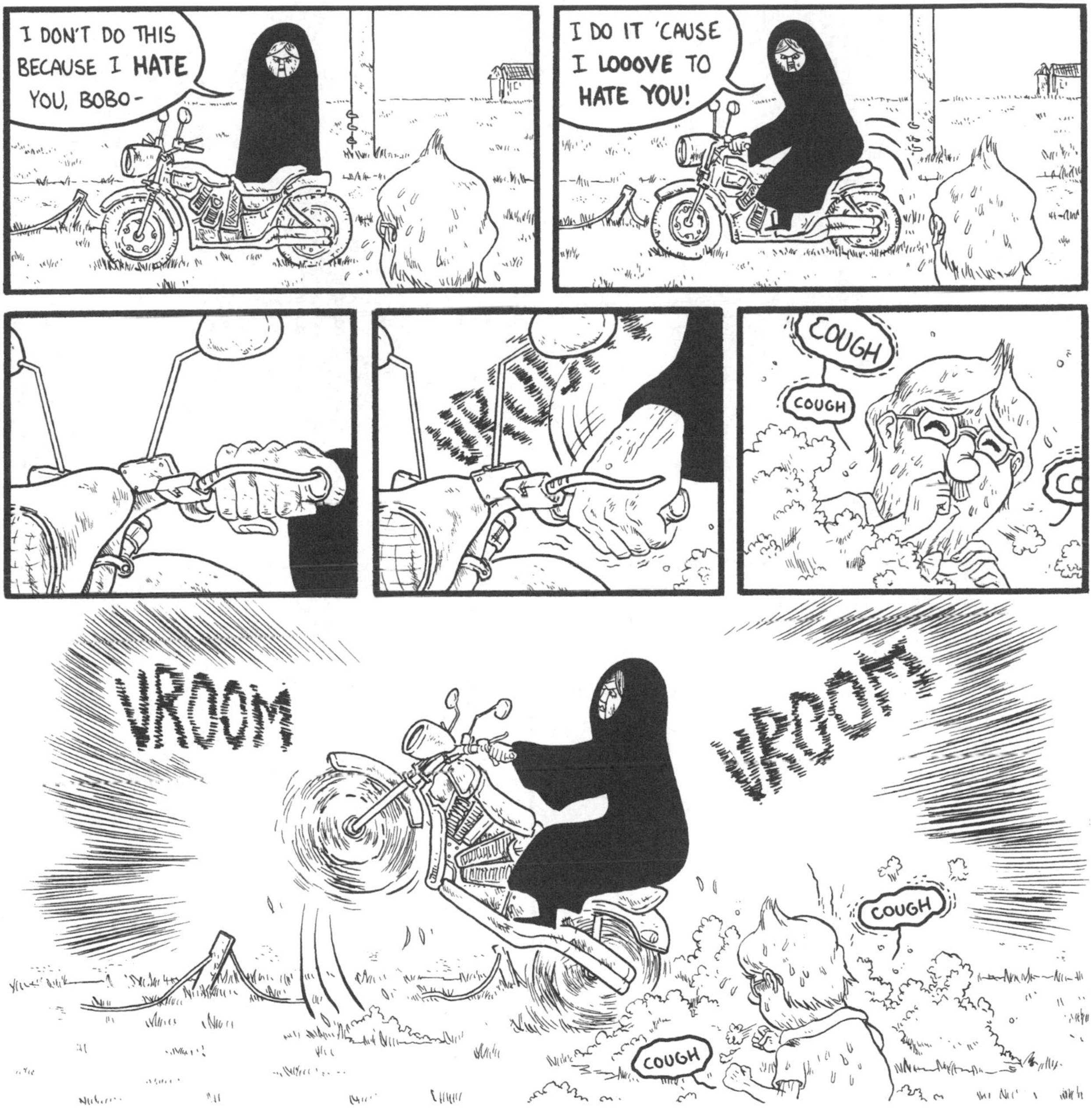
I DON'T DO THIS BECAUSE I HATE YOU, BOBO-
I DO IT 'CAUSE I LOOOVE TO HATE YOU!
COUGH
COUGH
VROOM
VROOM
COUGH
COUGH

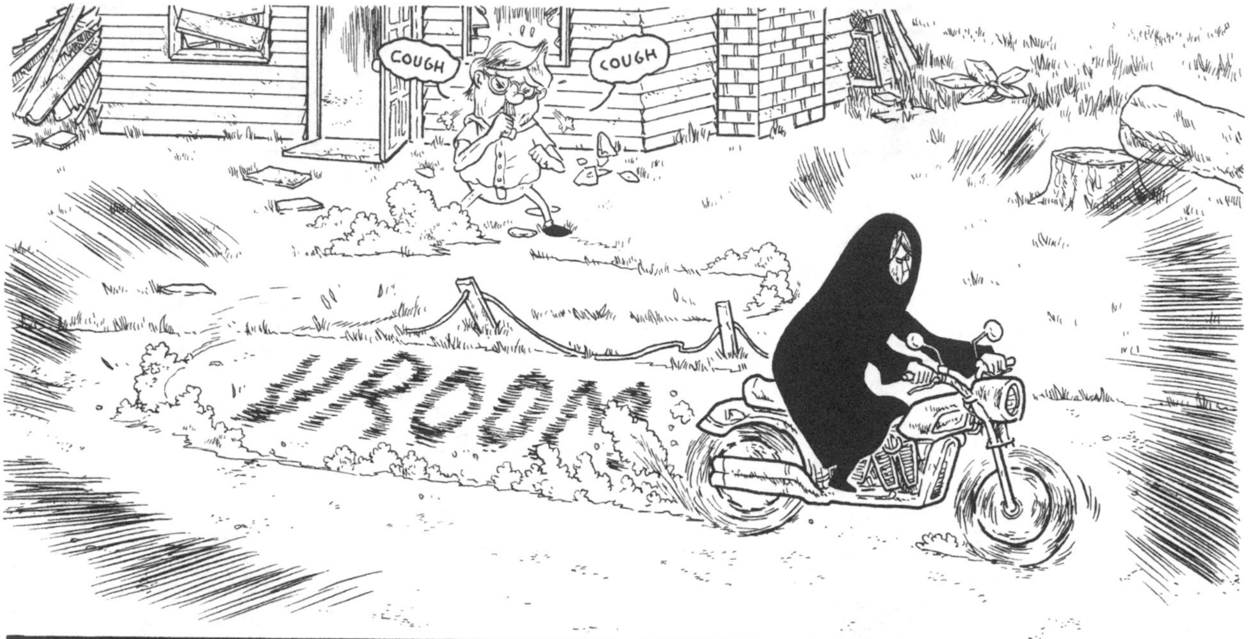
COUGH
COUGH
VROOM

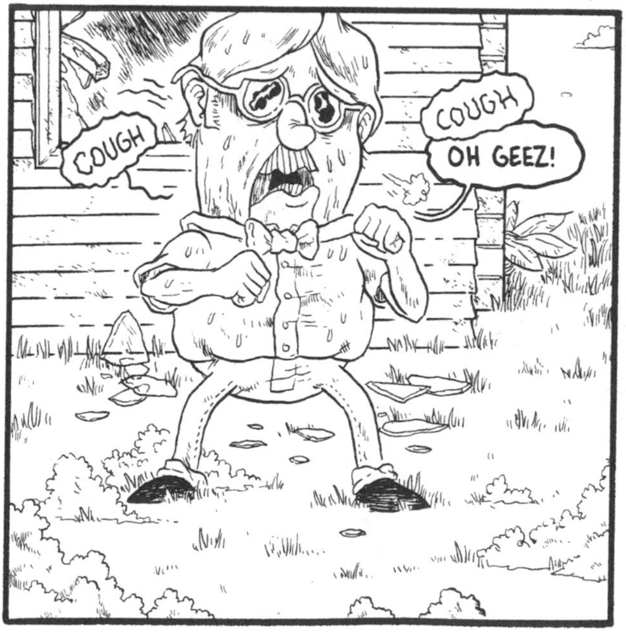
COUGH
COUGH
OH GEEZ!

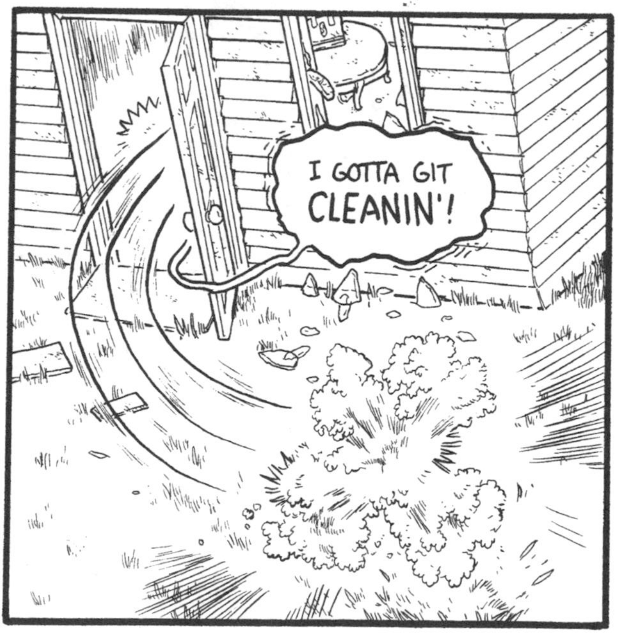
I GOTTA GIT CLEANIN'!

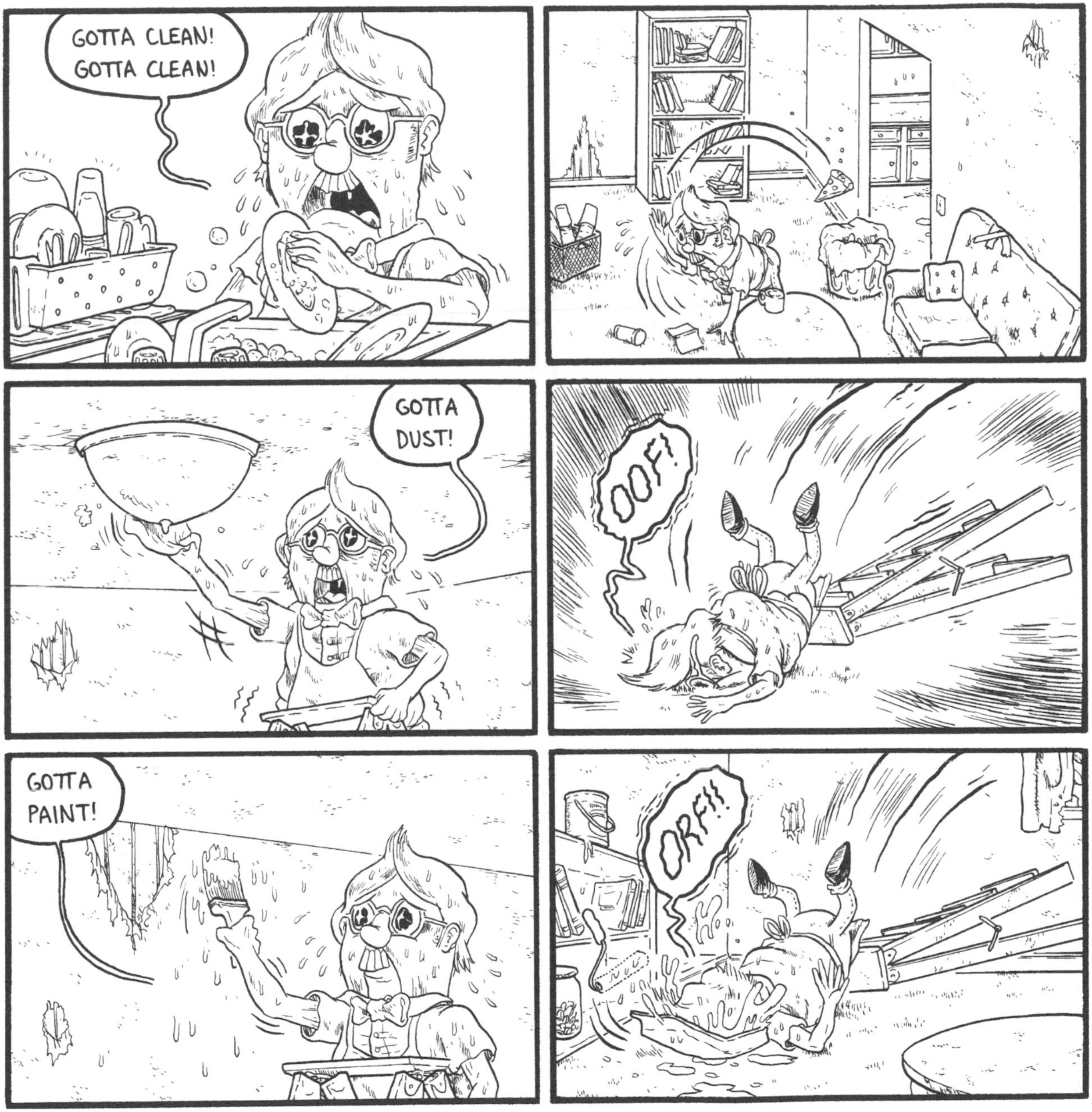
GOTTA CLEAN! GOTTA CLEAN!
GOTTA DUST!
OOF!
GOTTA PAINT!
ORF!!

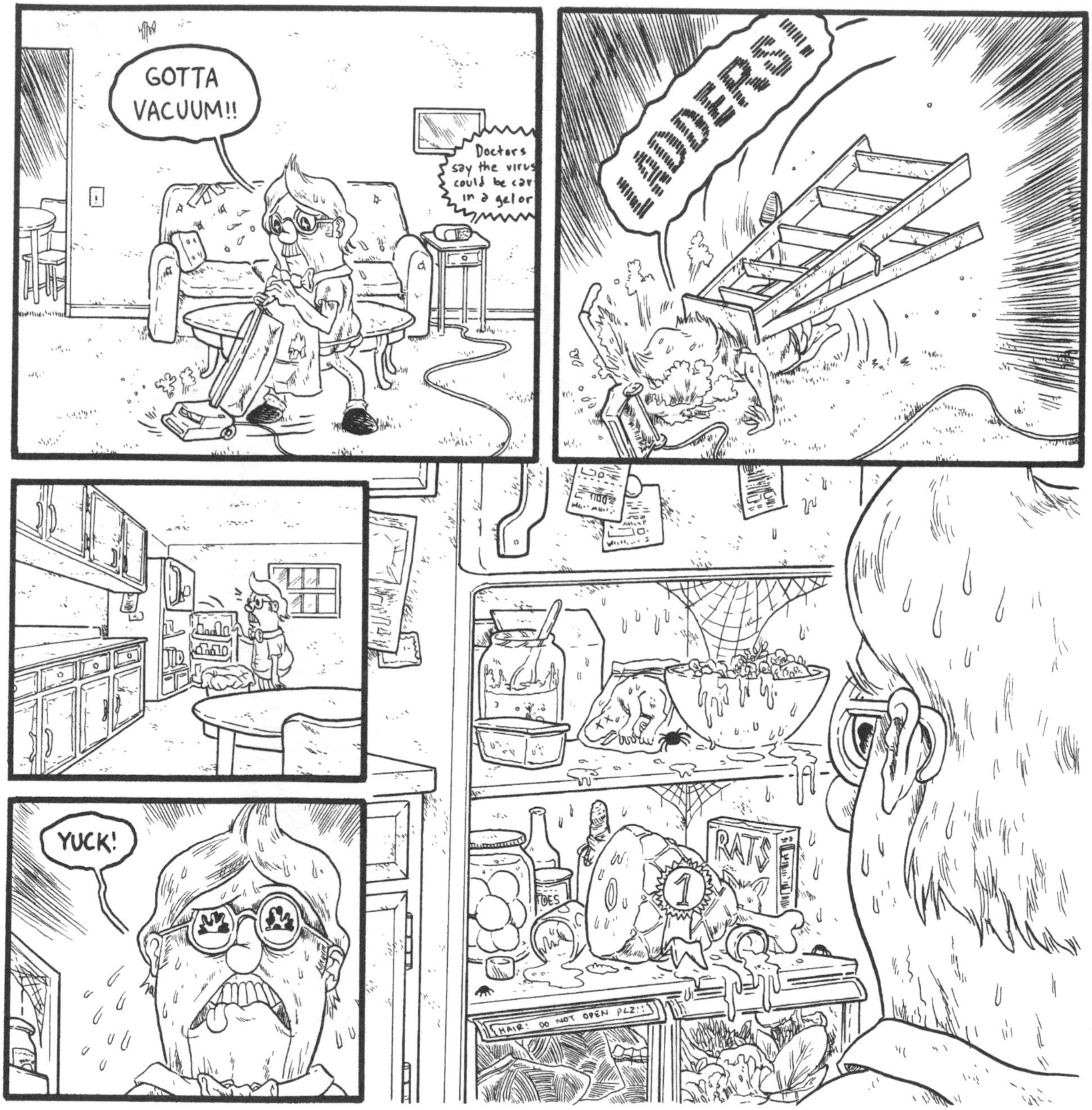
GOTTA VACUUM!!
Doctors say the virus could be car in a gel or
LADDERS!!
YUCK!
RATS
HAIR: DO NOT OPEN PLZ!!

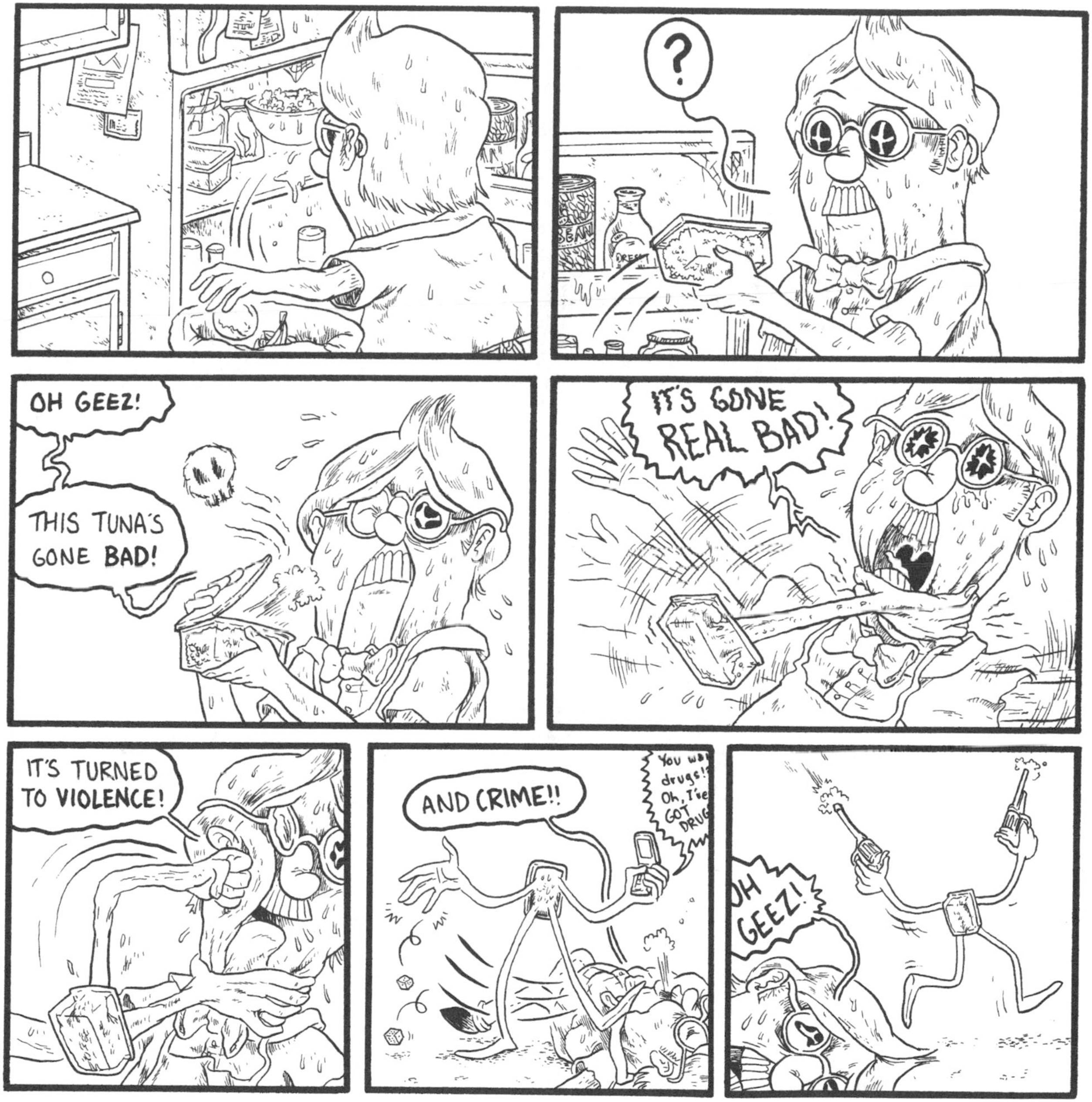
?
OH GEEZ!
THIS TUNA'S GONE BAD!
IT'S GONE REAL BAD!
IT'S TURNED TO VIOLENCE!
AND CRIME!!
You wa
drugs!? Oh, I've GOT DRUG
OH GEEZ!

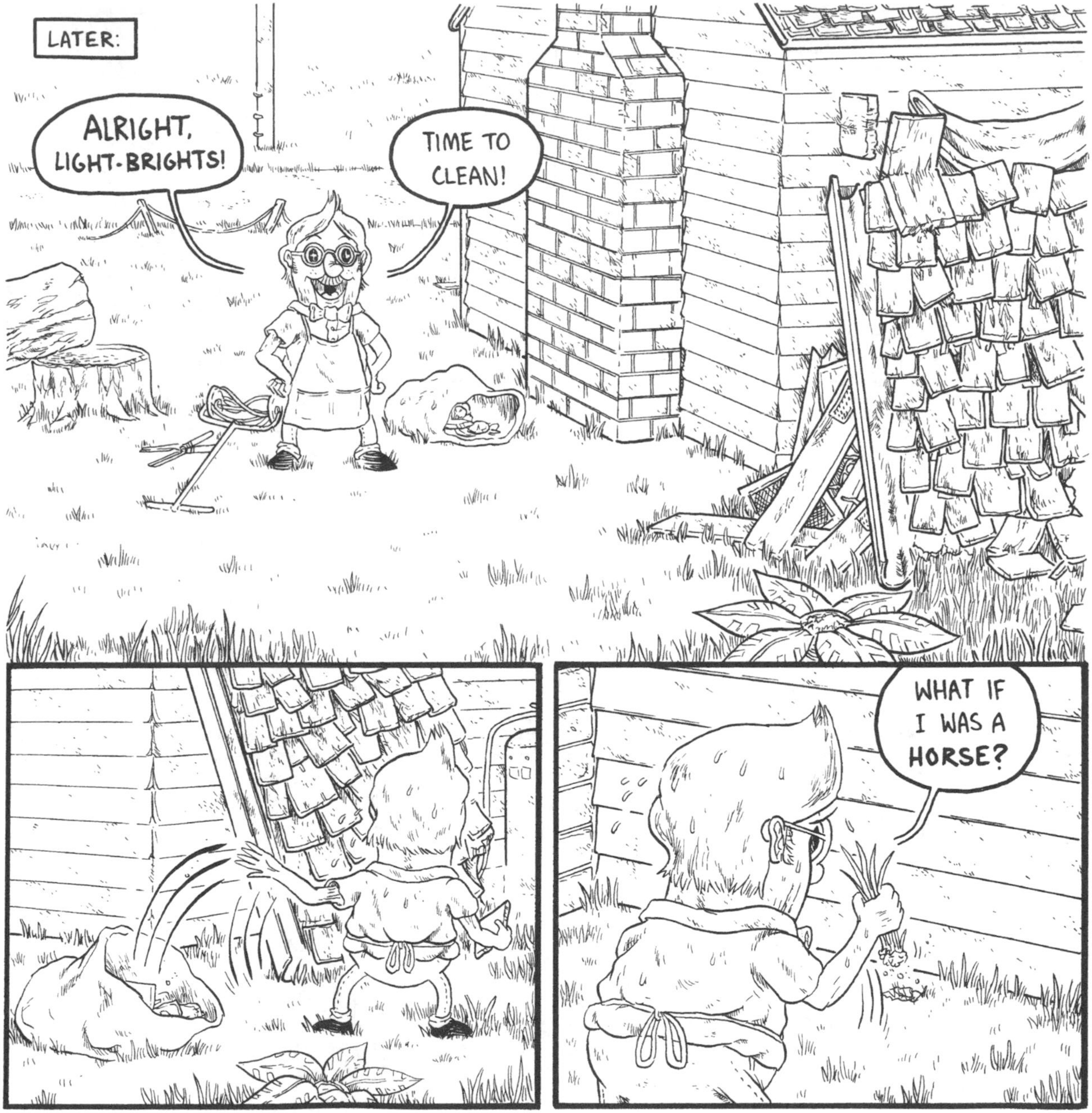
LATER:
ALRIGHT, LIGHT-BRIGHTS!
TIME TO CLEAN!
WHAT IF I WAS A HORSE?

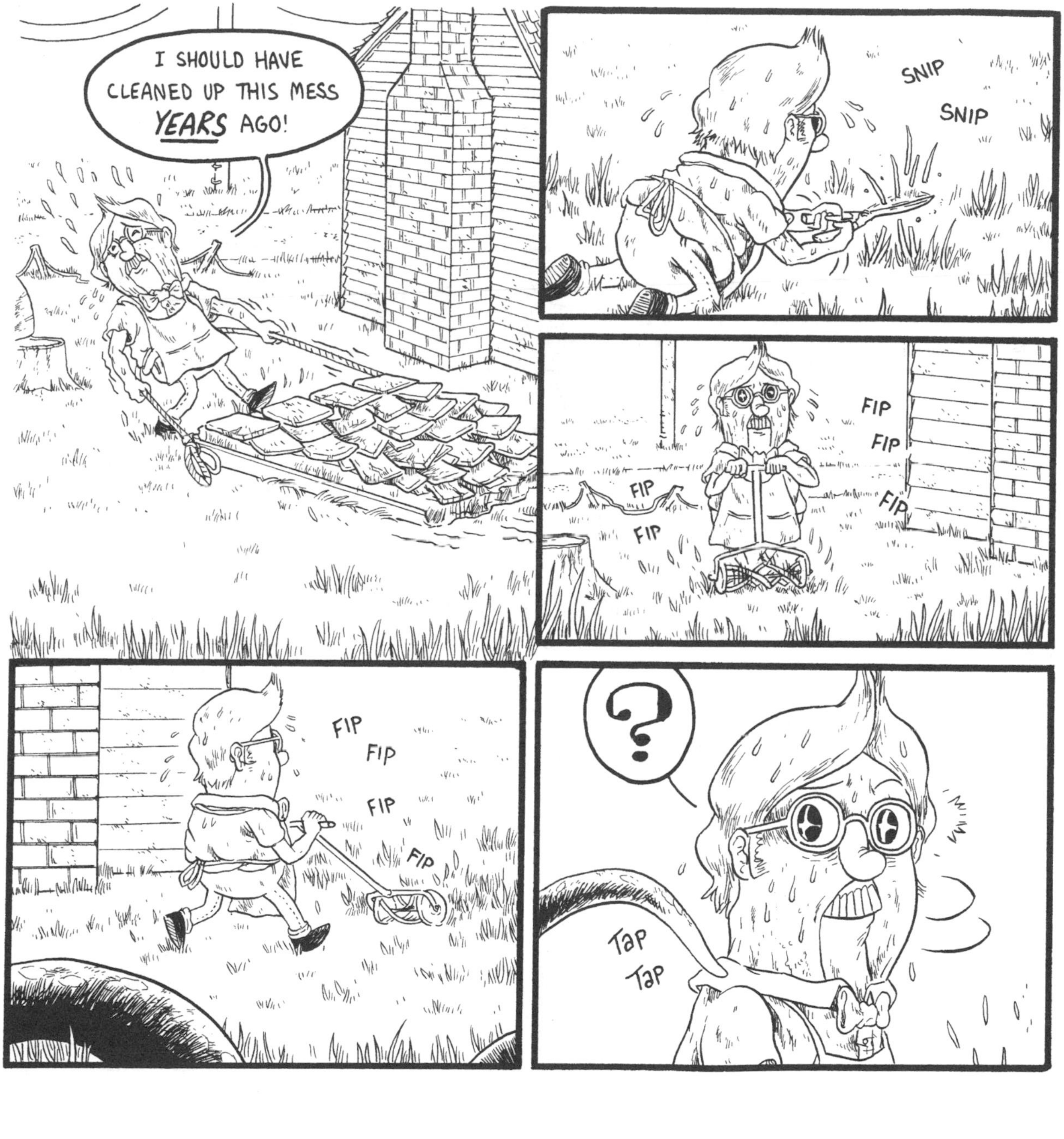
I SHOULD HAVE CLEANED UP THIS MESS YEARS AGO!
SNIP
SNIP
FIP
FIP
FIP
FIP
FIP
FIP
FIP
FIP
FIP
?
Tap
Tap

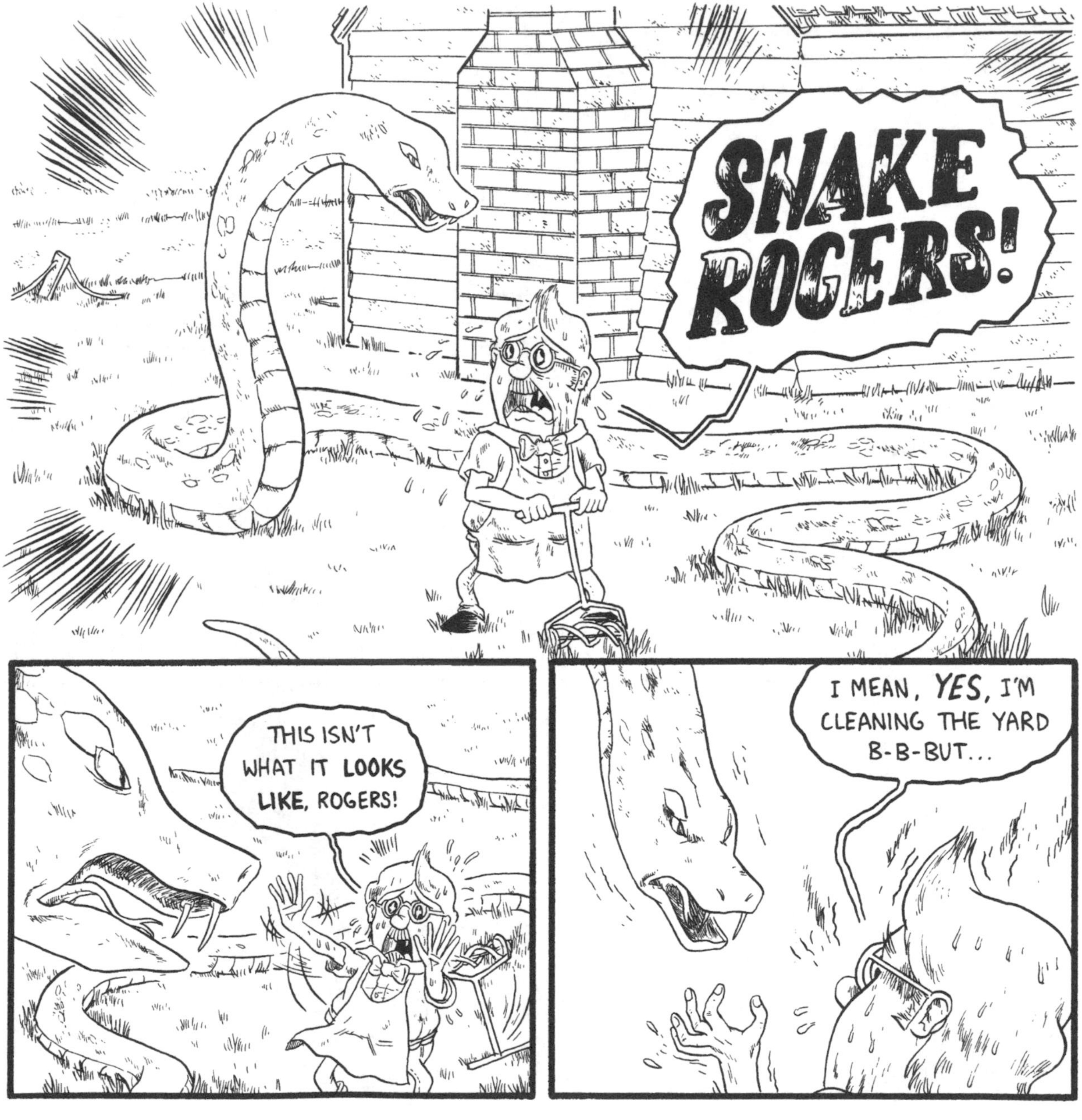
SNAKE ROGERS!
THIS ISN'T WHAT IT LOOKS LIKE, ROGERS!
I MEAN, YES, I'M CLEANING THE YARD B-B-BUT...

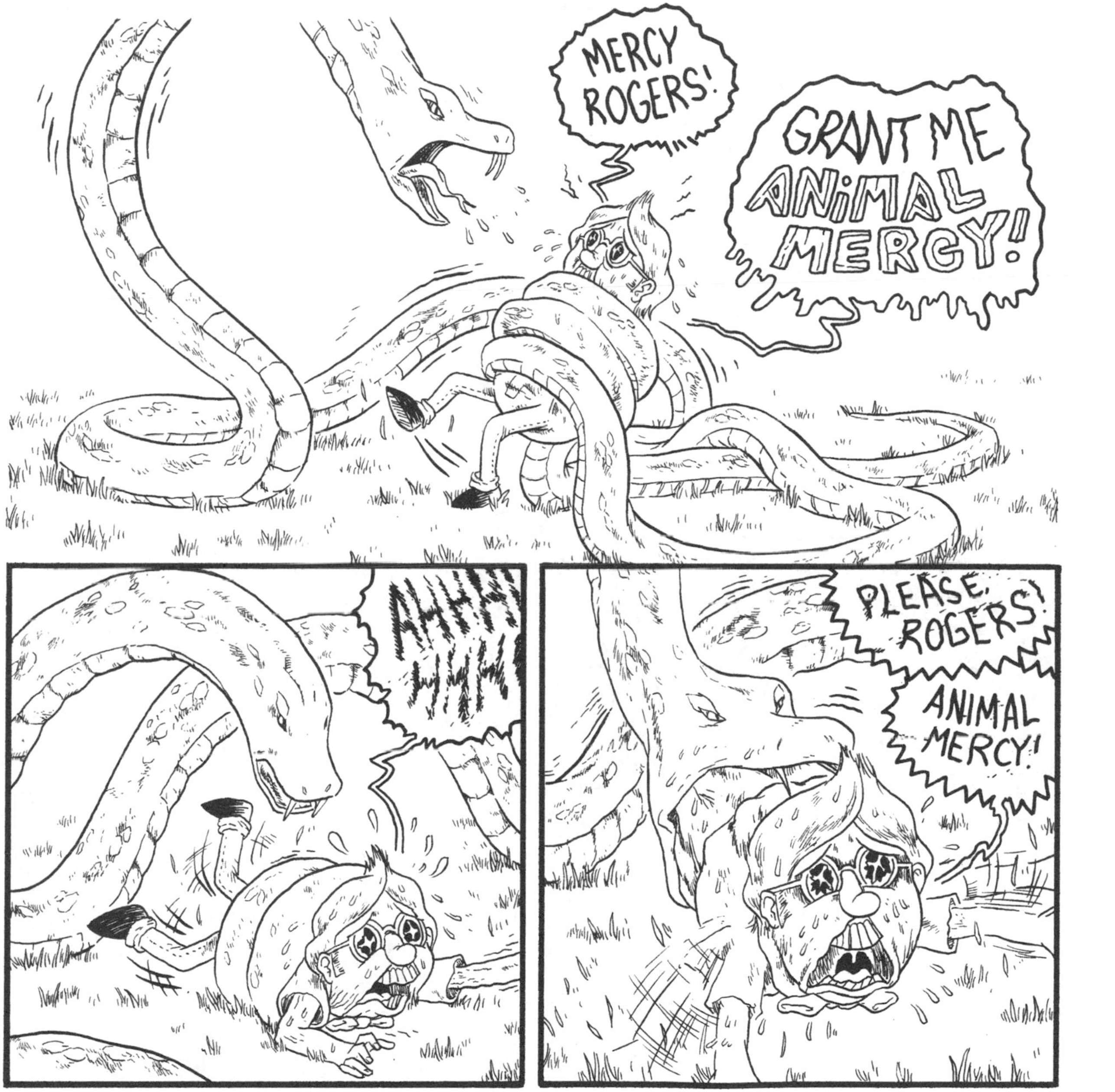
MERCY ROGERS!
GRANT ME ANIMAL MERCY!
AHHH
HHH
PLEASE, ROGERS!
ANIMAL MERCY!

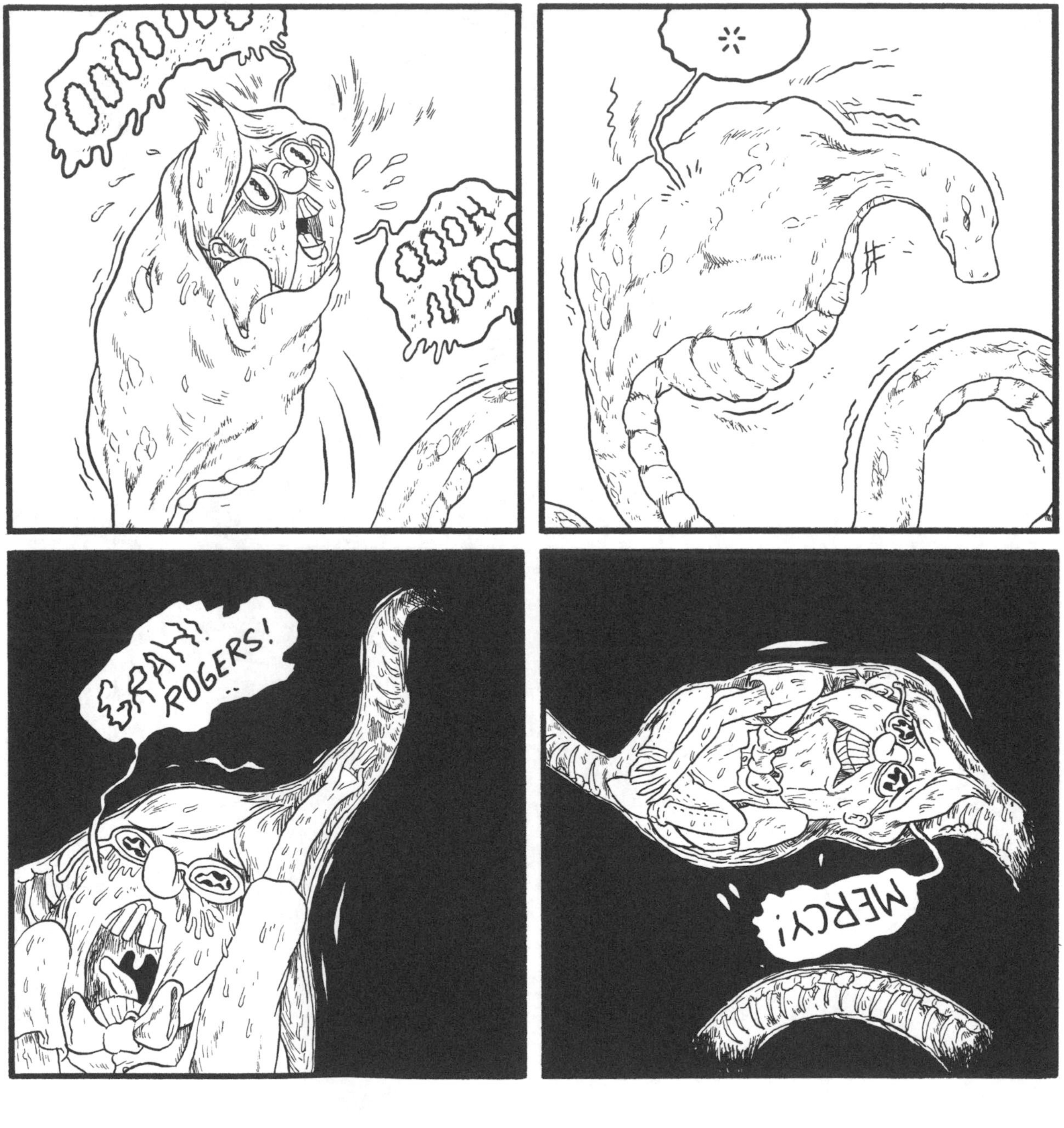
OOOOOOO
OOOH NOOOO
GRAH!! ROGERS!
MERCY!

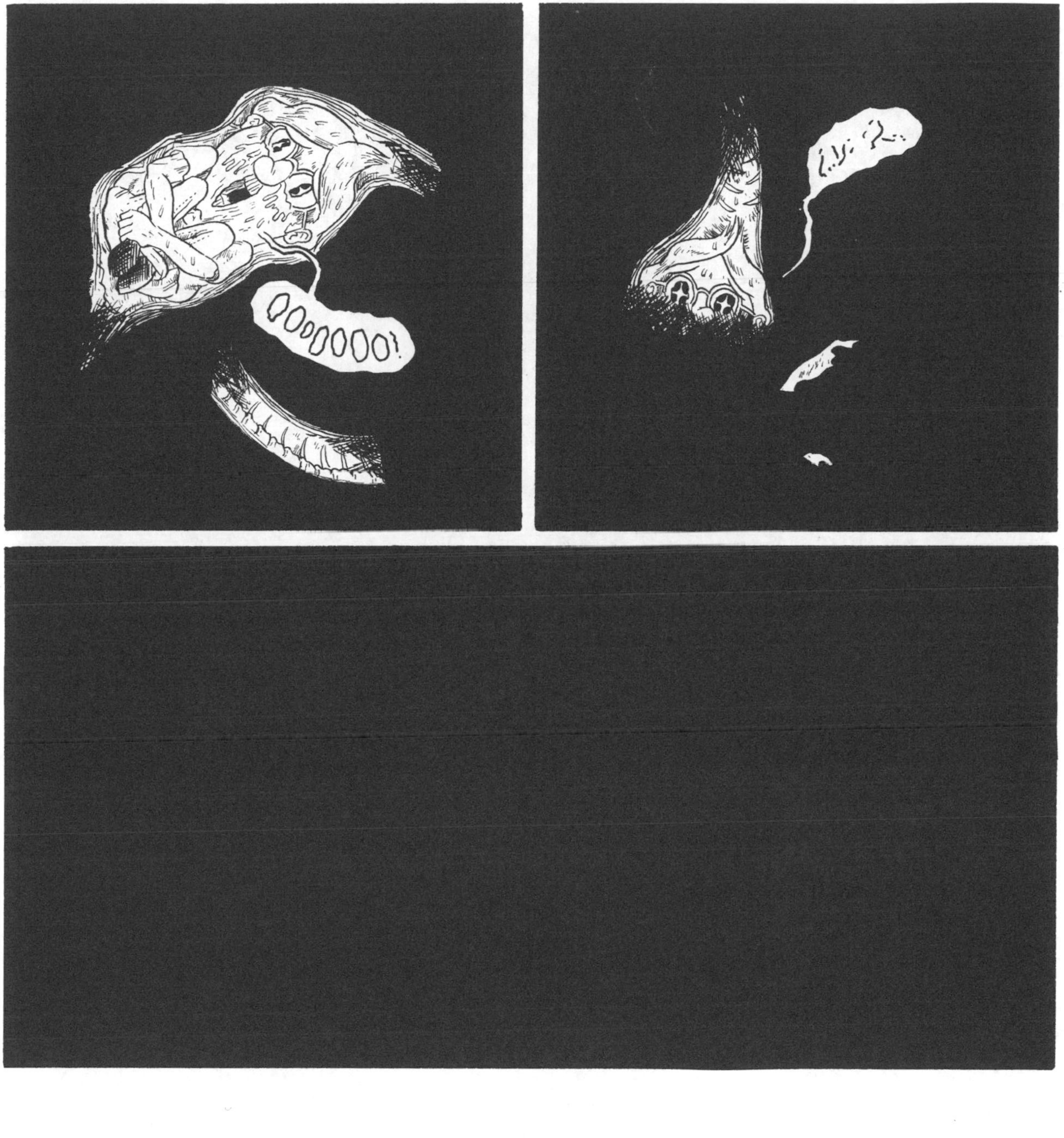
OOoOOOO!

OH GEEZ.

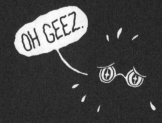

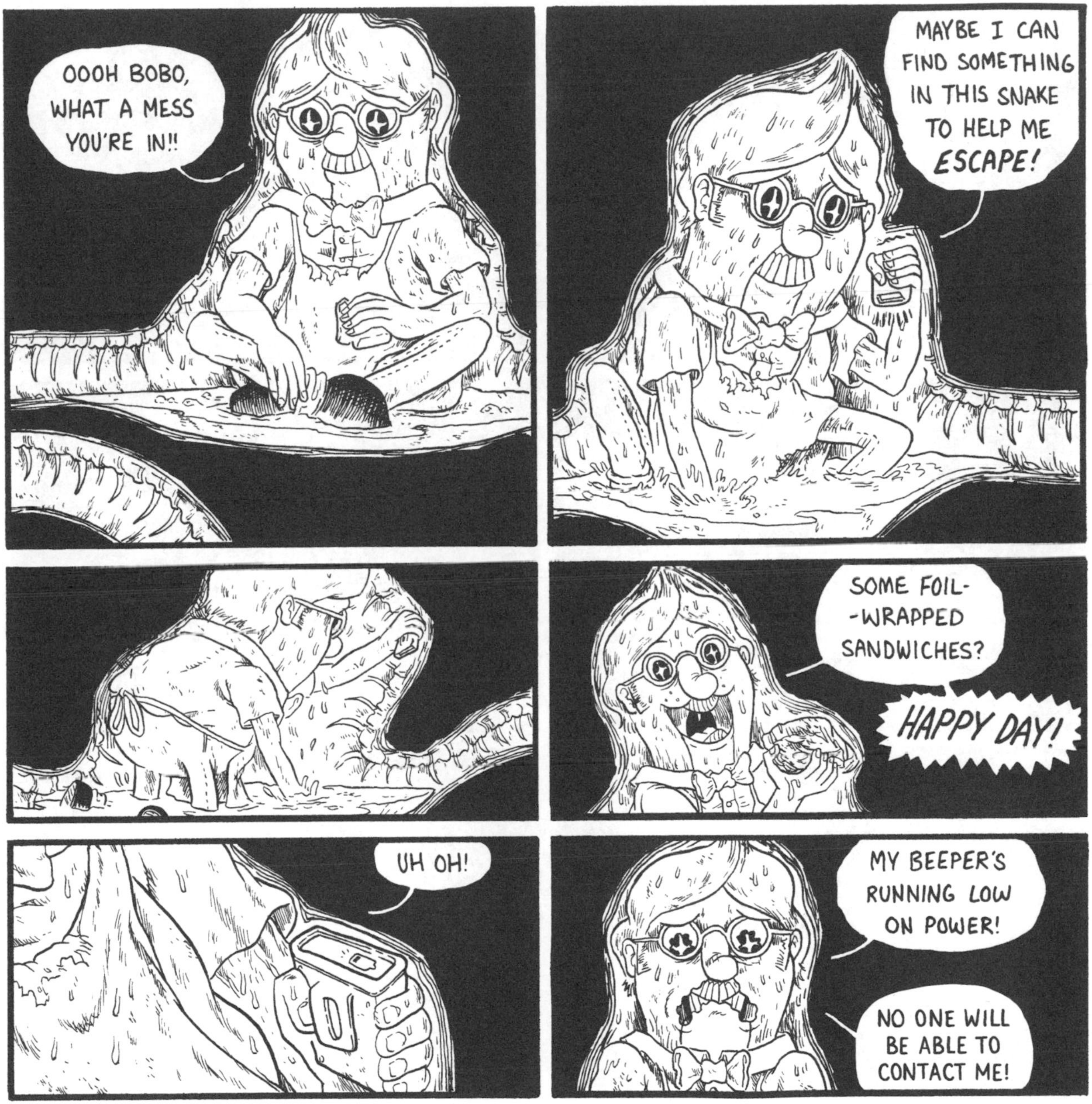
OOOH BOBO, WHAT A MESS YOU'RE IN!!
MAYBE I CAN FIND SOMETHING IN THIS SNAKE TO HELP ME ESCAPE!
SOME FOIL- -WRAPPED SANDWICHES?
HAPPY DAY!
UH OH!
MY BEEPER'S RUNNING LOW ON POWER!
NO ONE WILL BE ABLE TO CONTACT ME!

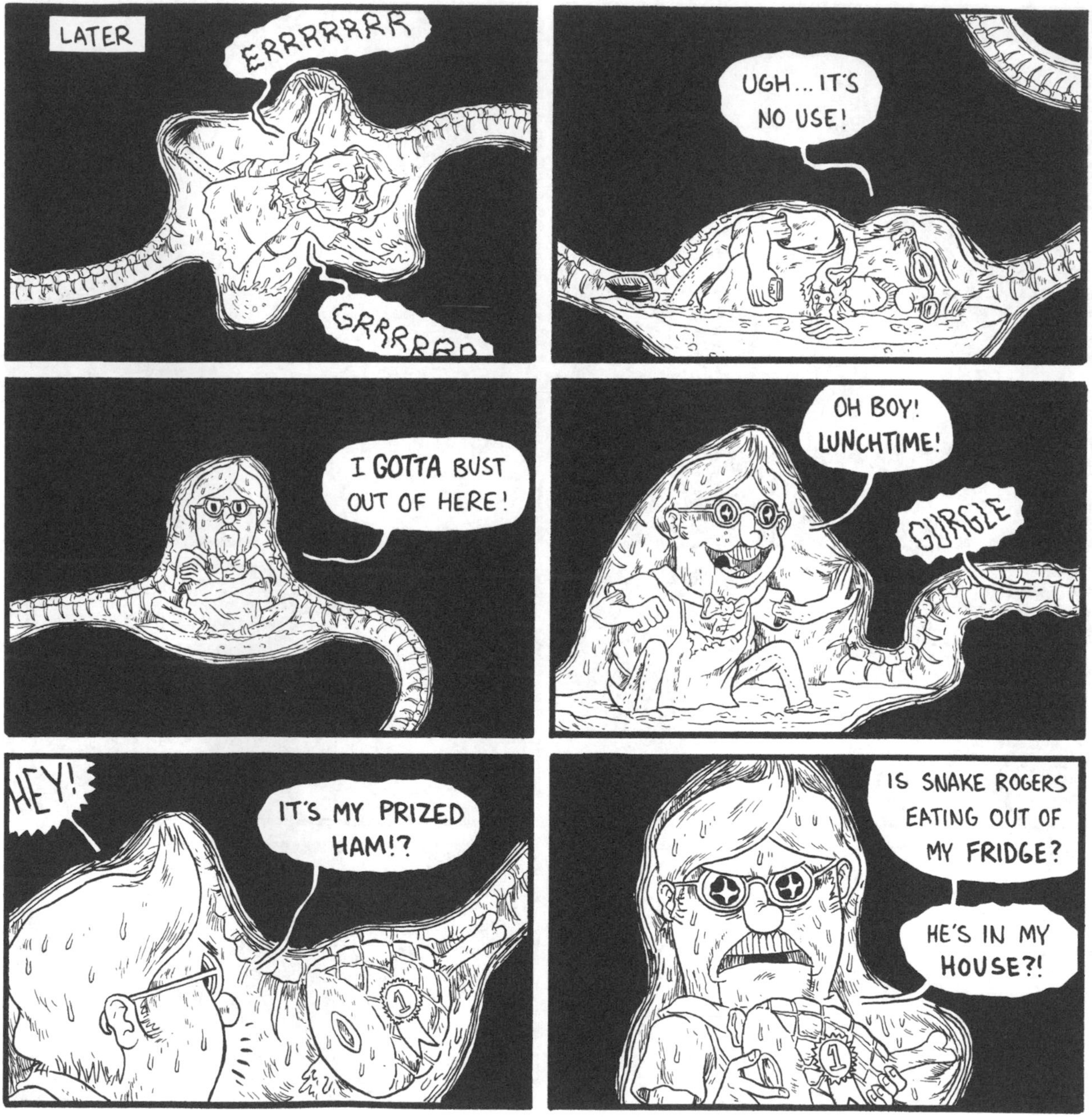
LATER
ERRRRRRR
GRRRRRRR
UGH... IT'S NO USE!
I GOTTA BUST OUT OF HERE!
OH BOY! LUNCHTIME!
GURGLE
HEY!
IT'S MY PRIZED HAM!?
IS SNAKE ROGERS EATING OUT OF MY FRIDGE?
HE'S IN MY HOUSE?!

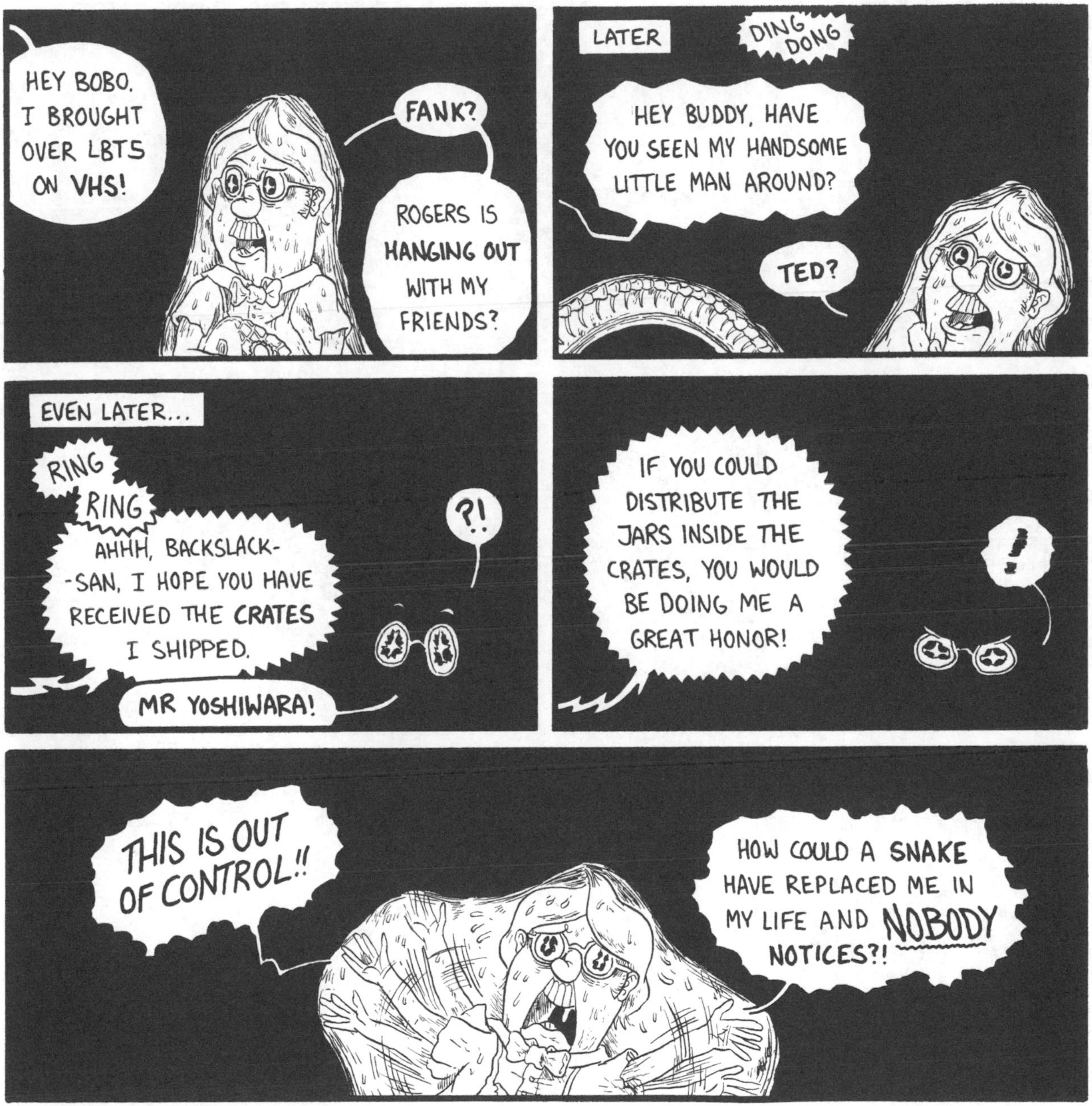
HEY BOBO. I BROUGHT OVER LBTS ON VHS!
FANK?
ROGERS IS HANGING OUT WITH MY FRIENDS?
LATER
DING DONG
HEY BUDDY, HAVE YOU SEEN MY HANDSOME LITTLE MAN AROUND?
TED?
EVEN LATER...
RING
RING
AHHH, BACKSLACK--SAN, I HOPE YOU HAVE RECEIVED THE CRATES I SHIPPED.
?!
MR YOSHIWARA!
IF YOU COULD DISTRIBUTE THE JARS INSIDE THE CRATES, YOU WOULD BE DOING ME A GREAT HONOR!
!
THIS IS OUT OF CONTROL!!
HOW COULD A SNAKE HAVE REPLACED ME IN MY LIFE AND NOBODY NOTICES?!

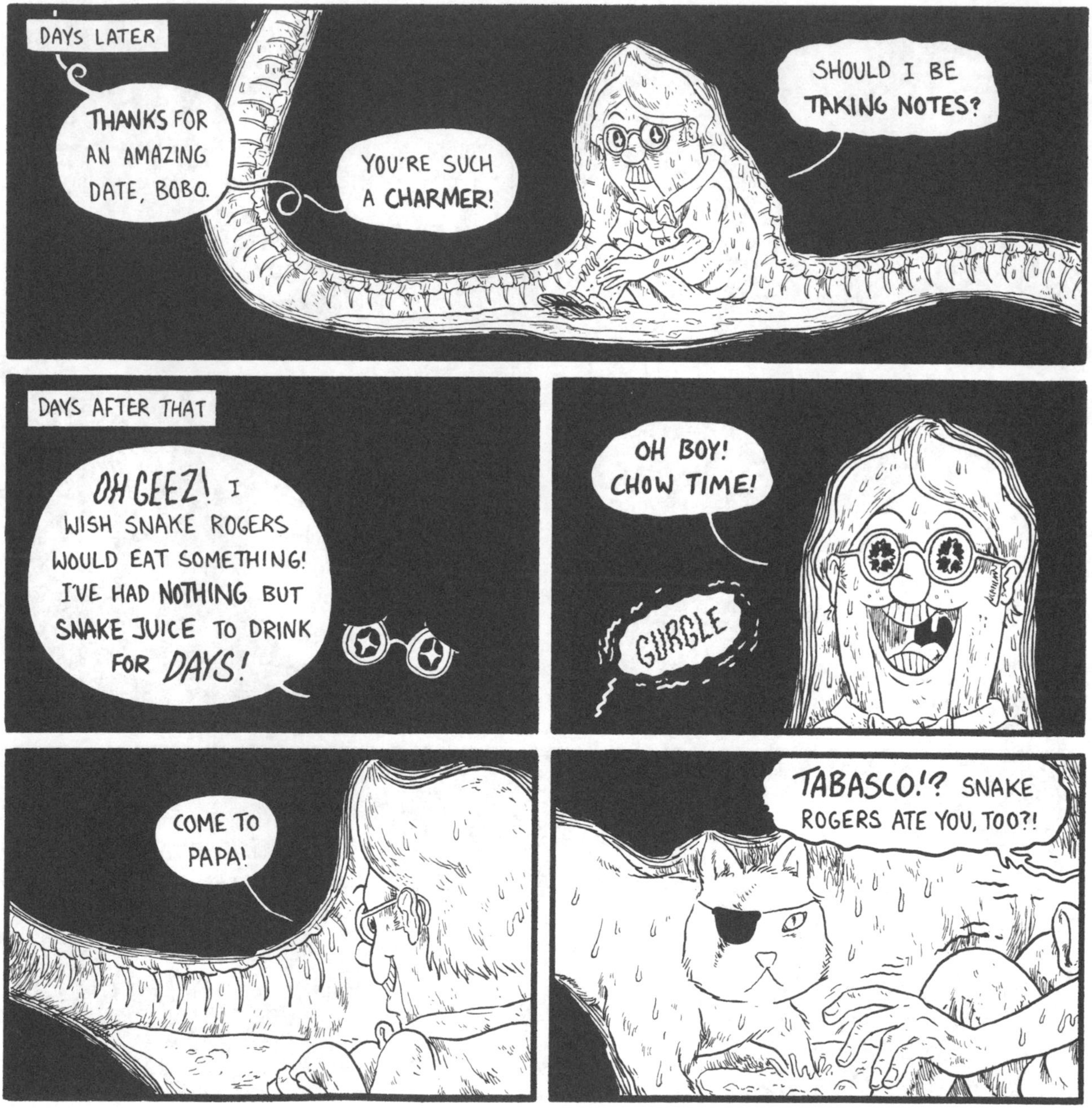
DAYS LATER
THANKS FOR AN AMAZING DATE, BOBO.
YOU'RE SUCH A CHARMER!
SHOULD I BE TAKING NOTES?
DAYS AFTER THAT
OH GEEZ! I WISH SNAKE ROGERS WOULD EAT SOMETHING! I'VE HAD NOTHING BUT SNAKE JUICE TO DRINK FOR DAYS!
OH BOY! CHOW TIME!
GURGLE
COME TO PAPA!
TABASCO!? SNAKE ROGERS ATE YOU, TOO?!

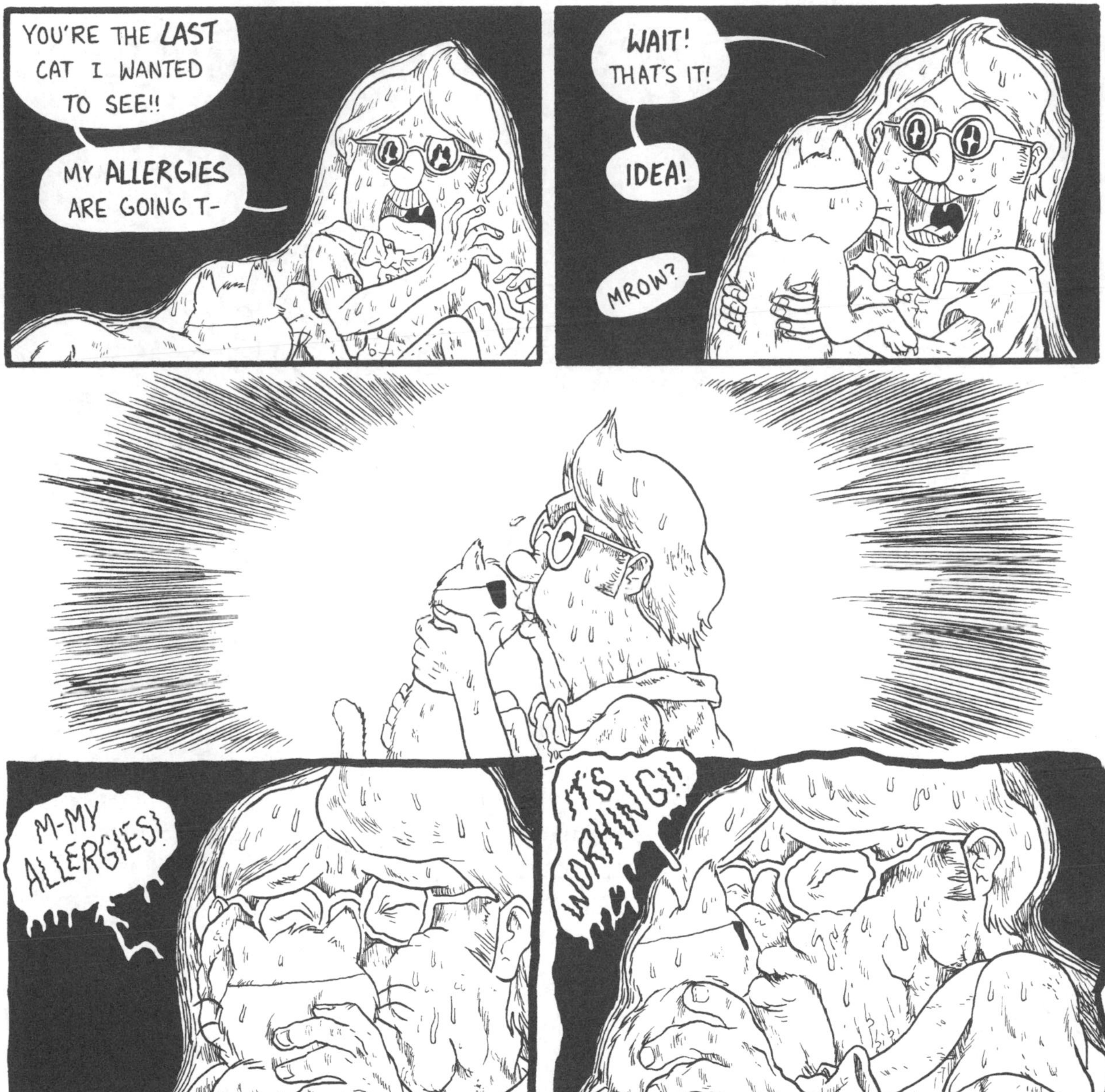
YOU'RE THE LAST CAT I WANTED TO SEE!!
MY ALLERGIES ARE GOING T-
WAIT! THAT'S IT!
IDEA!
MROW?
M-MY ALLERGIES!
IT'S WORKING!!

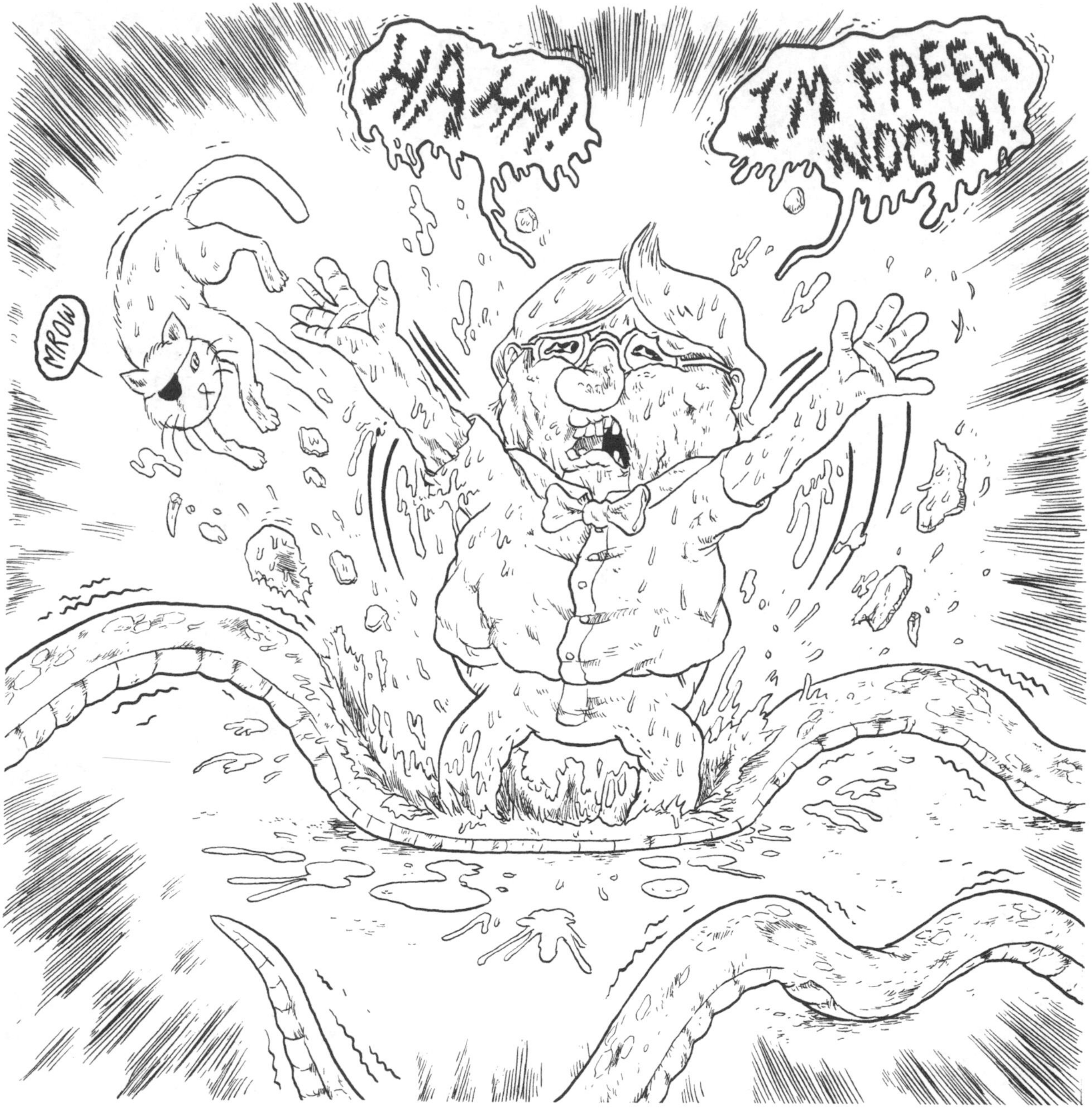

YAHH!
I'M FREEH NOOW!
MROW

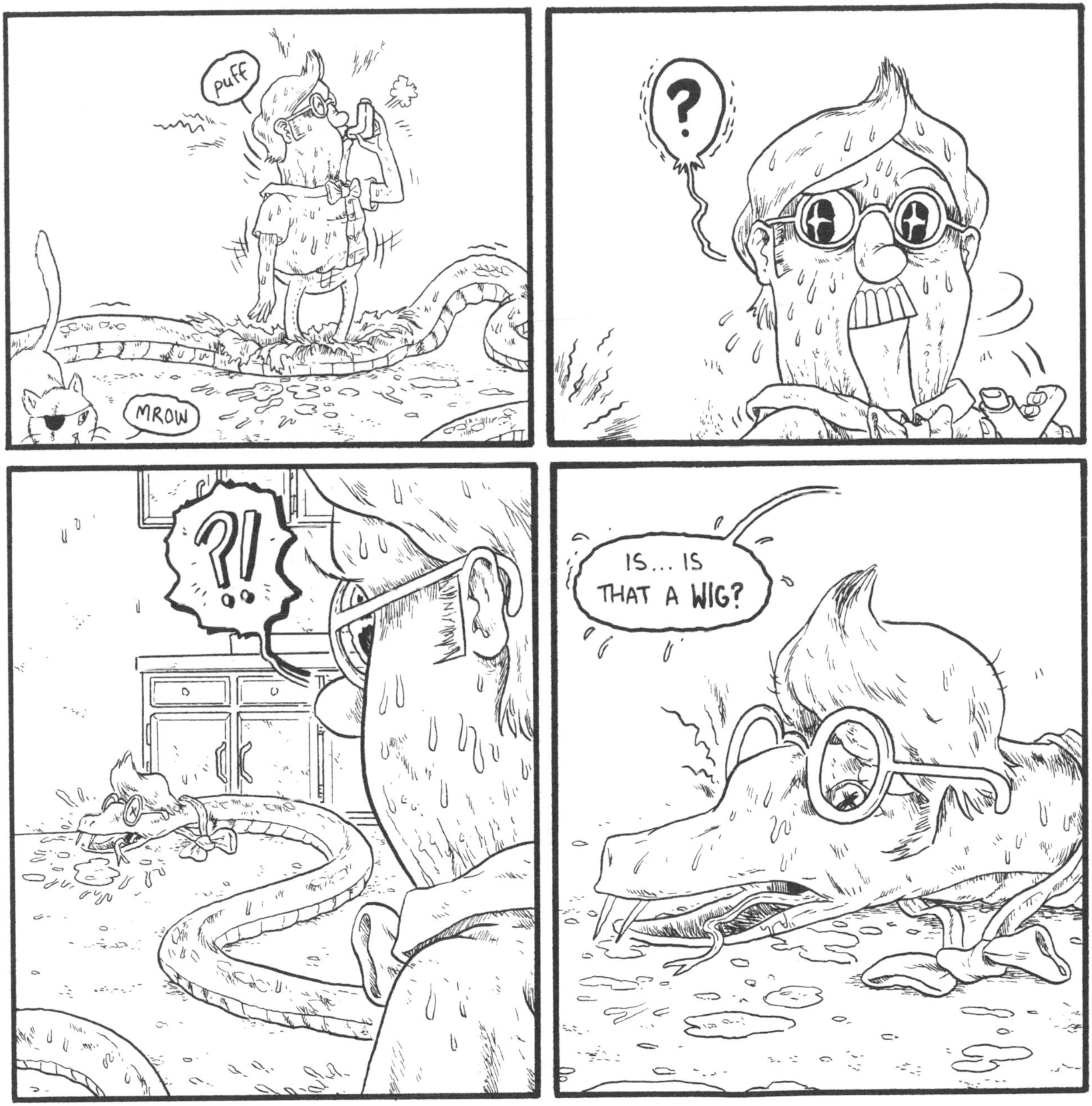
puff
MROW
?
?!
IS... IS
THAT A WIG?

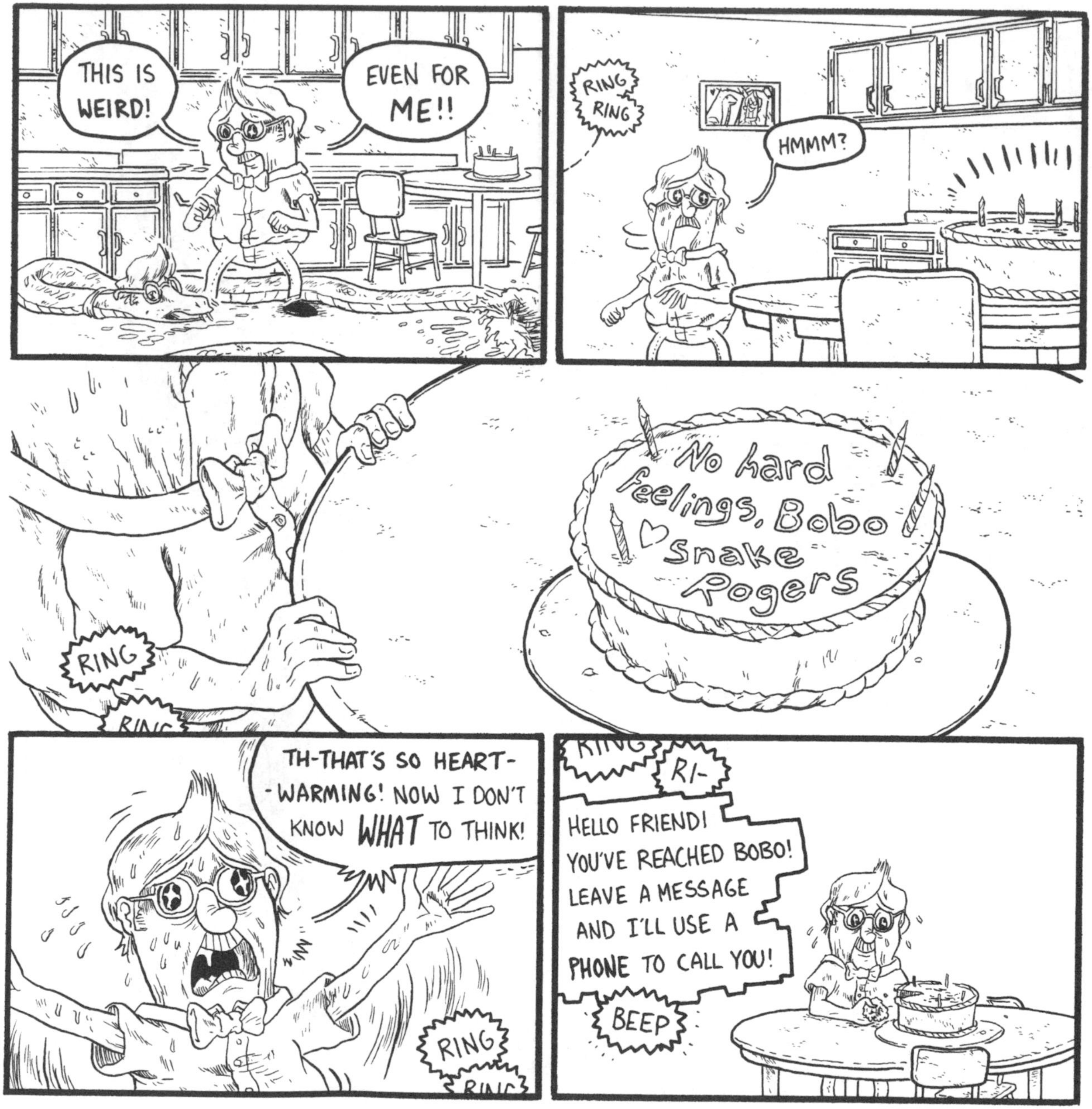
THIS IS WEIRD!
EVEN FOR ME!!
RING RING
HMMM?
RING
No hard feelings, Bobo
♡ Snake Rogers
TH-THAT'S SO HEART- -WARMING! NOW I DON'T KNOW WHAT TO THINK!
RING
RI-
HELLO FRIEND! YOU'VE REACHED BOBO! LEAVE A MESSAGE AND I'LL USE A PHONE TO CALL YOU!
BEEP

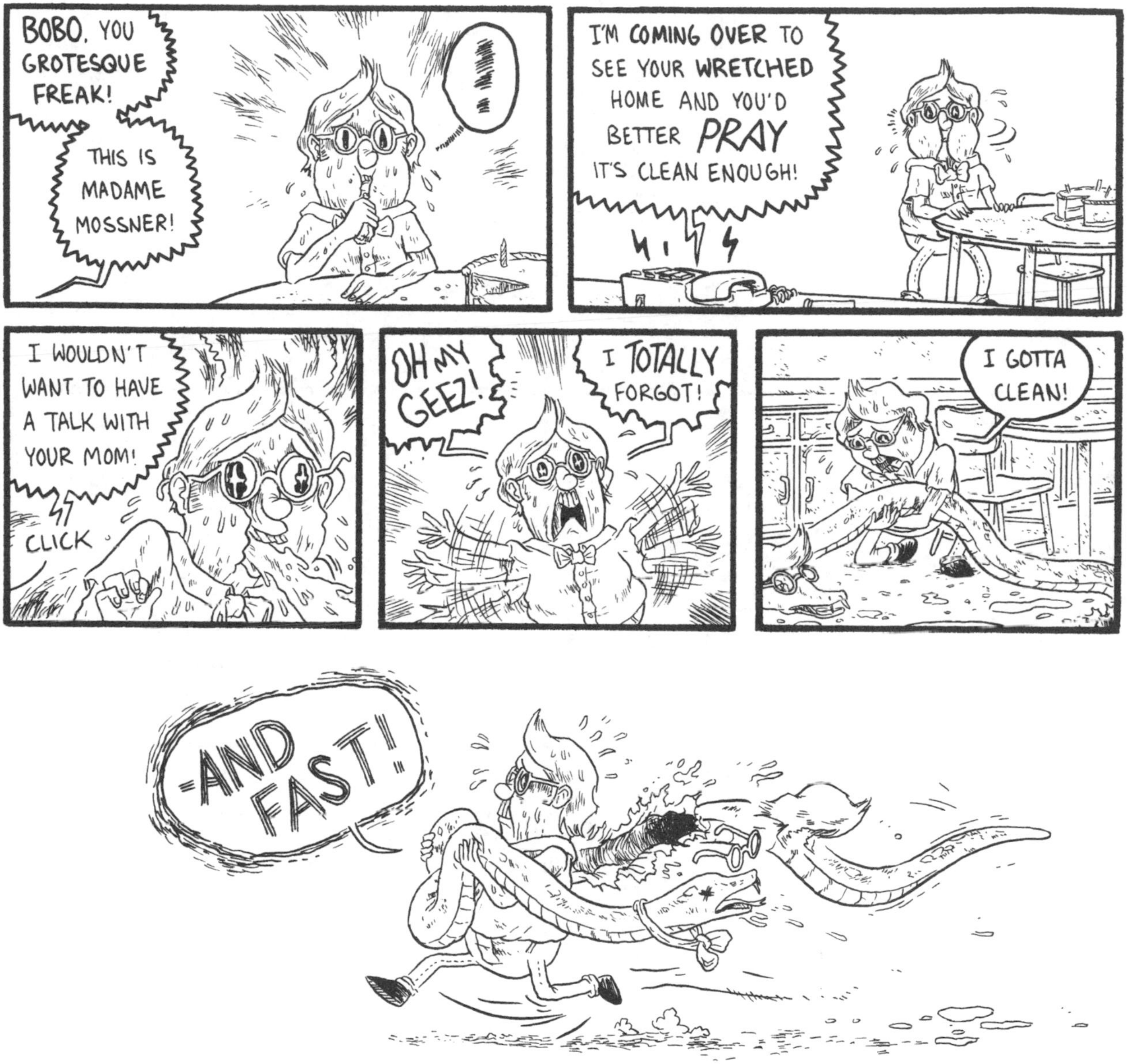

BOBO, YOU GROTESQUE FREAK!
THIS IS MADAME MOSSNER!
!
I'M COMING OVER TO SEE YOUR WRETCHED HOME AND YOU'D BETTER PRAY IT'S CLEAN ENOUGH!
I WOULDN'T WANT TO HAVE A TALK WITH YOUR MOM!
CLICK
OH MY GEEZ!
I TOTALLY FORGOT!
I GOTTA CLEAN!
-AND FAST!

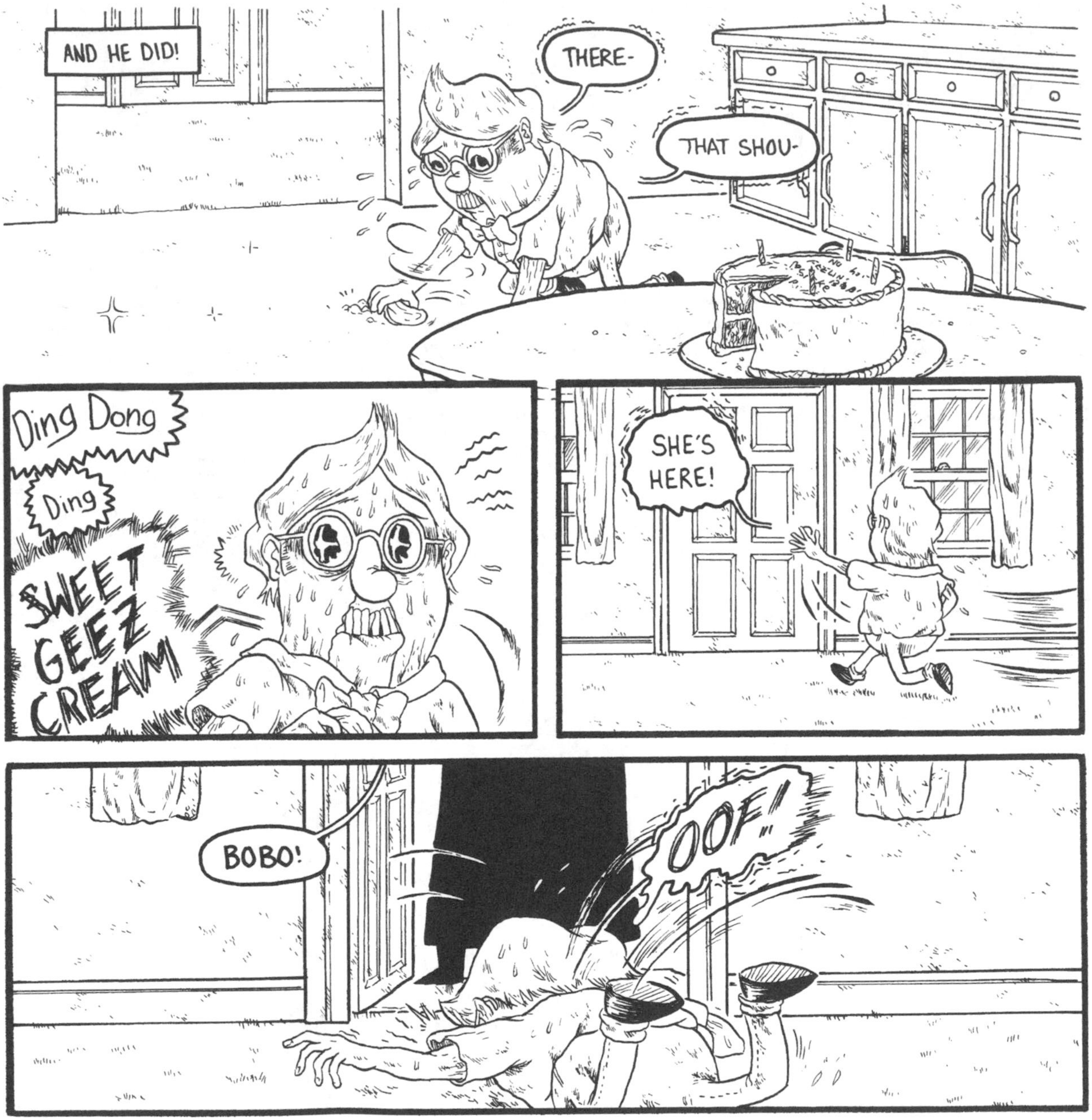
AND HE DID!
THERE-
THAT SHOU-
Ding Dong
Ding
SWEET GEEZ CREAM
SHE'S HERE!
BOBO!
OOF!!

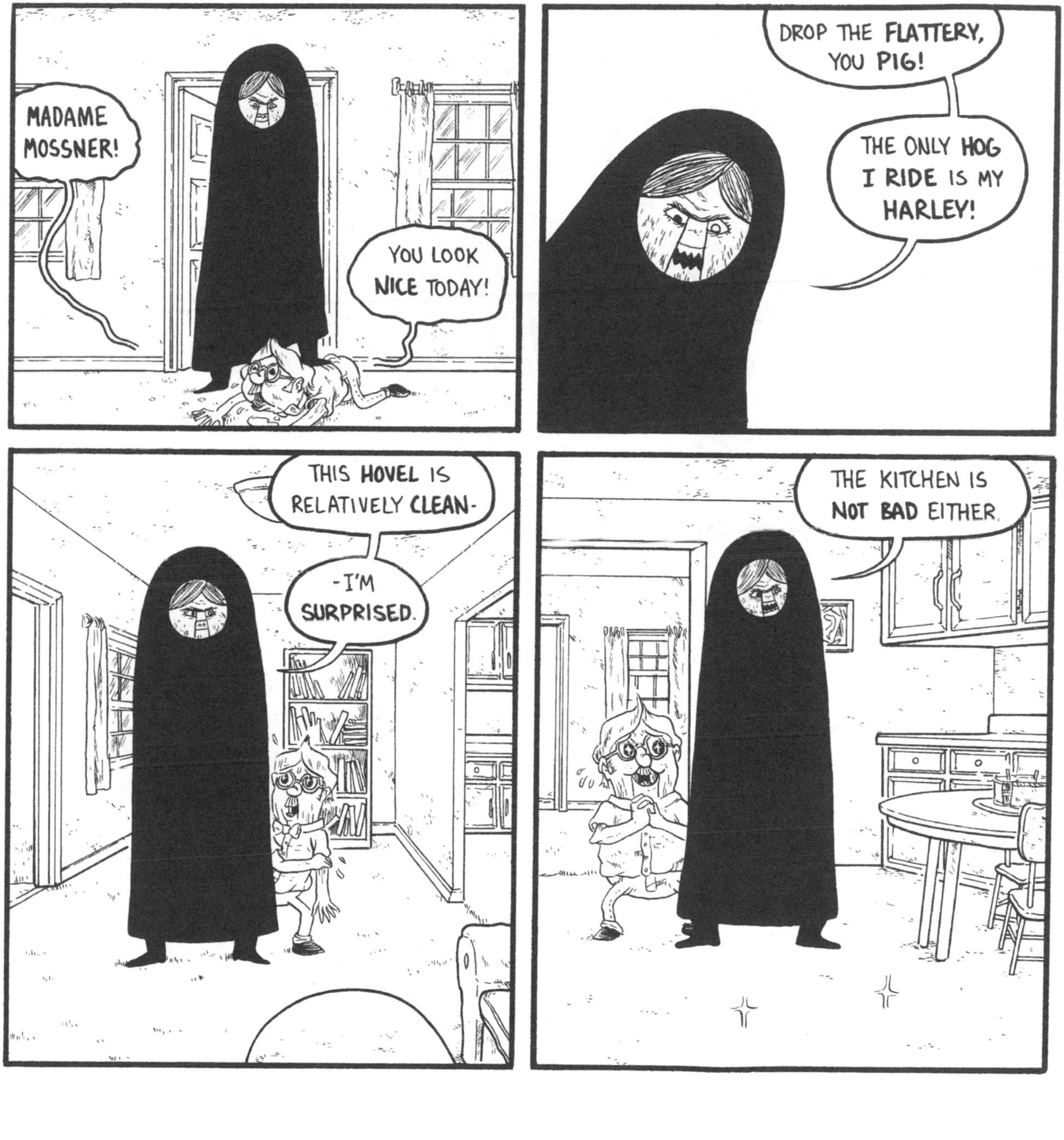
MADAME MOSSNER!
YOU LOOK NICE TODAY!
DROP THE FLATTERY, YOU PIG!
THE ONLY HOG I RIDE IS MY HARLEY!
THIS HOVEL IS RELATIVELY CLEAN-
-I'M SURPRISED.
THE KITCHEN IS NOT BAD EITHER.

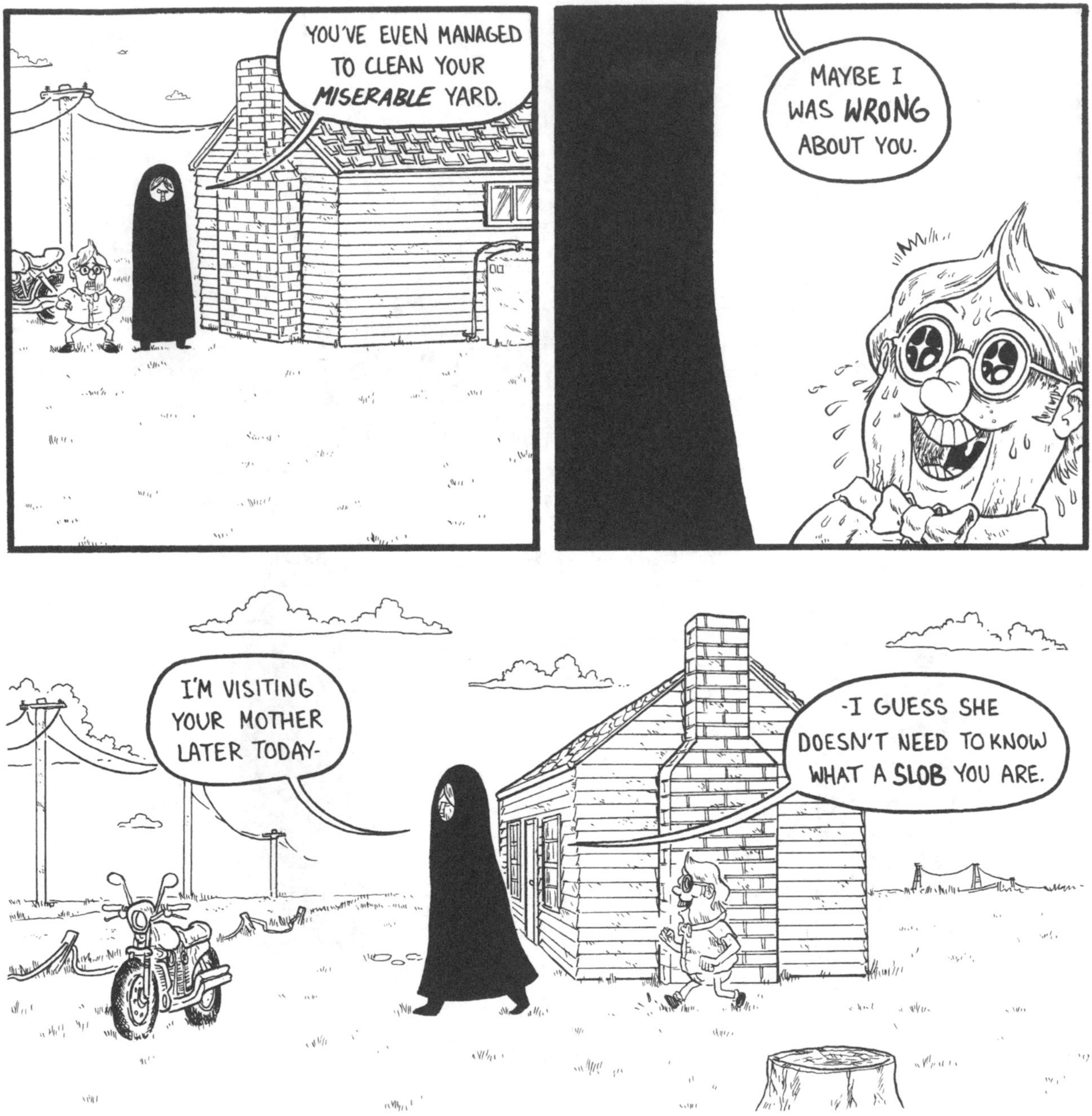
YOU'VE EVEN MANAGED TO CLEAN YOUR MISERABLE YARD.
MAYBE I WAS WRONG ABOUT YOU.
I'M VISITING YOUR MOTHER LATER TODAY-
-I GUESS SHE DOESN'T NEED TO KNOW WHAT A SLOB YOU ARE.

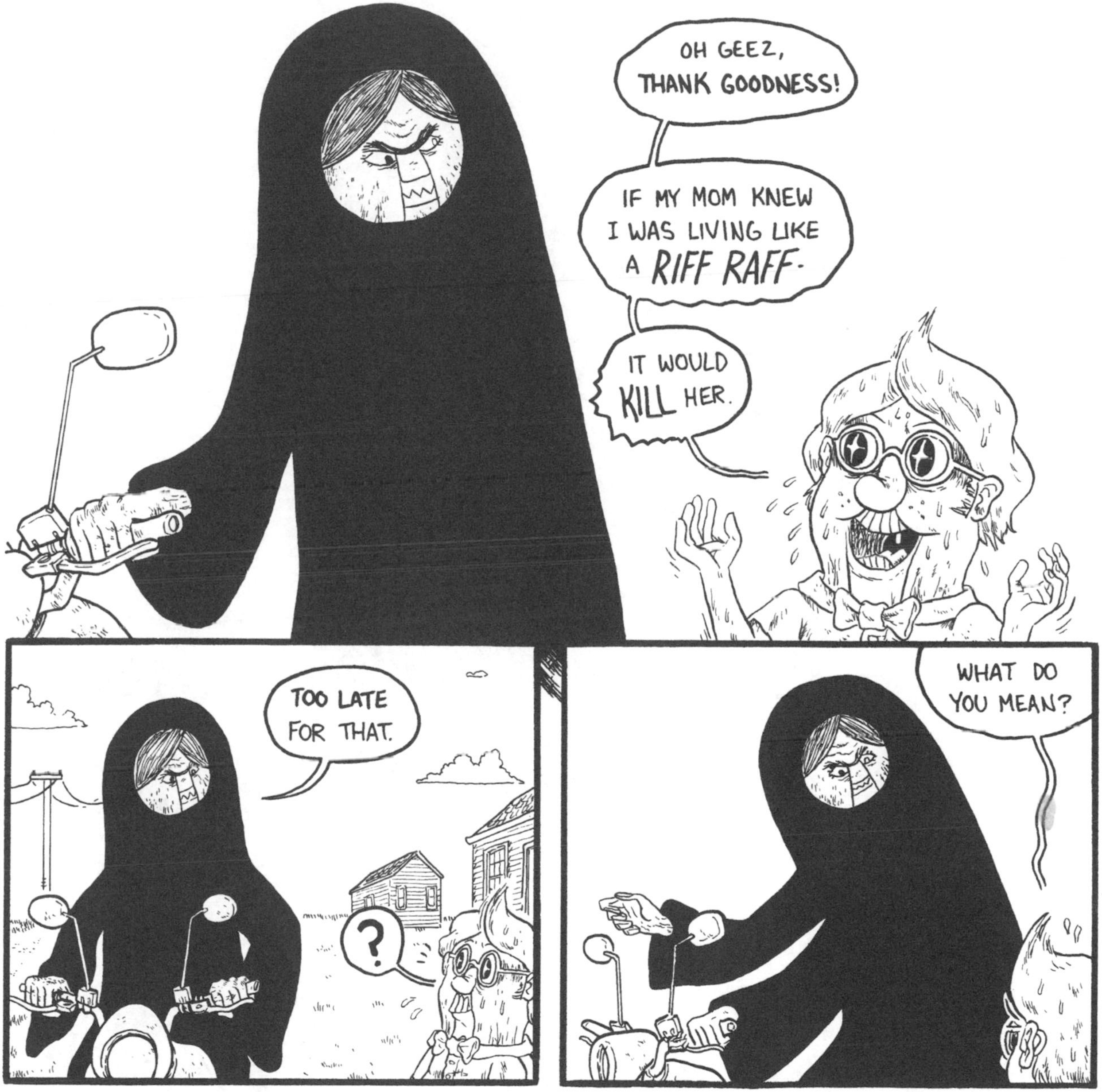
OH GEEZ, THANK GOODNESS!
IF MY MOM KNEW I WAS LIVING LIKE A RIFF RAFF-
IT WOULD KILL HER.
TOO LATE FOR THAT.
?
WHAT DO YOU MEAN?

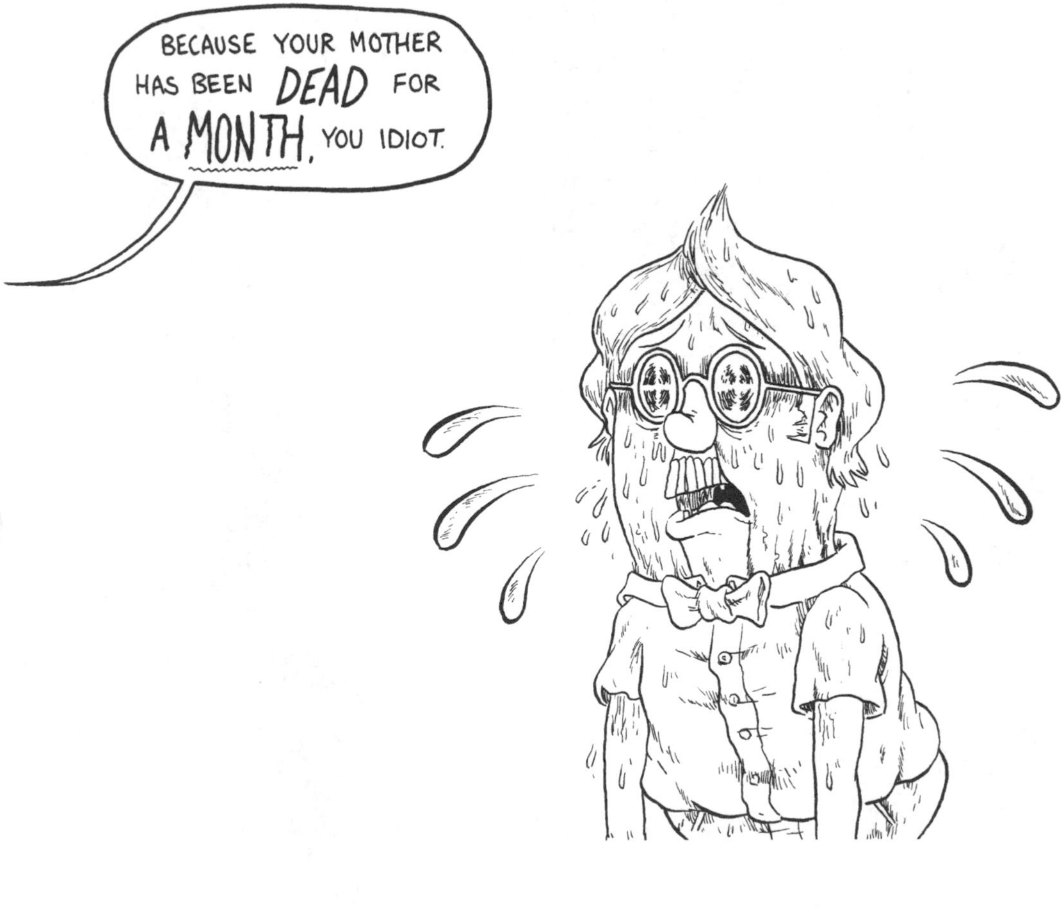
BECAUSE YOUR MOTHER HAS BEEN DEAD FOR A MONTH, YOU IDIOT.

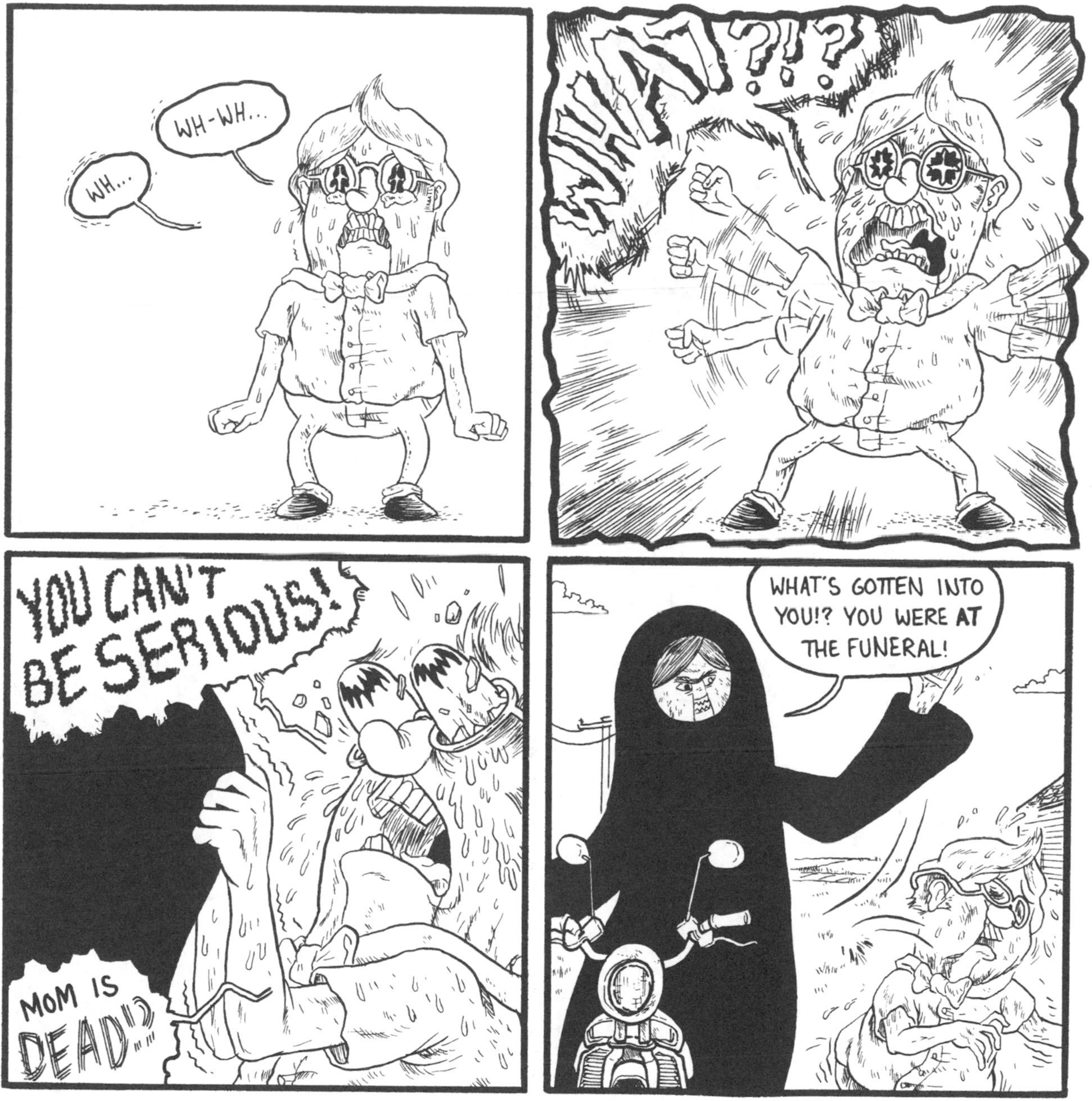
WH...
WH-WH...
WHAT?!?
YOU CAN'T BE SERIOUS!
MOM IS DEAD!?
WHAT'S GOTTEN INTO YOU!? YOU WERE AT THE FUNERAL!

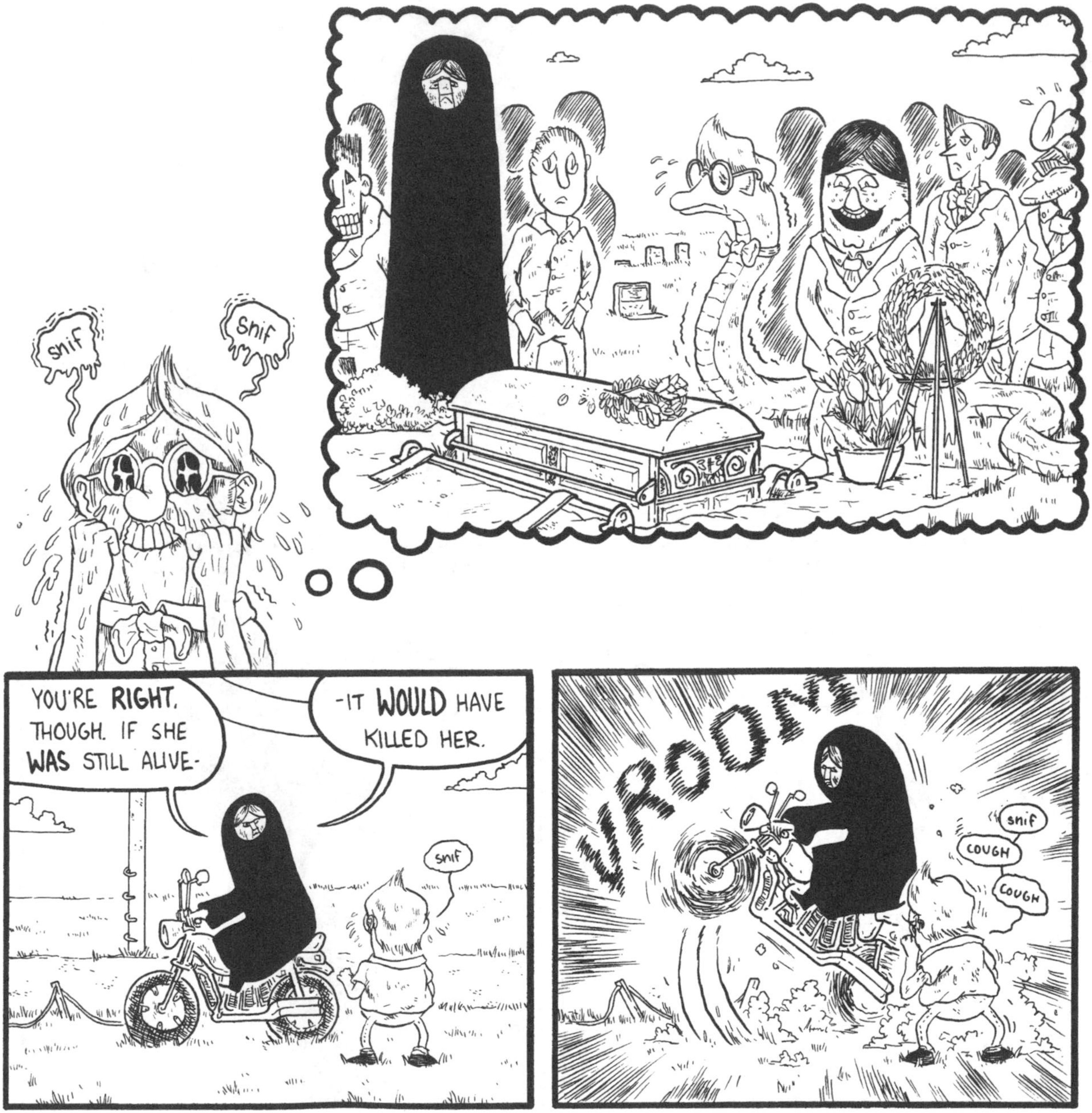
snif
snif
YOU'RE **RIGHT**, THOUGH. IF SHE **WAS** STILL ALIVE-
-IT **WOULD** HAVE KILLED HER.
snif
VROOM
snif
COUGH
COUGH

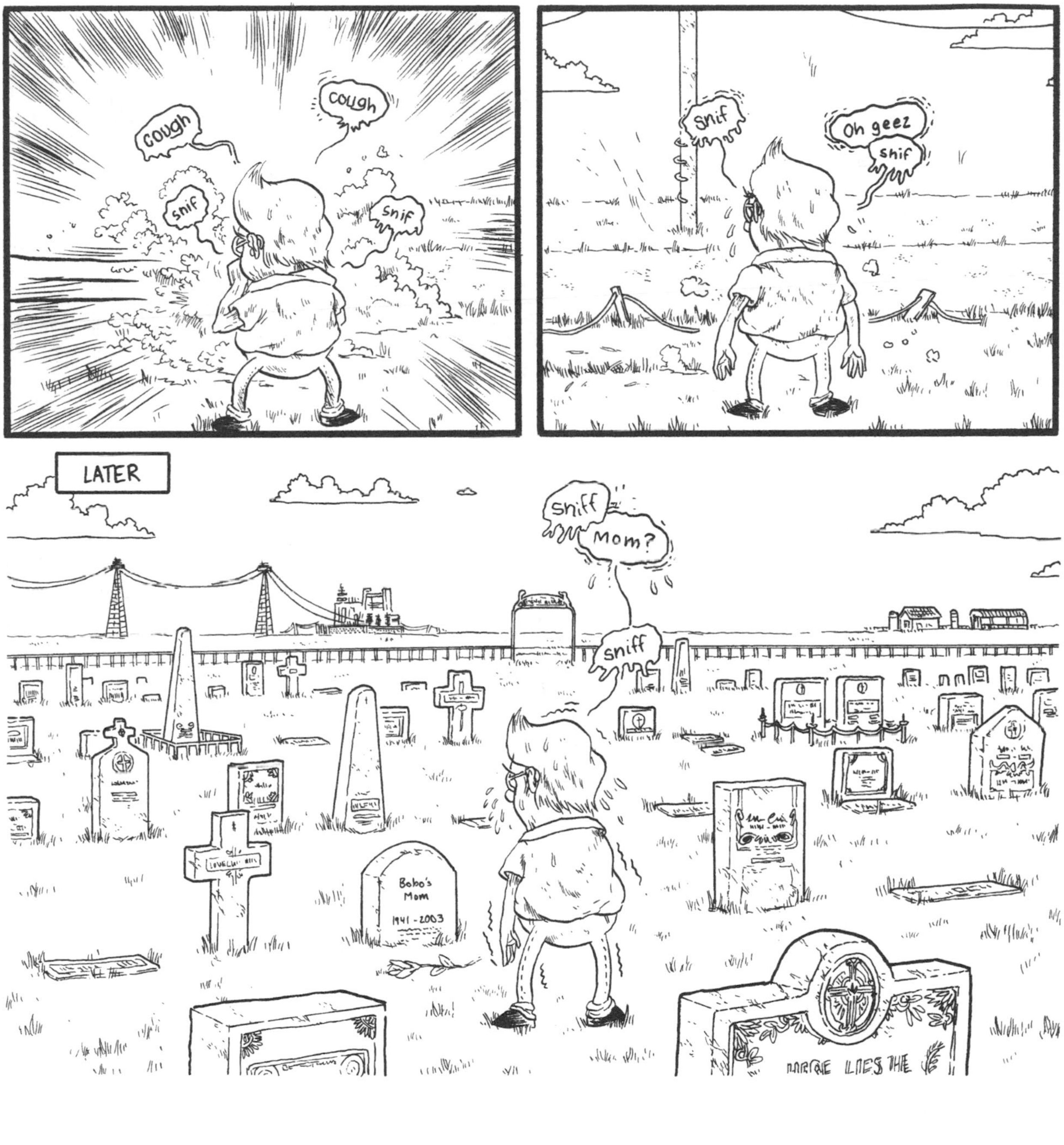
cough
cough
snif
snif
snif
Oh geez
shif
LATER
sniff
Mom?
sniff
Bobo's Mom
1941 - 2003
LIES THE

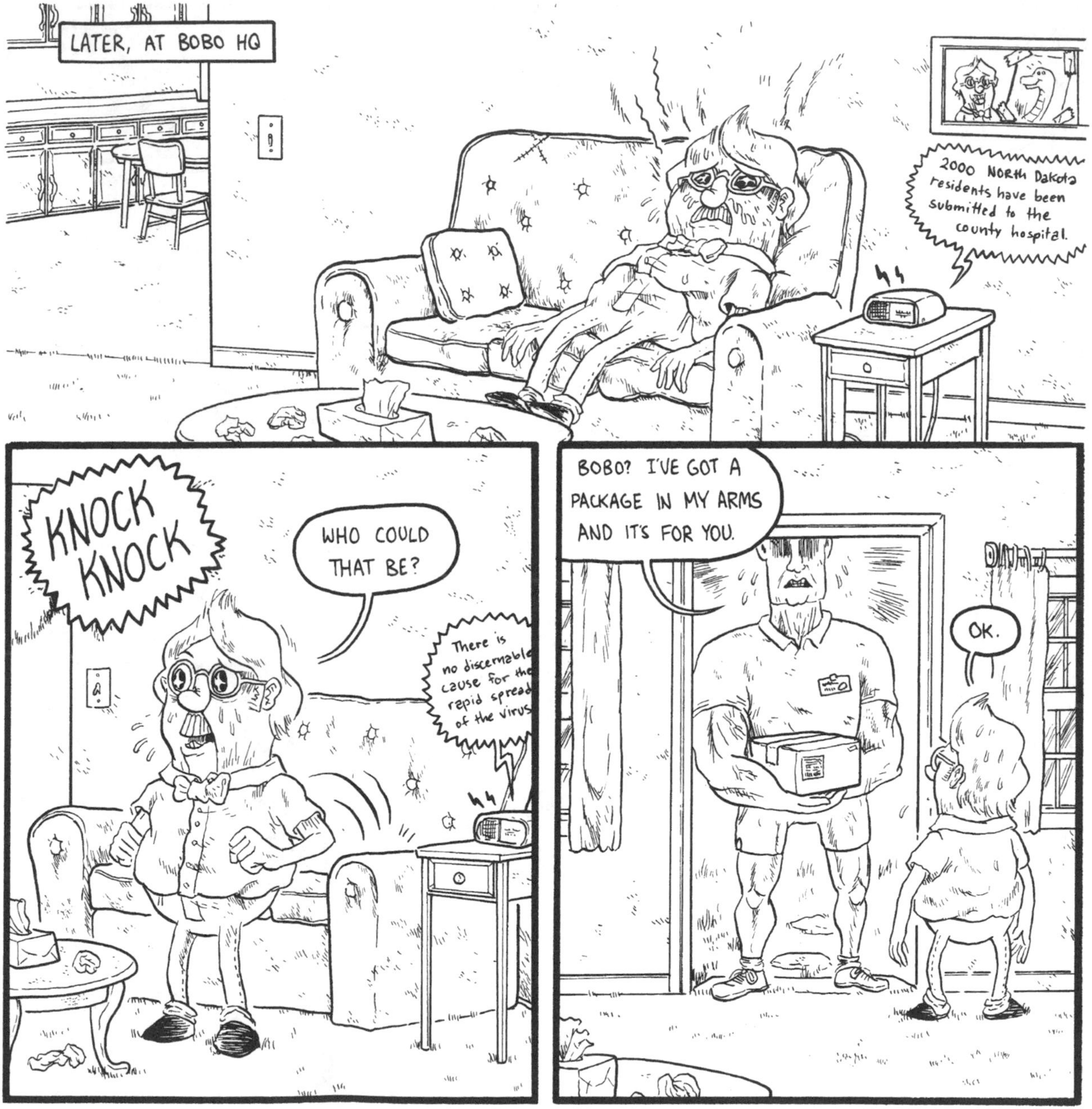
LATER, AT BOBO HQ
2000 NORTH Dakota residents have been submitted to the county hospital.
KNOCK KNOCK
WHO COULD THAT BE?
There is no discernable cause for the rapid spread of the virus.
BOBO? I'VE GOT A PACKAGE IN MY ARMS AND IT'S FOR YOU.
OK.

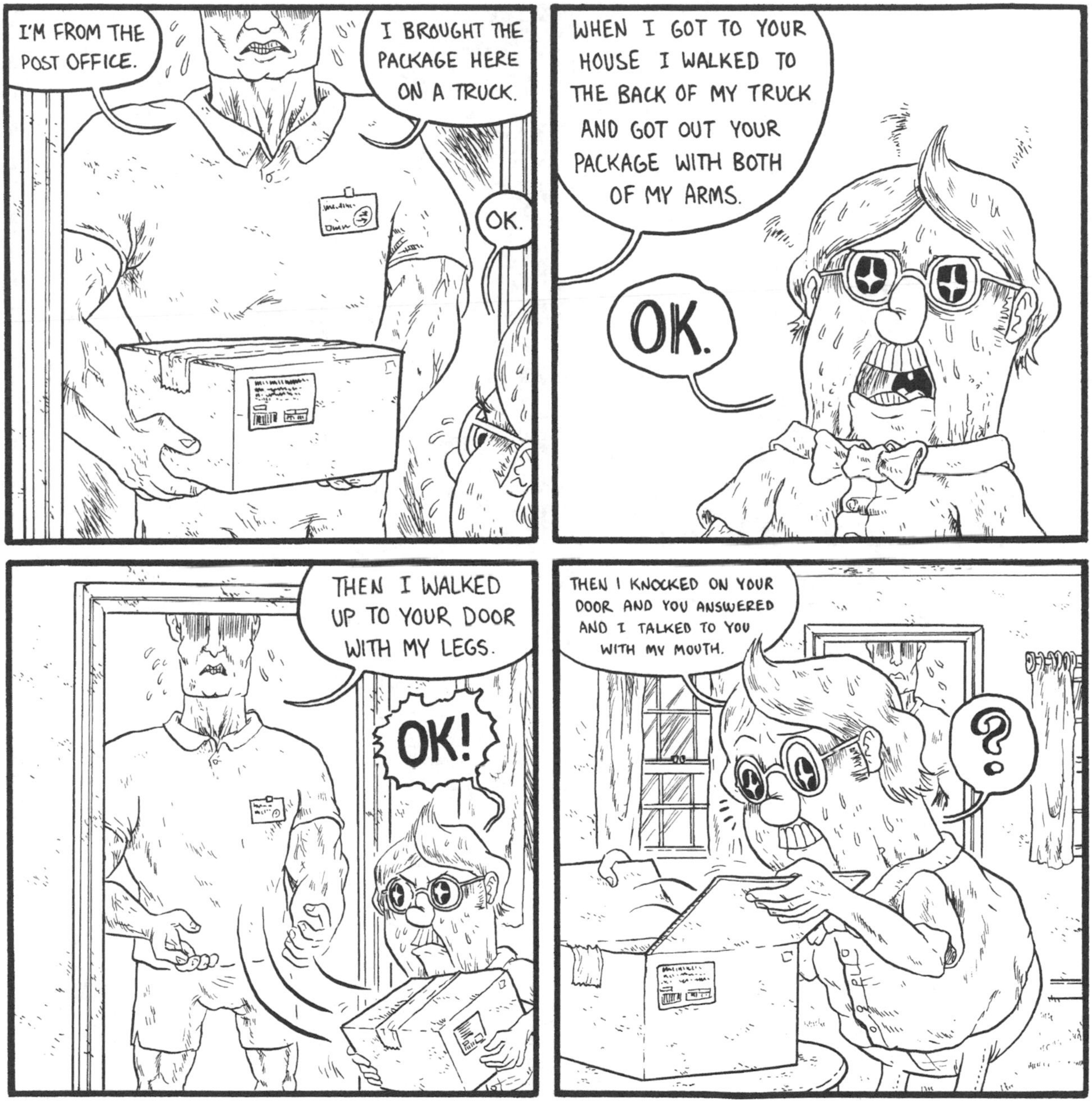
I'M FROM THE POST OFFICE.
I BROUGHT THE PACKAGE HERE ON A TRUCK.
OK.
WHEN I GOT TO YOUR HOUSE I WALKED TO THE BACK OF MY TRUCK AND GOT OUT YOUR PACKAGE WITH BOTH OF MY ARMS.
OK.
THEN I WALKED UP TO YOUR DOOR WITH MY LEGS.
OK!
THEN I KNOCKED ON YOUR DOOR AND YOU ANSWERED AND I TALKED TO YOU WITH MY MOUTH.
?

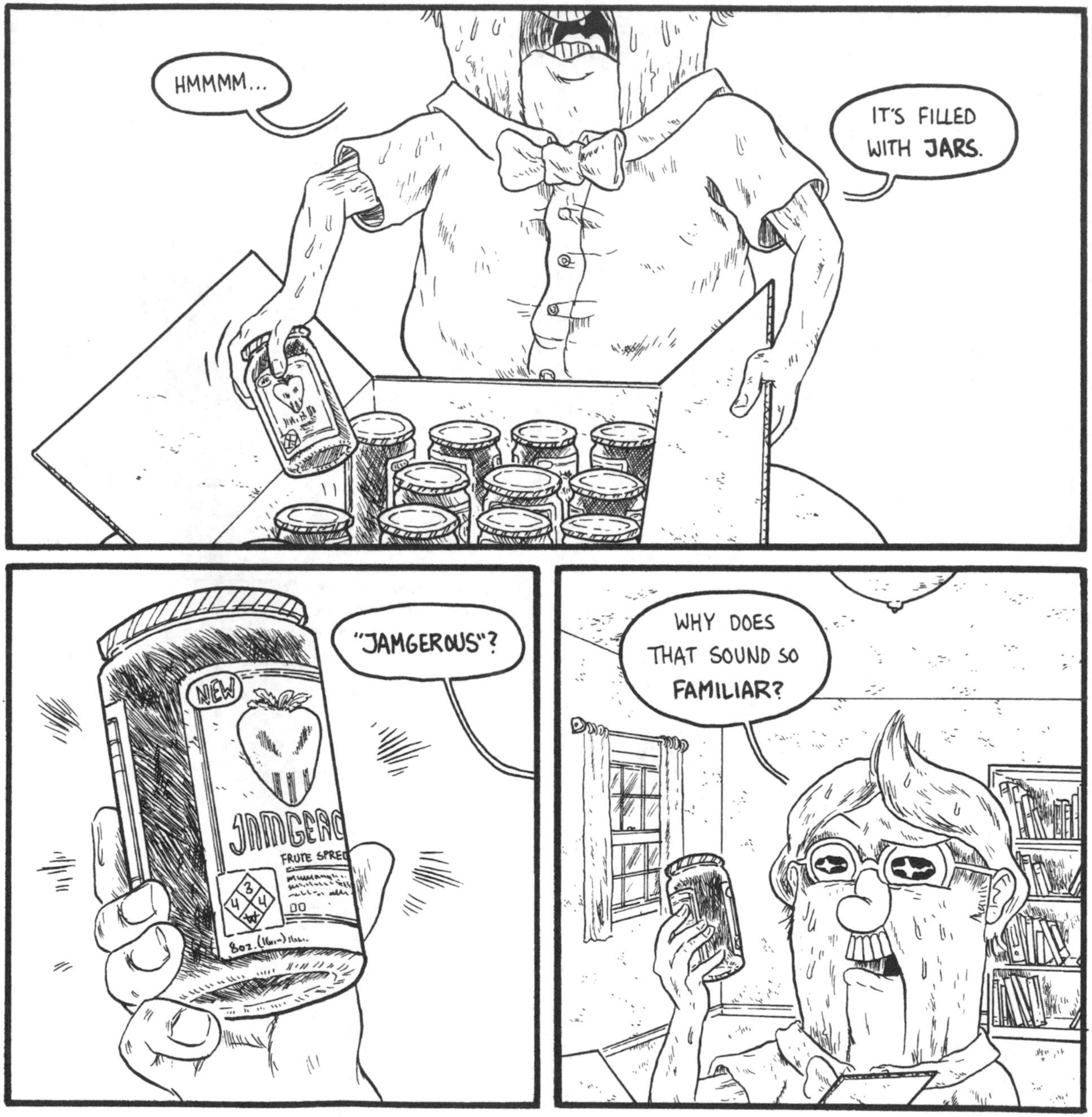
HMMMM...
IT'S FILLED WITH JARS.
NEW
"JAMGEROUS"?
WHY DOES THAT SOUND SO FAMILIAR?

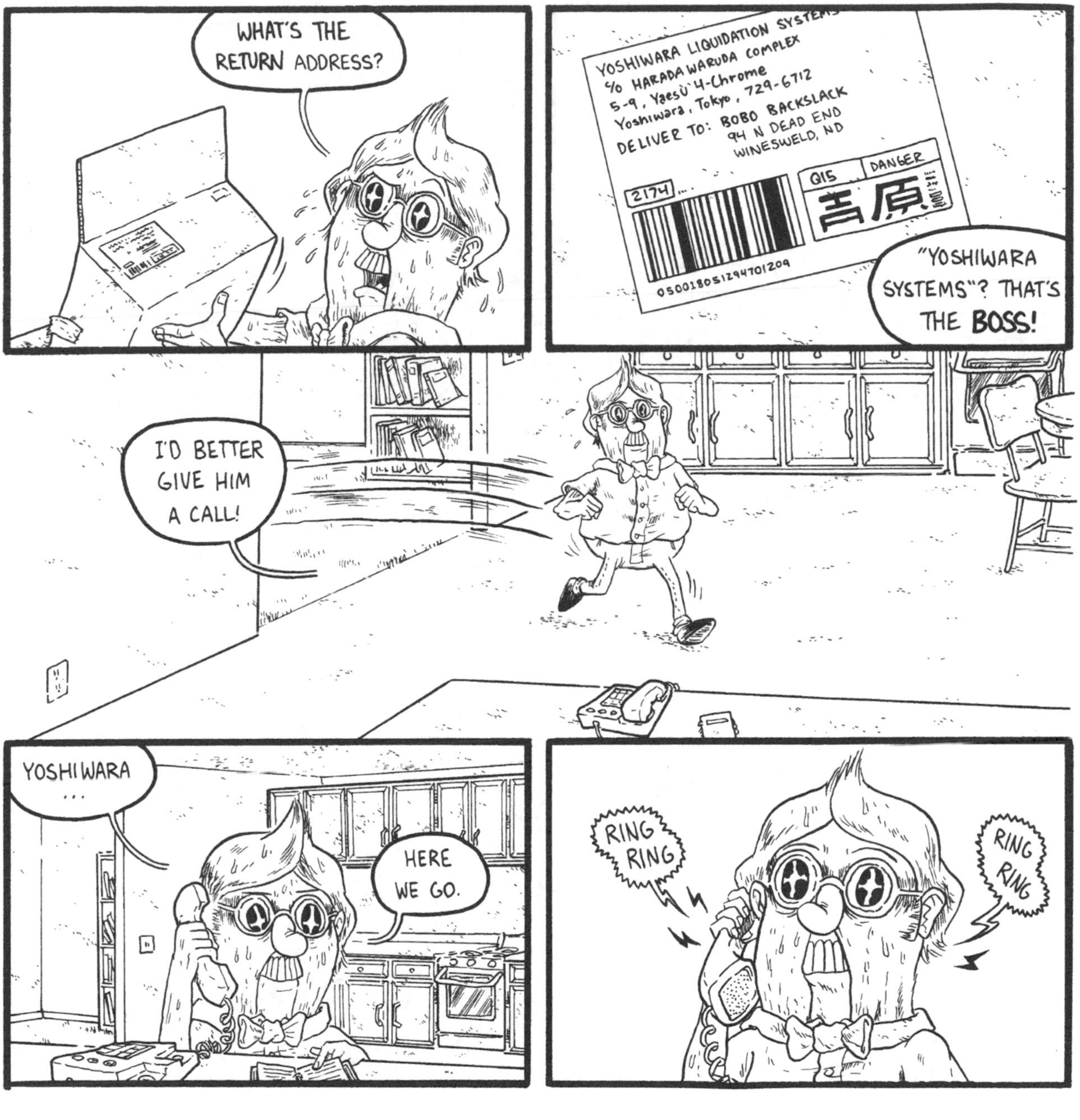
WHAT'S THE RETURN ADDRESS?
YOSHIWARA LIQUIDATION SYSTEMS
℅ HARADA WARUDA COMPLEX
5-9, Yaesù 4-Chrome
Yoshiwara, Tokyo, 729-6712
DELIVER TO: BOBO BACKSLACK
94 N DEAD END
WINESWELD, ND
2174
Q15
DANGER
吉原
050018051294701209
"YOSHIWARA SYSTEMS"? THAT'S THE BOSS!
I'D BETTER GIVE HIM A CALL!
YOSHIWARA ...
HERE WE GO.
RING RING
RING RING

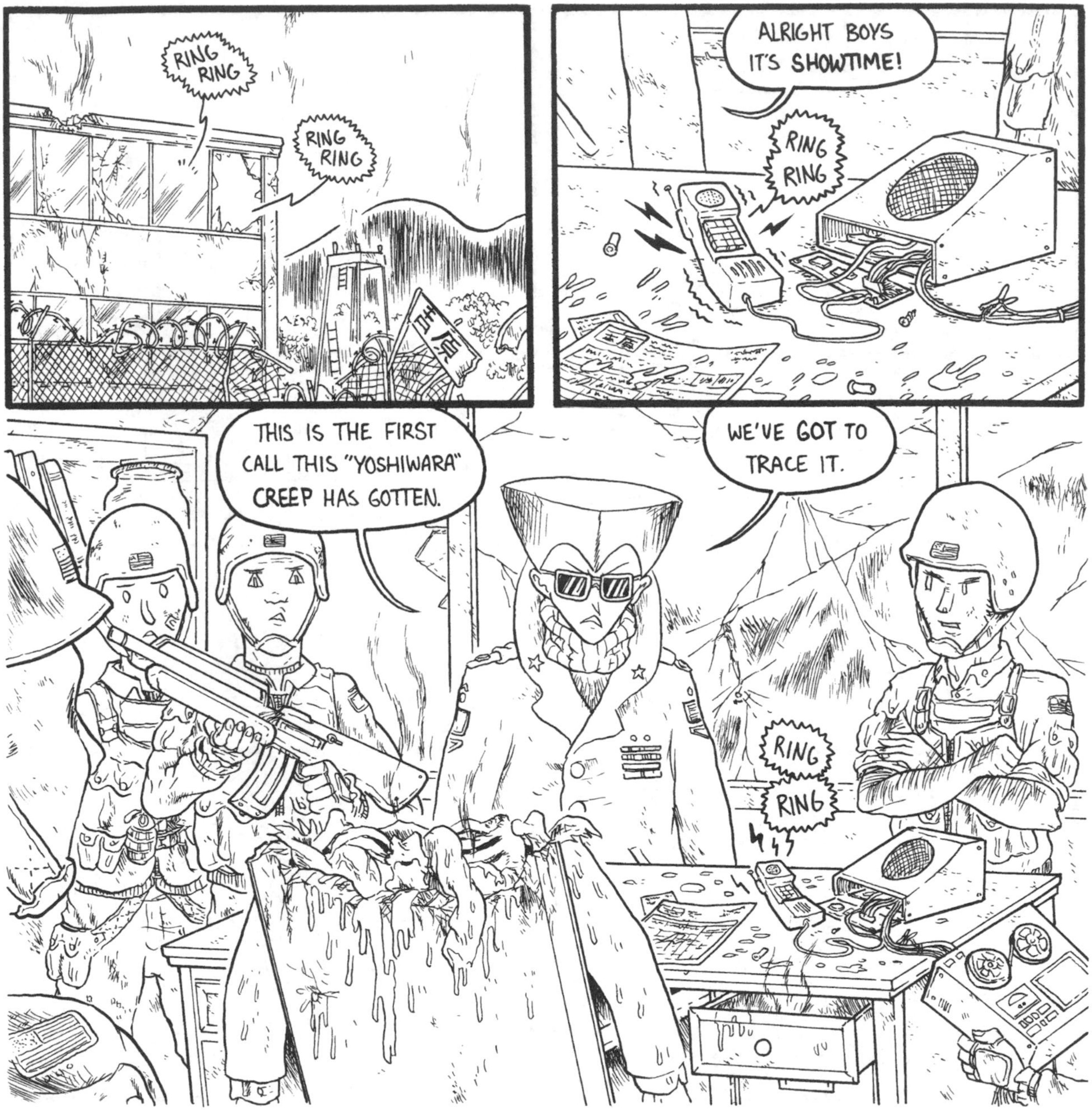
RING RING
RING RING
ALRIGHT BOYS IT'S SHOWTIME!
RING RING
THIS IS THE FIRST CALL THIS "YOSHIWARA" CREEP HAS GOTTEN.
WE'VE GOT TO TRACE IT.
RING
RING

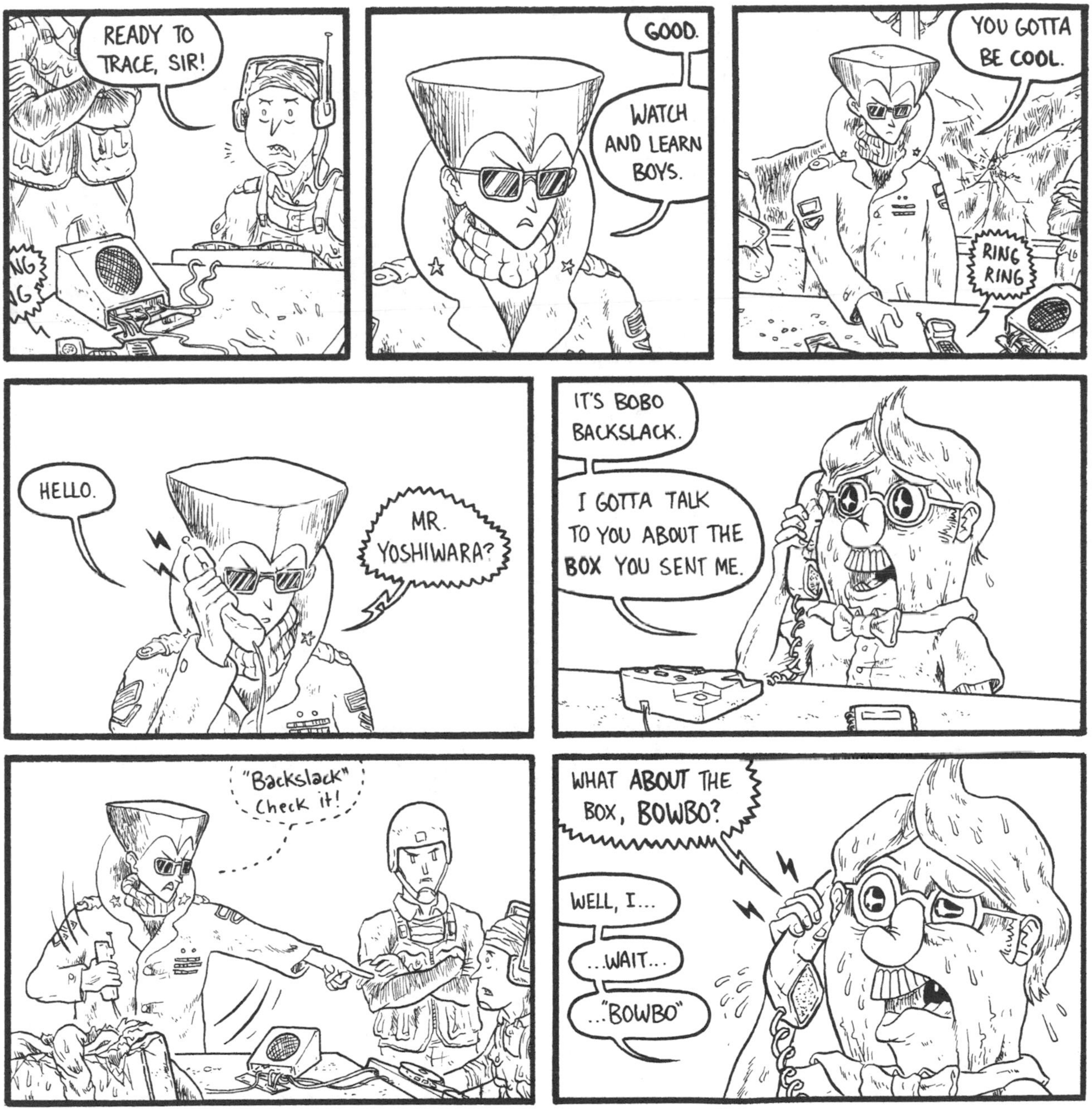
READY TO TRACE, SIR!
GOOD.
WATCH AND LEARN BOYS.
YOU GOTTA BE COOL.
RING RING
HELLO.
MR. YOSHIWARA?
IT'S BOBO BACKSLACK.
I GOTTA TALK TO YOU ABOUT THE BOX YOU SENT ME.
"Backslack" Check it!
WHAT ABOUT THE BOX, BOWBO?
WELL, I...
...WAIT...
..."BOWBO"

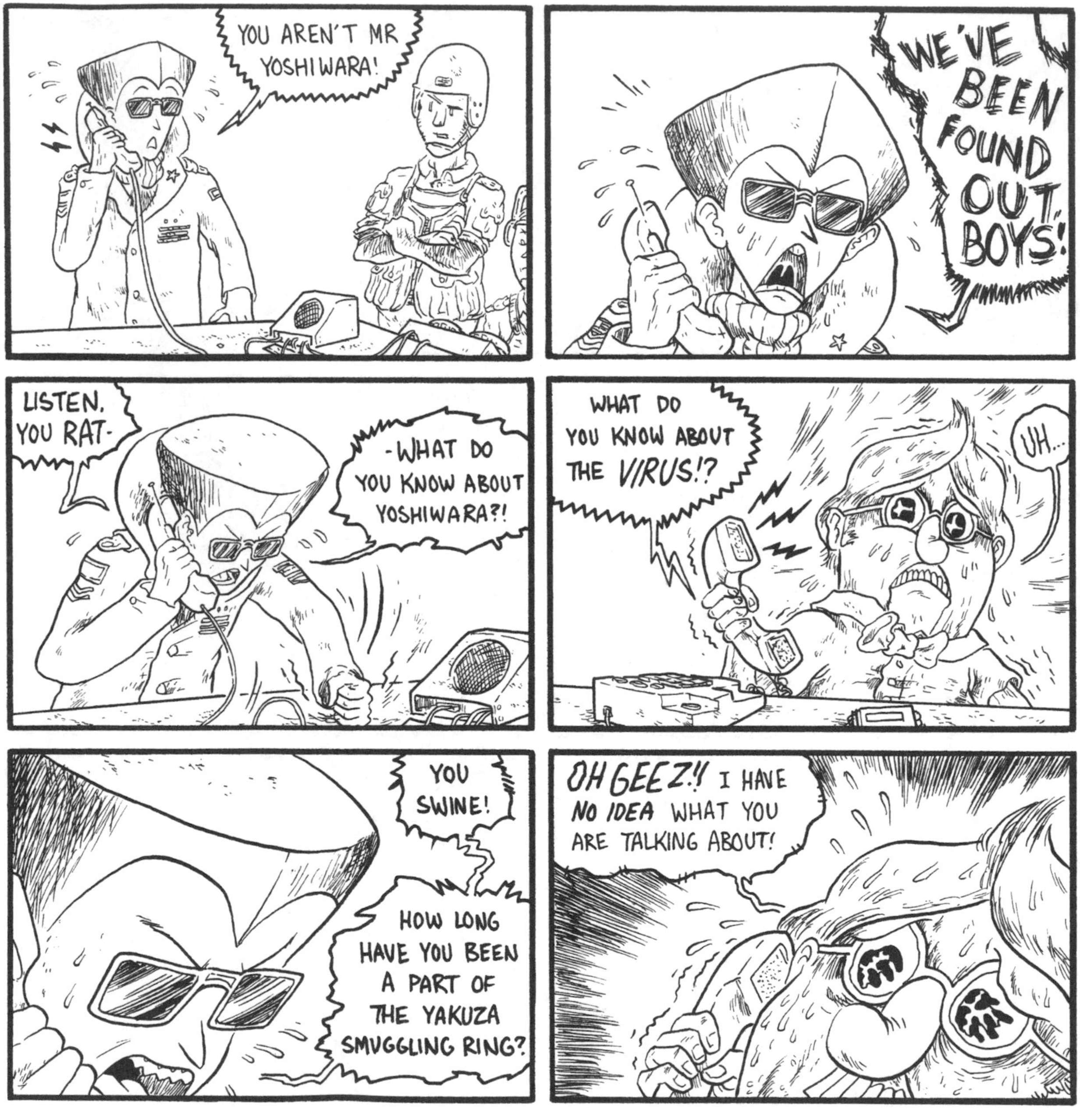
YOU AREN'T MR YOSHIWARA!
WE'VE BEEN FOUND OUT, BOYS!
LISTEN, YOU RAT-
-WHAT DO YOU KNOW ABOUT YOSHIWARA?!
WHAT DO YOU KNOW ABOUT THE VIRUS!?
UH...
YOU SWINE!
HOW LONG HAVE YOU BEEN A PART OF THE YAKUZA SMUGGLING RING?
OH GEEZ!! I HAVE NO IDEA WHAT YOU ARE TALKING ABOUT!

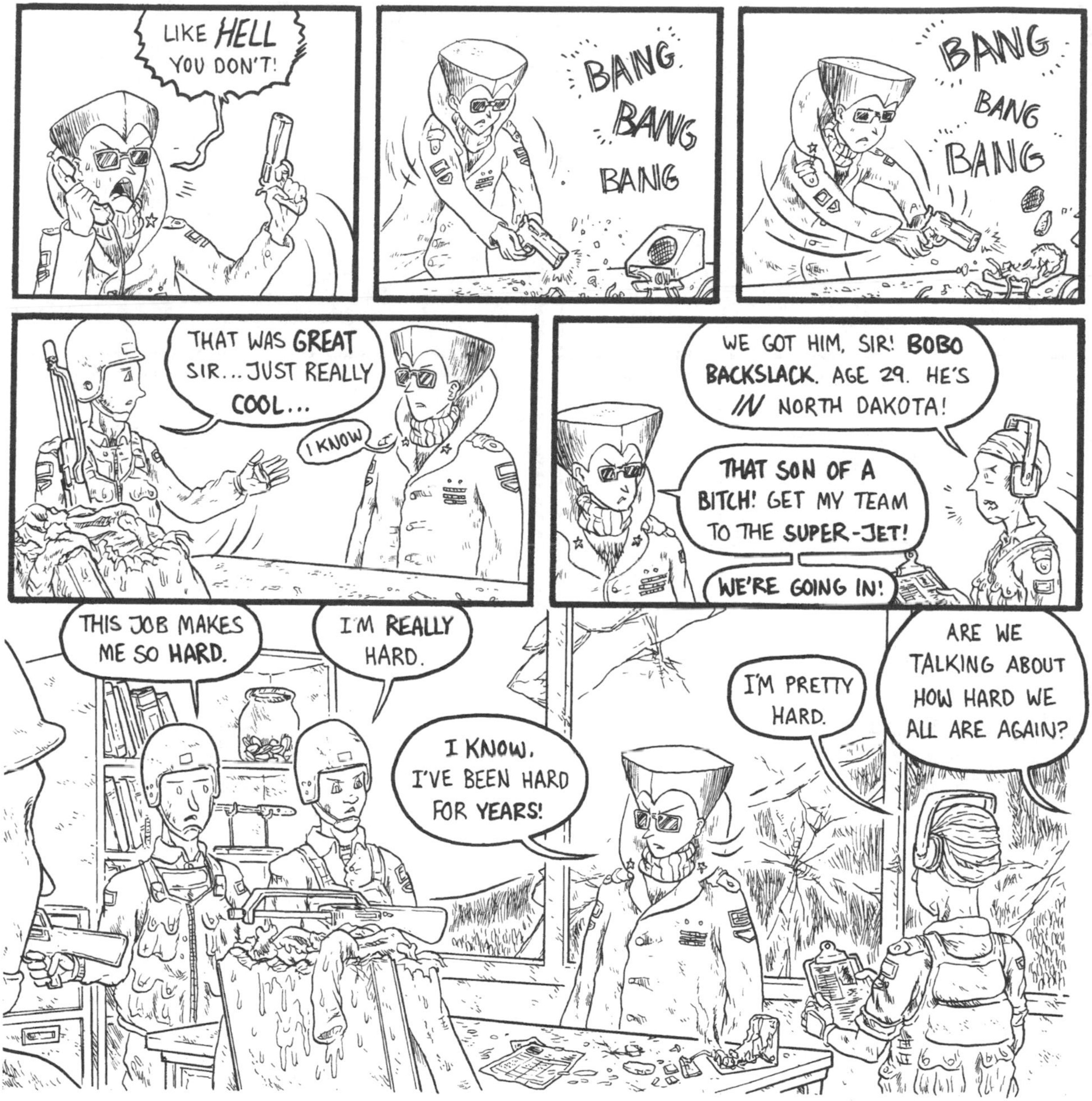
LIKE HELL YOU DON'T!
BANG BANG BANG
BANG BANG BANG
THAT WAS GREAT SIR... JUST REALLY COOL...
I KNOW
WE GOT HIM, SIR! BOBO BACKSLACK. AGE 29. HE'S IN NORTH DAKOTA!
THAT SON OF A BITCH! GET MY TEAM TO THE SUPER-JET!
WE'RE GOING IN!
THIS JOB MAKES ME SO HARD.
I'M REALLY HARD.
I KNOW. I'VE BEEN HARD FOR YEARS!
I'M PRETTY HARD.
ARE WE TALKING ABOUT HOW HARD WE ALL ARE AGAIN?

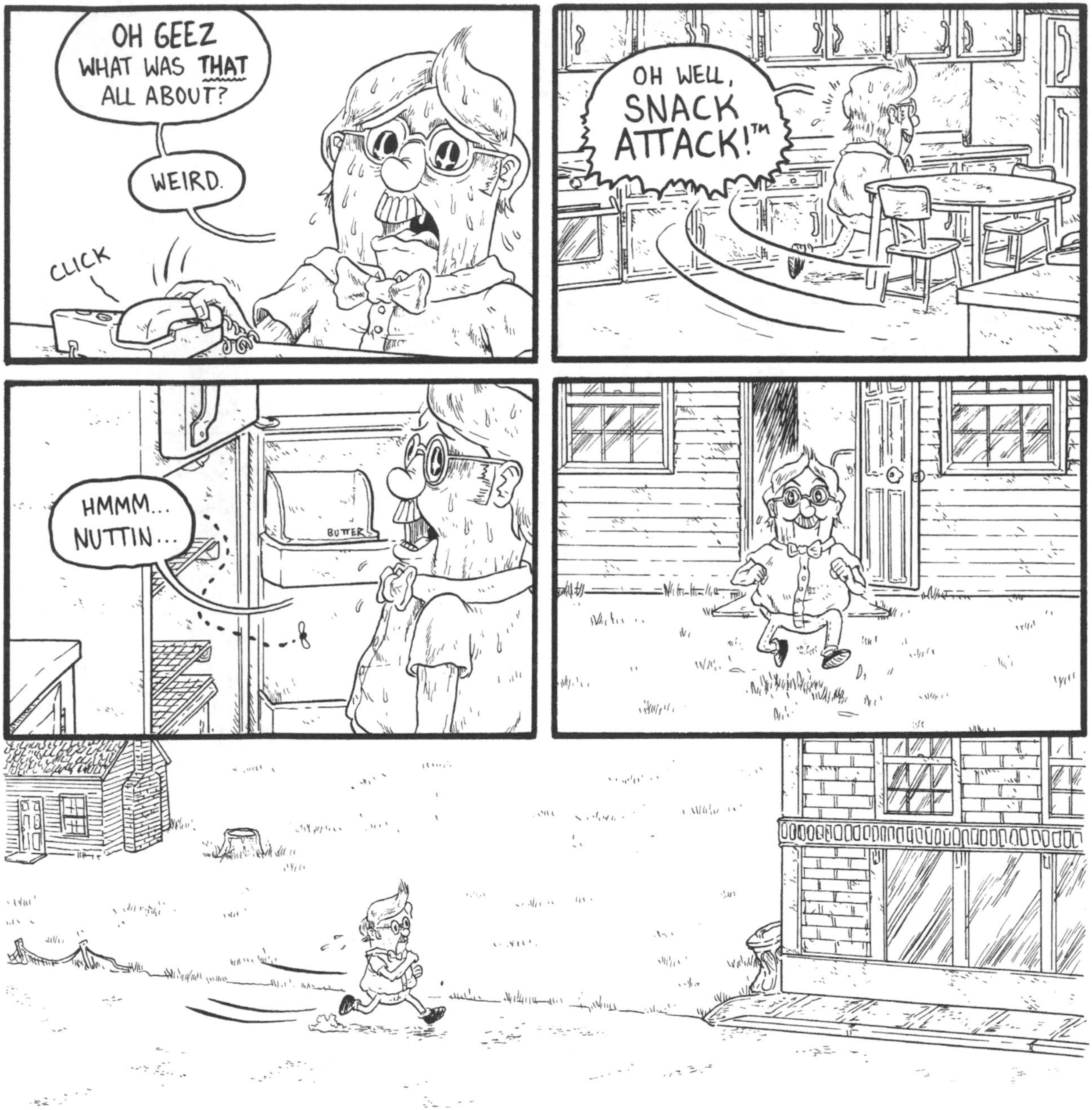
OH GEEZ
WHAT WAS THAT ALL ABOUT?
WEIRD.
CLICK
OH WELL,
SNACK ATTACK!™
HMMM...
NUTTIN...
BUTTER

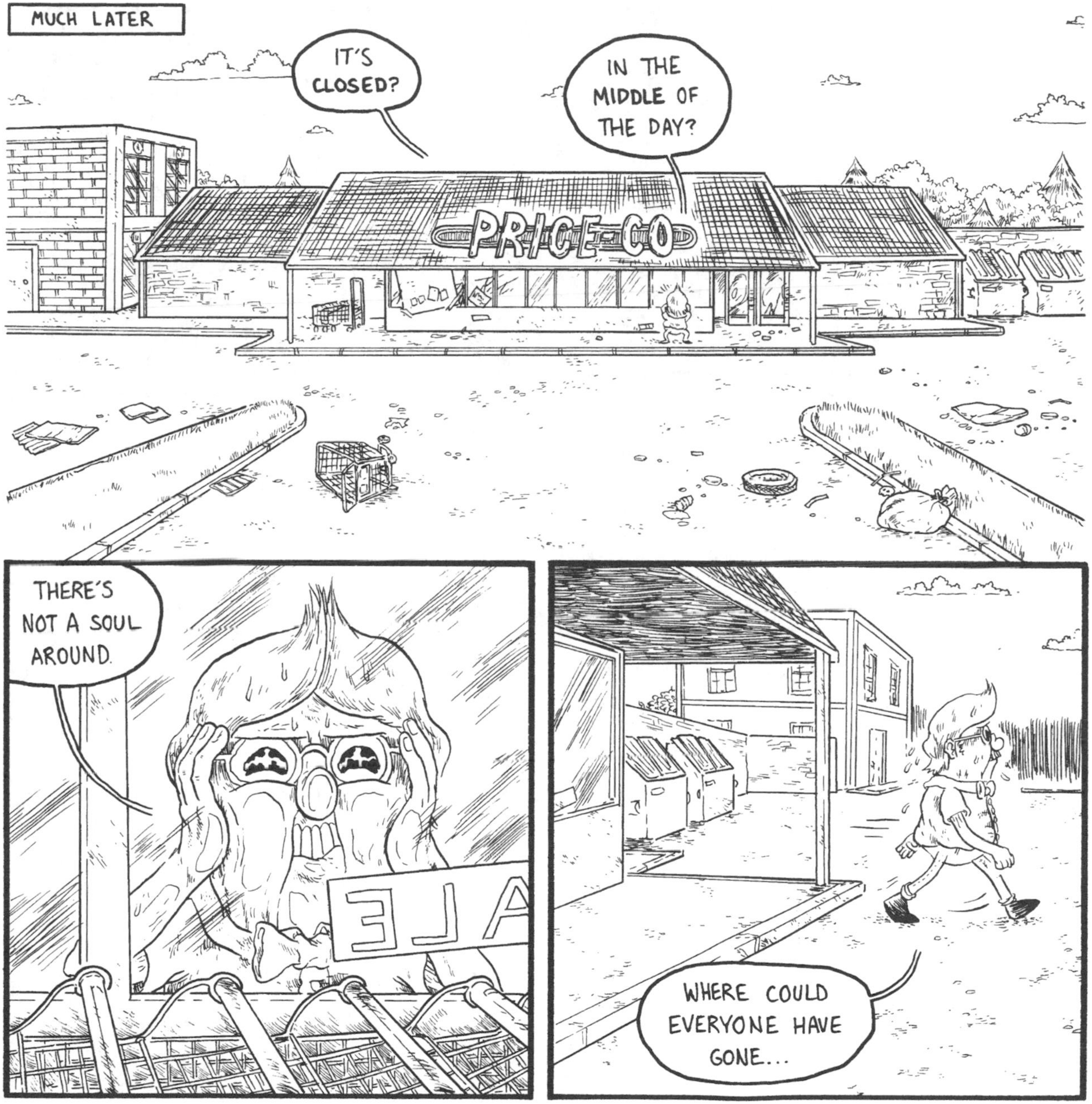
MUCH LATER
IT'S CLOSED?
IN THE MIDDLE OF THE DAY?
PRICE-CO
THERE'S NOT A SOUL AROUND.
WHERE COULD EVERYONE HAVE GONE...

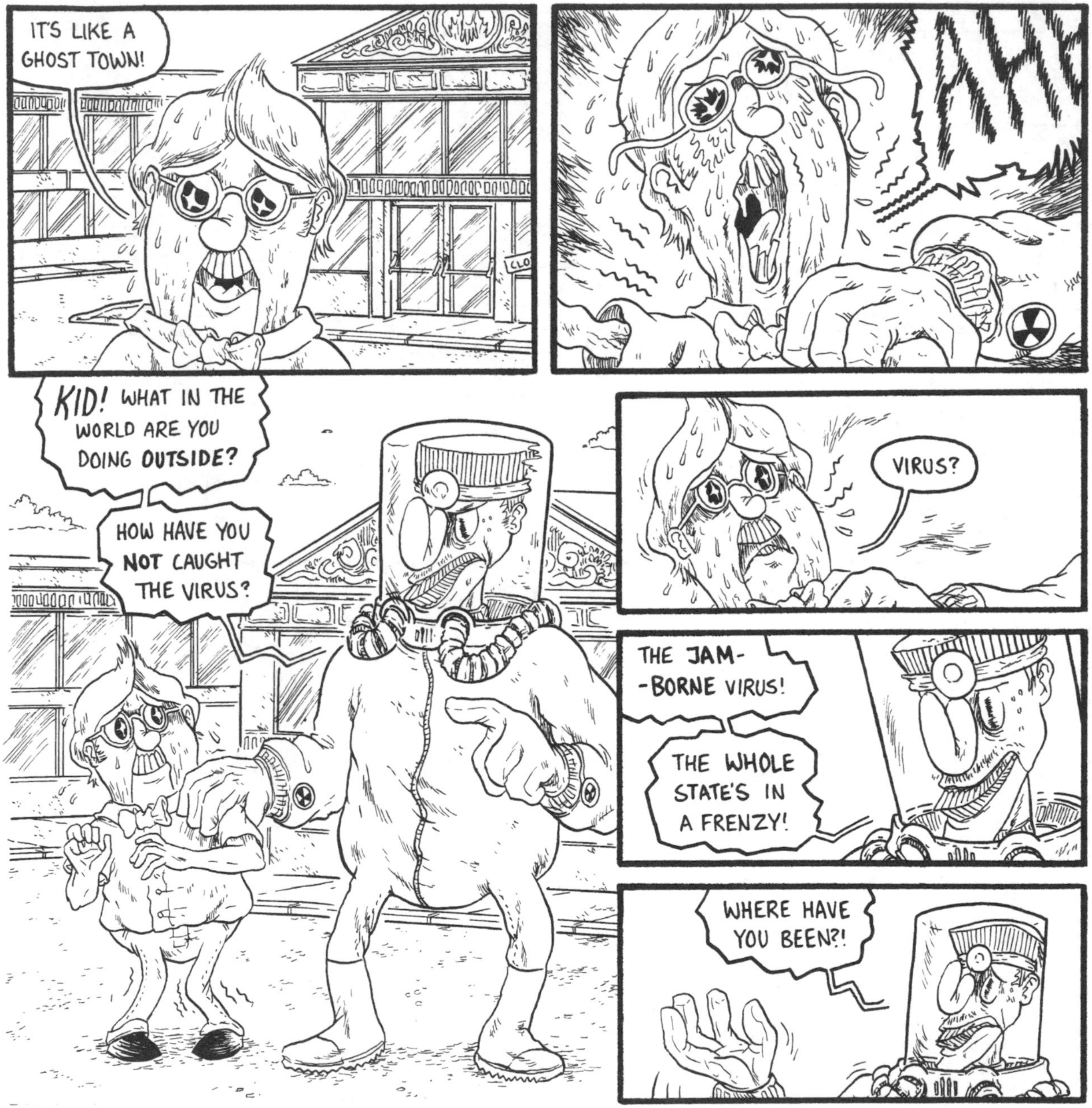
IT'S LIKE A GHOST TOWN!
AHH
KID! WHAT IN THE WORLD ARE YOU DOING **OUTSIDE**?
HOW HAVE YOU **NOT** CAUGHT THE VIRUS?
VIRUS?
THE **JAM-**
-BORNE VIRUS!
THE **WHOLE** STATE'S IN A FRENZY!
WHERE HAVE YOU BEEN?!

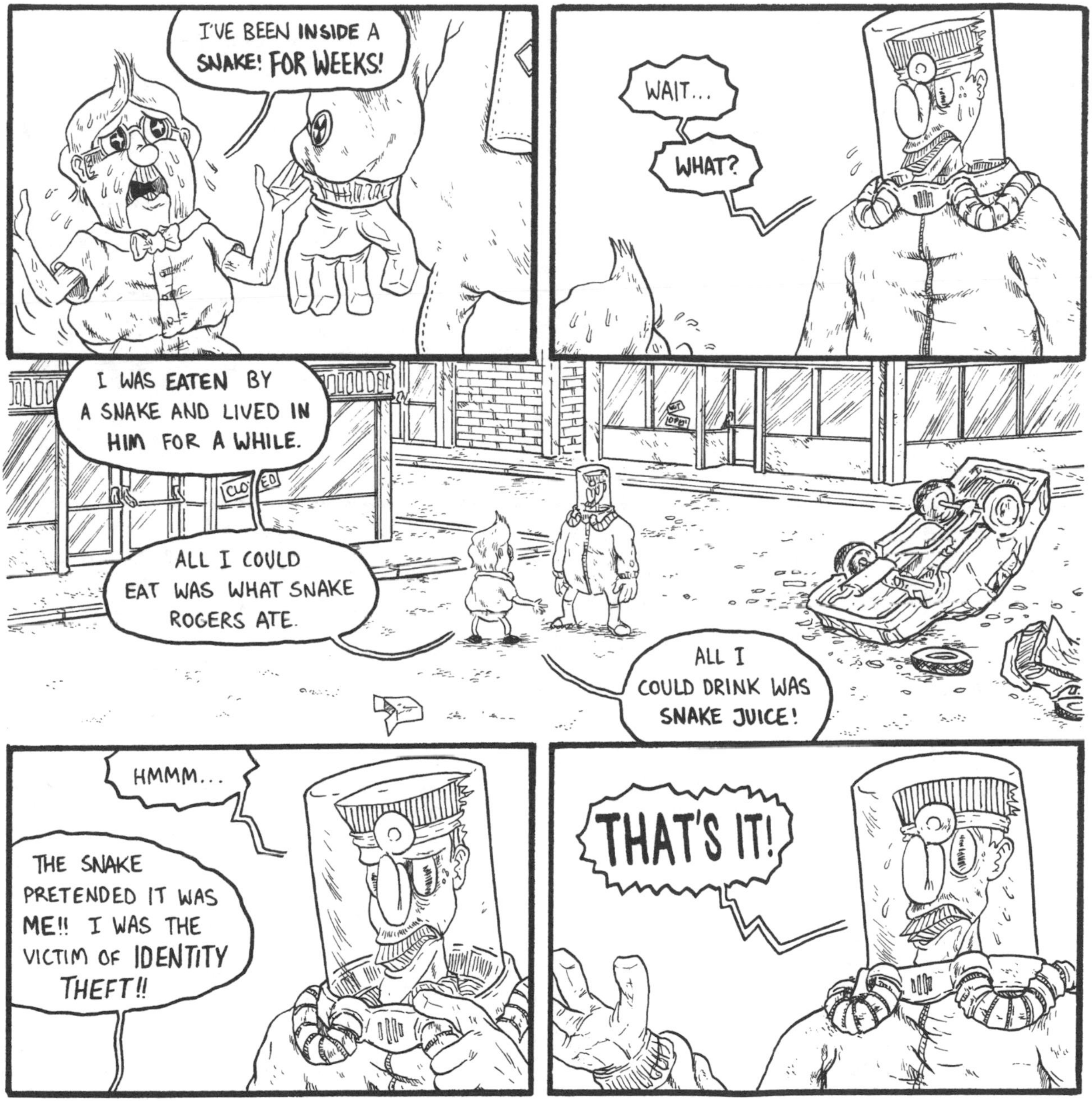
I'VE BEEN INSIDE A SNAKE! FOR WEEKS!
WAIT...
WHAT?
I WAS EATEN BY A SNAKE AND LIVED IN HIM FOR A WHILE.
ALL I COULD EAT WAS WHAT SNAKE ROGERS ATE.
ALL I COULD DRINK WAS SNAKE JUICE!
HMMM...
THE SNAKE PRETENDED IT WAS ME!! I WAS THE VICTIM OF IDENTITY THEFT!!
THAT'S IT!

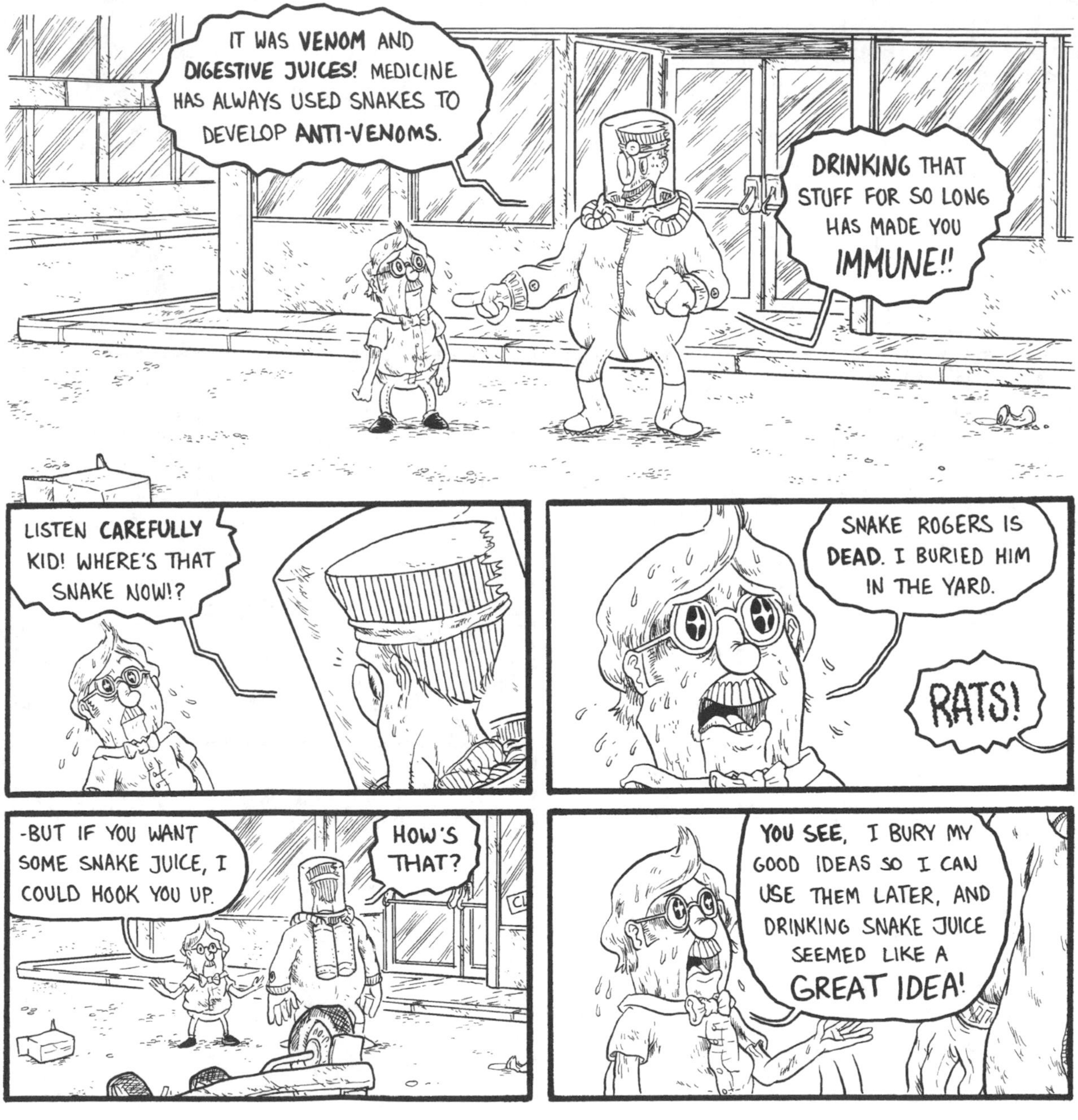
IT WAS VENOM AND DIGESTIVE JUICES! MEDICINE HAS ALWAYS USED SNAKES TO DEVELOP ANTI-VENOMS.
DRINKING THAT STUFF FOR SO LONG HAS MADE YOU IMMUNE!!
LISTEN CAREFULLY KID! WHERE'S THAT SNAKE NOW!?
SNAKE ROGERS IS DEAD. I BURIED HIM IN THE YARD.
RATS!
-BUT IF YOU WANT SOME SNAKE JUICE, I COULD HOOK YOU UP.
HOW'S THAT?
YOU SEE, I BURY MY GOOD IDEAS SO I CAN USE THEM LATER, AND DRINKING SNAKE JUICE SEEMED LIKE A GREAT IDEA!

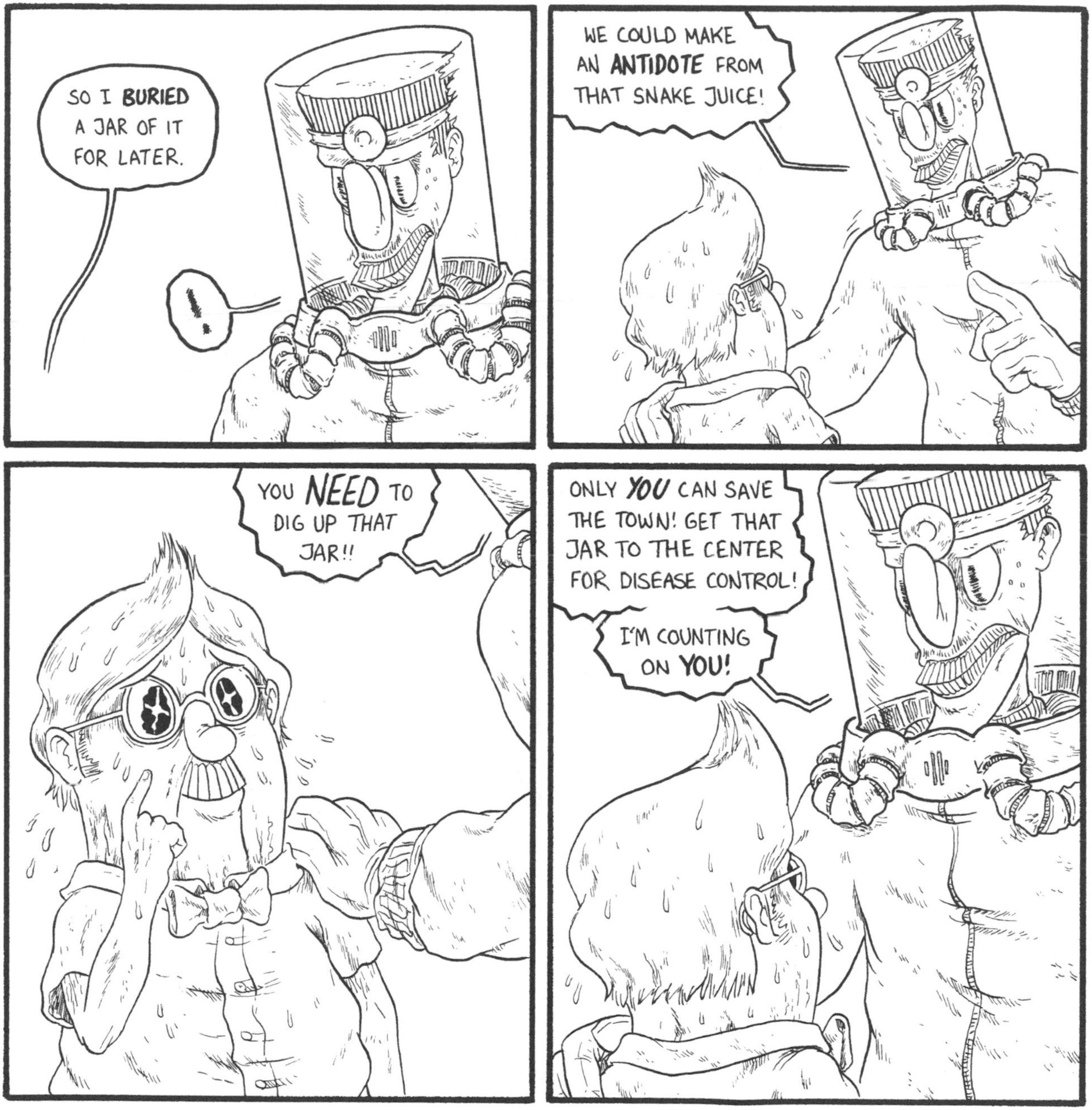
SO I BURIED A JAR OF IT FOR LATER.
WE COULD MAKE AN ANTIDOTE FROM THAT SNAKE JUICE!
YOU NEED TO DIG UP THAT JAR!!
ONLY YOU CAN SAVE THE TOWN! GET THAT JAR TO THE CENTER FOR DISEASE CONTROL!
I'M COUNTING ON YOU!

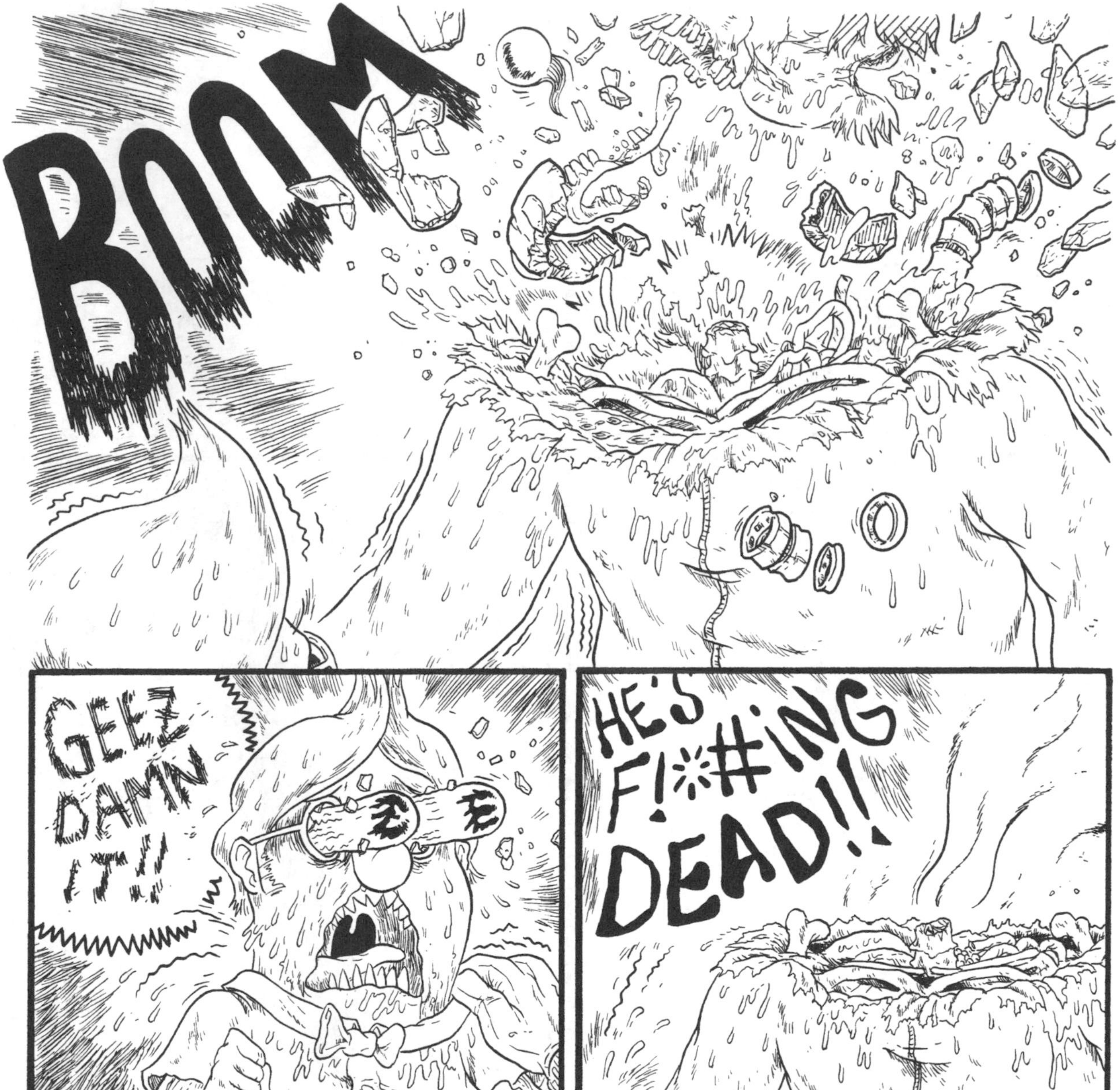
BOOM
GEEZ DAMN IT!!
HE'S F!*#ING DEAD!!

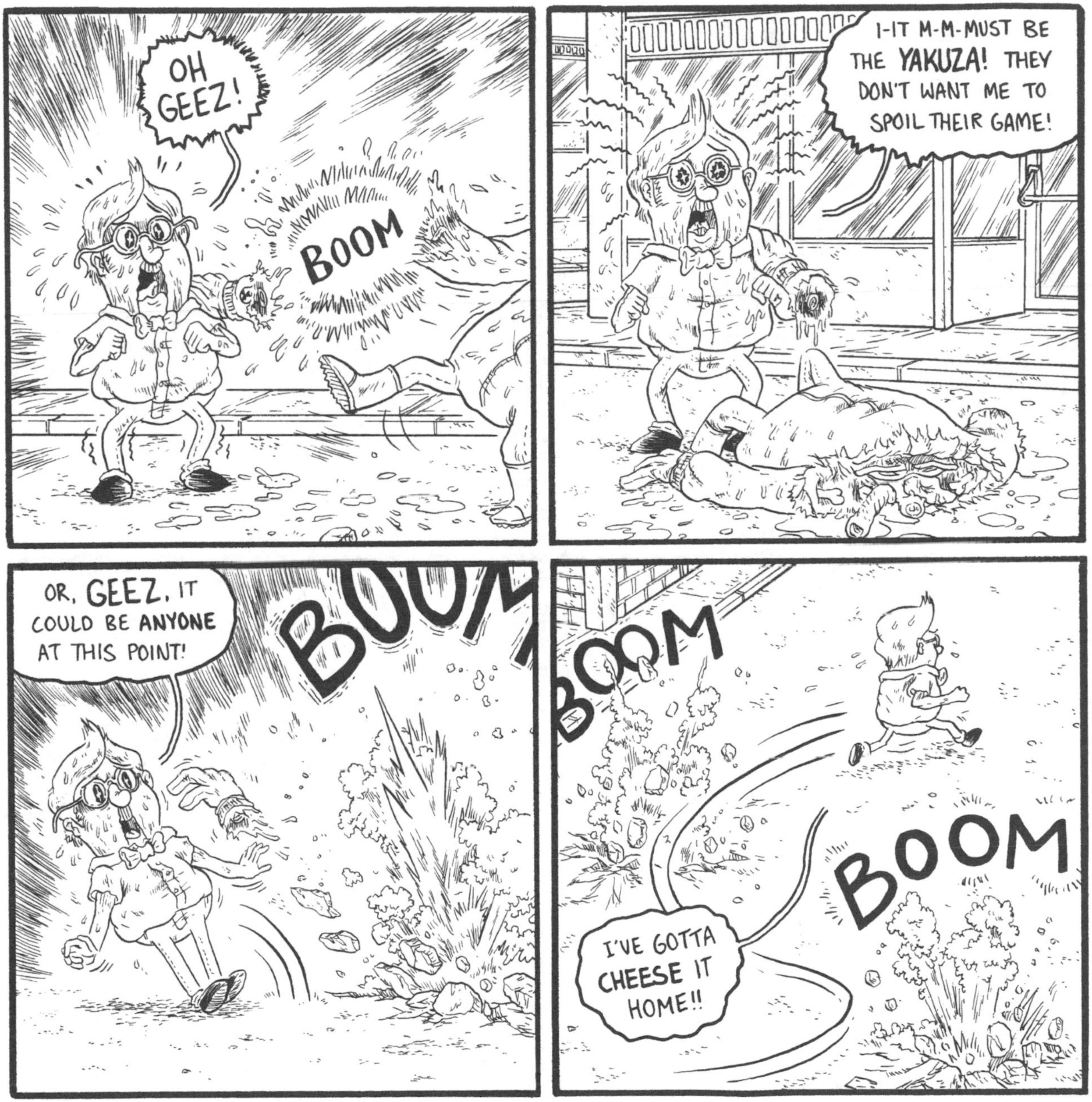
OH GEEZ!
BOOM
I-IT M-M-MUST BE THE YAKUZA! THEY DON'T WANT ME TO SPOIL THEIR GAME!
OR, GEEZ, IT COULD BE ANYONE AT THIS POINT!
BOOM
BOOM
BOOM
I'VE GOTTA CHEESE IT HOME!!

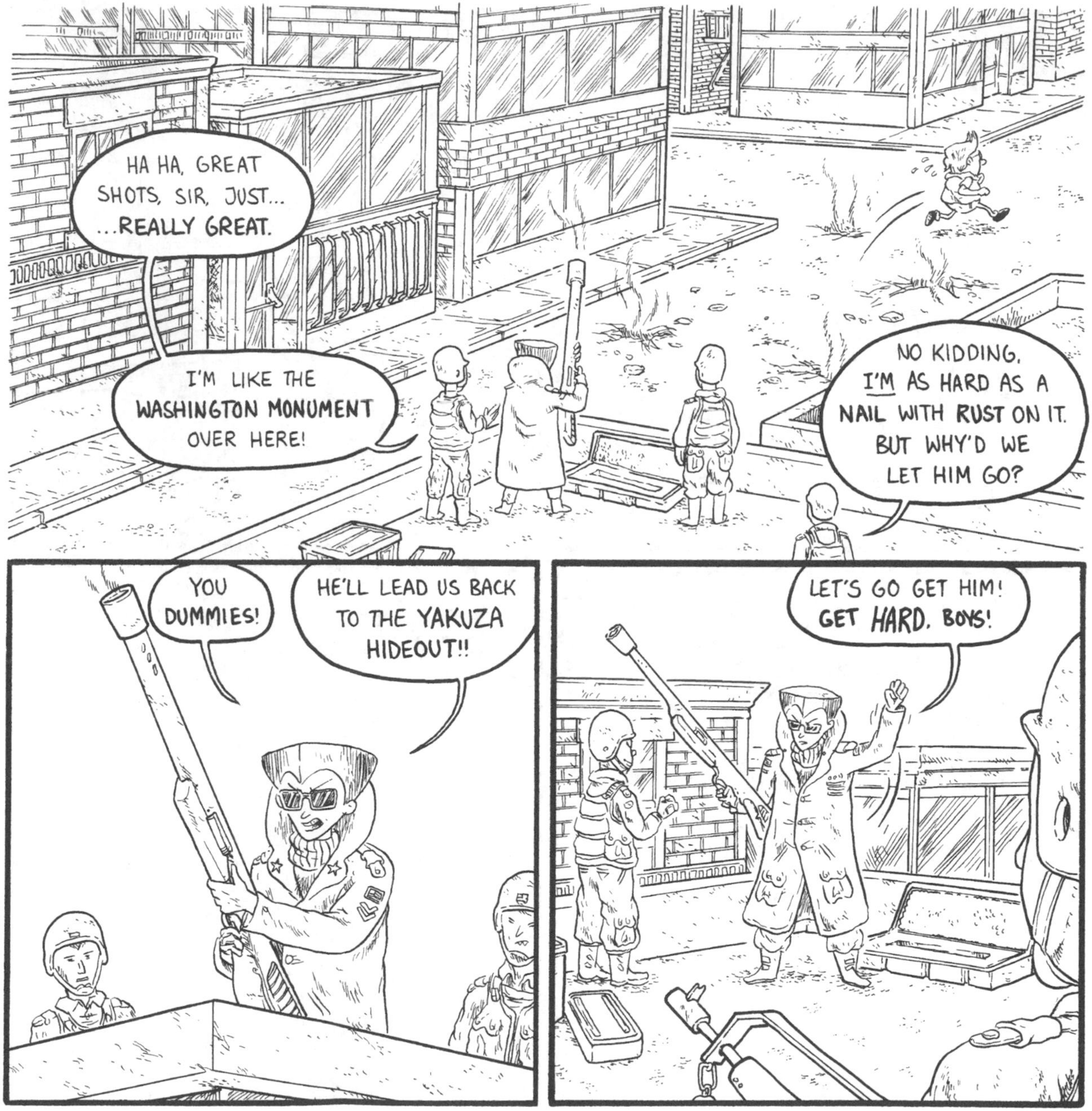
HA HA, GREAT SHOTS, SIR, JUST... ...REALLY GREAT.
I'M LIKE THE WASHINGTON MONUMENT OVER HERE!
NO KIDDING. I'M AS HARD AS A NAIL WITH RUST ON IT. BUT WHY'D WE LET HIM GO?
YOU DUMMIES!
HE'LL LEAD US BACK TO THE YAKUZA HIDEOUT!!
LET'S GO GET HIM! GET HARD, BOYS!

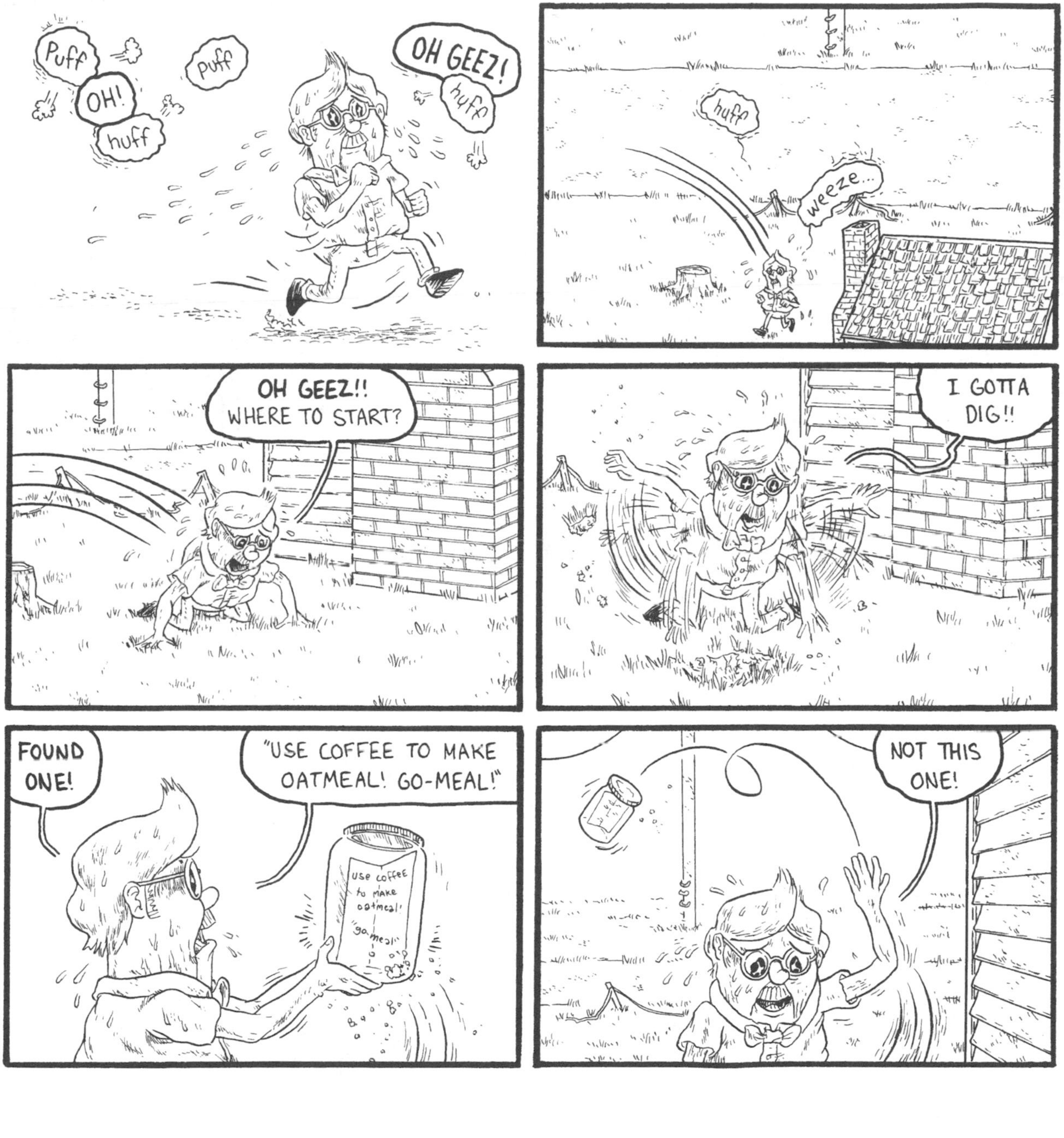
Puff
OH!
huff
puff
OH GEEZ!
huff
huff
weeze...
OH GEEZ!! WHERE TO START?
I GOTTA DIG!!
FOUND ONE!
"USE COFFEE TO MAKE OATMEAL! GO-MEAL!"
use coffee to make oatmeal! "go-meal"
NOT THIS ONE!

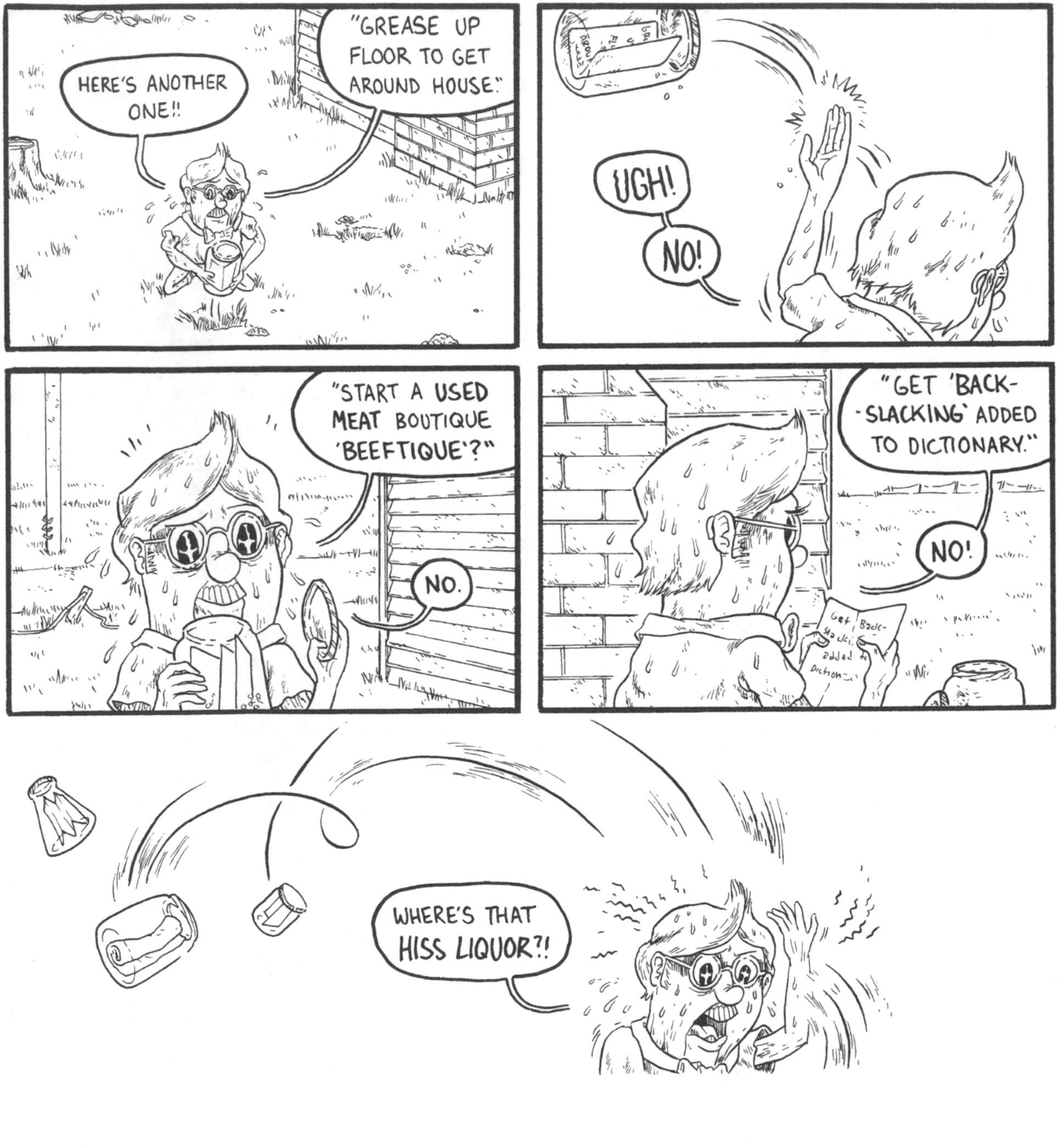
HERE'S ANOTHER ONE!!
"GREASE UP FLOOR TO GET AROUND HOUSE."
UGH!
NO!
"START A USED MEAT BOUTIQUE 'BEEFTIQUE'?"
NO.
"GET 'BACK-SLACKING' ADDED TO DICTIONARY."
NO!
WHERE'S THAT HISS LIQUOR?!

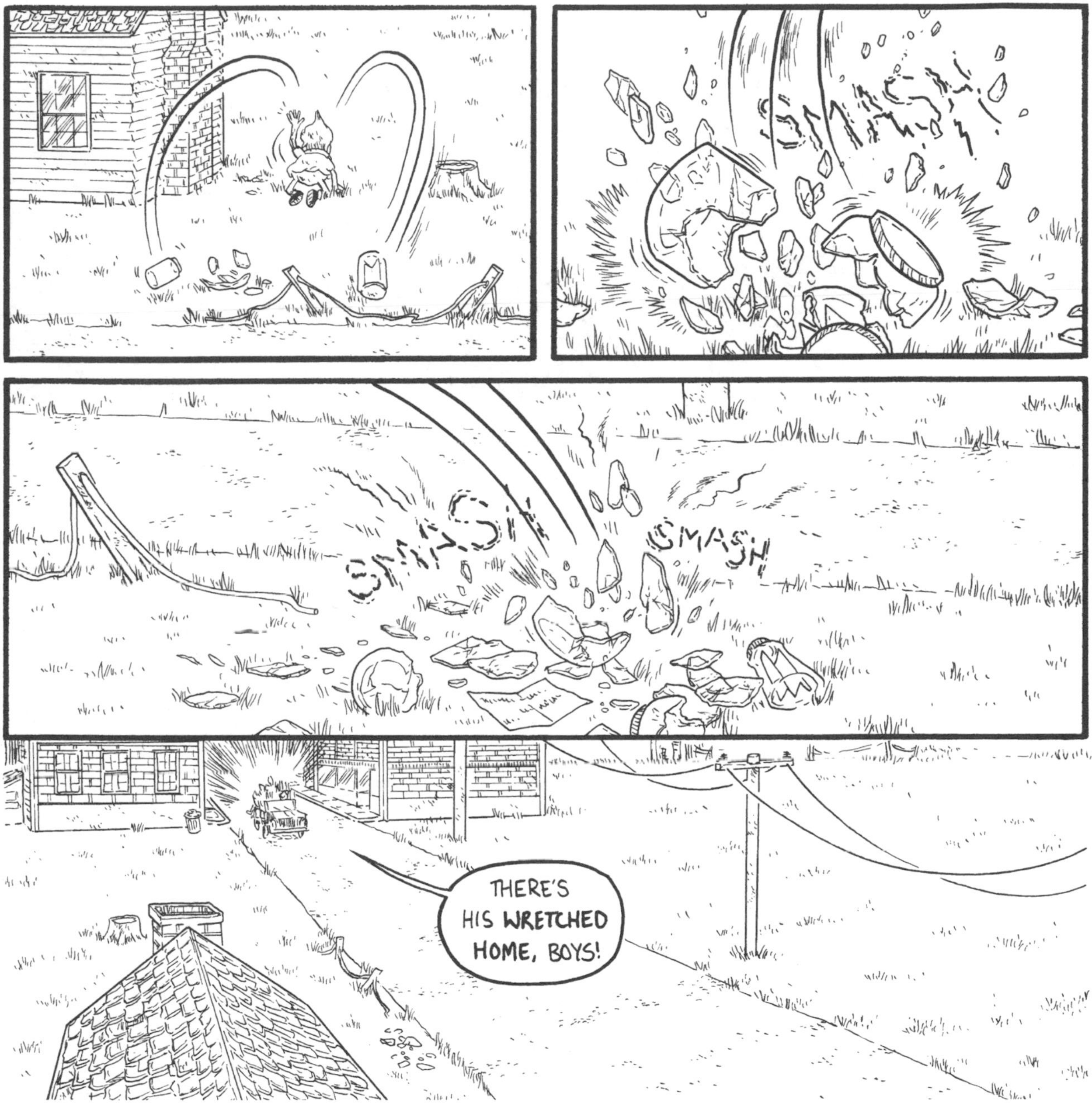
SMASH
SMASH
SMASH
THERE'S HIS WRETCHED HOME, BOYS!

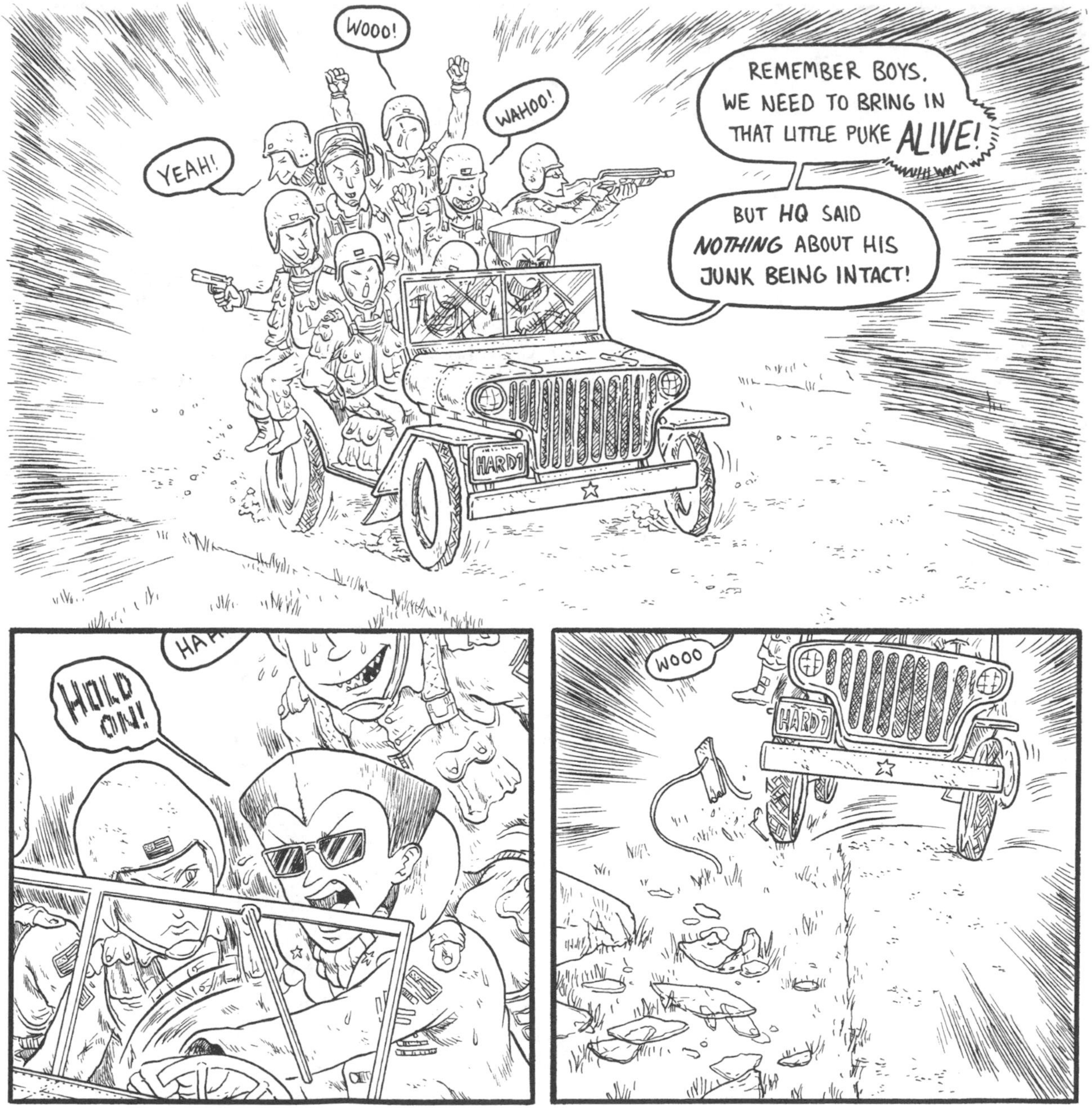
WOOO!
WAHOO!
YEAH!
REMEMBER BOYS, WE NEED TO BRING IN THAT LITTLE PUKE ALIVE!
BUT HQ SAID NOTHING ABOUT HIS JUNK BEING INTACT!
HARD1
HOLD ON!
WOOO
HARD1

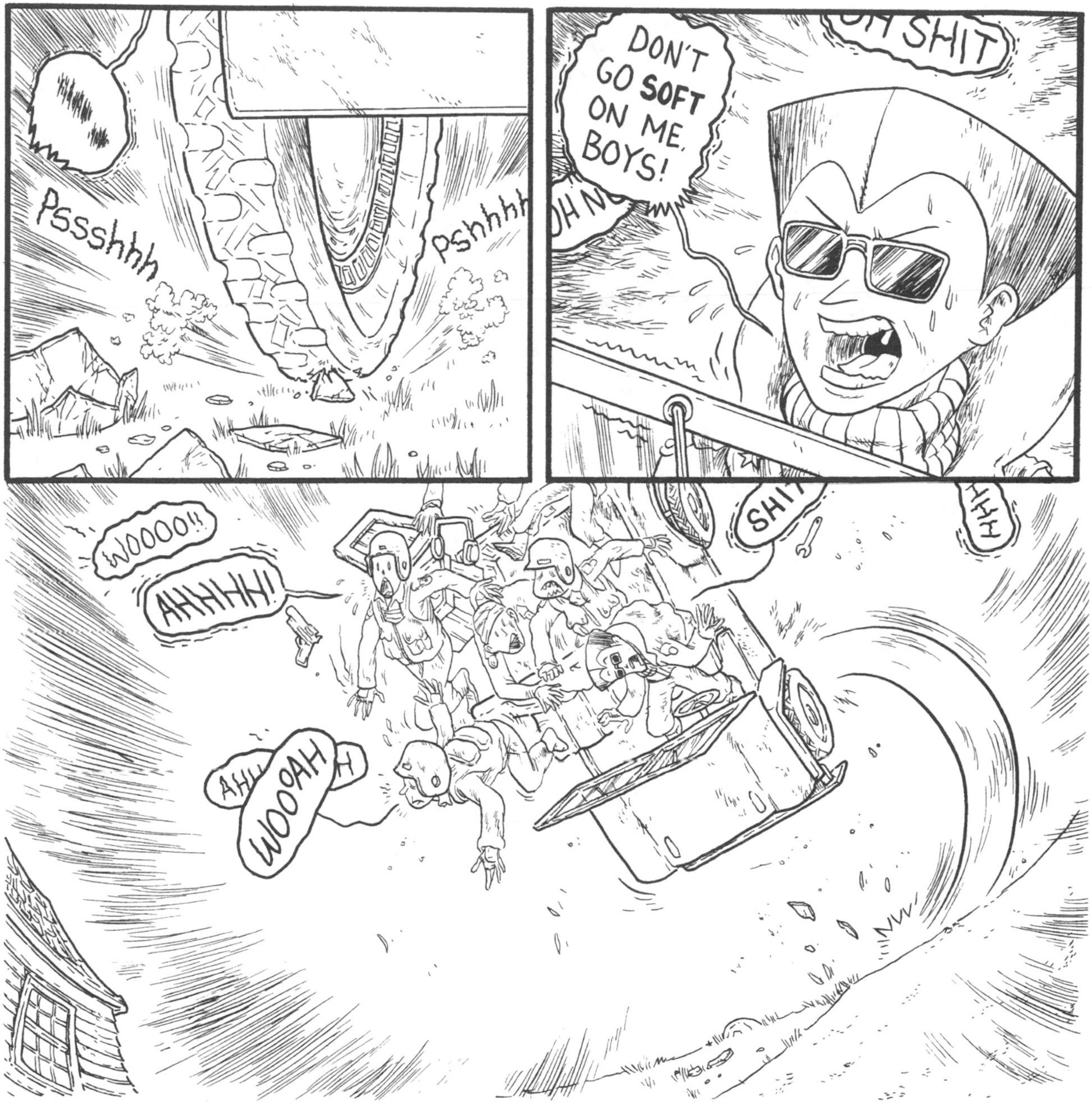
Pssshhh
pshhhh
DON'T GO SOFT ON ME, BOYS!
WOOOO!!
AHHHH!
WOOOAH

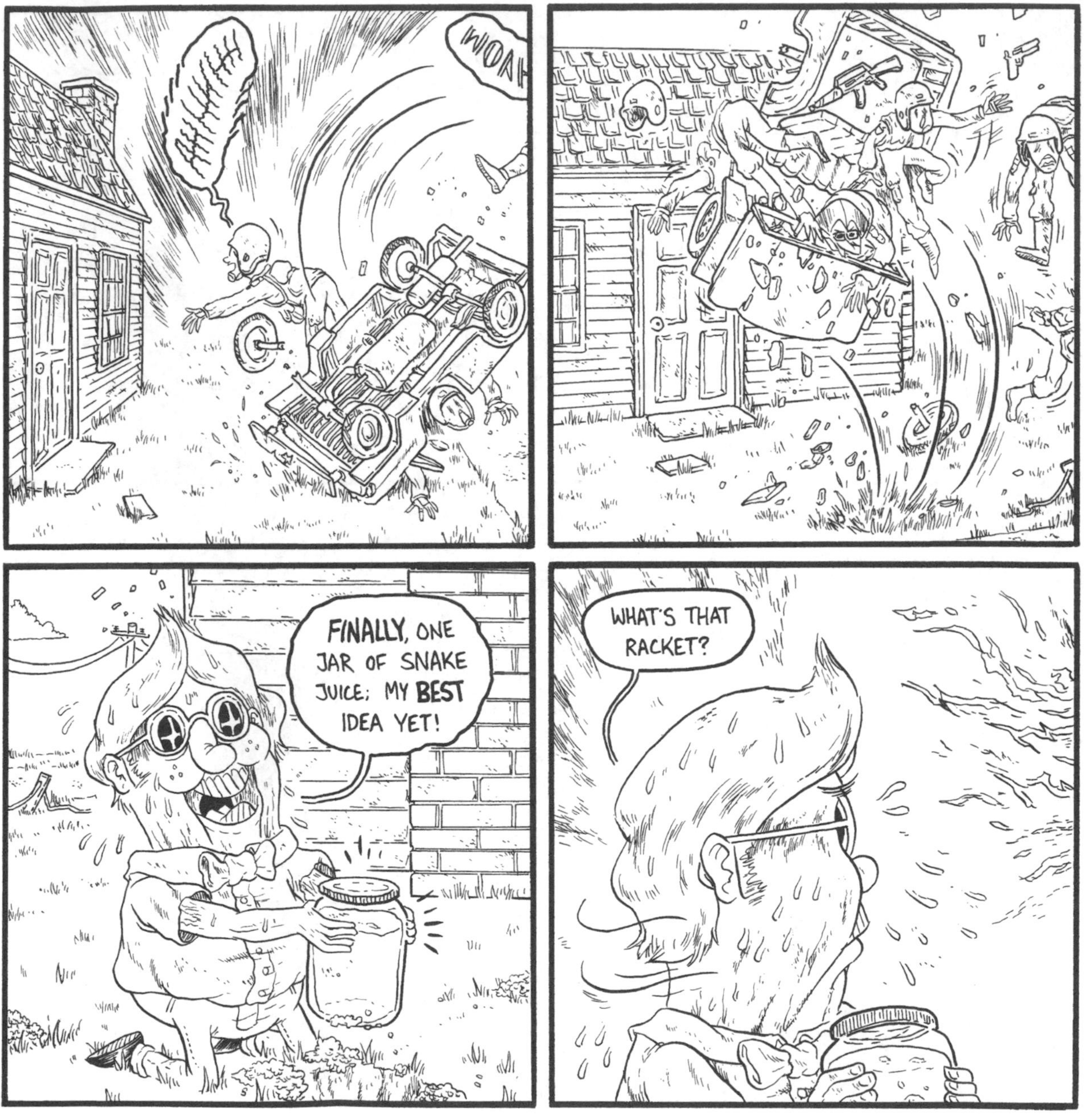
WOAH
FINALLY, ONE JAR OF SNAKE JUICE; MY BEST IDEA YET!
WHAT'S THAT RACKET?

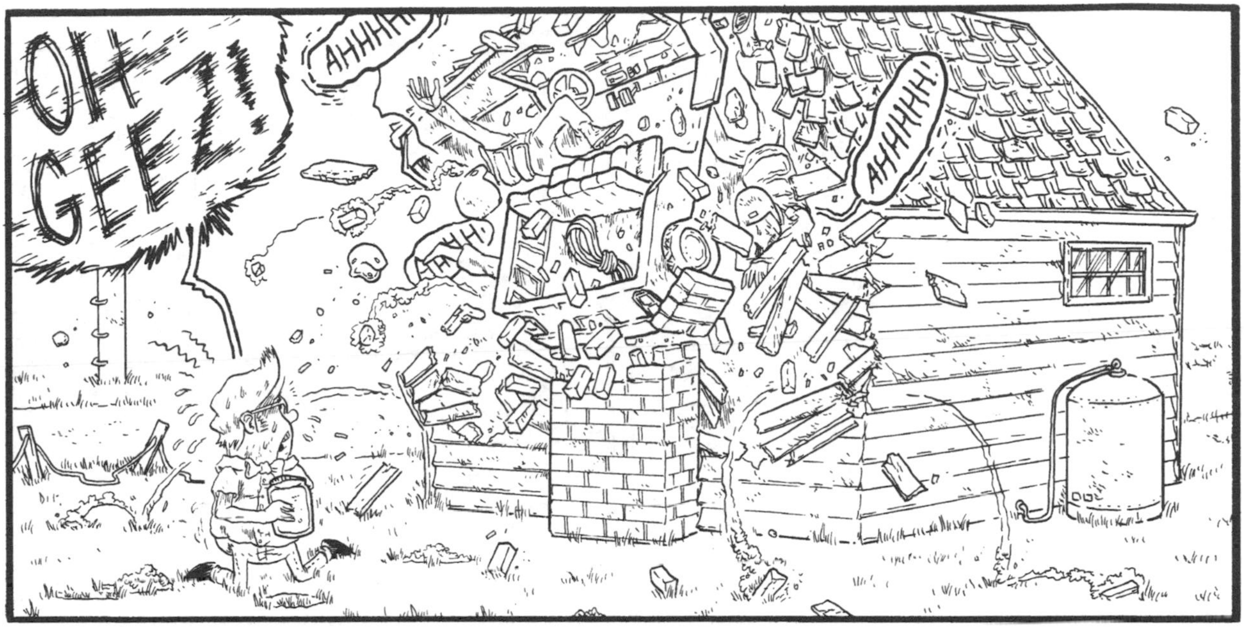
OH GEEZ!
AHHHH
AHHHHH!

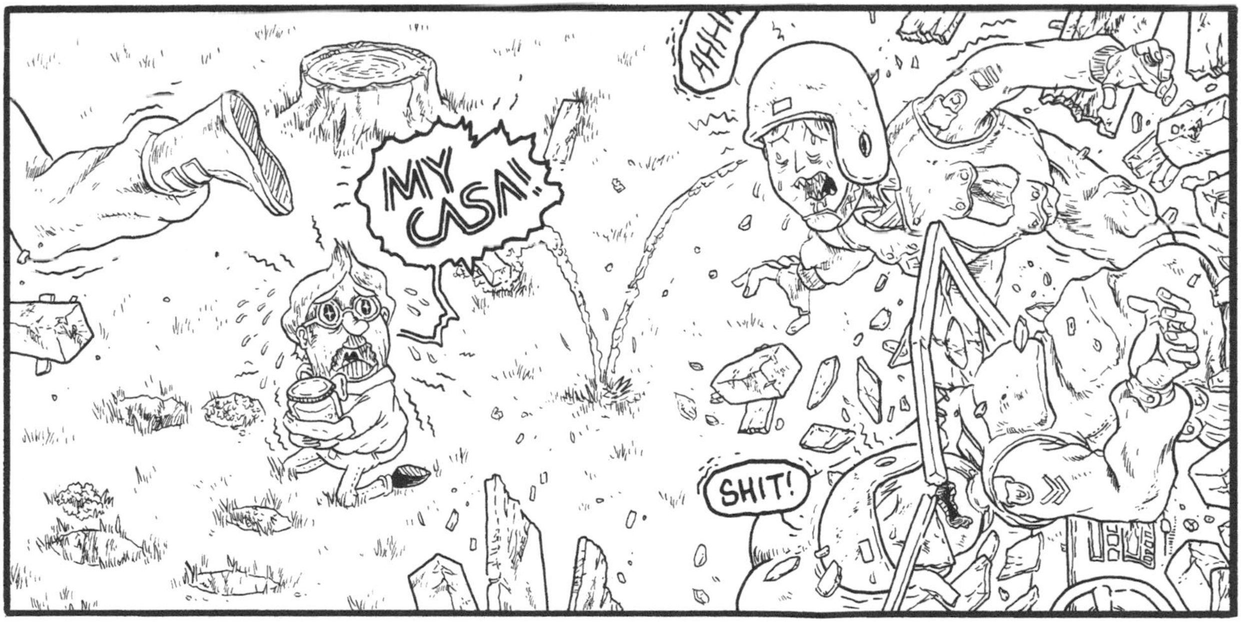
AHHH
MY CASA!
SHIT!

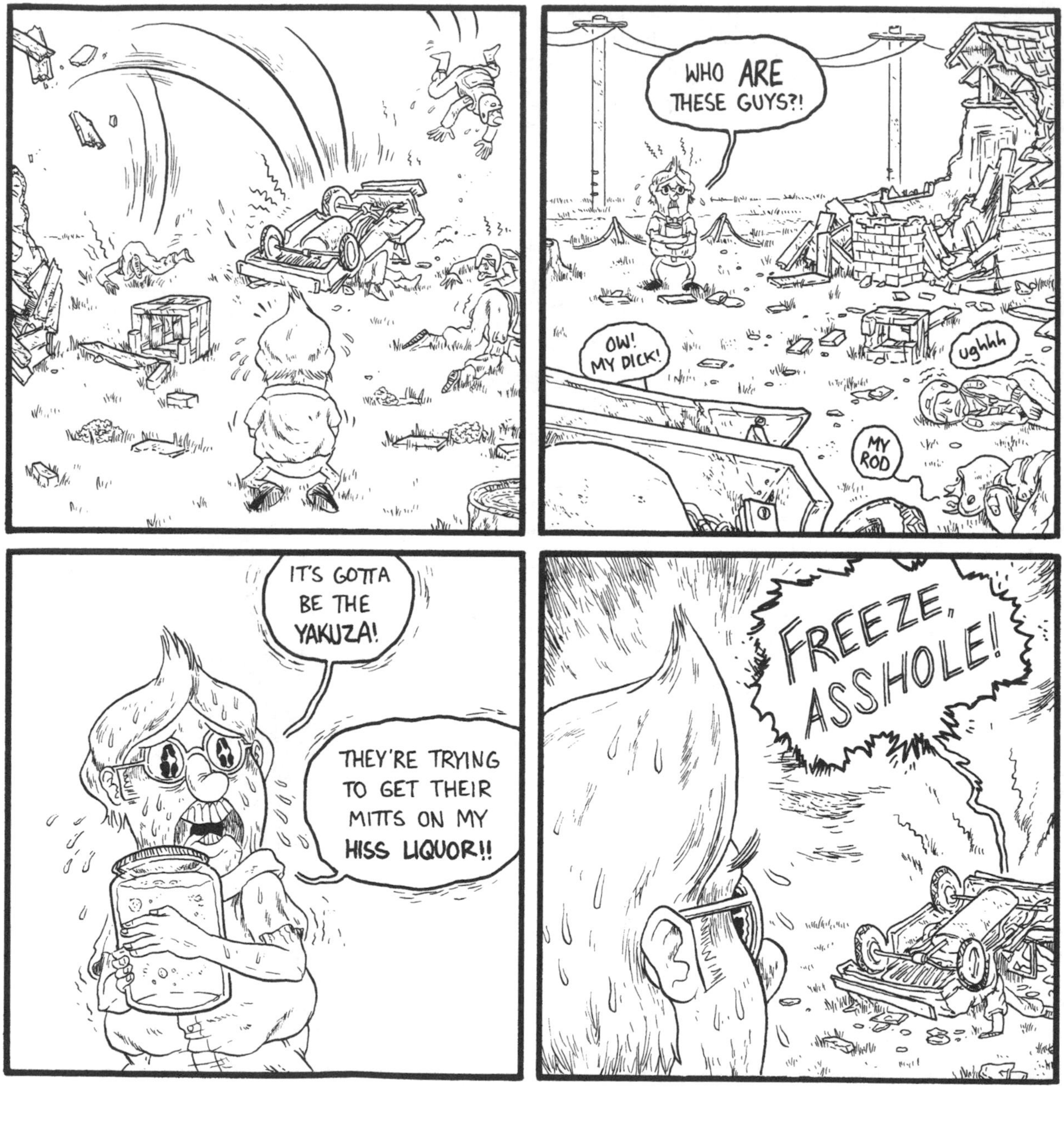
WHO ARE THESE GUYS?!
OW! MY DICK!
ughhh
MY ROD
IT'S GOTTA BE THE YAKUZA!
THEY'RE TRYING TO GET THEIR MITTS ON MY HISS LIQUOR!!
FREEZE, ASSHOLE!

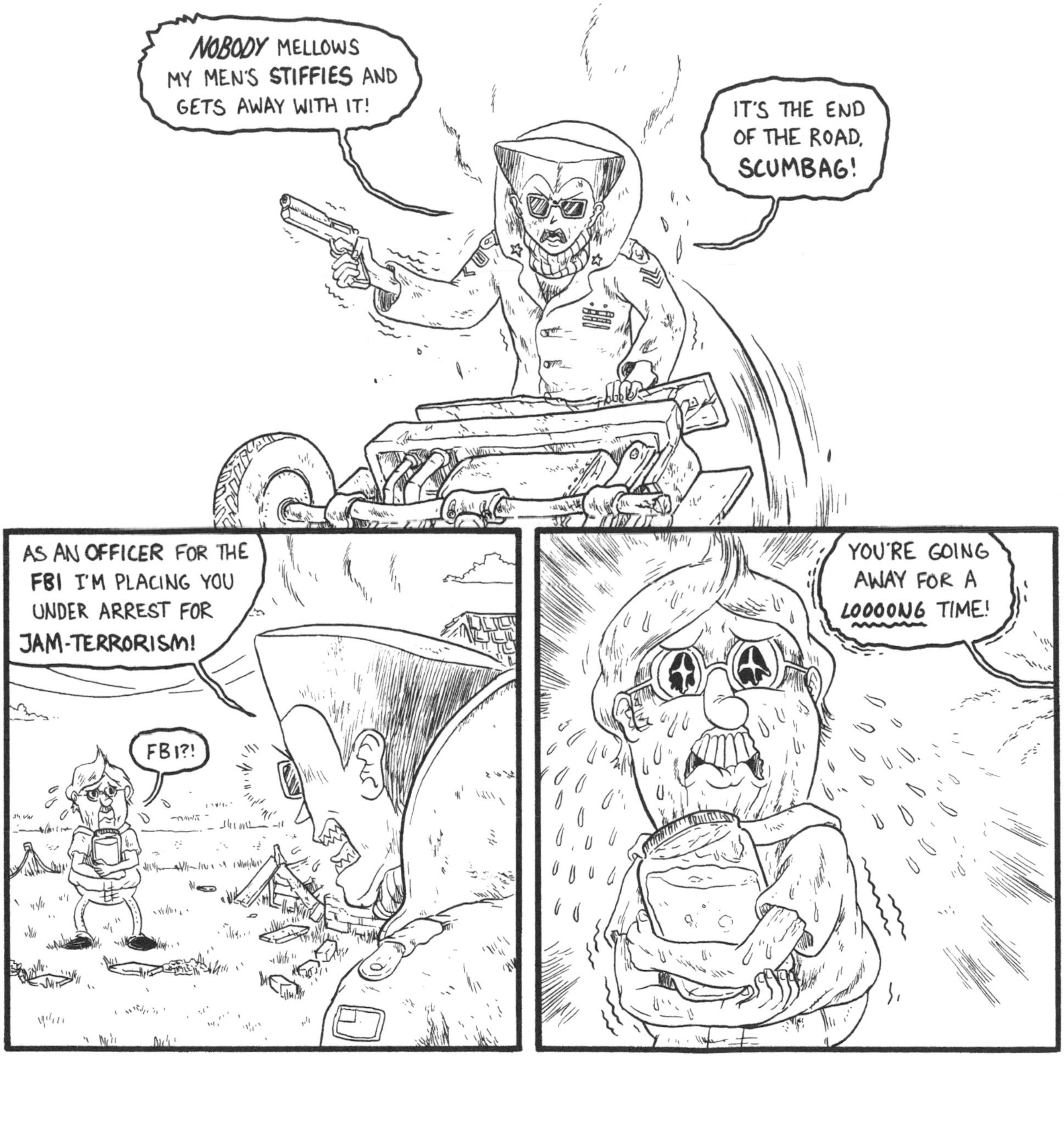
NOBODY MELLOWS MY MEN'S STIFFIES AND GETS AWAY WITH IT!
IT'S THE END OF THE ROAD, SCUMBAG!
AS AN OFFICER FOR THE FBI I'M PLACING YOU UNDER ARREST FOR JAM-TERRORISM!
FBI?!
YOU'RE GOING AWAY FOR A LOOOONG TIME!

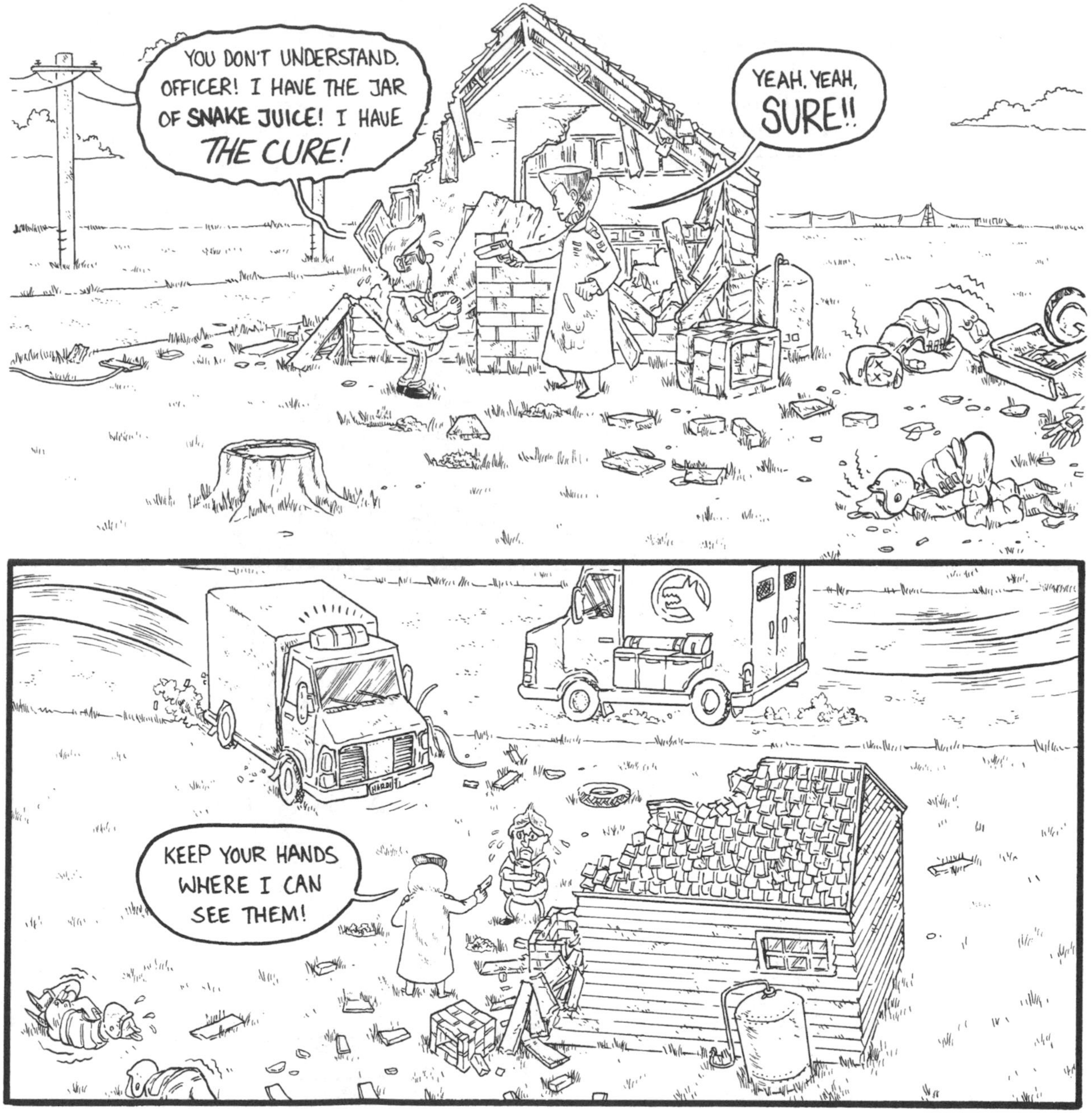
YOU DON'T UNDERSTAND, OFFICER! I HAVE THE JAR OF SNAKE JUICE! I HAVE THE CURE!
YEAH, YEAH, SURE!!
KEEP YOUR HANDS WHERE I CAN SEE THEM!

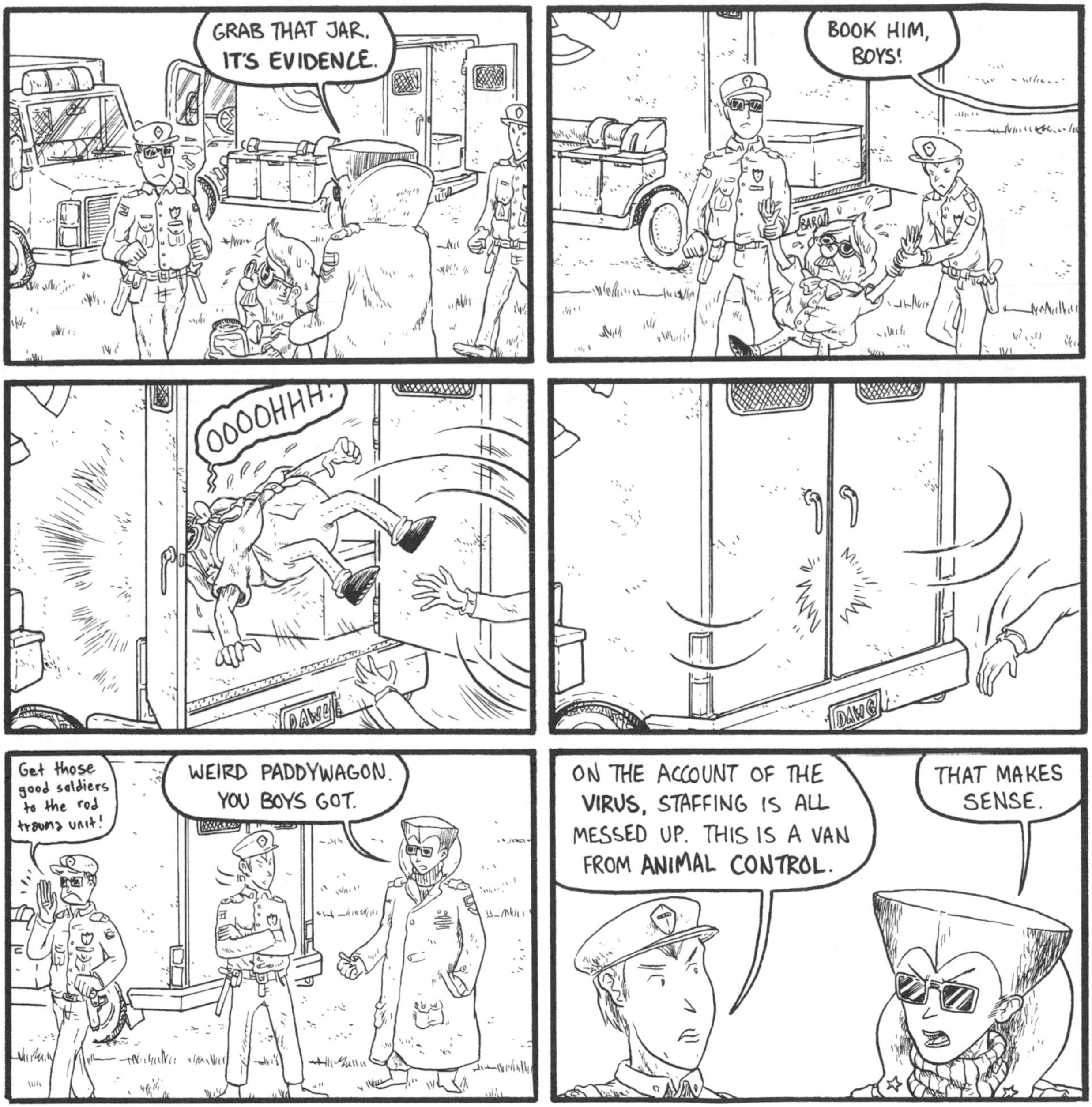
GRAB THAT JAR. IT'S EVIDENCE.
BOOK HIM, BOYS!
OOOOHHH!
DAWG
DAWG
Get those good soldiers to the rod trauma unit!
WEIRD PADDYWAGON. YOU BOYS GOT.
ON THE ACCOUNT OF THE VIRUS, STAFFING IS ALL MESSED UP. THIS IS A VAN FROM ANIMAL CONTROL.
THAT MAKES SENSE.

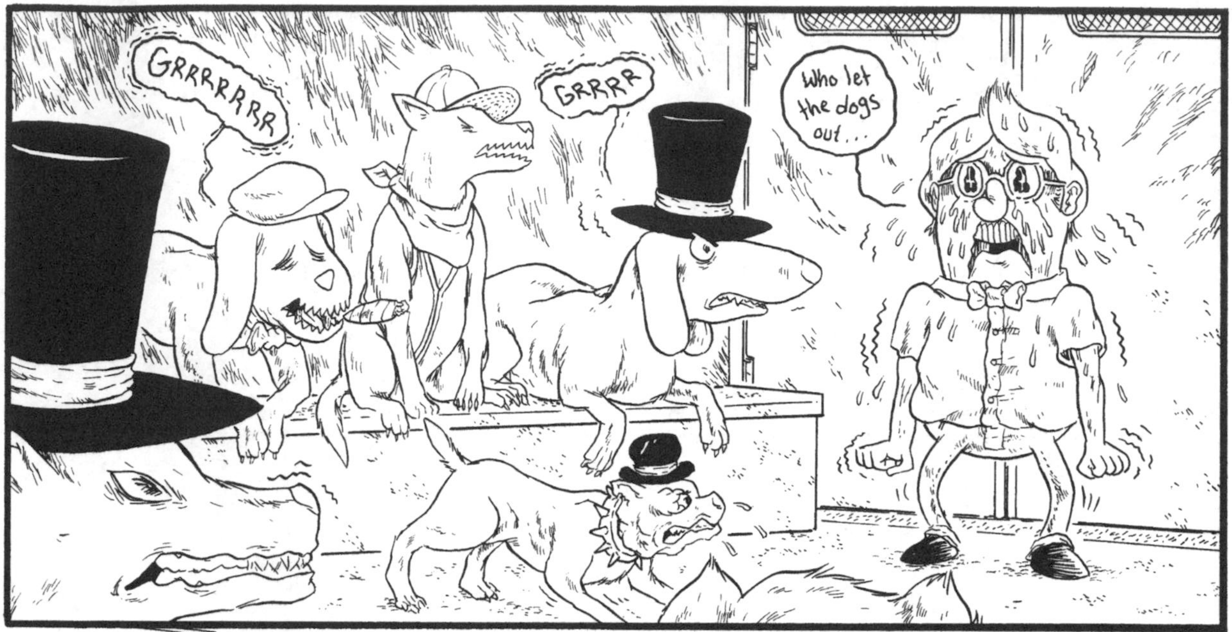
GRRRRRRR
GRRRR
Who let the dogs out...

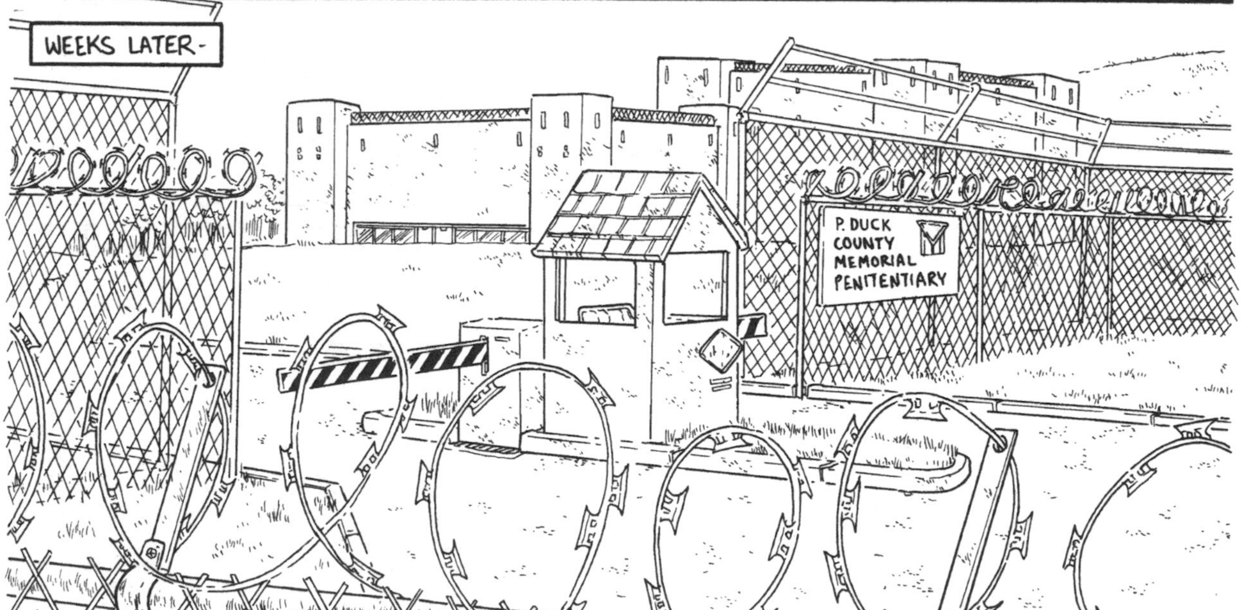
WEEKS LATER-
P. DUCK COUNTY MEMORIAL PENITENTIARY

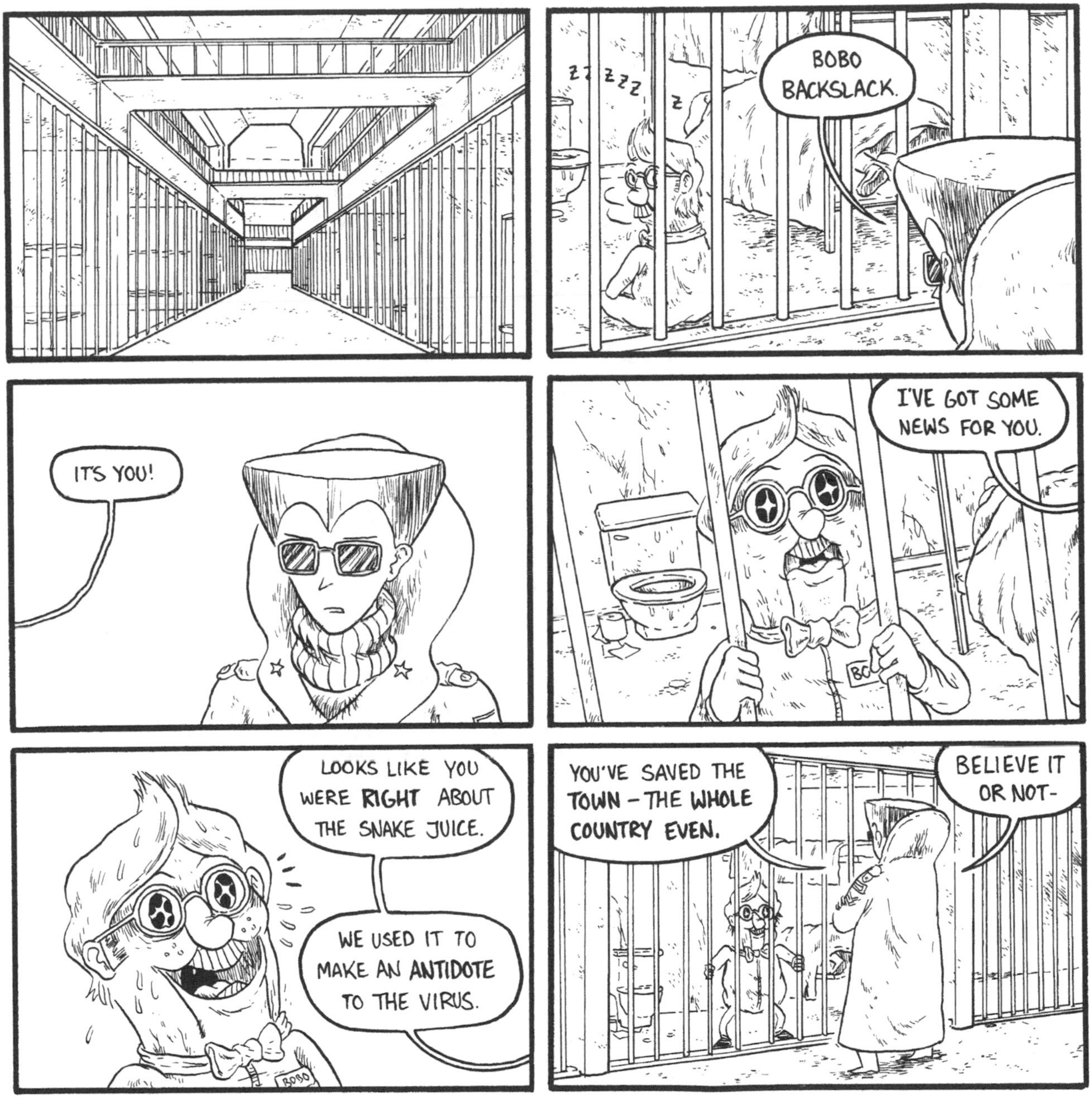

Z Z Z Z Z
Z
BOBO BACKSLACK.
IT'S YOU!
I'VE GOT SOME NEWS FOR YOU.
LOOKS LIKE YOU WERE **RIGHT** ABOUT THE SNAKE JUICE.
WE USED IT TO MAKE AN **ANTIDOTE** TO THE VIRUS.
YOU'VE SAVED THE **TOWN** – THE **WHOLE COUNTRY EVEN.**
BELIEVE IT OR NOT-

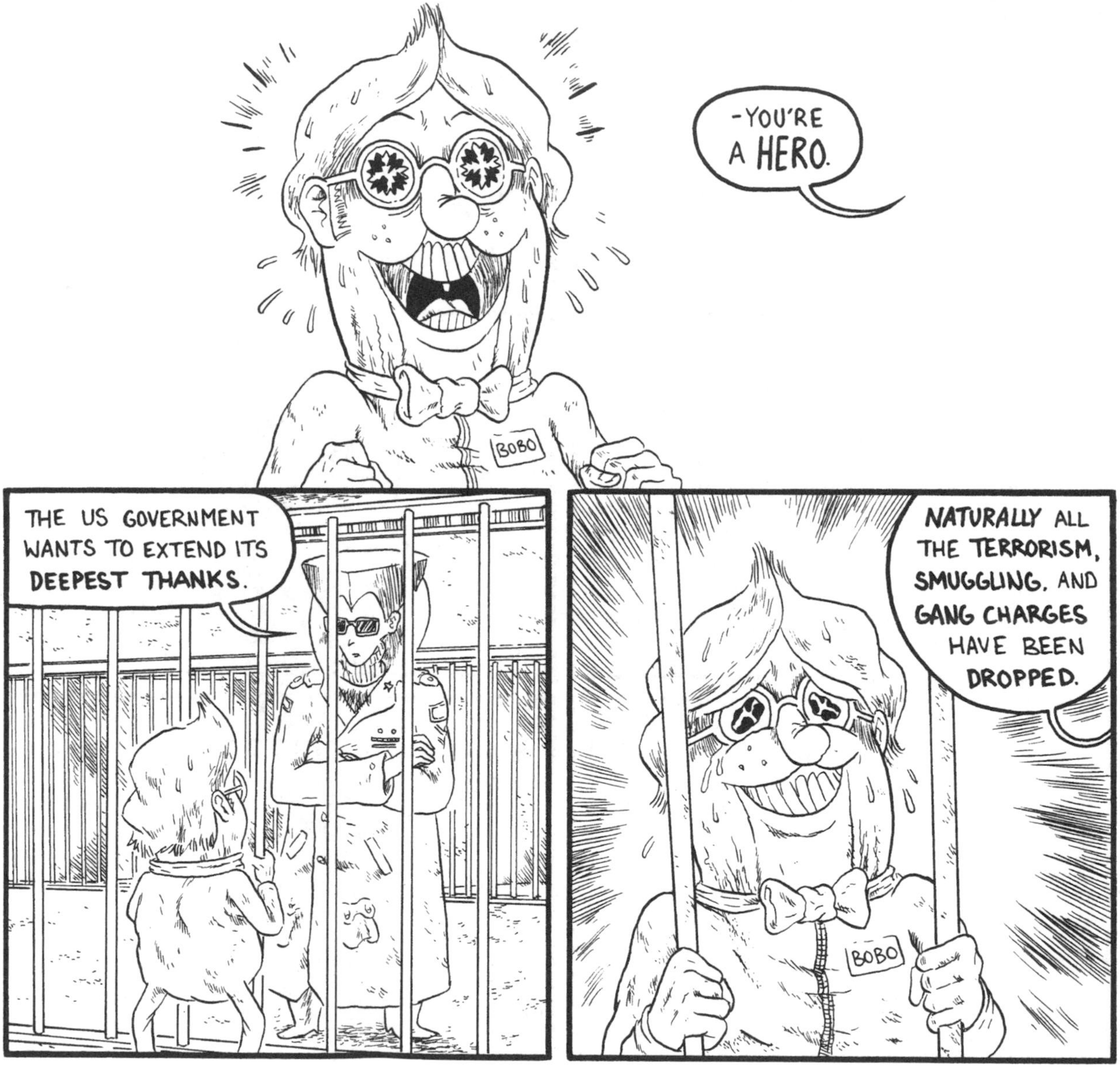
-YOU'RE A HERO.
BOBO
THE US GOVERNMENT WANTS TO EXTEND ITS DEEPEST THANKS.
NATURALLY ALL THE TERRORISM, SMUGGLING, AND GANG CHARGES HAVE BEEN DROPPED.
BOBO

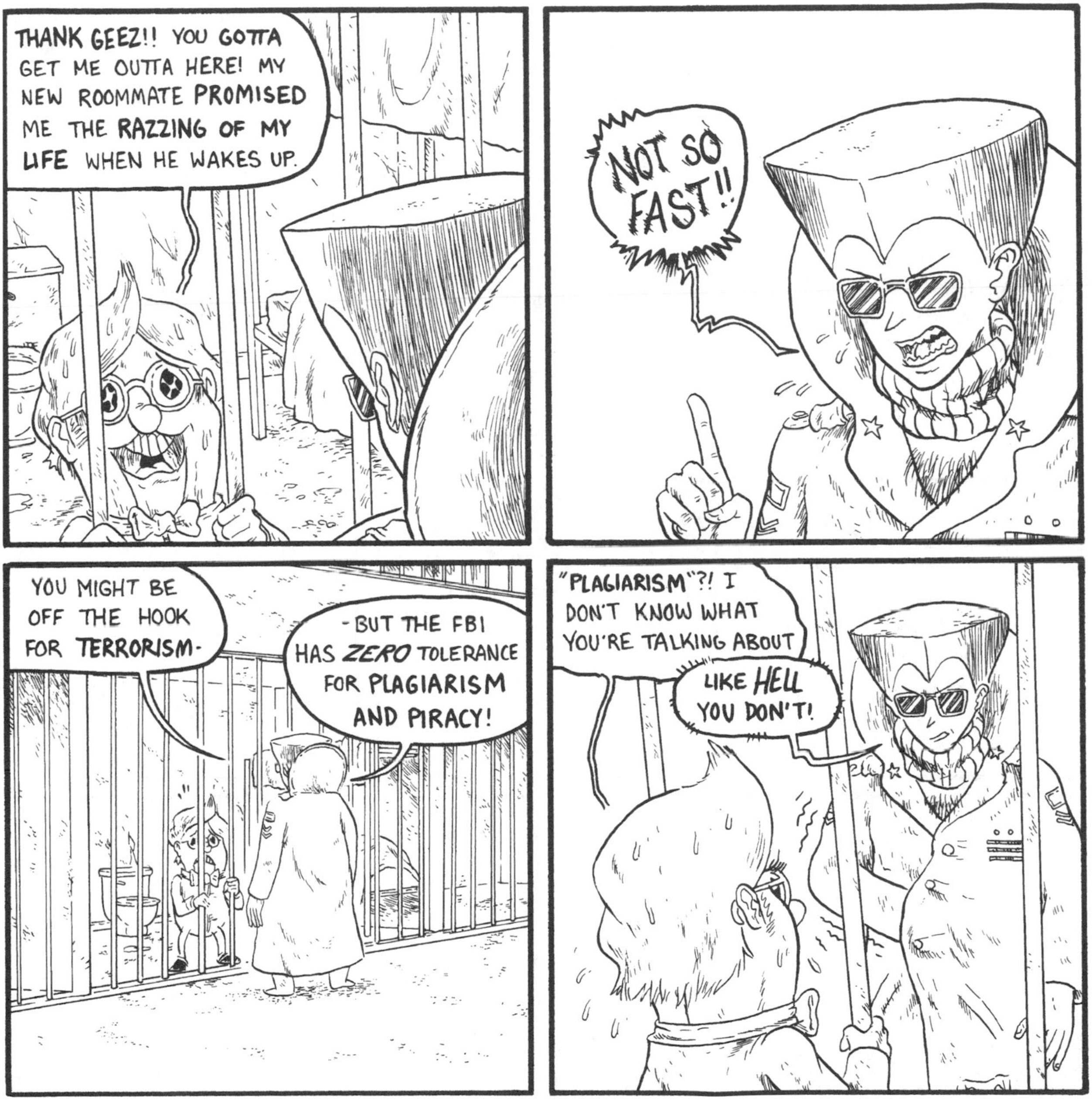
THANK GEEZ!! YOU GOTTA GET ME OUTTA HERE! MY NEW ROOMMATE PROMISED ME THE RAZZING OF MY LIFE WHEN HE WAKES UP.
NOT SO FAST!!
YOU MIGHT BE OFF THE HOOK FOR TERRORISM-
-BUT THE FBI HAS ZERO TOLERANCE FOR PLAGIARISM AND PIRACY!
"PLAGIARISM"?! I DON'T KNOW WHAT YOU'RE TALKING ABOUT
LIKE HELL YOU DON'T!

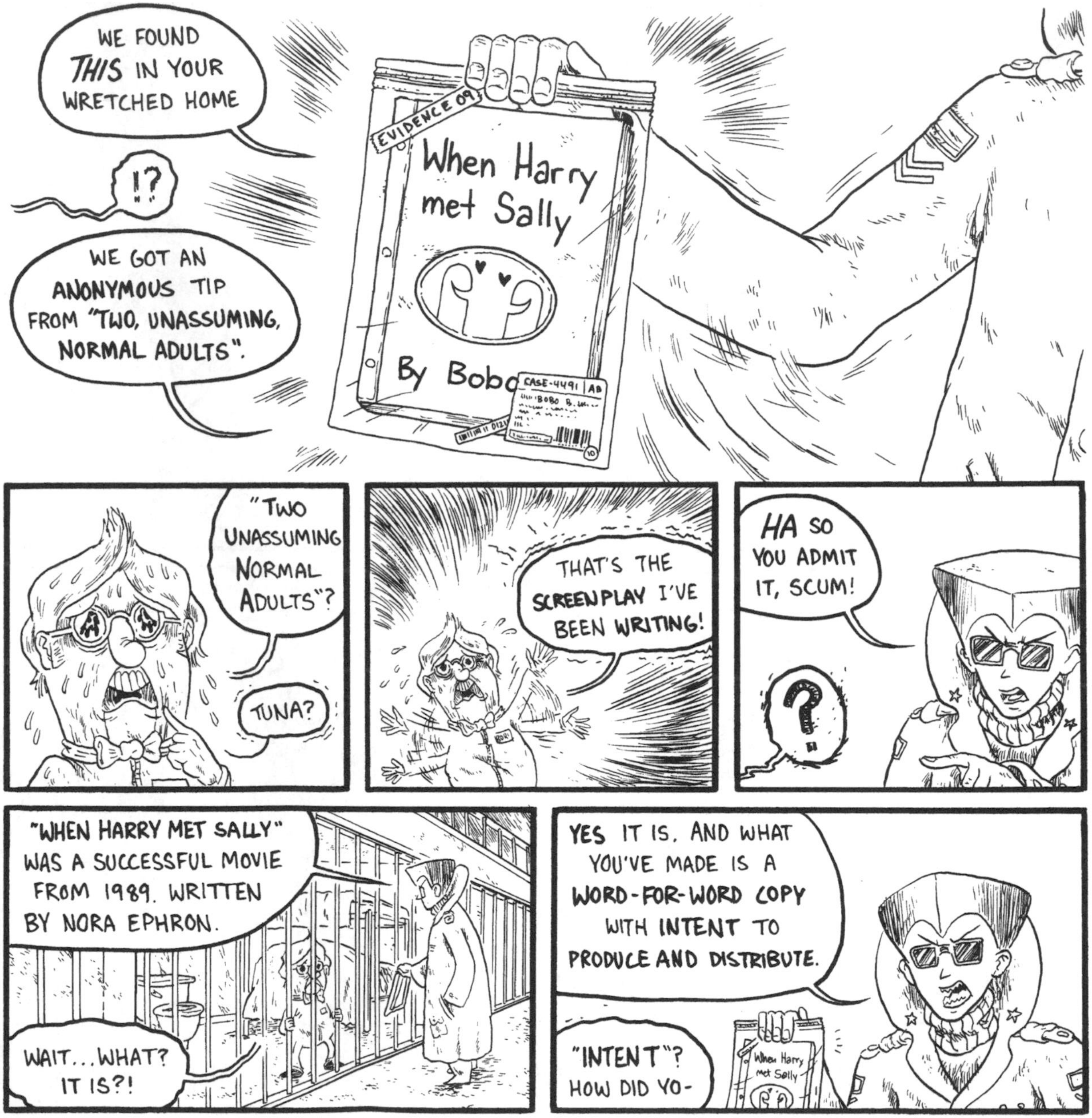
WE FOUND THIS IN YOUR WRETCHED HOME
!?
WE GOT AN ANONYMOUS TIP FROM "TWO, UNASSUMING, NORMAL ADULTS".
EVIDENCE 09
When Harry met Sally
By Bobo
CASE-4491 AB
"TWO UNASSUMING NORMAL ADULTS"?
TUNA?
THAT'S THE SCREENPLAY I'VE BEEN WRITING!
HA SO YOU ADMIT IT, SCUM!
?
"WHEN HARRY MET SALLY" WAS A SUCCESSFUL MOVIE FROM 1989. WRITTEN BY NORA EPHRON.
WAIT... WHAT? IT IS?!
YES IT IS. AND WHAT YOU'VE MADE IS A WORD-FOR-WORD COPY WITH INTENT TO PRODUCE AND DISTRIBUTE.
"INTENT"? HOW DID YO-
When Harry met Sally

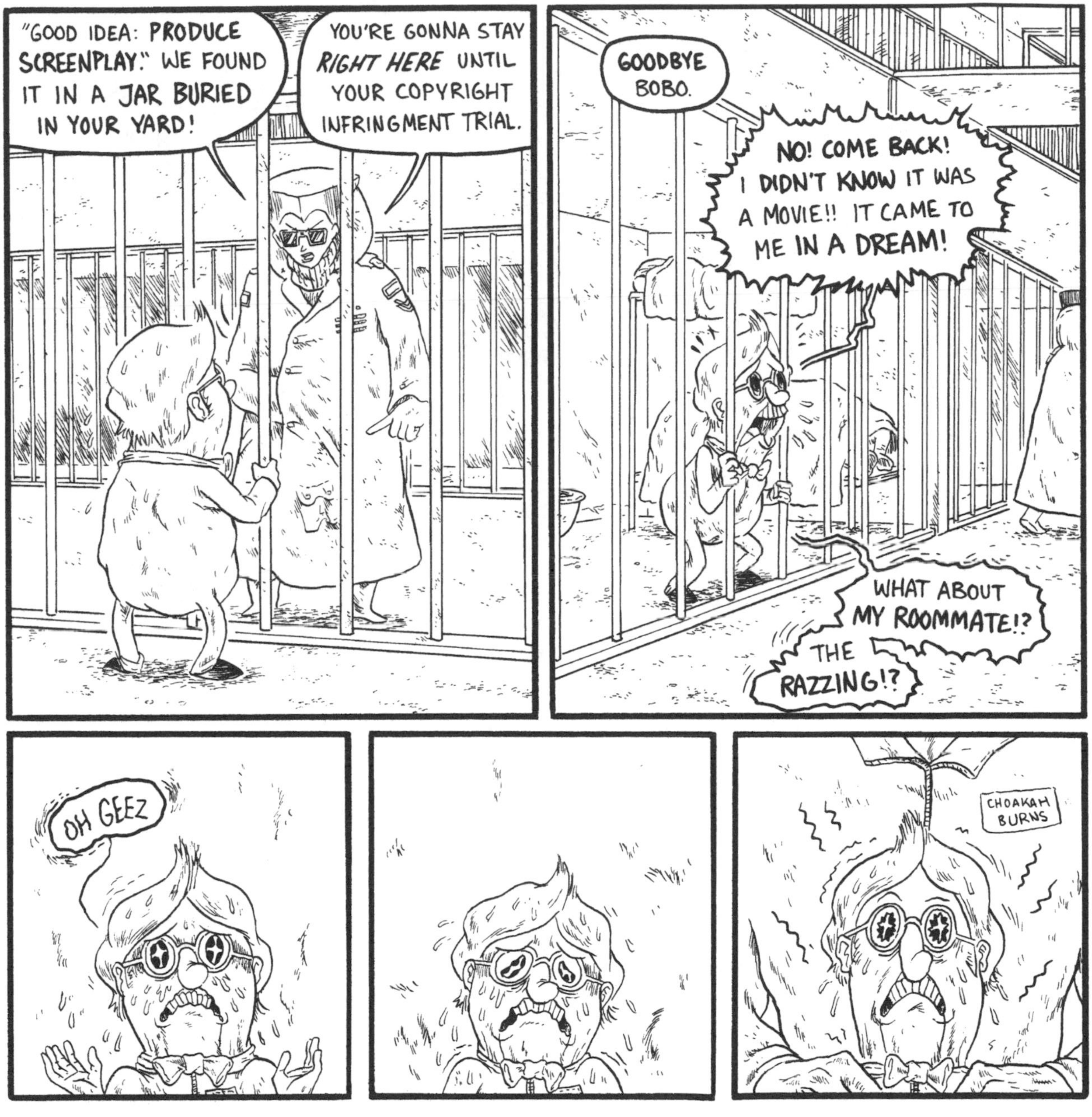
"GOOD IDEA: PRODUCE SCREENPLAY." WE FOUND IT IN A JAR BURIED IN YOUR YARD!
YOU'RE GONNA STAY RIGHT HERE UNTIL YOUR COPYRIGHT INFRINGMENT TRIAL.
GOODBYE BOBO.
NO! COME BACK! I DIDN'T KNOW IT WAS A MOVIE!! IT CAME TO ME IN A DREAM!
WHAT ABOUT MY ROOMMATE!?
THE RAZZING!?
OH GEEZ
CHOAKAH BURNS

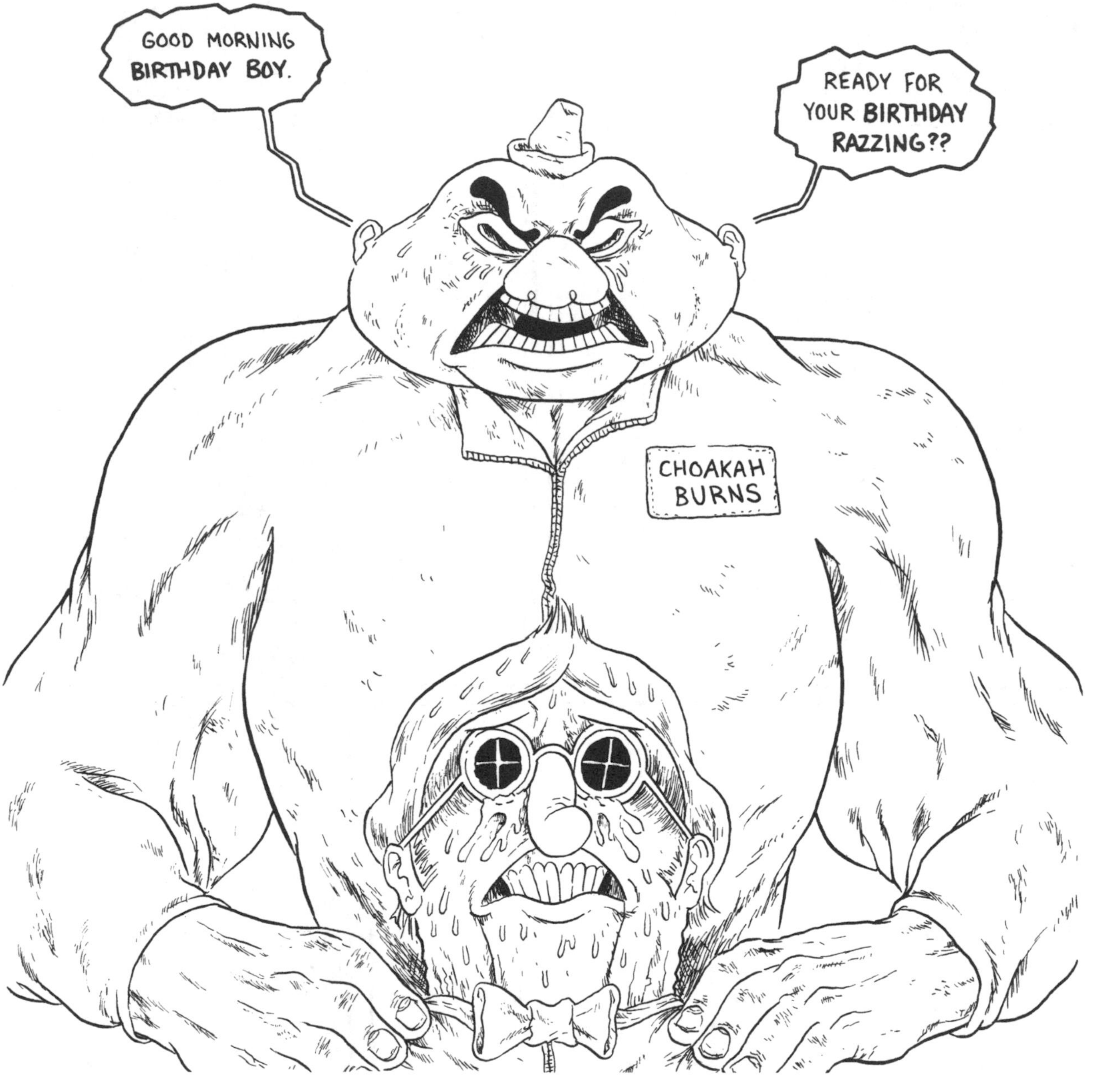
GOOD MORNING BIRTHDAY BOY.
READY FOR YOUR BIRTHDAY RAZZING??
CHOAKAH BURNS

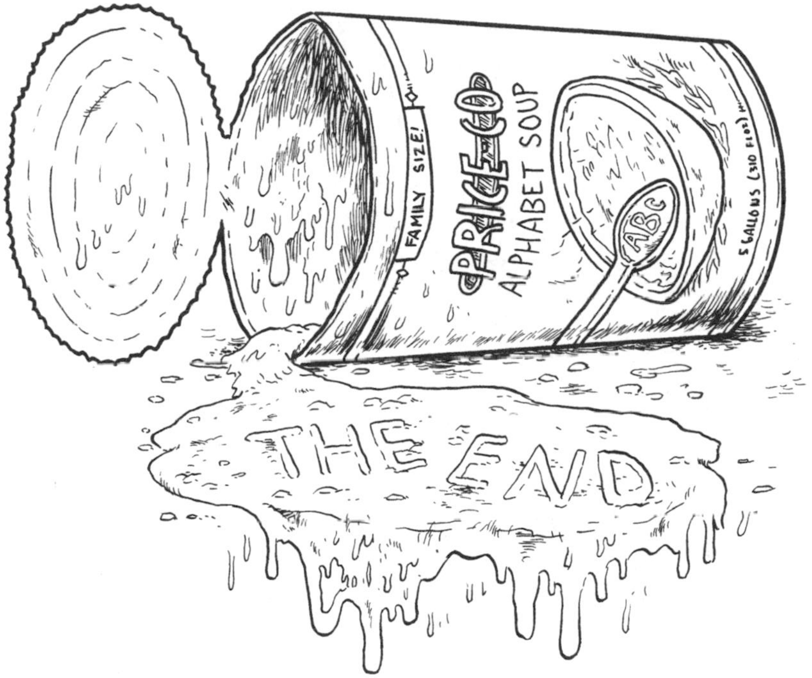
FAMILY SIZE!
PRICE CO
ALPHABET SOUP
ABC
5 GALLONS (310 FL OZ)
THE END

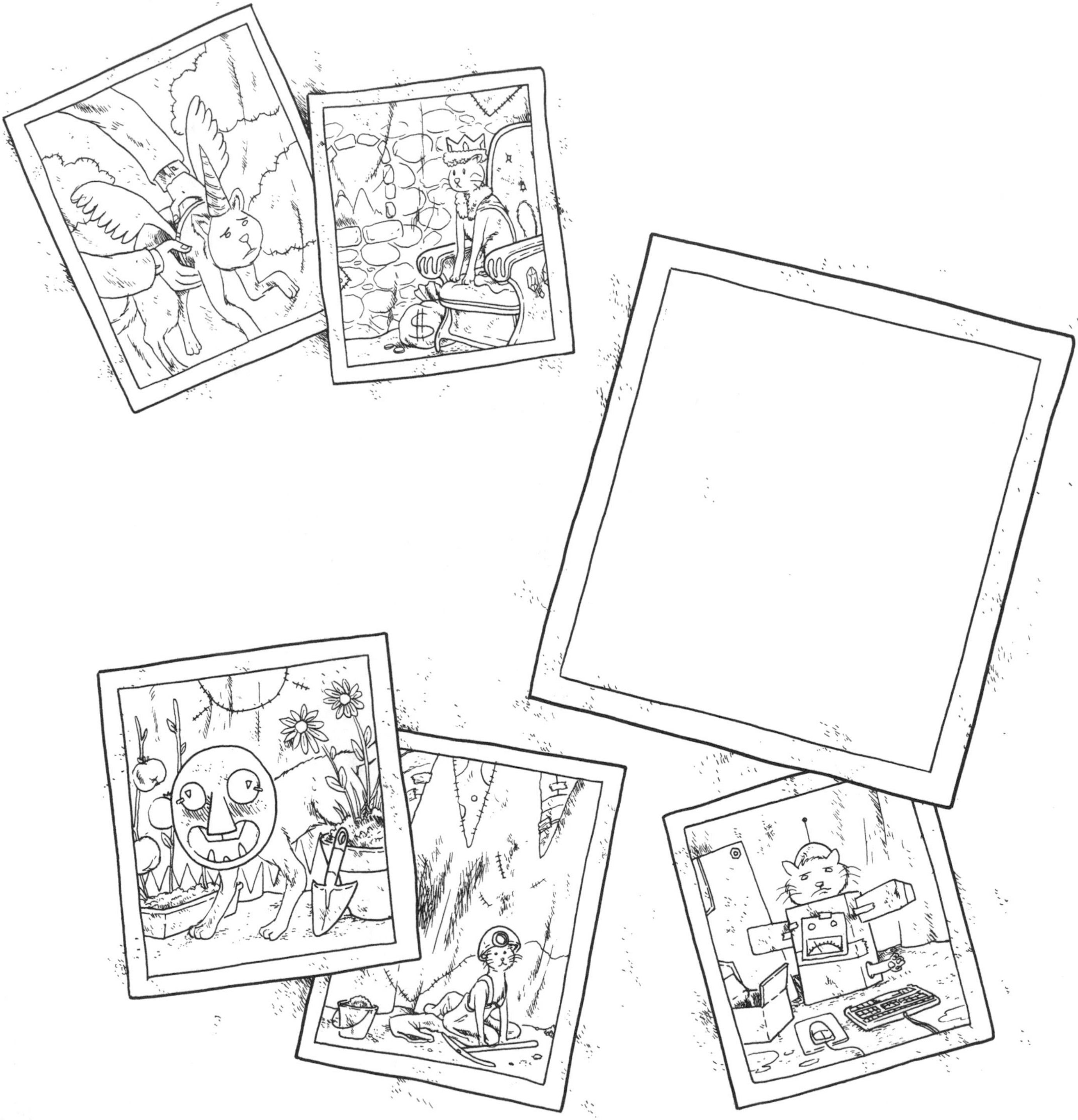

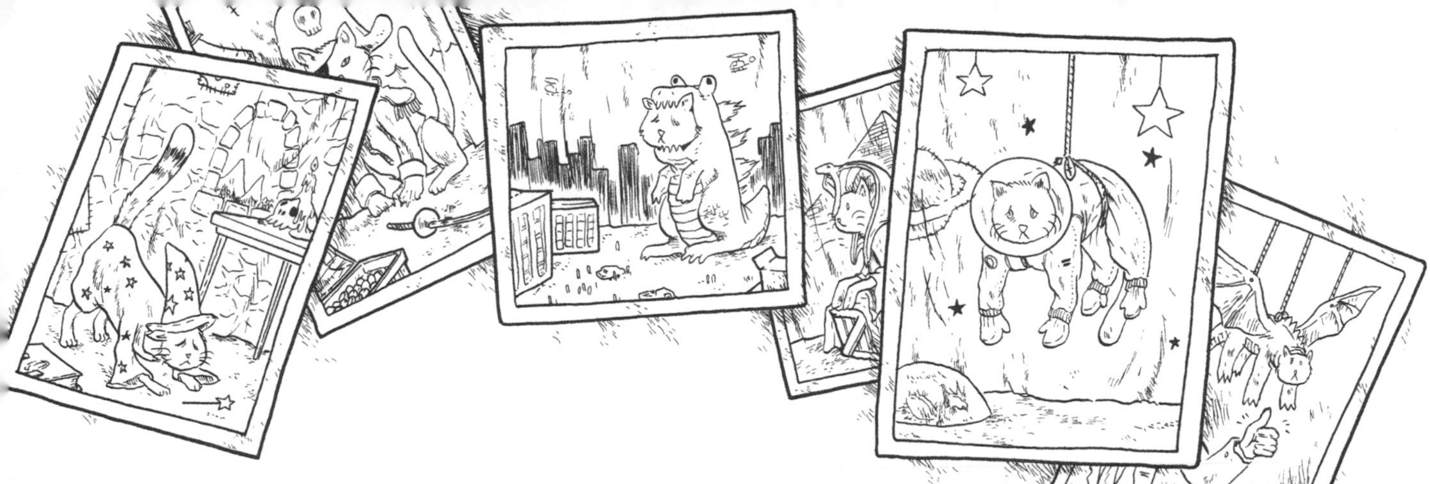
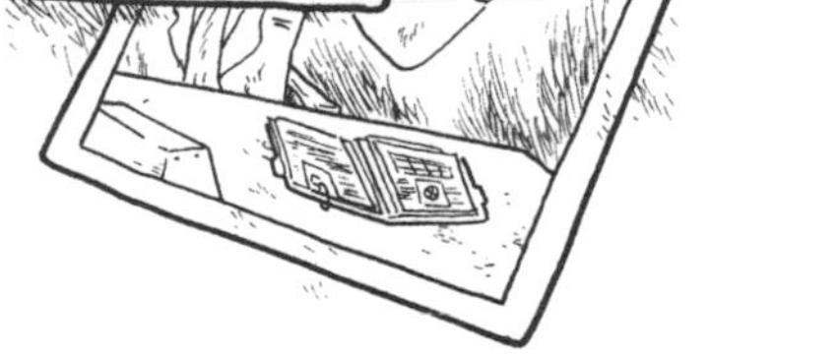

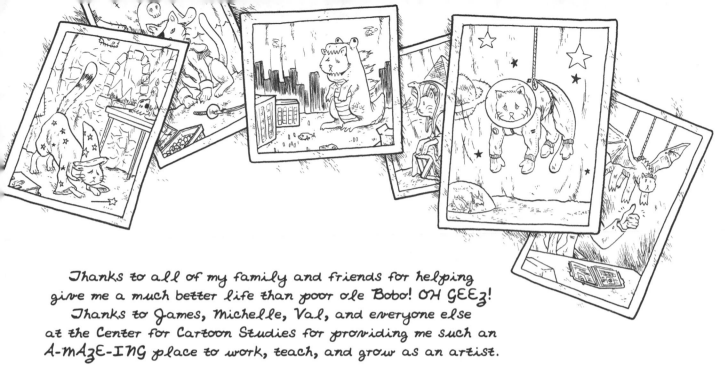

Thanks to all of my family and friends for helping give me a much better life than poor ole Bobo! OH GEEZ! Thanks to James, Michelle, Val, and everyone else at the Center for Cartoon Studies for providing me such an A-MAZE-ING place to work, teach, and grow as an artist.

Special thanks to Robyn C, Sophie G, Luke H, Laurel L, Josh L, Alec L, April M, Joyana M, Dakota M, Pranas N, Katherine R, Jeremy S, Laura T, Sasha and JJ for being a constant source of inspiration and support. I would be a mere husk of the person without you all.

And thanks to Jess for all her love and support.

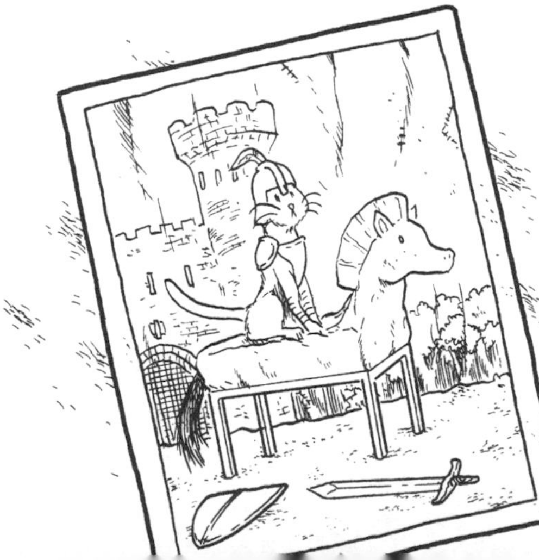
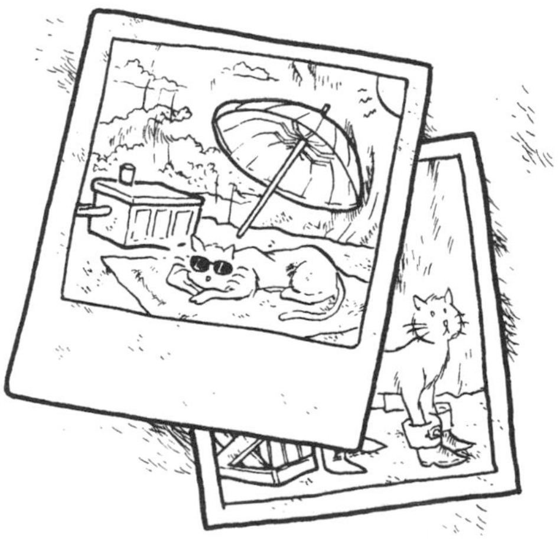

大切

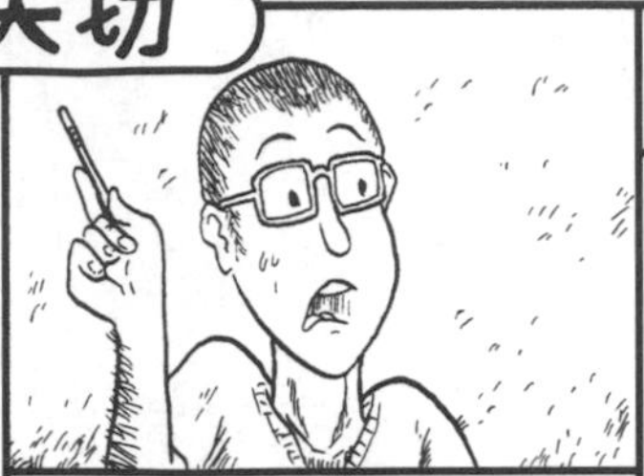

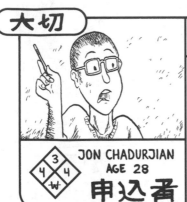

JON CHADURJIAN
AGE 28
申込者

ABOUT THE AUTHOR / 著者について

Jon Chadurjian was born and raised in Vermont. After completing his undergrad at the Savannah College of Art and Design, Jon moved to White River Junction, Vermont where we works and teaches bookmaking and screen-printing at the Center for Cartoon Studies. He is a huge fan of biking, hiking, and playing pinball. His ambition and overall cognizance of his surroundings makes him unsuitable for Operation “Jamgerous.”

APPLICANT 601-HWXXX0 REVIEWED BY H. WARUDA

REJECT

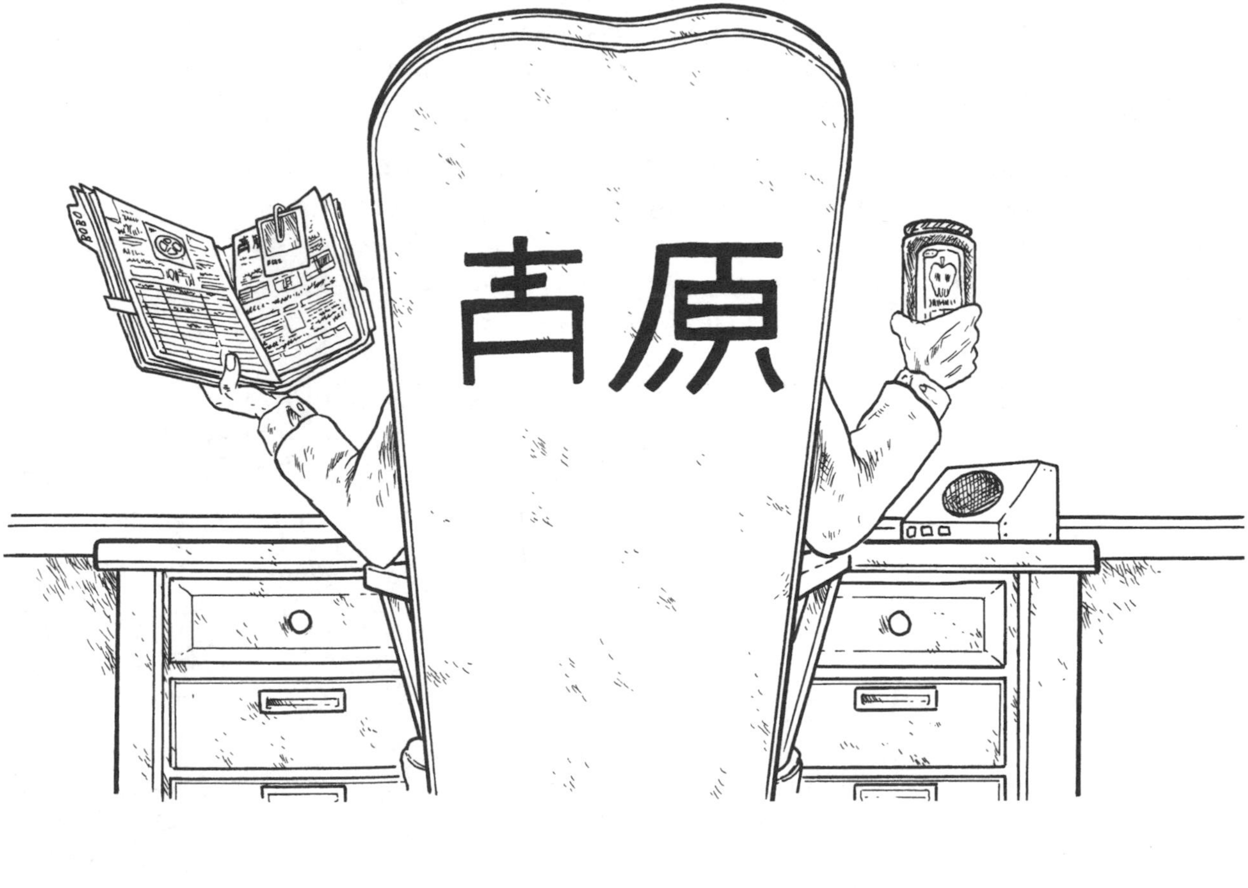
吉原